MODERN RAILWAYS

Geoffrey Freeman Allen

MODERN RAILWAYS

Geoffrey Freeman Allen

ELSEVIER-DUTTON PUBLISHING CO. INC.   New York

Published by
Elsevier-Dutton Publishing Co. Inc.,
2 Park Avenue,
New York,
N.Y. 10016.

© Copyright 1980 Basinghall Books Limited

Produced by
Basinghall Books Limited,
59 Cambridge Road,
Kings Heath,
Birmingham, England.

Designed by Roy Williams

ISBN 0-525-70727-1

Library of Congress Catalog No 80-65588

Printed in Hong Kong by South China Printing Co

CONTENTS

Rc-4 electric locomotive of the Swedish State Railways.

INTRODUCTION

The railway amateurs of the developed world used to be blinkered to what went on outside their own country. A Frenchman's railway interest generally faded around the Saar or Alsace–Lorraine just as most Englishmen's at the Channel ports. Rare in any language was the non-professional railway periodical which saw sales value in keeping its readership effectively briefed on operational and technological development abroad.

Nor were many professionals more broadminded. As recently as the mid-1960s the top brass of British Railways held a fairly overt view that the railways on each side of the English Channel were different industries, and that there was little the British railwayman could learn from the mainland. Similarly, North American 'experts' in the past have stolidly refused to acknowledge, let alone accept, advice or experience from across the oceans.

But over the past two years or so the barriers have been steadily yielding, partly thanks to trade and travel, partly because economic pressures have been forcing them down. In Europe, especially, the rising tides of international trade and the demands of its shippers for smart and reliable transits have been knitting the railways bit by bit into a recognizable Continental network, not just a circumstantial grouping of independent systems. And the container revolution has made some degree of common cause even between railways that are separated by oceans. Nor is it any longer only airlines, road passenger and freight operators who are sensible enough to buy standard vehicles from specialist international manufacturers, instead of obstinately and extravagantly insisting on doing their own 'research-and-development thing' as the railways did for so long. True, railways have a very long way to go before they attain the economical standardization of design evident in the airline industry, but trends since the 1950s have been encouraging. Not only is research more effectively co-ordinated, but international applications of the best design are becoming more numerous – and not only in the undeveloped world, where railways have necessarily bought off-the-shelf from the major countries. The trend is noticeable in Europe's freight stock, more and more high-capacity bogie vehicles of which are on a common type of bogie. But over and above component standardization, the widening market for the thyristor control expertise of the Swedish manufacturer ASEA and its embodiment in the Swedish Type Rc4 electric

French Railways Class CC6500.

locomotive, for instance, makes one optimistic that a standard European locomotive is not necessarily fantasy for all time.

All this and the newfound ease of travel are extending the horizons of amateur interest in railways by the month. Hence this book, which attempts to show how the major railways of the world are remoulding their operations to meet the severe challenges of the last quarter of the century, and the equipment they have evolved to attain their objectives.

The choice of railways for treatment has neces-sarily been restricted. Within the space limits pre-scribed I have preferred to deal with a few railways in some depth rather than a greater number more superficially. This decision has also given me room to explain some of the new technologies of the modern railway if only their fundamentals. They now need a book of their own to do them justice.

G. FREEMAN ALLEN
Laleham-on-Thames
December 1979

ABBREVIATIONS

AC	Alternating Current
AFC	Automatic Fare Collection
ANR	Australian National Railways
APT	Advanced Passenger Train
ASEA	Swedish engineering and manufacturing firm
ATC	Automatic Train Control
ATO	Automatic Train Operation
BART	Bay Area Rapid Transit
BDZ	Bulgarian State Railways
BLS	Bern–Lötschberg–Simplon Railway
BOB	Berner–Oberland–Bahnen
BR	British Railways
BTB	Bodensee–Toggenburg Bahn
BVZ	Brig–Visp–Zermatt Bahn
C&O	Chesapeake & Ohio Railroad (Chessie)
CIWLT	Compagnie Internationale des Wagons–lits et du Tourisme
CN	Canadian National Railways
Conrail	Consolidated Rail Corporation
CP	Canadian Pacific
CP	Portuguese Railways
CSWR	Cie Swiss des Wagons–Restaurants
CTA	Chicago Transit Authority
CTC	Centralized Traffic Control
DB	Deutsche Bundesbahn (West Germany)
DC	Direct Current
DMU	Diesel Multiple-Unit
DR	Deutsche Reichsbahn (East Germany)
DSB	Danish State Railways
DSG	German Sleeping & Dining Car Company Ltd
EMU	Electric Multiple-Unit
FDM	Frequency Division Multiplex
FOB	Furka–Oberalp Bahn
FS	Italian State Railways
hp	horsepower
HST	High Speed Train
Hz	Hertz
IC	Inter-City
ICC	Interstate Commerce Commission
JNR	Japanese National Railways
JOT	Junction Optimization Technique
JZ	Yugoslav Railways
kHz	kiloHertz
kmph	kilometres per hour
kV	kiloVolts
LMS	London Midland & Scottish Railway
LNER	London North Eastern Railway
LRT	Light Rail Transit
LRV	Light Rail Vehicle
LT	London Transport
MBTA	Massachusetts Bay Transportation Authority (Boston)
MGR	Merry-go-round (system of delivering coal)
mph	miles per hour
MTA	Metropolitan Transportation Authority
N&W	Norfolk & Western Railroad
NS	Netherlands Railways
NSB	Norwegian State Railways
NYC	New York Central
OBB	Austrian Federal Railways
PATH	Port Authority Trans-Hudson
PC	Penn-Central
PKP	Polish National Railways
PRR	Pennsylvania Railroad
PTE	Passenger Transport Executive
RA	Régime Accéléré
RATP	Paris Transport Authority
RENFE	Spanish National Railways
RER	Réseau Express Régional
RO	Régime Ordinaire
rpm	revolutions per minute
SAR	South African Railways
SBB	Swiss Federal Railways (also CFF)
SCL	Seaboard Coast Line
SEPTA	Southeastern Pennsylvania Transportation Authority (Philadelphia Rapid Transit)
SGP	Simmering–Graz–Pauker (Austrian manufacturers)
SJ	Swedish State Railways
SNCB	Belgian National Railways
SNCF	French Railways
SOB	Südostbahn
SR	Southern Railway
TALGO	*Tren Articulado Ligero Goicoechea y Oriel* (Spanish trains)
TDM	Time Division Multiplex
TECO	*Trenes Expresos de Contenedores* (Spanish freight container network
TEE	Trans-Europ Express
TEEM	Trans-Europ Express Marchandises
TEN	Trans Euro Nuit, Trans Euro Nacht, Trans Euro Notte etc.
TGV	Train Grande Vitesse
TOFC	Trailer on Flatcar (Piggyback)
TOPS	Total Operations Processing System
UHF	Ultra High Frequency
UIC	International Union of Railways
UMTA	Urban Mass Transit Administration
UP	Union Pacific Railroad
USRA	United States Railroad Association
VR	Finnish State Railways

A British Rail 5000hp Class 87 Bo-Bo emerges from Primrose Hill Tunnel, in northwest London, and begins the descent into Euston terminus with an express from Manchester, formed of BR's MkII series coaching stock, in the regular-interval inter-city service of the London Midland Region's 25kV AC electric network.

1.
BRITAIN: BIRTHPLACE OF INTER-CITY RAIL

The upsurge of road passenger and freight transport in the 1950s caught British Railways (BR) less well-armed to defend its traffics than many of its Western European neighbours. In large measure BR was the victim of historical circumstance, but some of its deficiencies were self-inflicted.

On the European mainland most railway infra-structures were so devastated and locomotive fleets and rolling stock so depredated that immediate reconstruction on a massive scale was inescapable if trains were to have more than a short-term role in postwar transport. Marshall Aid dollars were on offer from a benevolent United States of America for the job. So, given the means, most mainland railways happily seized the chance to modernize rather than merely to restore – in particular, to start the steady supersession of steam by diesel and electric traction.

Britain's railways had not been savaged by ground as well as air attacks. In places, certainly, British tracks were badly mauled by the Luftwaffe, but on nothing like the widespread scale or with such weight of bombs as those on the Continent suffered from Allied aircraft in the war's final years. There were scars to show after the war, but the tracks around them had been made good within days or weeks of the raid which inflicted the wound. Losses of loco-motives and rolling stock, too, had been compara-tively insignificant. Pushed to the limit and beyond in support of the war effort with the bare minimum of maintenance, the railways were depressingly run-down but they were thoroughly usable as a network. With capital and vital raw materials in short supply, successive British Governments therefore kicked the railways far down the queue for renewal and con-demned them to survival largely by 'make-do-and-

mend' for the first postwar decade. In that situation, naturally, there was little inducement to reconsider the traditional operational and commercial methods of running railways, even though by the early 1950s it was already clear that many of them were no match for the flexibility and economy of use auto-mobile technology was perfecting in postwar road vehicles.

A basic measure of essential renewal had to be conceded, however, and this was where British Railways voluntarily missed chances to reshape for the future. Although it had triumphantly persisted with steam development for high-speed passenger trains in the later 1930s rather than buy contem-porary German diesel streamliners, the LNER had broadmindedly recognized the subsequent vindica-tion of main-line diesel traction's superior economy and performance in the USA and was planning to

Britain's railways emerged from World War II almost unscathed compared with the destruction wrought on many European mainland systems.

dieselize its Anglo-Scottish services when it lost its identity in the 1948 nationalization of the British main-line railway network. Two more of the prewar 'Big Four', the LMS and Southern Railway (SR), were eyeing diesels with more than passing interest. But the newborn BR mechanical management short-sightedly decided to embark on a new generation of steam locomotive designs, confining diesel purchases to shunting locomotives. In other departments, too, BR built essentially to the style of a prewar railway, nowhere more so than in the capacity and charac-teristics of its freight equipment.

In general, postwar BR steam could barely regain let alone better prewar performance standards be-cause it became steadily more of an anachronism in the postwar industrial environment. Steam could no longer be guaranteed good coal; skilled men to drive and maintain it became progressively harder to

recruit as the manufacturing industry rapidly im-proved both its working conditions and its pay; and finally, given the restricted proportion of each work-ing day an individual steam locomotive can actually be employed in traffic because of its refuelling and maintenance demands, the men and resources needed to work a near-exclusively steam railway showed up in redder and redder ink on the balance sheet in an era when inflation was already incipient.

Not until 1955 was BR at last allowed to embark on a by-then dangerously overdue re-equipment plan on the grand scale. Regarding traction, the objective, very sensibly, was to electrify – and on the 25kV AC 50Hz method utilizing National Grid current at the industrial frequency which the French had per-fected since the war, not the 1.5kV DC system pre-viously endorsed for British main-line schemes; only on the Southern Region, so much of which had been

BR's first postwar electrification schemes – the SR excepted – were completed at 1.5kV DC, such as that from Manchester to Sheffield via the Woodhead Tunnel, where 2490hp Co-Co No 27003 pilots an 1870hp Bo-Bo on the Liverpool–Harwich Parkeston Quay boat train in the 1950s. The route's passenger service has since been abandoned and in 1980 the route itself faces closure.

electrified before the war on the low-voltage DC third-rail conductor system, would a different method be allowed for future extensions. Finally persuaded that steam had been outclassed both economically and practically by internal combustion engines, BR accepted that it must now buy main-line diesels; but on trunk routes they would be a stopgap pending ability to electrify.

For the rest of the 1950s and the early 1960s BR steadily lost control of its destiny. The 1955 Modernization Plan was new wine into old bottles. The trains might be diesel, instead of steam-hauled, and controlled by remotely operated colour-light instead of mechanically worked semaphore signals, but otherwise they would run to the same plan as those of the 1930s. As the 1950s faded it became clearer by the year that the costs saved by the new equipment were nowhere near enough to close the widening gap between revenue and expenditure. Some rural rail operations were so blatantly lossmaking, their traffic having ebbed away to more convenient road transport, that they were already clear candidates for closure. But where local and trunk traffic, freight and

Below:
One of BR's first postwar suburban electrification schemes – a 1.5kV DC electric multiple-unit of what is now Class 306-approaches Shenfield on a working from London's Liverpool Street in the autumn of 1949.
Bottom:
Plans of at least two of the pre-nationalization railways for main-line diesels were dropped by the newborn BR, but a handful of prototypes ordered by the LMS and Southern Railways was completed. Two of the SR's trio, the 1750hp Nos 10201 and 10202, head the 'Royal Scot' on the LMR in the mid-1950s.

passenger, shared the use of track and signalling the traditional means of railway costing failed to identify what was remunerative and what was not. Not recognizing that in the freight sector, especially, the character and quality of service and equipment styled in the 1930s mould had become uncompetitive, railwaymen tried to stop the drift of traffic to the road by underpricing. Since the services were already uneconomic, that only further aggravated the financial deterioration.

Matters became even worse when it was realized that electrification at the pace first envisaged was

way beyond the resources of industry as well as BR itself, that the soaring cost of steam demanded its immediate replacement, and that consequently diesels must be bought, untested and untried, in vast quantity at once. The price of this misadventure, inevitably, was teething traumas on a countrywide scale. Much time, effort and money was wasted before sound designs were developed and railwaymen had been thoroughly trained and the proper facilities established to operate the diesels efficiently. The pace of dieselization had to be curbed still more because the first main-line electrification from

London Euston to the Northwest overran its budget so extravagantly that successive Governments refused to authorize further schemes until the mid-1960s. It was the most hectic dieselization programme in world rail history; between 1958 and 1963 BR's steam power was cut by over 9000 locomotives to 7050, while in the same period just over 1900 main-line diesel locomotives and 1700 diesel railcar vehicles were added to stock (over 2400 of the latter were already at work by 1958).

But this book is intended to deal with *modern* railways. Why, then, rake over the 1950s and early

One of the most successful of the range of new standard steam classes built by BR before it dieselized was the Class 9F heavy freight 2-10-0. Despite 5ft-diameter driving wheels, it was timed at up to 90mph on some occasions when it was pressed into passenger service. No 92233 climbs to Ais Gill summit on the former Midland main line from Carlisle to Leeds, with a train of anhydrite for Widnes, in northwest England.

1960s? Because what happened then – which, one should emphasize, has had to be summarized very cursorily – explains why today's BR is so much leaner-looking than its contemporary Western European neighbours.

With private ownership of the railways until 1948 there was no concept in Britain of railways as a state-supported service, or for that matter a locally supported one. Although the 'Big Four' emerged from war service financially as well as materially exhausted, there was common conviction that they would break even as one state-owned network. Consequently the mounting deficits at the dawn of the 1960s were cause for acute political concern. In other countries with state-run railways, subsidies – to temper charges to selected classes of passenger or freight user, or to relieve railways of some of their infrastructure costs and put them on more equitable competitive terms with road transport – were established budgetary practice. In France, Italy, West Germany and many other countries the national railway system's published surplus or deficit was and still is the balance struck *after* absorbing these benefits. Thus the nominal loss of Western Germany's Deutsche Bundesbahn in 1978 was around £1200 ($2700) million, but its full cost to the country after taking account of a wide range of state compensations for mandatorily low fares, of contributions for level-crossing maintenance, of investment grants etc, was an incredible £4000 ($9000) million.

To Britons in 1960, on the other hand, every penny of operating cost, investment or loan interest which BR failed to cover out of its own revenue was loss. With that loss escalating into millions of pounds something must have been drastically wrong with the way BR was run. So in the early 1960s an industrialist from private industry, Dr (later Lord) Beeching, was put in charge with a brief to rethink the role of the railway in a motorcar age.

Beeching has an eternal niche in British history – and some worldwide repute too – for his ruthless axing of the country's rural railways. Within five years of his tenure as BR's chairman, from 1963 to 1968, he had lopped off a third of the route mileage run by passenger trains and shut nearly 1700 passenger stations. For a number of reasons, however, the eventual cost savings of that exercise were disproportionate to the political furore it excited. Much more significant were the economies in manpower and resources and the gains in competitiveness achieved in succeeding years as development after development was derived from a basic tenet of Beeching doctrine: that the economic unit of rail movement is a train, not its individual vehicles. Additional gains were made when modern marketing techniques were applied to these reshaped services.

Beeching's overriding concern was the under-utilization of increasingly costly assets inherent in blind following of traditional railway practice. As he himself put it at the time, 'Railways were developed to their fullest extent at a time when the horse and cart were the only means of feeding to and distributing from them. In order to provide for a large measure of rail participation in country-wide collection and delivery of small consignments – a task which they were never particularly well suited to do, and which they only did because the horse and cart were worse – the railways squandered their main advantages. They saddled themselves with the handling of light flows on a multiplicity of branch lines, and they sacrificed the speed, reliability and low cost of through-train operation, even over the main arteries of the system. In addition, this slow and semi-random movement of wagons necessitated the provision of an enormous wagon fleet, all of which had to be capable of coupling and running with one another and of going almost anywhere on the system. This, unavoidably, introduced great technical inertia, since the new railways had to match the old. In consequence, evolutionary change of rolling stock became very slow. The way out is to develop new services, with new rolling stock, not compatible with the old.'

Any freight service which dealt preponderantly in wagonloads was suspect. Aside from the commercial concern that any operation in which wagons were shunted from one train to another en route, perhaps several times, protracted transits and was vulnerable to unreliability, it was a question of the insupportable costs of such practice. It was this problem, particularly, that Beeching's researches clarified for the first time. Not only was the shunting expensive, but the wagons spent so much time loitering in yards and originating or destination sidings that they were averaging no more than a beggarly 70 miles or so under load every two weeks. That way of working was compounding the railway's competitive disadvantage, costwise, of having to maintain an elaborately staffed and controlled infrastructure entirely

Right:
The rural railway scene that disappeared after Beeching – in the dying years of BR steam an ex-LNER Class D40 4-4-0 trundles a local pick-up freight train over the former Great North of Scotland line near Elgin.
Below:
Diesel dawn – the first of the Western Region's diesel-hydraulics, the 2000hp NBL/MAN A1A-A1A No D600 *Active*, on a demonstration run for railway officers and the press between Paddington and Bristol on 17 February 1958. One of the least successful of BR's 'pilot dieselization scheme' designs, all five of the type were scrapped in 1967.

out of its own resources (in Britain, at least). But where the traffic flows were heaviest, both in passengers and freight, disciplined use of the railway's reserved roadway coupled with modern equipment's ability to shift huge tonnages at speed for a minimal train crew outlay gave it a decided edge over motor transport. The objective, therefore, must be the maximum of uninterrupted through-trainload movement over the minimum of track. Only by such concentration on low-cost operation, moreover, could a financial surplus be generated for ongoing investment in sophisticated track, signalling and vehicles.

To fulfil Beeching's plan, of course, BR had to be free to pick and choose its business and price as it judged fit. That concession was granted in the 1962 Transport Act; it released BR from the common carrier obligations imposed on all major railways in one form or another to curb any possible exploitation of their overwhelming superiority in the pre-motor

transport market. After that BR could, for example, refuse to deliver household coal by the wagonload to every local station yard and invite coal merchants to invest collaboratively in a few strategic, mechanized depots which could be served by the trainload and from which local delivery would radiate by road.

Away from the main British population and manufacturing complexes practically every British station demonstrates the outcome of Beeching's reforms and contrasts sharply with its counterpart in mainland Europe. At the average British station all that survives of a goods yard is the prints of sleepers all but obliterated by weeds, plus a one-time goods depot probably masked by the nameboards of some local entrepreneur who has leased or bought it for other use. The station may still deal in parcels sent by passenger train, but otherwise the neighbourhood's only contact with rail freight is through road vehicles which radiate from the nearest of the

system's limited number of less-than-wagon-load merchandise trans-shipment depots. On the other side of the English Channel, though, all but the most bucolic stations still sprout a foliage of sidings with an adjoining covered freight depot. A good many, in West Germany especially, will even have a diminutive diesel locomotive in permanent residence for shunting; the Deutsche Bundesbahn deploys some 1200 such 130hp diesel tractors in addition to a four-figure fleet of heavy yard shunters proper.

By and large mainland European railways still have a common carrier duty, and in one way or another are financially supported by the state in fulfilling it. Consequently they have been and still are much more solicitous for wagonload freight business than British Rail. This shows in the much greater number of private industrial as well as open station sidings they serve. Since 1960 BR has aban-

doned some 4000 private sidings because their business was preponderantly wagonload and sporadic, and now caters for around 2000. In West Germany the current total is over 10,000 and in France more than 9000, but whereas the DB's 10,000-plus sidings generate around 80 percent of the West German railway's freight, BR's 2000-odd are responsible for all but two percent of its total originating and all but seven percent of its total terminating tonnage – and practically all of it is in full trainloads.

Compression of BR's freight activity into full trainloads working from origin to destination has been pursued still more energetically in the Arctic like economic climate of the 1970s, and today a higher percentage of BR rail freight moves in block trains than anywhere else in Western Europe. The measure of its economy in resources can be judged from the record of BR's Western Region in 1975–77.

One of the big automated marshalling yards built at high cost under the 1955 Modernization Plan was Temple Mills, near Stratford in East London. In 1980 many of these yards were operating at far below their planned capacity – and in one or two cases used principally as storage space – because of BR's subsequent concentration on unit-freight-train operation.

A strength of BR's Freightliner operation has been its adoption by the motor industry for containerized exchange of components and assemblies between plants both in Britain and in mainland Europe. Complete, so-called 'company trains' are run for Ford from this terminal at Barking, near the company's Dagenham plant, to Harwich for container shipment to Zeebrugge for Ford plants in Belgium and West Germany.

Modernization Plan, the latter are now seriously under-employed because such a high proportion of BR's freight moves as intact trainloads from start to terminal – or is a *block working* in railway parlance. More than one of these yards, in fact, would never have been built had Beeching come to power earlier, but he did arrive in time to quash three more while they were still on the drawing board.

The second obvious contrast between BR and the other major European systems is the British system's meagre reserve of relief trackage and loops. Here again, overgrown trackbeds survive to underline how much has been lifted since the 1960s. Most was regarded as superfluous, expensive to maintain and signal, given the progressive concentration of traffic in trainloads of high-performance vehicles on key arterial routes.

Although he wanted out of the traditional handling of merchandise freight, Beeching was set on keeping a firm foothold in this, the fastest-growing of all freight markets as postwar consumer society evolved. To be both competitive and remunerative demanded a new approach: the marriage of local road collection and delivery with trainload trunk haulage, allotting to each medium the job it did most efficiently. The tool to effect the link was the high-capacity container. The main trunk flows of consumer-goods freight were aligned with BR's busiest main lines. Therefore the extra high-speed container trains could be operated at marginal run-on operating cost and the exercise promised to throw up enough surplus for heavy investment in custom-built container trains and road-rail container transshipment terminals in the main industrial and port areas. Also needed to justify that investment, however, was continuous revenue-earning use of the equipment.

Freightliner, launched in 1965, was the outcome. Conceptually, it was the equivalent of a conveyor-belt system for containers, with fixed train-sets of flatcars capable of express-train performance shuttling non-stop between pairs of strategically sited terminals. Massive gantry cranes spanning each terminal's tracks would guarantee the stipulated high rate of road-rail container transfer sufficient to promise overnight door-to-door transit between and match of production and distribution centres within 50–75 miles of a Freightliner depot. The expectation was that many of the big road hauliers would find it paid them to put their trunk traffic into Freightliner containers.

In the inland freight movement market BR's Freightliners have never quite lived up to their original prospectus, although they have certainly built up substantial containerized business in a variety of products, from Guinness stout to military equipment, which would otherwise have been lost to road. The reasons are various, but the most influential was underestimation of the costs of road collection and delivery of containers, and of the

In the wake of the oil crisis Western Region's freight tonnage slipped by five percent, but during the same period pressures for more economical operation clipped as much as 40 percent from the train-mileage run to shift the business.

Two more conspicuous differences distinguish BR from its European neighbours as a result of the focus on bulk flows between main commercial areas as prescribed by Beeching. One is that while the Continentals are still building huge and costly new automated marshalling yards, BR is not. Despite closure of so many old yards devoid of modern appliances and concentration of their work on several handsomely automated yards built under the 1955

minimum distance at which transport by Freightliner could realistically and economically compete with road. The latter has turned out to be nearer 200 miles than the 100 miles initially calculated. A side-effect of the expansion of Britain's motorways not fully foreseen was that firms would be induced to move their premises from cluttered and declining city centres to 'greenbelt' areas. That took them farther from Freightliner terminals and naturally magnified the deterrent of road transport movement costs to and from the railway depots.

Whatever Freightliners have missed inland, however, has been offset by their deep penetration of most sectors of the maritime container trade. More than half the boxes conveyed by the 200 1000-ton Freightliner trains which daily interconnect 36 terminals (11 of them privately owned) are moving from or to the country's container ports such as Harwich, Felixstowe, Southampton, Greenock and Liverpool. Whether the balance of Freightliner traffic will stay that way is another matter, for full application of European Economic Community restrictions on a heavy road freight vehicle driver's working day are estimated to trim road transport's productivity by as much as 20 percent before the 1980s are very old; that will drastically inflate the cost of domestic road trunk transport in Britain (it will make roll-on/roll-off road freight between Britain and Continental centres less attractive too). Freightliner trains are equipped to maintain 75mph on the open road, but intermediate stops for train-crew changes peg most end-to-end average speeds at around 50mph.

The Freightliner model has been adopted intact by a few other countries, notably Japan, but not to the extent BR hoped. The British wanted to see a European network of terminals interlinked by dedicated non-stop, Freightliner-type trains with container ships or train ferries bridging the maritime gap between Great Britain and the mainland. The whole journey was to be commonly priced to customers and centrally managed in such a way that a rate could be readily quoted for any reasonable door-to-door container movement within European boundaries. An international management company, Intercontainer, was set up and now numbers several countries without as well as within Western Europe. But it is little more than a sales organization, working within the individual rates of its member systems. Anxious not to prejudice their wagonload business, mainland European railways were wary of pricing container traffic as competitively as the British urged. Nor were they enamoured of BR's custom-built, articulated five-car Freightliner flatcar sets: a fault on one vehicle, they worried, would inconveniently immobilize four more. The other Western European railways certainly run many dedicated container trains and in several cases have terminals as comprehensively equipped for rapid road-rail transfer as BR, but many containers are carried on flat wagons adaptable to other traffic, and a substantial proportion of the container movement is by the wagonload, within the orthodox pattern of freight train operation. Until the late 1970s that applied to at least half the container traffic of West Germany's DB, which travelled on standard flat wagons innocent of container-locking devices and hence unable to run at anywhere near the 75mph of BR's Freightliners.

Britain's coal industry owes BR a lot for the 'merry-go-round' or MGR system of pit-to-power station coal feed. Without its reduction of transport

West Burton power station, on the River Trent east of Retford, Nottinghamshire, was the first to be fed with coal by trains of new high-capacity, automatic-discharge hopper wagons running in continuous circuit under BR's 'merry-go-round' system. A Class 47 diesel approaches the discharge bunkers, over which it will haul its train non-stop at a controlled 0.5mph as the wagons are automatically unloaded.

Above:
Merry-go-round in action – a loaded train traverses the discharge bunkers at Ferrybridge C power station in Yorkshire. At the side of the vacant track to the right can be seen the machines which engage the controls of the hopper wagons' bottom doors as the train passes at 0.5mph, opening them to discharge the coal through the grid between the rails to the bunkers below.
Below:
BR's latest diesel electric locomotive design in 1980, the 3520hp Class 56, essentially a heavy freight haulier.

costs coal would not have been the selected fuel for a number of Britain's latest electricity generating plants. Again the principle is essentially that of a conveyor-belt, with trains of high-capacity hopper wagons in continuous circuit between pit and power station. At the colliery the wagons are rapidly overhead-loaded, and if operation is smooth, an MGR train should not halt until it returns to the pithead empty for a fresh load. At the power station the track is laid out in a full circle which at one point bridges sub-surface coal bunkers. The Class 47 and 56 diesel-electric locomotives assigned to MGR duty are fitted with a slow speed control and the MGR wagons have discharge doors which are automatically activated by lineside apparatus. Thus an MGR train can inch steadily over a power station bunker and be auto-

matically unloaded, wagon by wagon, without stopping. In a further refinement perfected by BR (but the practical use of which was until recently blocked by railwaymen's union resistance) this slow passage of the unloading area can be unmanned, with the locomotive under remote control from the ground, so that the locomotive crew can economically be released for one of their rest breaks during the tedious unloading process. After unloading, the train completes its circuit of the plant area and goes straight back to the pit.

Merry-go-round is most highly developed in BR's Eastern Region, especially in the feed of 285,000-300,000 tonnes of coal weekly from some 30 collieries in South Yorkshire to three huge baseload power stations in the Aire Valley just to the east of the coalfield – Ferrybridge, Eggborough and Drax. For a variety of reasons connected with getting the right qualities of coal for efficient generation, the Eastern Region does not know until the Thursday of each week the collieries from which the power stations will draw in the following week and the tonnages involved in each case. Nevertheless within 24 hours a highly cost-effective train and train-crew plan is produced for the ensuing week.

It is achieved by feeding the data into a computer which is programmed to deploy a minimum number of locomotives, men and fixed hopper train-sets to fulfil the task, with the maximum possible amount of single-manning of locomotives within BR's agreements with the enginemen's union, and at the same time respecting all the practical constraints of colliery working hours, pithead and power-station track layouts, and so on. The average distance run by the MGR trains in this operation is only 20 miles, yet the efficiency of the computer's timetabling and of continuous circuit working, is such that the operat-

ing ratio of this whole MGR exercise is a remarkable 25 percent – in other words running costs are a quarter of revenue. One locomotive and train-set can make up to seven loaded trips in 24 hours and the biggest of the three power stations can take in up to 40 trainloads of over 1200 tonnes of coal in the scheme's standard 30-wagon train-sets during the same period. Now, using the much bigger TOPS central computer at BR's central headquarters, the technique is to be applied to a much bigger area of MGR operation shifting over 800,000 tonnes of coal weekly and involving 55 locomotives, 450 trainmen and over 5500 hopper wagons.

BR's heaviest regular trains serve the country's steel industry on MGR principles. When the British Steel Corporation decided to focus its production on five main centres in close proximity to new deep-sea ore trans-shipment terminals it was persuaded to invest its own money heavily in rail movement between coast and manufacturing plant. For this, the continuously circuiting ore trains are made up of tippler wagons with 100 tons loaded capacity and special rotatable couplings. The latter allow each wagon to be rotated or tippled sideways through an angle of 160 degrees so that its contents can be discharged without its being uncoupled from its neighbours. In BR's Western Region, between the Port Talbot ore terminal and Llanwern steelworks in South Wales, 27-wagon trains of these tipplers, permanently coupled and demanding haulage by a pair of Class 56 3250hp diesel-electrics, move 2000 tons of ore per trip, unload it within 45 minutes, then circle straight back to the coast for more. The conveyor-belt characteristic of this operation is emphasized by the fact that the local operating staff have a standing order to give the ore trains priority over short-distance passenger trains if timetable working

gets behind the clock; nothing must prevent the ore trains from completing their scheduled three round trips each working day.

The ownership of the tippler wagons by the British Steel Corporation and the latter's footing of the whole bill for the loading and unloading apparatus at Port Talbot and Llanwern needs stress. Held on a very tight investment rein by Government after Government since 1960 BR has striven to persuade customers with rail-suited trainload traffic to buy or lease their own high-performance, high-capacity wagons and set up their own loading and discharge plants. Recognizing the environmental advantage of trainload trunk movement of commodities like chemicals and building aggregates, the Government in 1974 supported the BR drive by offering potential clients 50 percent of the cost of equipping for bulk rail movement, but many had been convinced of the efficiency of BR's reshaped freight practice long before that and spent heavily from their own funds. In particular every major oil company acquired substantial fleets of 100-ton tankers and concluded long-term contracts to stream their products by rail from coastal refineries to inland distribution depots. Other important customers have been the chemical industry and firms quarrying material out in the country for roadbuilding and urban construction. Something like one-fifth of the total freight vehicle capacity deployed on BR today is privately owned and the proportion steadily rises.

This is just as well, because BR's own wagon fleet – drastically slimmed from over 850,000 vehicles at Beeching's accession to a mere 150,000 by the end of the 1970s – is on average the most outdated of any major European railway's. Too much of it is still of the same four-wheel, low-capacity pattern which set British railways apart from mainland European

The 100-tons-gross tank wagon has become prominent in BR's block freight train operations, chiefly for conveyance of oil products but also in chemical traffic. Trains of cryogenic tankers, one of them hauled here by No 87.022, regularly travel the LMR's electrified Euston–Northwest main line for the British Oxygen Company.

systems as long as 50 years ago. There is nothing wrong with a rigid four-wheeler *per se*. Latter-day wheel-and-rail technology has devised a two-axle frame and suspension that will run as sweetly and safely at up to 100mph as any bogie vehicle; such a four-wheeler is less expensive to build and maintain, proportionately to its capacity, than the bogie car and is more adaptable to the cramped layouts often encountered in private sidings. Thus a higher proportion of the latest freight vehicles operating on BR are four-wheelers than on some mainland European railways. The vital features of the modern British four-wheeler are first its long wheelbase, which affords a much bigger and more economical carrying capacity than the still prevalent short-wheelbase wagons of the immediate postwar era; and second that it is air-braked.

In the late 19th century the majority of the then-privately run railways of Great Britain opted for vacuum rather than air braking – and that primarily for passenger stock. Until the 1950s the greater part of British freight stock was built with nothing but handbrakes, so that on all too many goods trains a driver's braking resource was limited to his engine and any continuously brake-fitted wagons marshalled immediately behind it. Given the chance to modernize comprehensively in 1955, the then-BR chiefs quailed at the inconvenience of an all-line conversion to more efficient air-braking and thus hosts of new wagons and new diesel locomotives were built with vacuum braking. But with the rapid rise of passenger train speed a changeover to quicker-acting and less defect-prone air braking soon became necessary – but at considerably greater cost because it was so tardy. Thus many nearly new locomotives now required conversion. By the 1970s all new freight stock was constructed with air braking as a matter of course, but the wretchedly slow rate of new freight vehicle construction to which BR has been limited forced the system to enter the 1980s still using a residue of the old exclusively hand-braked wagons. And it will be the middle of the decade at least before the last vacuum-braked wagons are replaced.

It was not long after Beeching's withdrawal from railways that BR realized it could not afford a starkly draconian attitude to wagonload business. Un-

BR's present-day freight marketing aims chiefly for long-term, unit-train contracts under which the customer invests in his own terminals and rolling stock, like these special-purpose wagons which ship trainloads for Cleveland Potash from Boulby Mine in northeast Yorkshire. Where there is environmental as well as economic gain in such deals, 50 percent Government coverage of the customer's investment is available.

Above:
To stimulate its considerable
business in the shipment of
new cars from manufacturing
plants to distributors, BR
devised an articulated four-
unit double-deck car-carrier,
known as the Cartic 4, which
maximized payloads within
the limits of the British
loading gauge and permissible
wagon axleloads.
Left:
For its Speedlink service of
strictly timetabled,
controlled-capacity through
trains between major centres
for wagonload freight, BR has
produced a long-wheelbase
two axle wagon capable of
standard operation at 75mph.

profitable as it was, it helped share fixed track and
staff costs, which the rest of the freight operation
would have to shoulder *in toto* if all the wagonload
traffic incapable of reshaping into block train workings were voluntarily discarded. Furthermore much
of the wagonload contents was high-tariff merchandise, well worth keeping on rail – or more accurately,
worth recapturing, since so much had already been
lost due to the erratic performance of the traditional
wagonload system, with its badly dated equipment.

Three components were essential to the rebirth of a
fully competitive wagonload operation: a train plan
guaranteeing overnight service; high-capacity
75mph freight vehicles to implement it; and a control
system which both ensured optimum utilization of
resources to furnish such a quality service at tolerable
cost and assured customers that progress of their
consignments was instantly verifiable. The vehicles
were the long-wheelbase four-wheelers recently
mentioned, produced with varying types of open and
closed bodywork. And the train plan, marketed
under the brandname of Speedlink, was strictly a
centre-to-centre operation by tightly timed trains
between production and distribution railheads, or
between a port and an inland railhead.

The Communications Data Control centre of BR's TOPS system. Here all messages between TOPS terminals and the system's central on-line computer are monitored and converted into computer language.

En route Speedlink trains pass through no marshalling yards; a small proportion make one stop on the way at an intermediate town with worthwhile traffic potential to drop off or attach a ready-marshalled section of wagons. The gross load of each Speedlink train, moreover, is rigidly controlled so that there is no risk of operational delay from excess weight. Speedlink services are not confined to BR's own wagons; BR is eager to convey – and does – compatible privately owned vehicles via the Speedlink network, among them Continental European wagons arriving in Britain via the Zeebrugge-Harwich and Dunkerque-Dover train ferries. On one or two routes, furthermore, Speedlink and Freightliner sections are combined as one train where there is inadequate traffic to justify a separate working of either.

The control system overseeing Speedlink and a great deal else is TOPS (Total Operations Processing System), a computer-based system capable of continuously monitoring, recording and reporting every detail of traffic throughout the whole BR network. TOPS became operational during the late 1970s. In principle TOPS was devised by the Southern Pacific Railroad of the USA in the 1960s. It is a real-time system: that is, those using it – which can include freight customers – deal directly with the central computer apparatus which is always on line to receive data from and disseminate information to input/output terminals at every key centre on BR. From the data it is routinely fed on every vehicle movement and requirement by operators of the local terminals, the TOPS computer can instantly pinpoint the location of every loaded wagon and match the deployment of resources to demand with fine precision. Its monitoring capability is an invaluable asset to freight customer relations, but vastly more important is the considerable economy in use of resources that has accrued since TOPS was commissioned, not only through its finer tailoring of traction and rolling stock supply and of train service to demand fluctuations. For example, now that the daily mileage of every locomotive is accurately com-

mitted to the computer bank down to the last digit, maintenance schedules arbitrarily requiring all locomotives of a specific class to attend workshops after a given time in service are anachronisms. Schedules are now mileage-based, with the certainty that TOPS will call up each individual locomotive only when it needs attention. As a result countless BR locomotives nowadays are spending longer periods in traffic between essential depot or works visits in perfect mechanical security.

Expansion of the Speedlink network depends partly on the rate at which BR is allowed to invest in appropriate rolling stock. The obsolescence of so much of BR's freight equipment is one reason that the 1970s and 1980s balance of traffic which the Beeching administration envisaged for BR has not materialized. Given the full reshaping prescribed, the expectation in the early 1960s was freight sector growth but on the passenger side a holding operation – at best – against the progressive encroachments of air and motor transport. In the event, for reasons touched upon earlier, freight revenue slumped but inter-city passenger trains significantly enlarged their market share.

At the same time the country began to realize that passenger service closures on the scale and at the pace they were executed in the early 1960s had a domino effect. Each branch or secondary main-line service shutdown withdrew at least some connecting through traffic from the rest of the system, undermining the latter's economics and – as with rejected wagonload business in the freight sector – loading the remaining services with a higher share of overhead expenses. In the nature of the railway no closure instantly eliminated all the costs the service concerned had been incurring. Persistence with such clinical line-by-line evaluation could easily make the system contract to a trunk route skeleton, shorn even of its conurbation commuter lines, almost all of which were heavily in the red.

The country's 1968 Transport Act therefore formalized for the first time in British history the principle of public money support for socially necessary rail passenger services. To rationalize public transport as a whole in the provincial conurbations and to integrate its planning with that of highway, housing and industrial development in each area, the Act established Passenger Transport Executives, or PTEs, to function as agents of co-terminous local government authorities. Today there are seven PTEs: Greater Manchester, Merseyside, South Yorkshire, West Yorkshire, Tyne & Wear, Greater Glasgow and West Midlands. From central Government, BR draws annually a global sum known as its Public Service Obligation (PSO) grant, the level of which is fixed by the Government, to make good losses on socially necessary passenger services outside the PTE areas. Within the PTE areas BR runs local passenger services to the order of the PTEs, who specify the rail routes in their area to be served, frequency of service and fare scales to be applied, covering themselves any revenue shortfall on BR's outlay in covering their requirements. Contrivance of a similar arrangement for London has so far proved intractable, chiefly because the speed and frequency of BR's latter-day passenger operation has spread the capital's dormitory area at least 70, and in some directions as much as 100 miles, from the city centre. This brings the longer-distance commuters within the inter-city orbit, a market where BR is naturally reluctant to cede any control of service planning, pricing or marketing.

Stabilization of the passenger network under the 1968 Act, its guarantee of financial support and the business growth stimulated by the vanguard of today's high-speed passenger services, made 1969 a milestone in British Rail history. For the first time the country's railways took more money from passengers than freight. It has stayed that way ever since.

The regular-interval frequency which is a cardinal principle of BR's contemporary passenger operation – and which has been a key factor in its success – has been gratefully adopted by one mainland European railway after another. Some, like West Germany's DB and Holland's NS, have even borrowed BR's Inter-City brandname untranslated, though the Swiss Federal Railways have mutated it to 'Inter-Ville'.

Credit for the concept, however, really belongs to the prewar Southern Railway. When the SR in the

1930s extended its ramified low-voltage DC third-rail London suburban electrification to the South Coast resorts, it applied to the newly electrified main lines precisely the same operating practices which had been so successful on the short-distance routes: a strictly patterned, hourly-interval service with standard multiple-unit train-sets, quickly turned round at terminals because they were double-ended; this combined convenience of use for the customer with maximum use of assets and optimal employment of train-crews.

Before World War II Britain's railways had clung

Above: Two German firms have built (for leasing) fleets of high-capacity vans for international traffic via train ferries. They are the biggest possible within the BR loading gauge.

Below:
An SR inter-city multiple-unit of two Class 491 sets propelled by a Class 430 1460hp four-car motored unit arrives at Bournemouth from Waterloo.

to a few places in the world table of fastest daily trains – though by 1939 the British entrants were lagging far behind the front-running American and German diesels – with a specially nurtured elite of services like the 'Silver Jubilee' and 'Coronation' streamliners of the LNER. But between them and the bulk of the British train service there was quite a yawning gulf in end-to-end speed. For a good many postwar years BR's express passenger service was equally unbalanced, though the highest prewar average speeds were not yet recouped.

From the 1960s onward, however, selectivity was out. Any step-up in speed must apply commensurately to the whole range of a route's inter-city services to avoid waste of track capacity by creating operational 'vacuums' between trains of widely divergent pace as well as to enhance the overall salability of the service. Obviously some trains would still have an end-to-end speed edge over the rest – at peak travel hours, for instance, business trains between the far provinces and London would be making fewer intermediate stops and of necessity be timed to give their clientele the maximum period at destination to transact their affairs. By then French Railways, with the benefit of immediate postwar main-line electrification, had clearly demonstrated the attraction to the commercial world of high-speed morning and evening trains affording Parisians a comfortable business day in, for instance, Lyons and Lille – or vice versa – without having to spend the night away. But the line speed of the whole service must be standardized.

The switch from temperamental steam power to more predictable diesel and electric traction made the policy still more rational, though the outcome on dieselized routes has never been immaculate because as yet BR's scope for investment has not permitted acquisition of sufficient traction units with individual power ratings of the magnitude needed to transform a whole service. Even now BR's 125mph High Speed Diesel Train units, the HSTs, have to share tracks with expresses hauled by locomotives limited to 90–100mph and of which the total power/train weight ratio is much less generous, so that their accelerative competence is well below an HST's.

The initial target for all key routes was a minimum start-to-stop average speed between cities of 75mph. This was seen as the absolute baseline, in conjunction with an easily memorable and fixed-interval service of hourly frequency, for effective competition with the door-to-door speed and convenience of an automobile exploiting the new motorways. But with time the economic as well as the straight commercial advantage of speed emerged: the faster each journey, the more journeys could be completed in a working day with the same set of coaches and locomotive, not

Two generations of BR coaching stock – the early MkI type in the 08.10 Liverpool–Newcastle passes Batley behind diesel No 40.070 in April 1977; and (inset) the latest MkIII (buffet car excepted) speeds from Birmingham to Euston alongside the M1 motorway behind a Class 86 AC electric locomotive.

necessarily on the same route. The economic benefits would be maximized on electrified routes, of course, because it needed exploitation to the full of an electric traction unit's near-continuous availability for work and optimization of every inch of track capacity to amortize the high capital cost of setting up the catenary. Since they demanded no extra vehicles or locomotives, the extra trains timetabled as a result of the quickened tempo of working would be operated at marginal added cost in maintenance, crewing and energy. The extra seats they created could therefore be sold at a discounted fare.

That may be a hazardous over-simplification of the economics, but it is essentially the basis on which the present-day BR Inter-City timetable (without world peer for its combination of speed, frequency, network breadth and distances involved) has been built up and priced with an astute mix of full and cheap fares styled to balance peak and off-peak loads, and to appeal to the purse of each attainable market sector. Japan's Shinkansen trains, described in a later chapter, are superior in speed over many inter-city sections and run at comparable or in some cases higher frequency, but the Shinkansen network is not yet as wide-ranging as BR's high-speed Inter-City enterprise. In 1979 West Germany's DB rebuilt its Inter-City timetable on an hourly basis, but for reasons outlined in a subsequent chapter cannot yet match BR for end-to-end speed.

The operators of the East Coast Route from London to industrial Yorkshire, the Northeast and Scotland were pioneers of BR's intensive, fixed-interval Inter-City service over the island's longest distances, but the concept first fully bloomed with the 1966–67 completion of the 25kV AC London Midland Region electrification from London Euston to the West Midlands and Liverpool and Manchester in the Northwest. After an infuriating period of Government hesitation the catenary was at last continued to Glasgow to complete conversion of the Anglo-Scottish West Coast Route in 1974. Since then, depressingly, succeeding Governments have unbuttoned the electrification purse only for commuter schemes around London, so that by the end of the 1970s BR was languishing in seventeenth place among the world's national railways for percentage of total route-mileage electrified – a miserable 20 percent, less than the electrified component of Spain's far-from-affluent RENFE or of such Eastern Bloc systems as Poland's PKP and Bulgaria's BDZ. But the deepening energy crisis seems likely to make Britain's political masters more amenable to fresh main-line electrification in the 1980s.

By the end of the 1960s the London Midland electric service – the first on BR to be marketed not only with a sheaf of discounted off-peak fare offers but also with the whole panoply of modern marketing aids including TV commercials (ever since BR's chief promotional tool) – had doubled previous rail passenger carryings between London and the North-

west. Sustained 100mph running and point-to-point average speeds of up to 80mph accumulated 75 percent of the route's travel market and drove the domestic airlines to thin out their flights between London and both Liverpool and Manchester.

Today service between London Euston and each of these two northwestern cities is hourly the whole day long, with extra peak trains. Journey time for the $188\frac{3}{4}$ miles to Manchester is generally about two hours and 35 minutes inclusive of intermediate stops, and is two hours and 40 minutes for the $193\frac{1}{2}$ miles to Liverpool. Over the $113\frac{1}{4}$ miles between London and the West Midlands city of Birmingham, notwithstanding a parallel motorway (Britain's first), traffic growth has stimulated a doubling of service to half-hourly frequency since the electric trains' debut. Standard time for this itinerary, two intermediate stops included, is one hour and 37 minutes. At the start of the 1980s the London Midland's electric Inter-City timetable was studded with over 160 start-to-stop schedules daily averaging 80mph or more up to a peak of 88.8mph over the 65 miles between Rugby and the London outer suburban railhead of Watford Junction.

Denied the electrification it had been glibly promised in the 1955 Modernization Plan, BR's East Coast route from London to the North achieved near-comparable levels of speed and inter-city frequency at lower first cost by a combination of (a) infrastructure work to realign speed-limiting curves and respace signalling for extended braking distance, which fettled up four-fifths of the $268\frac{1}{4}$ miles from London Kings Cross to Newcastle for 100mph running, and (b) investment in 22 diesel-electric locomotives of unique provenance. These, the 3300hp English Electric 'Deltics', BR's Class 55, are the only main-line locomotives in world history so far to have successfully exploited a diesel engine originally conceived for marine use. It is the unusual triangular configuration of the Napier opposed-piston high-rpm engines, created for fast naval patrol craft, which bestowed their class name on the 'Deltics'. The engine was so compact that a pair could be embodied in each locomotive to produce the 3300hp output in a six-axle Co-Co machine with 105mph top speed for a total weight of only 105 tons, a very impressive power/weight ratio for a diesel locomotive at the time of the 'Deltics'' emergence in the early 1960s.

Step by step the East Coast Inter-City timetable was accelerated and intensified on the fixed-interval basis until by 1973 the 'Flying Scotsman' was linking London and Edinburgh, $392\frac{3}{4}$ miles apart, in $5\frac{1}{2}$ hours; and nine trains each way between London and Newcastle were on an *average* end-to-end schedule for the $268\frac{1}{4}$ miles of $3\frac{3}{4}$ hours, stops en route included. The schedules featured point-to-point average speeds as keen as 83mph for the $204\frac{1}{2}$ miles from Darlington in northeastern England, to Stevenage, the new town on the northern perimeter of London.

More daily mileage in traffic was squeezed out of

the 'Deltics' than from any other BR diesel type. Without deft work diagramming that manoeuvred the locomotives on to a remarkably high proportion of the East Coast route's expresses in relation to the size of the 'Deltic' fleet, the overall speed standard of the service would have been unattainable. At the zenith of the 'Deltic' operation it was commonplace for one locomotive to accomplish both a return and a unidirectional London–Edinburgh trip totalling almost 1180 miles within 24 hours.

The speed and intensity of BR's Inter-City service has not been attained without a sacrifice of some traditional conveniences. It was remarked earlier that it is the extraction of marginal use from assets which generates the scope for marketing at variable prices. Productivity of coaching stock, therefore, is as critical as that of locomotives. To optimize it a train-set must be adaptable to market demands not only at different periods of the day but also on dif-

ferent routes, so that it can be slotted into whatever trips most conveniently fulfil the timetable specification and simultaneously secure the maximum possible daily mileage from the vehicles. This presupposes standardization of train formats, which in turn rules out detachment or attachment of through coaches to and from places off an arterial Inter-City route. But in any event BR's terminal stations have neither the platforms nor the approach layout capacity to divorce arrivals and departures in a service of present-day intensity. The highest possible proportion of incoming train-sets have to be cleaned and revictualled at the platform, then turned round as a departure, not hauled away to carriage yards for servicing. This also makes train-set standardization imperative.

In consequence there is less sectionalized train working on BR than on any other European system – even than in a country of still shorter inland

The East Coast Route's 3300hp Class 55 'Deltic' diesel-electrics spearheaded the high-speed drive of the 1960s in non-electrified territory. No 55018 *Ballymoss* climbs out of Newcastle past Chester-le-Street with the 14.45 Edinburgh–Kings Cross in July 1976.

In Britain there is no tradition of municipal contribution to the cost of new stations as a civic asset, such as there is in mainland Europe. BR's only hope of mitigating the cost is to associate such schemes with commercial development, though possibilities there have lately been limited by new taxation laws. Consequently Britain has lately seen few new stations on the scale of London's Euston, the concourse of which is seen here.

distances like the Netherlands, where the timetable makes considerable play with the assembly and dispersal of multiple-unit sections. Gone are trains like the Southern Region's 'Atlantic Coast Express', which dropped off coaches for seven or eight different branches to holiday resorts in Devon and Cornwall en route from London's Waterloo Station to Plymouth. Many journeys once possible by through coach or train from London now entail interchange at some point between the Inter-City network and a local service, often a diesel multiple-unit, though the nuisance is mitigated by a much quicker end-to-end journey time despite the change en route. A compensatory benefit of train-set standardization is the availability of restaurant or fixed buffet services on a higher proportion of BR trains than anywhere else in Europe.

Economic pursuit of standardization has also killed off every British Pullman train bar one, the 'Manchester Pullman'. In face of the ascendant quality (including air-conditioning in both classes) of Inter-City services in general the Pullmans could only find a premium-fare market in the morning and evening business peaks, which kept them unacceptably idle throughout the middle of the day. Other casualties have been the majority of British train names, robbed of credibility when the rest of the

service on their route was uplifted to similar standards of speed and accommodation, and when one could often see their train-sets turned round within an hour or so to form an anonymous working on the same or perhaps a humbler route. At the end of the 1970s only a score or so survived. Some, like the 'Flying Scotsman' or 'Royal Scot' endured because the name had a historical cachet with marketing value abroad as well as at home. Other titles were preserved to underline a train's styling in speed, timing and pattern of stops for a specific local market – for instance, the 'Hull Executive'.

The trend of BR passenger business in the late 1960s indicated as a rule of thumb that each mile-an-hour of improved average speed on a given route generated a one percent rise in traffic volume. But it looked in the early 1970s as though orthodox electric and diesel-powered equipment was up against the speed limit of existing BR infra-structure. Of Britain's early 19th century railway builders only Brunel presciently laid down a main line, that of the Western Region from London Paddington to Bristol, which was to prove nearly ideally aligned for 20th-century 100mph-plus trains over much of its distance. On the rest curves too frequently interrupted opportunities for sustained bursts of high speed, and significant junctions for converging or intersecting traffic hampered main-line traffic. More accelerative punch was obtainable from electric traction for quicker recovery from these checks to continuous speed to shorten end-to-end times; but as already described Government brows tended to knit at fresh electrification proposals.

At that time a diesel locomotive, packing equivalent power, looked unattainable within a tolerable all-up weight, even if proven engines of the required power could be bought off the shelf. And another vexing problem had surfaced: the track was wilting under the continuous pounding of intensive 100mph use by orthodox diesel- and electric-powered trains (the West Germans were stopped short in the quest for 125mph by the same experience). Was emulation of the Japanese – construction of brand-new trunk lines, custom-built for exclusive use of passenger

The 'Manchester Pullman' on the electrified LMR main line was at the start of the 1980s the sole survivor of Britain's Pullman trains; the rest had been sacrificed to the new high-speed, regular-interval pattern of inter-city service with standard train-sets.

trains – the only way to lift the speed ceiling further? If so, BR could abandon the quest. No British Government, whatever its political hue, would countenance the massive cost of such a project in highly urbanized Britain.

The speed limit a curve enforces on a passenger train is the maximum for tolerable passenger comfort, not safety. There is a margin within which the limit can be raised quite substantially provided the cant, or superelevation of the track through the curve is increased to control the effects of centrifugal force. But where a line is used by traffic with a wide speed range the degree of cant has to be a compromise between the ideal for the fastest and the slowest, or excessive cant to indulge higher express passenger speed will have the slowest trains inflicting intolerable wear on the inner rail of the curve. Build a line exclusively for passenger equipment of fixed design, like the French in their Paris-Lyons TGV discussed in the next chapter, then 160mph is feasible over curves almost as demanding as those of a motorway, because the cant can be ideally matched to the behaviour of ultra low-centre-of-gravity vehicles of immaculately standard design.

On an existing, mixed traffic infrastructure more pace can be won for passenger equipment without increasing curve superelevation by inducing an un-

natural extra degree of cant in the vehicle body – in other words, by installing in the vehicle a body-tilting device that is automatically actuated to the required degree by gyroscopic or other sensors which detect entry into a curve and measure its parameters. As discussed later in this book, several railways have developed automatic body-tilting equipment, but only one or two look set to adopt it in series production equipment. First, it is expensive and adds weight to modern vehicles already encumbered under both heads by the air-conditioning apparatus now regarded as essential inter-city equipment by major railways. Second, full advantage cannot be taken of the extra pace won by body-tilting on a busy mixed traffic route unless the latter's humblest trains are somehow re-equipped to raise their speed commensurately (or else they are thinned out). If you widen the speed band between the fastest and slowest of a route's trains you reduce the number of trains it can carry. The fastest will either catch up more quickly or get further ahead of the slowest and thus considerable route-mileage will be left bare of trains.

BR is one system intent on widespread use of automatic body-tilting, in its Advanced Passenger Train, or APT. This is designed to run at 150mph on existing British Inter-City routes, though certain technical factors are bound to inhibit APT operation

The prototype, gas turbine-powered Advanced Passenger Train unit, APT-E, runs parallel to the M1 motorway during mid-1970s trials on the main line from London St Pancras to the East Midlands.

The driving trailer end and a second-class saloon interior of one of the three pre-production APT-P units with 25kV AC electric power. In the interior view note the pronounced taper of the exterior walls, essential to achieve a cross-sectional outline that will not foul adjoining tracks when the coach is tilted abnormally on curves.

In the centre of the APT-P driving desk, showing '125', is the transponder-activated display which keeps the driver continuously advised of the maximum speed within which he can run; this varies from normal limits because of the APT's higher speed capability through curves.

at top speed in public service until the 1990s at the earliest. In design detail the APT is the most revolutionary of all the 100mph-plus equipment yet unveiled by the world's railway industry. Apart from automatic body-tilting it features a suspension system which positively 'steers' the wheel-sets of its extraordinarily long articulating bogies into and through curves, eliminating juddering contact between flange and railhead. This system is the product of exhaustive research into the inter-action of wheel and rail by engineers at BR's Derby research centre, the biggest and most comprehensively equipped in the Western railway world. To enable the APT to operate safely at 150mph within the braking distances of existing BR signalling, a hydrokinetic brake is applied to the APT for the first time in rail history. Claimed by the designers to be the most efficient means of rapid but smooth deceleration, the hydrokinetic brake is most simply understood as a turbine in reverse, opposing the pressure of fluid trapped between stationary and rotating discs to

movement and dissipating the moving vehicle's energy as heat. Lightweight aluminium alloy body construction and assiduous weight-saving in every component, together with articulation of adjoining coaches by a single bogie, has trimmed the weight of each APT power car to 69 tons and of each passenger car to 23 tons, more than 25 percent less than that of a BR MkIII coach with equivalent seating capacity.

A prototype APT now in Britain's National Railway Museum at York (it was tested up to a maximum of 152mph on the Western Region, between Reading and Swindon) was gas turbine-electric. But even if the selected turbine plant had been fully developed by its makers (it was not) the oil price explosion has now made turbine power the most expensive form of rail traction, instead of predictably the cheapest as it appeared in the 1960s. So the first production APTs will be electric, for the 25kV AC main line from London Euston to the Northwest and Scotland via the West Coast.

But APT history is a depressing chronicle of second, third and even more design thoughts, of practical testing stymied by labour unions on one pretext or another and of Government hesitation over investment. At the start of 1980, 13 years after the project was first revealed and eight years after completion of the turbine-powered prototype four-car set, all BR had to show in hardware was three pre-production train-sets (classified APT-P), which were to begin evaluation in public London-Glasgow service during the year.

Each APT-P set marshalls a pair of 4000hp power cars in the centre of the unit, flanked by articulated six-car trailer sets of passenger accommodation each ending in a driving trailer. Total weight of the unit is 456 tons. An 8000hp twin power pack is essential to realize the 150mph peak performance of the APT and its unusual central placing in the formation is

dictated by the desirability, with automatic body-tilting vehicles, of feeding current to both power cars from a single pantograph; that would be decidedly impractical if the power cars were distanced from each other at the extremities of the unit. Since there is no public passageway through the power cars this arrangement incurs the extravagence of separate catering facilities in each passenger trailer set.

No production sets are likely to be built in this format for a decade or more however, because of belated recognition that the APT's maximum speed potential is unrealizable without heavy additional expenditure in two fields. Every major railroad now accepts that drivers cannot be left reliant on intermittent observation of lineside signals where trains are running regularly at 125mph-plus; ground and vehicle equipment to produce a continuous visual display of signals aspects ahead on the cab driving console is essential. Second, a number of APTs at full tilt within one current feed section will impose a combined power demand beyond the capacity of the existing power supply equipment; squadron service at 150mph will be impossible without costly modification of both catenary and trackside apparatus, though there is some hope of eventually lifting APT-P top operational speed to 135mph with the present lineside equipment.

Prospects of Government approval for BR expenditure on either prerequisite for 150mph in daily service are remote at the time of writing. For immediate series production, therefore, the APT will be slimmed down to a single power unit coupled to eleven passenger trailers. This format will have a power/weight ratio adequate for 125mph top speed and, given the APT's enhanced pace through curves by comparison with conventionally suspended rolling stock, to run the 401 miles from London to Glasgow in four hours and ten minutes inclusive of two intermediate stops for an end-to-end average of 96.2mph, compared with five hours by the previous locomotive-hauled 'Royal Scot'. Naturally, a single power car can be switched from the centre to one end of the formation, whereupon the extravagance of a second restaurant-kitchen unit in the train can be discarded; but the change involves redesign of the power car with a driving cab — yet another revision to protract the already tedious research and development history of the APT.

At the end of the 1970s BR was urging Government approval for construction of 70 APTs at a cost of about £2¼ million a set, to convert the entire Inter-City service from London to the Northwest and Glasgow (a total takeover is essential, of course, to optimize the APT's characteristics, otherwise the new trains will be persistently held up by conventional equipment making slower speed over curved stretches of the route). But the mid-1980s are now the earliest practical date for full APT service out of London's Euston. Until then the West Coast Anglo-Scottish route must soldier on at the speed levels set with electrification in the late 1960s — effective enough at that time, but by the late 1970s a much less virile match for British Airways' walk-on shuttle service between London Heathrow and Glasgow.

From two other London terminals, however, 125mph service — or 'Inter-City 125', as BR brands it — is already the natural order. The traction is diesel with which, remarkably, BR was not only running faster than under catenary in the late 1970s but operating daily at point-to-point speeds surpassed only for the moment by Japan's newly built and electrified Shinkansen.

At the end of the 1960s, when the translation of APT theory into proven mass production hardware was looking a far longer haul than first estimated, BR took a fresh look at the economics and practicalities of higher speed with conventional equipment. The reappraisal proved that alliance of the research department's evolving running-gear science with continuously welded track to a stringent specification, plus more easing of speed-hampering curves in locations where realignment was not formidably expensive, would make sustained 125mph running feasible over mileages sufficient to cut end-to-end journey times substantially on some key routes, and for an outlay which the gains would comfortably remunerate. The only other critical requirement was high power and lightweight vehicle construction to endow the trains with enough accelerative punch to reach the line speed limit as quickly as possible.

The outcome was the High Speed Diesel Train, or HST, a fixed-formation unit of nine (Class 253) or ten cars (Class 254). In this passenger vehicles of BR standard MkIII type are enclosed by a pair of

One of the diesel-alternator HST train-sets, with 2250hp power units front and rear, which BR operates in its 'Inter-City 125' service to achieve timetable frequencies and average speeds surpassed only by Japan's purpose-built Shinkansen electric high-speed lines at the start of the 1980s.

An 'Inter-City 125' HST coasts into London Paddington on a morning service from Bristol. Inset: Second-class saloon of the fully air-conditioned MkIII coach which forms the passenger-carrying vehicles of an HST.

streamlined power cars each housing a 2250hp Paxman Valenta engine driving electric traction motors via an alternator and rectifier. Total weight of a nine-car Class 253 unit is 383 tons, so that the power/weight ratio is a healthy 11.75hp/ton, 25 percent more favourable than that of a Class 55 'Deltic' locomotive-hauled train with equivalent seating capacity. From a dead start on level track it is enough to whip an HST up to 100mph in $3\frac{1}{2}$ minutes and 125mph in little more than $5\frac{1}{2}$ minutes.

The first Class 253 HSTs were assigned to the Bristol and South Wales routes from London's Paddington Station, in BR's Western Region, where a few realignment touches to Brunel's superbly engineered route offered them scope for over 70 miles' 125mph running from London's outskirts to Swindon checked only by an 80mph restriction through Reading, and more 125mph territory further west on the South Wales line. In South Wales itself and over the final stretch of the Bristol route the route characteristics peg speed at 90mph, so it is over the London-Swindon sector that the Western's HSTs – three an hour each way throughout the day, with supplementary workings in the business peaks –

display the most effervescent pace. The weekday Western 'Inter-City 125' timetable is sprinkled with nearly 90 start-to-stop runs timed at more than 90mph up to a peak of 103.3mph for the 41.3 miles between Swindon and Reading. On 10 April 1979 one of the Western's HSTs eclipsed the fastest regular Japanese Shinkansen schedule, taking advantage of a path free of any temporarily speed-restricting work on the track to gobble up the 94 miles from Paddington to its first call at Chippenham in a fraction over $50\frac{1}{2}$ minutes start to stop at an average of 111.6mph, but without exceeding 125mph. This was the work of a standard train-set on a normal weekday service, the 09.20 Paddington-Bristol.

In 1979–80 more HSTs arrived on the Western to assume the bulk of the Region's other prime Inter-City service, from Paddington to Plymouth and Penzance in England's far Southwest. This route, unfortunately, is too persistently sinuous for economical reconstruction to take full advantage of the HST's potential. At the start of the 1980s, moreover, a substantial proportion of its mileage had yet to be converted to the multiple-aspect colour-light signalling under control of a few strategically-sited, push-button electronic signalling centres which has been a pivotal feature of BR modernization since the 1950s. This resignalling is improbable before the mid-1980s – another measure of the rigid ceiling clamped on BR's rate of investment – and consequently end-to-end averages in excess of 80mph are as yet unattainable on the Paddington-Plymouth route. Because of physical route constraints, moreover, the HSTs are unlikely to be allowed more than 110mph top speed on this route.

To digress briefly from HSTs, by the end of the 1970s two-thirds of BR's basic network – that is, with secondary branches excluded – or about 7500 route-miles were controlled by multiple-aspect colour-light signalling. The total included whole trunk lines – from London Euston to Glasgow, 401 miles; London Kings Cross to Edinburgh, $392\frac{3}{4}$ miles; and London Paddington to Swansea, $212\frac{1}{2}$ miles. The advent of the transistor and other developments in electronics has steadily compacted the size of signalling components to the extent that up to 500 track-miles of running line and their trains can be supervised from a single signalling centre. The Edinburgh installation, for instance, takes in 220 route-miles and almost 440 track-miles of running line; the push-pull buttons on its console actuate no fewer than 1200 different route-settings and their appropriate signals in the territory the centre controls. On BR's Southern Region, the London Bridge centre, which commands the most intensive of all the capital's electric commuter operations, takes complete control of the working in the London suburbs and signals from there to destination the dense flows of trains converging from seven different routes, then diverging to four different termini – London Bridge itself, Holborn Viaduct, Cannon Street and Charing Cross. The reaction of trains on low-current circuitry in the tracks not only informs the signalmen of the position and progress, section by section, of every train in their territory through the illuminated track diagram display facing them, but also identifies each train visually by its working timetable number via the train describer system (the working of which is briefly described in a discussion of the DB's Frankfurt signalbox in Chapter Three).

Apart from immeasurably improving train operating efficiency because signalmen and traffic regulators in these centres can supervise such a wide tract of railway and anticipate conflicts of advancing train paths which might lead to a signal check, the new technology is impressively labour-saving. And this gain increases as signal engineers are emboldened to enlarge the control area with each new scheme. For instance, whereas the London Bridge project took in 147 track-miles, superseded 16 existing signalboxes and saved over 80 staff, the subsequent Southern Region scheme establishing a centre to control the ramified approaches to another very busy London terminus, Victoria, will embrace 267

track-miles handling nearly 1400 trains daily and make as many as 36 existing signalboxes redundant. The Victoria resignalling, in fact, is probably the most ambitious of its kind the railway world has yet seen.

Computers have already been introduced into signalling to sift the input to the train describer system, process the data to activate the signalmen's visual displays and also to adapt it suitably for accurate real-time information to passengers via station platform train indicators. The next step is to apply the computers to the decision-making and traffic regulatory work of a signalbox. As described in the book's final chapter, this is much easier to achieve

Exterior and operating floor interior of the London Bridge electronic signal centre which controls 150 miles of running lines and over 900 possible routings, protected by 550 main signals, at the crowded SR approaches to three London termini from the southeast London suburbs.

on a metropolitan or rapid transit passenger railway, where the route layout is comparatively simple, and the trains standard and running to a repetitive pattern. Here, completely automated operation is already practicable and on some systems only a stage or two away from actual realization. It is not so simple on a main-line surface railway, with its many conflicting flows of varied traffic and the assortment of commercial priorities. Nevertheless BR has one of the systems well forward with development in this area. The signalbox at Glasgow Central is the test-bed for a BR system known as JOT (for Junction Optimization Technique), which counsels the signalmen on the priorities to accord incoming trains and how they should be platformed for maximum efficiency and best use of the terminal's capacity.

British Rail's high-speed Inter-City operation grabbed second place in the league table of the world's fastest daily trains – beaten only by the electric Shinkansen of Japan – when the diesel HSTs were introduced to the East Coast main line from London Kings Cross to the North in the late 1970s. End-to-end timing was spectacular enough, with the 'Flying Scotsman' cut to a four hour 37 minute schedule for the London-Edinburgh distance of $392\frac{3}{4}$ miles inclusive of an intermediate call at Newcastle. But each day the 08.00 Kings Cross–Edinburgh and 09.05 Kings Cross–Leeds were now scheduled to sprint the $48\frac{3}{4}$ miles from Stevenage to Peterborough in $27\frac{1}{2}$ minutes start-to-stop at a mean speed of 106.25mph. Eighteen HSTs each way daily between London and Newcastle averaged only three hours 13 minutes transit time for the $268\frac{1}{4}$-mile journey inclusive of stops, with a fastest schedule of two hours 55 minutes, representing an end-to-end average of 92mph. Frequency and speed between London and the West Riding cities, Leeds and Bradford, were only marginally less impressive.

Seating in the fully air-conditioned HSTs is entirely in open saloons, a configuration which BR has standardized in its Inter-City equipment, and every unit of both classes embodies both a buffet-bar and a kitchen for full meal service; in the Western sets the two facilities are combined in one vehicle – a compression deemed adequate for catering demand on BR's shorter Inter-City routes – but in the East Coast sets they are in separate cars. The HST buffets and kitchens were the first new catering vehicles BR could secure authority to build since the 1950s (construction of modern air-conditioned sleeping cars employing the MkIII coach bodyshell was also excluded from BR's plans by investment constraints until 1979). They put a long-overdue end to the anachronistic mismatch of serenely-riding, air-conditioned saloons of recent build with noisily rough restaurants and buffets of 1950s vintage that was a serious flaw in BR's prime Inter-City services for most of the 1970s.

The economy of the HST's double-ended, fixed-formation consist, with its aptitude for quick terminal turnrounds and high daily mileage, has 'dis-benefits' too. In face of business growth aggregating as much as 37 percent in second-class passenger-miles and 46 percent in first after only two years of Western 'Inter-City 125' operation, even a timetable intensified by as much as 40 percent in total of daily trains has come up with inadequate capacity to prevent overcrowding at peak travel periods of the day or week. Within so limited a formation, moreover, space cannot be yielded to a separate restaurant car. The HST buffet-kitchen separates first- and second-class accommodation and proffers full meal service only at first-class seats. It was envisaged that a few of the latter would be held in reserve for potential second-class diners, but the heavy first-class travel demand stimulated by the HST service quality has pre-empted the entire space at that end and second-class HST travellers are effectively restricted to the range of take-away hot dishes available from the buffet car's microwave equipment.

Left:
Dinner is served in a first-class saloon of an HST in BR's 'Inter-City 125' service.
Right:
BR's train catering service is the most extensive on European railways. Besides kitchen service of full meals at seats every 'Inter-City 125' train-set has a capacious buffet-bar for takeaway service of wares that includes a variety of hot snacks quickly prepared on demand in microwave ovens.

Throughout the steam age Britain's railways designed and built the greater part of their locomotives and rolling stock themselves. BR's workshops lacked both the technical experience and the capacity to cope with the huge demand for diesel and electric traction ensuing from the 1955 Modernization Plan, however, and much of the new power was initially built by the country's private-sector industry. By the 1970s BR's own plant was again monopolizing the domestic business, re-equipped and retrained to deal in the new power – and also quite sizeable enough to cater for BR's drastically curbed latter-day rate of investment and still have room to handle a substantial export trade in traction and rolling stock.

The critical problem confronting BR as this is written is that the mass of new equipment acquired so rapidly under the 1955 Plan comes crowding up for renewal in the early 1980s, predicating a rate of re-investment far beyond the ceiling currently imposed by the Government. The most worrying area – apart from that of freight stock discussed earlier – is short-distance passenger stock. At the close of the 1970s the only conurbation commuter services in the country with rolling stock of post-1960 design were the few electrified since the 1955 Plan. Only in 1979 did the Southern's intricate, far-ranging third-rail DC suburban system on the south side of London's Thames River begin to receive smooth-riding new sliding-door train-sets to initiate – but only to initiate – supersession of its huge fleet of 1950s-vintage multiple-units with slam doors at every seating bay. Just as obsolescent and run-down now are the 3000-odd, largely bus-engined diesel-mechanical multiple-unit railcars of various interior layouts which were acquired two decades ago. Refurbishing is restoring a little ride quality, but even the reconditioned units are mediaevally noisy and rough-riding compared with the standards of BR Inter-City.

A replacement diesel-electric multiple-unit is on the drawing-board and a prototype was building in 1979, but at a prospective production cost of £650,000 per set, apprehension is rife that both Government and PTEs will opt for abandonment of many diesel railcar services in favour of road buses. A possible ray of hope is a much cheaper alternative under experimental development by BR's research department: the marriage of a standard British Leyland

The intensity of BR's Inter-City service demands not only very high-quality track maintenance but extraordinary means for track surveillance, such as this coach which can electronically measure and record 12 different track conditioning factors at speeds up to 125mph. It covers over 80,000 miles of track a year.

Below:
A 100mph, 2700hp Class 50 diesel-electric heads a locomotive-hauled Inter-City express on the WR.

Above:
Exterior and interior of one of the latest generation of open-saloon, sliding-door electric multiple-units for conurbation suburban services. This is the Class 508 for the third-rail DC network of the Southern Region.

Below:
Maid of all heavy work in BR's diesel traction fleet is the Sulzer-engined 2650hp Class 47 diesel-electric Co-Co, which is both freight haulier and inter-city power, with 95mph maximum speed. No 47.417 moves a morning express to Edinburgh out of Aberdeen in September 1977.

bus body and power plant with sophisticated four-wheel rail underframe and suspension to create a vehicle already proved a 'sweet runner' at 75mph on rails and capable of production in a multiple-unit version. This was priced at no more than £150,000 ($300,000) in 1979. In 1980 the US Federal Railroad Administration imported one for demonstration service in New England between Concord, New Hampshire and Lowell, Massachusetts.

At the start of dieselization BR's Western Region, pursuing the idiosyncracy of its private enterprise forerunner the Great Western Railway, gouged grudging approval out of BR's mechanical chiefs to follow German diesel-hydraulic practice in its main-line locomotives, though the rest of the system went exclusively diesel-electric from the start. The last of

the Western's diesel-hydraulics were scrapped in the 1970s, however, and the Region now conforms with all-line practice. After the Class 55 'Deltics', now ousted from their front-rank East Coast passenger work by HSTs and nearing life-expiry, BR's most powerful diesel locomotives are a 1976 acquisition, the Class 56 Co-Cos of 126 tons apiece with a single GEC diesel 3250hp engine which is arranged and geared specifically for freight haulage, though the design was evolved from the earlier and essentially mixed traffic Class 47. A purely freight haulage design is being created *ab initio* in the Class 58, programmed for series production from 1982. By then it is expected that reliable single engines will be capable of installing the Class 58 with up to 4000hp output. A Co-Co, this new class will break fresh stylistic ground among BR's high-power diesels by discarding a full-width car body for a simpler bonnet between the two end cabs, with an external walkway on each side of the locomotive for ease of access to the machinery.

Most powerful passenger hauliers in the diesel stud are 50 2700hp Class 50 Co-Cos with a single English Electric 2700hp engine and 100mph top speed. All were concentrated on the Western Region at the end of the 1970s, but in 1980 reconstruction of a number with 3520hp engines to achieve an accelerated service between London St Pancras, the East Midlands and Sheffield was under consideration. By far the most numerous of BR's higher-powered diesels and the most versatile, covering a wide spectrum of assignments from inter-city trains on non-electrified routes to merry-go-round coal hauls, are the Class 47 Co-Cos, each engined with single Sulzer 2650hp machine and arranged for a maximum of 95mph.

BR's 25kV AC electric locomotives, visually, are very closely related in outline. All are Bo-Bos. In the 1960s BR's electrical chiefs saw no need to build into their first designs the short-term reserve of power the French embodied in their locomotives. The early Bo-Bo classes of around 3000hp continuous rating, therefore, are nowadays allocated chiefly to the London-Midland's secondary work in electrified territory. The Inter-City expresses and Freightliners are entrusted almost wholly to Class 86, a 3600hp design of 1965 of which 58 were subsequently modified as Class 86/2 with improved suspension and a 4040hp rating, and the longer-wheelbase 5000hp Class 87 of 1973.

The 5000hp of the Class 87s, however, has proved inadequate since the extension of AC electrification into Scotland spanned the lengthy 1 in 75 of Shap incline in the Cumbrian fells and the similarly graded Beattock bank north of the Anglo-Scottish border with catenary. In autumn and winter climatic conditions can undermine adhesion seriously on these hills, so much so that double-heading of Freightliner trains exceeding 1000 tons has become *de rigueur* even with Class 87s. To avoid this BR has had a more powerful electric Co-Co on the drawing board for several years, but as yet there is no hint of a firm order.

One of the two pre-production series train-sets built for French Railways' 160mph Paris–Sudest TGV line rests at Paris Gare de Lyon during its early trials on existing main lines in 1979. The new TGV line itself is due for full commissioning by the end of 1983

2.
FRENCH RAILWAYS ARE POISED FOR THE WORLD SPEED CROWN

Restrained by a statutory limit of 120kmph (74.5mph) on their steam trains and with main-line electrification (at 1.5kV DC) as yet continuous only on the routes from Paris to Le Mans and from Paris through Bordeaux to the Spanish border at Hendaye, the French were lagging behind the Americans, Germans and British in rail passenger speed up to the outbreak of World War II. But within a decade of the peace they were world leaders. They were jostled off that pedestal by the first of Japan's new Shinkansen, the New Tokaido Line, in the 1960s and edged even out of Europe's top spot by Britain's 'Inter-City 125' diesel trains in the late 1970s, but by the mid-1980s they will yet again outdistance the rest of the world comfortably with a new 160mph railway from Paris to Lyons.

As soon as the war was over French Railways (SNCF) set out determinedly not only on a main-line electrification programme as rapid as resources would allow, but on a complementary redesign of main-line operation to optimize the high reserve of power in mind for the new electric traction. Centre-piece of the operational plan was to be a high-speed passenger service. As yet no demand had surfaced on the European mainland for the kind of hourly interval service which is a hallmark of contemporary British and German inter-city timetables. The French traditionally embarked upon long-distance journeys in the morning, at midday or in the evening – and to a considerable extent still do where rail travel is concerned; on the longer-distance SNCF routes the timetables tend even now to be barer of departures in mid-morning and afternoon than elsewhere in Western Europe except for Scandinavia, Spain, Portugal and Greece. In its timetable redraft the SNCF could thus gain an appreciable amount of end-to-end pace by grouping or 'flighting' the prime morning, midday and evening inter-city trains the length of each main line and, as far as possible, clearing their paths of freight and slower-moving passenger trains for the passage of each 'flight'.

The scheme was facilitated by the greater freedom from junctions and conflicting traffic flows of most SNCF trunk routes compared with those of, say, BR or West Germany's DB. Although the few traditional transversal main lines of the SNCF, such as those from the Atlantic ports in Northwest France and from the Southwest and Spain to the Rhône valley have been joined by a newcomer or two in recent years – Le Havre, Rouen and the navigable Seine to the industrial Northeast, for instance – the social and commercial axes of French social and commercial traffic are predominantly radii from Paris. Except to the north of the capital the SNCF's trunk routes encounter few significant junctions in the great expanses of agricultural land until they encounter the rail complexes of major provincial cities.

So, with its first postwar 1.5kV DC electrification complete from Paris to Lyons in 1951 the SNCF ushered Europe into the 70–75mph range of inter-city end-to-end average speed as early as the winter of 1952. But though Europe's postwar scarcity of coal had the French Government as well as the SNCF eager for ongoing electrification, the first costs of setting up current supply and catenary were daunting. The Paris-Lyons scheme had absorbed them quite comfortably because it was the system's busiest trunk route, but they bulked more disconcertingly on the putative balance sheets of future projects.

The capital cost deterrent was relaxed when the SNCF's electrical engineers refined to perfection a traction system that could adapt high-voltage alternating current at the industrial frequency straight from the national supply system to the use of the direct current motors which were most practical in rail locomotives. That greatly reduced the scale and cost of lineside supply installations and permitted less ponderous and hence cheaper catenary and catenary structures. Also promised by the new technology were superior adhesion characteristics and efficiency in the locomotives themselves. The advantages were then immeasurably enhanced by the 1950s adaptation of materials such as germanium and silicon for semi-conductor rectifiers, whereby the apparatus to mutate the AC line supply to a DC traction motor on the locomotive was strikingly reduced in size and weight. Now a 4000–5000hp AC four-axle locomotive of less than 100 tons' all-up weight became a practical proposition.

The next milestone was evolution of compact multi-voltage traction equipment, enabling a locomotive to operate with equal facility and on near-standard output of power under AC or DC wires (and if necessary at varying voltages in each case) which could give it the freedom of Western Europe's electrified network (the 3kV DC of Belgium and Italy, and the 15kV $16\frac{2}{3}$Hz AC of West Germany, Switzerland and Austria as well as the 1.5kV DC of France and the Netherlands and France's new 25kV 50Hz). This enabled the SNCF to pursue AC and DC electrification in parallel as logistics and local circumstances dictated.

The AC system spread across the industrial north of the country from Le Havre through Paris to Strasbourg and Basle, but south of that line, apart from fingers of AC reaching south to the Paris–Lyons trunk route and a pocket of AC in Savoie which was the system's early postwar test-bed, the new catenary was at first exclusively DC. Infills within this southern network, such as electrification of the lateral route from Bordeaux to Montauban, junction with the trunk route from Paris to Toulouse just north of the latter city, and of the Rhône right bank line to supplement the left bank trunk route and double capacity through the thriving industrial area between Lyons, Avignon and Nîmes, are still being executed at 1.5kV DC. But latterly extensions on the periphery have been at 25kV AC. The projections beyond Marseilles along the Côte d'Azur shore to the

Italian border at Ventimiglia, and from Le Mans to Rennes, the first stage of electrification into Brittany, to Nantes and France's Atlantic ports, are cases in point.

By the start of the 1970s the pace of SNCF electrification had significantly slackened and the French seemed committed to high-power diesel traction in a number of areas where traffic levels could not generate the predicted return on investment in catenary in those days. Since then the oil-price explosion, the gathering energy crisis and fresh advances in electric traction technology have rescaled the balance sheet. In 1969 electric current cost the SNCF twice as much as diesel fuel for a given haulage effort, but by 1977 electricity was already 17 percent cheaper and since then oil has become steadily dearer; as more French electricity is generated by nuclear power the gap will widen. For reasons touched upon later in this chapter the latest breed of electric locomotive with thyristor control of traction power has halved the traction maintenance requirement in terms of man-hours per miles run. Consequently routes which failed the viability test a decade ago are now being or about to be electrified.

Early in the 1980s the Bordeaux–Montauban electrification and that from Narbonne to the Spanish border crossing at Cerbère, already under way at the start of the decade, will be finished and complemented by conversion east of Lyons to finish the web of catenary in Savoie. All the key transverse routes in the South will then have been electrified as well as the main radials from Paris and high-power diesels will be redundant in the southern half of the country. That will still leave nearly 70 percent of SNCF route-mileage dieselized, but the electrified remainder (roughly half DC, half AC) will be moving over three-quarters of the traffic. (*En passant*, these statistics hint at the huge extent of rural SNCF mileage that remains open for a meagre one or two passengers or freight trains a day.) The SNCF is now set on continuing electrification to the end of the century, by which time there may be 50 percent more AC than DC catenary. Schemes in draft include the creation of orbital routes north and south of Paris, to reduce the freight load on the capital's peripheral network but also to nourish new cross-country inter-city routes.

In the 1950s and 1960s the main thrust of the SNCF's inter-city passenger policy was directed to the establishment of *rapides* between Paris and major provincial cities in the morning and evening travel peaks and to a lesser extent at midday. For the most part they were first-class only and on all of them a supplementary fare was levied. This approach harmonized with the international 'Trans-Europ Express' concept formulated by the Netherlands Railways chief of the 1950s, den Hollander, and put into practice by a consortium of the French, West German, Belgian, Netherlands, Luxembourg, Swiss and Italian national railways in 1957 (TEEs sub-

sequently penetrated Austria and Spain as well). The aim was the same: to forestall the seduction of highly remunerative business traffic by the Continent's fast-evolving tracery of air services. Speed and high quality of accommodation and amenities were seen as the most effective competitive weapons, supplemented on the TEEs by a reduction of frontier rigmarole on the train to eliminate the interminable halts at border crossings to which air travellers were immune.

Sadly national self-interest frustrated realization of a good deal of den Hollander's ideal and admirable prospectus. He dreamed not merely of fixed, predictable TEE standards of speed and comfort, but of standard equipment, staffing and administration under a supra-national management. Instead each country right from the start built TEE equipment to its own taste. Some were superb like that of West Germany's DB, some pedestrian like Italy's diesel multiple-units (which the Germans, who had to host them on the Milan–Munich 'Mediolanum' TEE service, disparaged as 'The Lorries') and the near-standard diesel railcar sets which were the SNCF's first contribution to the TEE pool while it mulled over vehicle designs that would be economically adaptable to its domestic supplementary-fare *rapide* fleet. The TEE image was muddied still more when purely domestic inter-city services were admitted to the network and the TEE logo embellished, for instance, Italian electric multiple-unit equipment.

Even if den Hollander had had his way entirely though, it would probably not have prolonged the life of the longest-distance TEEs. By the late 1970s their end-to-end carryings were negligible, their passengers almost entirely joining them only for sectors of the trains' itinerary. One by one they were being killed off as the major railways concentrated on their individual domestic inter-city markets. Today the TEE is becoming a first-class category of each country's inter-city operations.

The shop in the bar car of one of the mid-1960s stainless-steel, air-conditioned train-sets built for the 'Mistral'. Originally an elegant unisex hairdressing salon operated in a room on the far side of the shop, but that and a train secretarial service were abandoned a decade later for lack of custom.

Above:
A 5900hp BB15000 Class Bo-
Bo under 25kV AC 50Hz
catenary, hauls the Paris–
Strasbourg 'Stanislas' TEE
of 'Grand Confort' stock.

Right:
A four-voltage 6100hp
CC40101 Class Co-Co in
charge of one of the Paris–
Brussels–Amsterdam TEEs.

Several of the SNCF's exclusive *rapides* have
already gained TEE preferment. First to be upgraded, in 1965, was the best-known of France's
postwar expresses, the midday 'Mistral' each way
between Paris, Lyons, Marseilles and Nice. Its
repute was established when the SNCF allotted it
Europe's first postwar 80mph schedule as early as
1957 following the Paris–Lyons electrification and
assignment to the 'Mistral' of new stainless-steel,
air-conditioned stock with improved air braking
that allowed a line speed limit uplift from 140 to
150kmph (87.5–93mph) over stretches of the Paris–
Lyons main line. Stainless steel, then very fashion-
able for bodywork, is no longer so, incidentally. Its
cost in materials and construction methods has
escalated too sharply. At the same time the advance
in coachbuilding technology has obtained equivalent
collision-shock resistance by more economical building styles, combined with polyurethene paints which
have been developed to a high degree of efficacy
against corrosion without need of multi-layer
application.

The election of the 'Mistral' as a TEE was only
logical when it was re-equipped a second time with
the SNCF's first generation of locomotive-hauled
TEE stock. The first batch of these handsome
vehicles – the SNCF's last inter-city cars in stainless
steel – was produced in 1964 for one of the most
successful of all TEE exercises, that from Paris to
Brussels, The Hague and Amsterdam. At only 195
miles from each other, Paris and Brussels were ideally
related for a quality rail service and Brussels' adoption as the Common Market capital made the
premium-fare travel market between the cities still
more lucrative. Twice intensified since its inception,
the Paris–Brussels TEE service now totals two morning, one midday and three evening trains each way
daily, two with sections that continue to and from
Amsterdam, and all but one connecting the French

Top:
Bar car of a Paris–Brussels–
Amsterdam TEE train-set.
Above:
The driving desk of an 8000hp
CC6500 Class Co-Co electric
locomotive, with 125mph
maximum speed capability.
Note the slot on the driver's
main power controller for his
working documents, so that
he has his schedule always
clearly in view.

and Belgian capitals in under 2½ hours. Fastest is the 06.44 'Memling' from Paris, which takes only two hours 21 minutes for an end-to-end average speed of just on 83mph.

To digress, however, mark the 'Memling's' departure time. In the postwar development of European inter-city service the SNCF boldly pioneered very early starts and terminal arrivals almost up to midnight, sensing that the business market would gladly tolerate them if the rewards included substantial time for affairs at a quite remote city without a night away – or at least with return to base in time for five or six hours in their own beds. One should add that a factor encouraging this SNCF policy was the city-centre residence of a far higher proportion of the trains' potential customers than of the counterpart clientele for British Rail's trains. So, while the

SNCF's early *rapides* stream straight out of Paris, BR, now that it too is scheduling early and late high-speed business trains, stops many of them at outer London park-and-ride railheads for the better convenience of the majority of executives living in the suburbs.

Electrically hauled throughout, today's 'Mistral' covers the 676.2 miles between Paris and Nice in nine hours and 13 minutes southbound and seven minutes less northbound, which postulates an end-to-end average of 74.3mph despite nine intermediate stops – the one at Marseilles involves a reversal. This is achieved despite the fact that it is customarily a 14–15 car rake as far as Marseilles; in fact, so consistently high is its patronage, even though it is first-class only, that it demands a relief TEE to tail it from Paris to Marseilles every Friday. The beautifully riding, air-conditioned TEE coaches are elegantly and most comfortably furnished. The train-set includes both restaurant and buffet, the latter in an unusual car which also houses a small confectionery, journal and fancy goods shop and rooms that once served as a train secretary's office and unisex hairdressing saloon for a decade; however, the SNCF discarded the two latter flourishes for lack of worthwhile custom in the mid-1970s.

The SNCF attitude to line speed has always been conservative. Only since the 1960s has a maximum of 100mph been admitted over some stretches of the electrified trunk routes; over the greater part of these lines the ceiling on reasonably aligned track is 87.5 or 93.8mph, and insistence on observance of the limits is strict, even when there is lost time to be recovered. Tachographs in every traction cab which chart speed continuously are mute witnesses no engineman can refute.

In that light the scale of acceleration on some SNCF routes since 1960 is remarkable, even allowing for the electrification factor. The Paris Gare de l'Est–Strasbourg route epitomizes the advance. Before its electrification in 1962 the day's fastest train took six hours 40 minutes over the 315 route-miles between the two cities. Today no more than 40 percent of the distance is passed for 100mph, yet the morning 'Kleber' TEE from Strasbourg reaches Paris in three hours 56 minutes (the eastbound 'Kleber' is only a minute slower) for an end-to-end average speed of just over 80mph inclusive of a two-minute halt en route at Nancy.

Sustainment of a mean pace so close to the line speed limit is partly attributable to the inbuilt power of SNCF electrics and the infrequency of junctions with conflicting movements to threaten signal checks, as already mentioned. But it also owes a great deal to the disciplined driving techniques instilled into SNCF enginemen. The power of their machines is for rapid acceleration to the line speed limit. Once that has been reached the *mécaniciens* are trained to use their controller to hold the pace steady, which means exploiting momentum and conserving energy downhill, but opening the taps wider up-grade. The logs of SNCF express trains over mileage unhampered by severe speed restrictions invariably display a consistency of speed irrespective of gradient which contrasts sharply with most records, for instance, of BR Inter-City runs. Improvement on scheduled point-to-point times is only countenanced when there are lost minutes to recoup, whereas BR's attitude to an ebullient driver who sprints up to a timing point ahead of the clock is usually indulgent.

At the start of the 1980s 125mph was admissible on parts of two SNCF trunk routes. The French have been set on high rail speed since the start of their postwar modernization – their still impregnable world rail speed record of 205.6mph was set successively by Nos BB9004 and CC7107 in trials on the ex-Midi main line south of Bordeaux as far back as March 1955, which seems hardly credible – but their progress into the three-figure bracket has been one of methodical, step-by-step research, development and evaluation of every necessary equipment component the whole way. So it was 1967 before 31 miles of the Paris–Toulouse main line between Les Aubrais and Vierzon, on the Orleans cut-off, were fitted out with track devices to actuate the continuous driving-cab display of signal aspects and sophisticated automatic train braking control which the SNCF then held necessary for regular 100mph-plus operation, and six Class BB9200 DC locomotives were modified for 125mph operation over this section.

The only scheduled public service timed at this speed between Les Aubrais and Vierzon, though, was and still is a first-class-only flier inaugurated that year between Paris's Austerlitz and Toulouse, the 'Capitôle', at first run once daily each way but within a year expanded by prompt market response

to a morning and evening train in each direction; all are now TEEs. With the benefit of that 125mph sector the southbound 'Capitôle du Soir' reels off the 250 miles from Paris to the first stop at Limoges in two hours 50 minutes at a start-to-stop average of 88.2mph. But further south pace is curbed as the Toulouse route curves through and hurdles the ridges flanking the rivers flowing from the Massif Central to the Atlantic. Even so all four 'Capitôles' link Paris and Toulouse, 443 miles apart, in only a few minutes more than six hours. Leaving Toulouse at 07.41, a Toulouse executive can be in Paris by 13.48 and have over three hours for business before the 17.44 departure of the 'Capitôle du Soir', which will decant him in Toulouse at 23.48.

Of late, however, French businessmen have become progressively less inclined to spend as much as 12 hours of the day in a train. The time economy of air travel for a 400-mile journey more than compensates for the airport tedium, the plasticized catering and muscle-cramping confinement of an air journey. End-to-end use of the 'Capitôles' is not what it was, though the trains thrive well enough on intermediate traffic to escape the eclipse of the 'Rhodanien', a near replica of the 'Mistral' which the SNCF was emboldened by the latter's success to inaugurate in 1971 on a breakfast-time path from Marseilles to Paris with an evening return. By the later 1970s the 450-ton 'Rhodanien' train-set was all too often conveying only a score of passengers south of Avignon and it was abandoned as a first-class-only TEE in 1978.

This further stressed the imperative need of more speed to retain a healthy share of the premium-fare market between Paris and the more remote provincial cities. Automatic body-tilting, of the kind adopted in BR's APT and described in the previous chapter, was one possible means. This was provided

The first SNCF train to run regularly at 125mph – the Paris–Toulouse 'Capitôle' of 1967. It is headed by BB9288, one of six locomotives of this class specially modified for this first high-speed operation and liveried deep red and white to match the train-set, which apart from its exterior style and equipment with electromagnetic track brakes was (except for its restaurant car) formed of the standard, non-air-conditioned coaches of the period.

in the SNCF's second-generation TEE locomotive-hauled coach design, the so-called 'Grand Confort' type, which made its debut at the outset of the 1970s. Internally furnished with the same degree of spacious luxury as the 'Mistral'-type vehicles, the 'Grand Confort' coaches are distinctive externally for their two-tone red-and-grey livery enlivened by orange lining, and for their upward-tapering cross-sectional profile, essential to keep the inner bodyside of the vehicle within the loading gauge when the body is canted beyond the attitude of a conventional vehicle in negotiation of a curve.

But only one 'Grand Confort' coach was actually equipped with the body-tilting mechanism. The rest of the fleet was delivered and remains conventionally mounted on its running gear – though one should add that the latter's bogies, one of the items in which the steady evolution of French rolling stock technology has achieved particularly impressive results, keep the vehicles as they are near-flawlessly smooth-riding through curves as well as on tangent track. That apart, both categories of SNCF TEE stock are in the author's opinion the most effectively sound-insulated coaches currently running on European

Below:
One of France's two fastest trains at the start of the 1980s, the 'Etendard', speeds behind a CC6500 beneath the peculiar portal-shaped catenary supports with which the old Midi Railway was electrified to Bordeaux. It was under these 1920s structures that the SNCF staged their 205.6mph world speed record in March 1955.
Right:
Close-up of a Class CC6500.

rails. So far as the SNCF is concerned the economic and operational arguments against equipping an elite of rolling stock for ultra-high-speed on a mixed traffic route, rehearsed in the discussion of BR's APT, seem to have ruled out any further interest in automatic body-tilting.

'Grand Confort' stock now graces several French TEE services, but one instinctively associates it with the first to which it was applied, the co-holder of the French daily rail speed title on the eve of the 1980s. Most favourably speed-aligned of all French trunk routes is that from Paris Austerlitz to Bordeaux, so much so that the SNCF found just over 200 route-miles of it fit for 125mph operation by modern equipment given comparatively minor adjustments. In the late 1960s, moreover, the French had concluded that 125mph was the practical ceiling of speed on its mixed-traffic trunk routes, and that within that limit continuous cab signalling was expendable; security would be adequately protected by a far less costly modification of the signalling to afford 125mph trains advance warning of a cautionary signal ahead through a flashing green aspect backed up by a cab warning activated by track mounted devices. The balance sheet looked acceptable enough to pair the SNCF's latest 8000hp Co-Cos and 'Grand Confort' coaches on a long-distance service strikingly faster than anything experienced in Europe up to that time.

The outcome was the 'Aquitaine' and yet again, as between Paris and Toulouse, the market response soon warranted adding a sister train, the 'Etendard', to create a morning and evening service each way. The evening trains, the 'Aquitaine' outward from Paris and 'Etendard' inward from Bordeaux, glide the 359.8 miles non-stop in three hours 50 minutes at an average of 93.8mph, which makes them the fastest long-distance trains in mainland Europe. However, their morning partners stop intermediately. Between two of its calls, St Pierre des Corps and Poitiers, the southbound 'Etendard' is set a 37-minute time for 62.8 miles, which demands a start-to-stop average speed of 101.8mph.

The 'Aquitaine' and 'Etendard', TEEs both, were for several years solitary members of the 125mph club on the Bordeaux line. This opened a much wider gap in speed between them and the main body of Paris–Bordeaux expresses than exists between any

trains in BR's 'Inter-City 125' operation, for instance. In the summer 1979 timetable the southbound breakfast-time 'Etendard' was followed out of Paris by the 'Sud Express' taking four hours 24 minutes over a non-stop Paris–Bordeaux journey, while the evening 18.50 'Drapeau' was allowed 23 minutes more to reach its first stop at Poitiers than the morning 'Etendard', even though the latter had the handicap of a stop at St Pierre-des-Corps on the way. But whereas the 125mph trains were usually 11-car formations of 570 tonnes, the others were 15-car loads of 750–800 tonnes. At last, with completion of a Paris–Bordeaux motorway in 1980, the SNCF was to equip a fleet of 60 of its new 'Corail' coaches (to be described shortly) for 125mph and to introduce some limited-load dual-class fliers at near-'Aquitaine' speed between Paris and Bordeaux in the 1980–81 winter.

It gradually became a tenet of SNCF commercial practice in the later 1950s and 1960s to trail the exclusive *rapides* on each route with a standard dual class train not too badly outclassed in speed, but the supplementary-fare elite were still nurtured so obsessively that the French image of inter-city rail travel moved perceptibly up-market. In the 1970s market research awoke SNCF management to the fact that a worrying percentage of the postwar middle-class generation had dismissed the railway as a mode either for their seniors and betters or else for the blue-collar masses, and was becoming wedded to the automobile.

The first significant SNCF move to halt this trend and reshape an inter-city service on a near-standard pattern of pace and comfort combined with enhanced frequency came with the introduction of gas turbine-powered multiple-units to the Paris–Caen–Cherbourg route in 1970. At the time the compact, lightweight turbines evolved for helicopters by the aerospace industry held high promise for the advance of speed on routes where traffic levels could not support electrification economically. The Turbomeca Turmo III turbine employed in the SNCF's first series of train-sets, Type ETG, together with its hydromechanical transmission and anciliaries was less than one-third of the weight of a diesel engine of equivalent output; moreover, the whole turbine power plant assembly occupied nearly one-fifth less floor space. Married to lightweight bodywork, therefore, turbine traction could offer not only a high power/weight ratio for smart acceleration to and maintenance of high speed on well-aligned track, but also vehicles with low axleloading and a low centre of gravity which could make a good pace over sinuous routes. The turbine's characteristically higher fuel consumption than that of a diesel of comparable output was in those days, of course, no cause for serious concern – a trifling discrepancy quite easily accommodated in the balance sheet by the turbine unit's higher availability for work and hence its capability of generating more passenger seat-miles over a given period of revenue-earning service.

The SNCF's first breed of gas turbine multiple-units, the ETG, transformed the Paris–Caen–Cherbourg service in 1970.

The four-car ETGs, with a 1150hp turbine in one power car and a 450hp diesel engine in the other to boost the $175\frac{3}{4}$-ton unit's acceleration from rest, were arranged for 112mph maximum and fitted with electro-magnetic track as well as conventional air brakes to secure rapid deceleration from three-figure pace. (Electro-magnetic track brakes, a common component of European mainland high-speed rolling stock since the 1960s, are spring skids suspended just above the rails from the equalizing beams of bogies which derive their retarding effect from magnetic strength generated when they are energized by windings connected to the vehicle's electrical system; at around 30mph they are cut out, leaving conventional air brakes to complete the deceleration to a stand.) With some sections of the route from Paris Gare St Lazare to Nantes fettled up for 112mph and some 100 miles of the remaining 196 to Cherbourg made fit for 100mph, the ETGs were assigned to a revitalized timetable of consistent quality and speed; they were nearly 20 percent faster than the schedules before their debut. Though the mid-afternoon timetable was and still is sparse, frequency otherwise was at a higher level than the French norm. The ETGs rode sweetly at the highest speeds; their entirely open saloon accommodation, supported by a neat 14-seater self-service cafeteria, was brightly and comfortably furnished; and in short order they garnered a great deal of extra patronage and goodwill from the Normans.

So successful were they that in the mid-1970s the ETGs had to be supplanted on the Paris–Cherbourg route by the later, more capacious and fully air-conditioned five-car units of Type RTG, each of them exclusively turbine-powered with a 1100hp engine at each end. The RTGs, most of which at the end of the decade were based at Caen for Paris–Cherbourg, Lisieux–Trouville–Dives and a few Paris–Calais services, were originally created for France's important transversal lines, from Lyons to Nantes, Strasbourg and Bordeaux; but on the Lyons–Nantes route their appeal soon outran their seating and in 1977 they had to give way to loco-motive-hauled trains of the new Corail stock, dis-cussed below. The ETGs, which by the end of their Paris–Cherbourg career had to be operated in multiple on some services to cope with the traffic, have repaired to the threshhold of the French Alps, where at the end of the 1970s they were mostly deployed in the network ranging east of Lyons to Grenoble, Chambéry, Annecy and St Gervais-les-Bains (the junction for the picturesque, third-rail DC narrow-guage line of the SNCF which clambers up the Chamonix valley past the foot of Mont Blanc, then threads a vertiginous pass and descends rapidly into Switzerland's Rhône valley at Martigny).

The French alone have applied gas turbine power to production train-sets with conviction and success. The US passenger train operators, Amtrak, bought a batch of French-built RTGs, then supplemented them with a series of home-built (but essentially to the French specification by Rohr Industries of Cali-fornia) vehicles. Both types are outliving the over-innovatory Turbotrains which Canadian National and the Americans took from United Aircraft; their chequered career is summarized in a later chapter.

Before the Shah was ousted, more were marketed to the railways of Iran, which for a brief period in 1975–76 essayed with a wild excess of ambition to operate one regularly on a 100mph start-to-stop timing in the course of its Tehran–Mashhad journey – and that on single track in a largely desert environment.

Sadly the oil price explosion has aggravated the penalty of the turbine's fuel thirst so severely that all the other advantages of a turbine-powered unit are outweighed. The balance has been pulled back some way, following an analysis which demonstrated an RTG's ability to observe Paris–Caen–Cherbourg timings with only one turbine cut in for over half the journey, by replacing Turmo IIIF 1100hp engines with Turmo XIIs of 1610hp. With this more potent power plant almost the whole run can be made on a single turbine at the cost of inflating the schedule by only three or four minutes. This cuts fuel costs by nearly one-third and also reduces total running expenses significantly because more intermittent use of the turbines allows a lengthening of time between overhauls. But this is remedial work to avoid premature sidetracking of the turbine trains, not an advance that will keep turbine traction in the future reckoning of world railway planners.

Except for those covered by the gas turbine train-sets, almost all the SNCF's trunk routes were still deploying a noticeable proportion of pre-World War II coaches in their two-class domestic inter-city services in the early 1970s: and all-year round, not just in the winter sports or July–August peaks when all France seems to decamp to the holiday areas and relief trains pack SNCF main stations and tracks. In the second half of the decade, however, the scene was transformed as the SNCF founded its bid to recapture the middle-class travel market on a massive infusion of new fully air-conditioned, 100mph coaching stock in an elegant external livery of two-tone grey with orange doors. Officially designated VTU75, the stock has been popularly promoted under the brand-name 'Corail', a contraction of *'Confort + Rail'* but also a visual pun since the dominant interior colour of the second-class internal decor is coral. In these vehicles French second-class travellers were blessed with full air-conditioning for the first time, journeys in RTGs alone excepted.

At first configuration of the VTU stock was entirely open saloon in both classes. Side-corridor compartment stock classified VU75 was built within the same body-shell and liveried similarly, but essentially for international operation (one might add that the structure has also been adapted to a new fleet of air-conditioned *couchette* coaches). Subsequently a hard-core 25 percent of the SNCF's clientele evinced such an emphatic preference for compartments that the French modified their attitude in the late 1970s. Nearly 400 Corail coaches of both classes with this configuration were ordered to allow a mix of roughly two-to-one between saloon and compartment vehicles on the longest domestic inter-city itineraries.

Unlike BR, which groups the seats around tables in its MkIII coaches, the SNCF have opted for a bus or airliner arrangement in both classes of Corail saloon, with small pull-down tables in each seatback. The outcome, with 88 seats packed into an 86.6ft Corail second-class as against 72 in a 75ft BR MkIII second-class, is noticeably less knee-room in the former – but then the BR design is commonly acclaimed in Europe as prodigally generous to the second-class customer, especially as on most key trunk routes the SNCF levies supplementary fares on second- and first-class traveller alike in one or two peak-hour Corail-equipped trains as a load-spreading device which BR has so far eschewed. For instance, the second-class passenger from Paris to Nancy has to pay an extra Ffr12 to ride the 07.45 from Gare l'Est rather than the 06.45, while on the 125mph Paris–Bordeaux Corail trains mentioned earlier the extra fee may be a TEE level of Ffr 48. On the Paris–Metz/Nancy and Paris–Marseilles route, incidentally, some Corail open saloons were fitted up with closed-circuit TV screens for passenger entertainment in the autumn of 1979.

Catering was another department in which the SNCF followed the airline model in its Corail stock, constructing no restaurant cars in the same mould but fitting a proportion of both firsts and seconds with airliner-type galleys in recesses adjoining the entrance vestibules to serve tray meals at seats. This was one more downhill step in the degradation – by no means confined to the French – of an amenity which used to be one of the most appealing wares in the whole rail travel shop-window. The Corail fleet also includes bar cars, incidentally.

Inflation has had a markedly more severe impact on train catering than on eating-places on the ground, firstly because the price and upkeep of a new railway coach has risen even more sharply than that of new

Interior of a first-class saloon in one of the later RTG turbine-powered multiple-units, examples of which were exported to the USA for operation by Amtrak and also to Iran and Egypt.

Catering in many SNCF inter-city services nowadays is by self-service cafeteria under the brandname 'Gril-Express'. Compared with a conventional restaurant car the cafeteria can be staffed more economically and, because it is continuously open for trade, turn over more sales in a journey.

parnasse and St Lazare termini in Paris and the Lyons-based turbine train-sets, though that leaves CIWLT still presiding over more than 80 percent of SNCF train catering.)

Waiter service of traditional kitchen-cooked meals is increasingly confined to TEEs and other supplementary-fare or prime-time *rapides*. They can be counted upon to hold a sizeable market prepared to pay what it costs nowadays to sustain a creditable standard of gastronomy on wheels. A more economical alternative, essayed by several mainland European railways but most widely exploited on the SNCF and West Germany's DB, is the self-service cafeteria car, which scores on two counts so far as the operator is concerned: it can function throughout a journey, drawing in a continuous flow of customers instead of isolated peak loads at main meal hours; and because the customer load is spread and the culinary activity is essentially labour-saving, the vehicle can be staffed much more frugally than an orthodox kitchen-restaurant car, so that the turnover generated per unit of staff is valuably increased. With modern microwave ovens to resuscitate pre-prepared, deep-frozen dishes a range of three or four hot entrees can be produced to near-immediate order from a very compact and minimally staffed kitchen; this main dish can be supplemented with a selection from the wide variety of cold foods and drinks in the counter display units. West Germany's rail catering company, the DSG, offers an astonishingly long list of hot dishes in its cafeteria cars considering the size of the latter's production area. The SNCF's cafeteria cars, brandnamed 'Gril-Express', are not quite so enterprising.

The list of new devices which have performed faultlessly in a static installation but have developed unforseen frailties when subjected to the rugged environment of a rail vehicle is long. Modern electronic kitchen equipment is one of the latest defaulters. BR have been plagued by failures in the all-electric kitchens of their 'Inter-City 125' HSTs and the SNCF seems to have had unhappy early experience with its Corail galleys, which at the end of the 1970s were restricted to dispensing cold meal trays. That was the last straw for first-class customers of the Paris–Lille inter-city service, who underlined for the SNCF the fine commercial judgement still required where economy in train catering is an issue.

After its 25kV AC electrification in 1959 the SNCF made a showpiece of the 161.3-mile Paris–Lille line's business service, equipping it with high-speed *rapides* including telephone connections with the national network amongst their amenities, and scheduling one of the trains at 84.9mph between two of its intermediate stops – a postwar world record at the time (the train telephone facility on this route has since been discontinued, as its use fell far short of its renewal when the equipment became obsolete in 1979). Thereafter this was always one of the SNCF's more prestigious passenger operations. But the

buildings; and secondly because, in the nature of railway operation, catering cars cannot always be rostered to a sequence of trains that will allow them to get in service of three main meals a day. With its staff only partially employed compared with their counterparts on terra firma, train catering has thus taken a proportionately harder knock from wage escalation. On really long-distance European mainland routes, too, staff invariably need to be lodged overnight away from home, which compounds the disproportionate crewing expense.

To revert to the question of capital cost, an orthodox inter-city coach with seating in 1979 ran out at £200,000 to £250,000 ($450,000–$560,000) in a production run, so that with all its specialized equipment a catering car will set the purchaser back £350,000+ ($790,000+). Assuming a life expectancy of 25 years and, say, 125,000 miles of operation annually, it would run up another £1 million-worth ($2¼ million) of maintenance expenses before it was retired – altogether a massive amount to recoup from margins on a meal service that may not necessarily be served the whole day long.

Within only a decade of World War II the International Wagons-Lits Company (CIWLT), purveyors of train catering and overnight sleeping cars to almost all Western Europe since the late 19th century – Britain and Germany were the outstanding but not the only exceptions – could see clearly that private enterprise would never again make enough from restaurant cars to fund renewals as a strictly commercial investment. That eventually forced CIWLT's client railways in 1962 to take over responsibility for upkeep of existing cars, for the costs of renewals and for matching quality of catering-car environment to that of the rest of the train. CIWLT retained responsibility for only the provisioning and staffing of the cars, and naturally the catering itself. (On the SNCF-owned cars, CIWLT surrendered its monopoly of those tasks when its agreement fell due for renegotiation in 1973; three other companies now cover respectively trains radiating from the Mont-

average inter-city speeds of today's journeys of 200 miles or less make the balance sheet of restaurant-car meal service less and less happy reading, because there is barely time for one sitting en route at the civilized pace of Gallic eating. So, upon re-equipment of the route with the new Corail stock the SNCF boldly reduced the catering to tray service from the galleys. But the trays stayed frosted in the galleys. Lille businessmen would have none of them and reacted so bitterly that in the autumn of 1978 the SNCF had to turn smartly about and introduce three TEEs each way with full meal service at every seat in the peak-hour paths between Paris and Lille.

In its other sphere of rail business the role of the International Wagons-Lits company had also been reduced. As with restaurant cars, CIWLT found it progressively harder to finance construction of new sleeping cars from berth revenue, while simultaneously the need of new cars to satisfy emergent demand for good-quality second-class overnight accommodation became more critical by the year. Here too, therefore, the French, West German, Swiss, Italian, Belgian, Dutch, Austrian, Danish and Luxembourg railways formed a consortium in 1971 to lease and assume full upkeep and marketing responsibility for all existing sleepers both of CIWLT and of the West German company, DSG, on the international circuits, and to shoulder the required new building. As CIWLT almost simultaneously came to a similar agreement with French and Italian Railways over internal sleeper operations in those countries, the negotiations left it only with a staffing and housekeeping role in overnight travel throughout Western Europe, except in the case of its cars plying within Austria or from Austria into Eastern Europe. Consequently the historic Wagons-Lits livery of midnight blue with elegant 19th century gold lining and lettering is slowly but steadily being

effaced on Europe's internationally peregrinating sleepers by the nine-country consortium's new purplish blue with stark contemporary white lining and its 'TEN' logo, which handily expands into the same brandname in practically all their languages – 'Trans Euro Nuit', 'Trans Euro Nacht', 'Trans Euro Notte', etc. So far, however, DSG has clung to its own livery of deep red.

Since the end of the 1950s Western European sleeper construction has focussed on the so-called 'Universal' configuration, in which each compart-

A modern 'Universal'-type sleeper wears the 'TEN' logo of the Western European sleeping-car pool.

SNCF's latest air conditioned second-class *couchette* accommodation.

The 160mph Paris–Lyons TGV Sudest line takes shape. Its construction features several viaducts but not one tunnel, because the high performance of the train-sets has allowed the civil engineers to hug the ground contours with frequent and sharp changes of gradient.

ment is quickly convertible to first-, second- or tourist-class use. So far as ex-CIWLT pattern stock is concerned, the most comfortable is the Type T2S car, in which the 17 compartments have three berths arranged vertically; for single, first-class occupancy only one is let down, for second-class two and for tourist-class three. The objection to this arrangement is that married couples cannot buy a compartment to themselves at the tourist berth rate. This was solved by interlocking 18 compartments, duplex-fashion, in the Type T2; all can accommodate two berths but – in the view of many, especially in Germany – at the cost of overmuch sacrifice of room for manoeuvre within the compartment. For that reason, single first-class occupancy of a lower T2 compartment is about one-third cheaper than sole use of a T2S room.

Most striking testimony to the SNCF's determination to broaden the market base of its inter-city passenger product is the new 160mph passenger railway, the TGV Sudest (TGV standing for *Train Grande Vitesse*), taking shape between Paris and Lyons for opening by late 1983. Except that a handful of its train-sets will be exclusively first-class for key business services, the new line will operate entirely with a single type of train-set of unvarying accommodation quality in both classes run at a standard average and top speed. Under the last two heads the TGV Sudest will be the fastest railway in the world by a handsome margin.

In the 1960s the SNCF realized that if traffic growth on its Paris–Dijon–Lyons trunk route, the most important of all because it was the rail path through or to 40 percent of France's population, continued at its present rate, it ran the risk of self-strangulation by the 1980s. Heavy investment to increase the capacity of the existing infrastructure by extending its quadruple tracking was unappealing, because the route is not one of France's best-aligned and the scope to uplift inter-city passenger train speeds when they had more track space to themselves was consequently restricted. Given the rural, agricultural character of so much of central

France it looked much better value for money to custom-build a new, segregated route for passenger traffic.

For reasons already discussed in the context of automatic body-tilting, dedication exclusively to immaculately standard train-sets of the high power/weight ratio and low gravity-centre realized by the latest traction and lightweight vehicle technology would drastically simplify the design of the infrastructure and trim its initial cost. Without recourse to automatic body-tilting the engineers could curve the line almost as sharply as an *autoroute* and still provide for negotiation of the bends at speeds far in excess of 100mph without remotely discomforting passengers, let alone prejudicing their safety. And they could indulge gradients as steep as 1 in $28\frac{1}{2}$, compared with the normal *autoroute* limit of 1 in 25, again without any sacrifice of speed. In fact, new *autoroutes* and TGVs could practically and economically be constructed in parallel on a common line of route – and indeed are over one 35-mile and another nine-mile stretch of the Paris–Lyons course. Other putative TGV schemes cherished by the SNCF envisage much longer-distance exploitation of this concept.

With such a degree of grading and curving licence, of course, the TGV builders have been able to hug the ground contours and avoid costly earthworks and bridges to an extent previously inconceivable. There is not a tunnel the whole way; where the existing line bores through the crest of the Burgundy hills before Dijon the TGV soars over it nearly 1000ft higher up. The cripplingly high costs of driving a new railway through conurbations which the Japanese have incurred in the Shinkansen have been avoided; for the first $18\frac{1}{2}$ miles out of Paris the TGV trains will use the existing tracks from Gare de Lyon and they will rejoin the existing network $4\frac{1}{2}$ miles from the centre of Lyons. Since the superseded main line will cater for intermediate traffic the TGV will have only two stations en route, at Montchanin and Mâcon, and between start and finish of its new track only three junctions with the old route, two of them engineered and smoothly curved for negotiation at no less than 137mph by TGV trains diverging from the new line. This naturally facilitates traffic and regulation of the entire route from a single control centre. Since speed is intended to be a consistent 160mph from end to end of the new track, up the stretches of 1 in $28\frac{1}{2}$ as well as on the level, lineside signalling would be quite unacceptable; drivers will work entirely from a continuous control desk display of aspects activated by coded low-frequency currents passed through the running rails and picked up and translated by receivers and decoders on the train-sets.

The ten-car 25kV AC TGV train-sets embody all the exhaustive and methodical research, development and testing in laboratory and out on the track of high-speed rail components that the SNCF and the French rail supply industry have pursued for over two decades, ever since the one-off 205.6mph exploits of 1955 demonstrated that there was up to 200mph potential in the marriage of flanged wheel and steel rail. Most spectacular of the pre-production test-beds was the five-car prototype unit, TGV001, built in 1972, which ran for over 34,000 miles at more than 125mph and up to a peak of 198mph before it was retired in 1978 on the eve of delivery of the first two TGV sets proper. The production sets, in which two independently bogied power cars with an aggregated output of 8750hp flank an articulated eight-car passenger unit, the whole weighing only 380 tonnes, closely resemble TGV001 in outline. The outstanding difference is that TGV001 was turbine-powered, whereas the production train-sets are electric.

Pivotal to the original TGV concept was the compatibility of its train-sets with the rest of the SNCF trunk network, so that they could continue beyond the new line and let as many as possible of France's southeastern cities – and major Swiss and possibly Italian cities as well – benefit from the vastly quicker pace to be realized between Paris and Lyons. The SNCF forecasts that by the mid-1980s a third of

all long-distance rail travellers converging on Paris will have come part of the way on the TGV, so far-reaching will be its impact. In the late 1960s turbine traction looked likely to offer the required versatility at least cost. But no longer. The bulk of the TGV train-sets are multi-voltage – 25kV AC for the new line and 1.5kV DC for negotiation of the existing routes. (DC output is half that available on AC, all that is needed to run at the maximum line speeds of the existing system.) Six of the first bunch of 85 production train-sets, though, are triple-voltage for through working under Swiss 15kV 16⅔ Hz catenary.

A TGV driver will always be in supreme control of the train, but with the benefit of numerous auto-mated aids so that he is distracted as little as possible from concentration on the road ahead, on his cab signal display and on the battery of fault detector lights on his driving console. The SNCF has put a high premium on instant recognition of incipient faults and remedial action in its TGV driver training, for obvious reasons. An immobilizing breakdown will have far more serious impact on the TGV than other main-line services, not only because of the new

One of the two pre-production TGV train-sets on proving trials during 1979. Each ten-car set packs a total output of 8750hp for a train weight of only 380 tonnes.

TGV001, the 6500hp gas turbine-alternator-powered five-car unit was completed in 1972 to test the traction and vehicle technology for the new high-speed railways. When it was retired in January 1978 it had run more than 15,000 miles on existing main lines at over 160mph, up to a top speed of 198mph.

line's operational speed and frequency of trains, but because the only refuges in which a failed train can be sidetracked are at the two intermediate stations. Elsewhere it will be a case of resorting to single-track working round the blockage. Against that sort of emergency each track is reversibly signalled throughout – or *banalisé*, to use the French term that has gone into world railway parlance because the SNCF was the first to adopt the practice intensively – with high-speed crossovers at intervals to switch trains from one track to the other.

One TGV driver's aid deserves particular mention. The gradient profile of the new line is as jaggedly serrated as a cluster of stalagmites, since the route engineers have followed the contours of the terrain as closely as possible. Slopes can veer swiftly from the gentle to a short stretch of the severest 1 in 28½ and switchbacks are sometimes sharp. To negotiate all this at a constant 160mph without waste of energy a driver would have to concentrate almost single-mindedly on dexterous manipulation of his controls. To avoid this the TGV train-sets are fitted with a device which senses gradient changes. The driver selects a controller position suited to the general characteristics of the section through which he is running and the apparatus will automatically ensure that the current feed is marginally adjusted as necessary to hold the pace steady for the minimum consumption of energy.

Regular patrons of the 'Mistral' and other high-

grade *rapides* on the old Paris–Lyons main line will pay for the forthcoming speed with a sacrifice both of comfort and of amenity. Adequate seating capacity in the TGV train-sets' slender, low-slung bodies – laid out as open saloons in both classes – could only be bought with Corail-type furnishing. And Corail experience notwithstanding, catering at the time of writing is to be limited to galley service of tray meals, supplemented by a compact bar for drinks service, because the drastically curtailed journey time rules out anything more pretentious.

The southern half of the TGV, accessible from the present main line by one of the three TGV junctions, was due for commissioning in late 1981 to enable inauguration of public TGV train service on partially accelerated schedules. But when the whole of the new route is operational in late 1983 the standard TGV transit time for the revised route-mileage of 264.1 miles from Paris Gare de Lyon to Lyons will be slashed to two hours flat, which postulates a phenomenal start-to-stop average speed of 132.1mph. Two examples will serve to demonstrate the equally striking ripple effect of the TGV on more remote cities. TGV trains continuing beyond Lyons to Marseilles, 483 miles from Paris, will make the port in 4¾ hours from the capital instead of the 6½ hours attained by the fastest conventional *rapide* in the late 1970s. And Geneva will be brought within 3¼ instead of 5¾ hours of Paris. In conjunction with the Rhône left-bank electrification mentioned earlier,

city centre to obviate tiresome changes into and out of the Paris Metro were aired immediately after World War I, but the motivation to pursue them was lacking until the rapid spread of dormitory suburbia and the establishment of several new towns on the city's perimeter after World War II. This concentrated the minds of Government, local and transport authorities wonderfully, and engendered a co-operative approach to the project previously unimaginable. The scale of the ensuing enterprises can be gauged from the fact that since 1962 the local authority administering the conurbation (denominated the Ile-de-France Regional Council since 1976) has been earmarking over a quarter of its whole annual investment for the city's rail transport improvements; and to that huge sums of state money have been added. In the four years 1974–77 alone the total outlay from all sources on Paris railways – that is, the Metro run by the city's transport authority, RATP, as well as the SNCF's suburban services – was in the vicinity of £1 billion ($2.25 billion). On top of that, one ought perhaps to add, day-to-day operation of the system is substantially subsidized in subservience to social policy, to peg fares generally and discount them to specific categories of passenger; the RATP covers barely half its expenditure from revenue.

So far as standard loading-guage railway construction was concerned, the first step was to project a new deep-level, limited-stop line on an east-west route beneath the city centre. Begun in 1960 this first 1.5kV DC overhead electric *Réseau Express Régional* (RER) line from St Germain-en-Laye in the west to Boissy-St Léger in the east came to full fruition at the end of 1977 when its central link under the heart of Paris was forged through Châtelet-les-Halles. This transversal is above the surface at its suburban extremities and connected to the main

moreover, the TGV will endow the SNCF with four modernized tracks practically the whole way from Paris to the Mediterranean coast.

In the later 1970s the French were investing even bigger sums than those laid out on the Paris–Lyons TGV in the expansion and betterment of railways within the Paris conurbation. Schemes to project new standard loading-gauge railways through the

Examples of the attractive and remarkably spacious styling of the city-centre stations of the deep-level, main-line-gauge RER lines that cross Paris underground. Platform facilities below ground at Gare de Lyon (left) include a buffet.

A train-set of the first generation of RER stock at Nation.

the various interests involved hit on the sensible alternative of interconnecting the expanding SNCF suburban networks on both sides of the city via the already-built east-west RER line. Focal point of the scheme is Châtelet, where one of the most remarkable underground railway complexes in the world has been taking shape. From a huge concourse 820ft long, 260ft wide and a transfixing essay in modernistic decor, no fewer than 34 escalators lead to and interconnect the immediately sub-surface Metro lines with the four island platforms of the seven-track RER station below them. By the mid-1980s trains from around a dozen lines connecting all four compass quarters of Paris suburbia (and amongst other things directly linking by through train the city's two major airports, Charles de Gaulle in the north – via Roissy – and Orly in the south) will converge on Châtelet, where the complex underground layout will have to cope with a throughput of at least 70 and perhaps as many as 100 trains in each morning and evening peak hour.

The other major components of this breathtaking project are the reconstruction of Gare du Nord and Gare de Lyon and their approaches to segregate tracks collecting interconnecting trains from their respective suburban networks; these tracks then tunnel on to feed into the Châtelet junctions. Both terminal schemes are massive projects in themselves. At Gare de Lyon one side of the station has been reconstructed on four levels, to free more of the surface platforms for the growing weight of

SNCF network, which amongst other things has allowed rail fans to charter an 'Aquitaine' train-set complete with 8000hp Co-Co locomotive for the novel experience of sailing underground through the centre of Paris in the full panoply of TEE style.

The formidably escalating costs of urban tunnelling enforced a reappraisal of the original plan for two completely new north-south RER lines. Instead

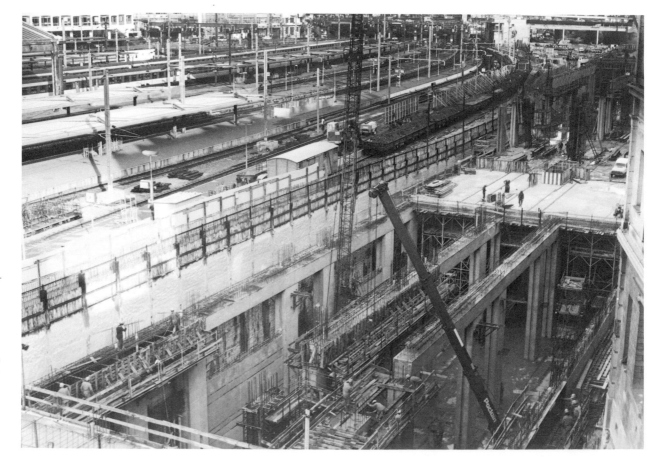

The mammoth engineering works in progress at Paris Gare du Nord in 1979 were commissioned to create a sub-surface station for the new 'Interconnection' lines to the city-centre interchange of RATP and SNCF routes below ground at Châtelet. Apart from this construction at the terminus more massive works were in progress at the station's approaches to reorganize flat, flying and burrowing junctions and project tracks from the surface down to the new sub-surface platforms.

development which is transforming rail transport in and through the centre of Paris. (The RATP's Metro, anyway, is treated in a subsequent chapter on urban rapid transit.) And space permits only a glance at the latest equipment of the SNCF's surface suburban system, which is worked partly by multiple-units and partly by locomotive-powered push-pull sets. Mainstay of the multiple-unit fleet are the low-slung stainless-steel-bodied sets evolved in various series since the early 1950s, all with high-density open saloon layout embodying good standing as well as seating room. The class designations of the 1.5kV DC units are numbered in the Z5000 range, those of the 25kV AC sector in the Z6000 series. Despite the essentially short-distance character of their accommodation, units of this kind have been assigned to regular as well as high-season extra workings over quite considerable distances from Paris, for instance to Orleans, 75 miles out. However, in 1979 they were supplanted on that job by what are probably Europe's fastest push-pull locomotive-powered sets, a match of specially modified Corail coaches including driving trailers fronted by a cockpit-style cab with selected BB9200 locomotives repainted in co-ordinating Corail livery, all passed to run at up to 100mph (similar combinations, but employing 25kV AC BB16000s, have been applied to some Paris-Rouen-Le Havre services).

The newly opened line from Paris Gare du Nord to Roissy (for Charles de Gaulle airport) was the stage for the debut of the Paris network's latest multiple-unit, the 25kV AC Type Z6400, on which the stainless-steel finish has been enlivened with a broad blue band at window level and the more modern, deep-windowed cab front by a band of bright yellow featuring the SNCF logo above the bufferbeam. These, too, are high-performance units, with an aggregate of 1580hp output in each four-car set's

The elegant new Class M179 dual-voltage electric multiple-unit created for the 'Interconnection' services below Paris between the Gare du Nord and Gare de Lyon suburban networks of the SNCF and the RATP system.

main-line movements (which will increase with the TGV's inception) by carving out a new suburban terminus at the third level below the Metro; at the lowest stratum are the platforms for trains proceeding to Châtelet.

To satisfy a rather intricate operational specification for the interconnecting services – because of varying surface and sub-surface platform dimensions and differing control systems, for instance, let alone contrasting traction current supply systems in different SNCF suburban sectors – design of a special dual-voltage 1.5kV DC/25kV AC multiple-unit was essential. Designated M179, the first of these very elegantly styled and liveried multiple-units was nearing completion in 1979; they are high-performance four-car aluminium-bodied sets with an acceleration rate of 2.8ft/sec , which is necessary to cope with gradients as steep as 1 in 24 on parts of the new network.

Unfortunately the author has only space to summarize the biggest projects of the multifaceted

Right:
A 1.5kV DC electric multiple-unit of the Z5300 series for suburban services of the SNCF.

two power cars to ensure steady 75mph capability up the often steep gradients of the Roissy line.

Increasingly prominent on the busiest Paris suburban routes – those radiating from Gare St Lazare and Gare du Nord in particular – are push-pull seven- or eight-car trains of the double-decker coaches which, uniquely in Western Europe, the SNCF put into quantity production in the 1970s (though as the 1970s faded the Italians decided to have their own industry build to the same design). By the end of the decade the Paris system was already deploying over 500 of these very distinctive bi-levels, as conspicuous for their bold orange-banded grey livery as their rounded bulk, within which seating space can be found for as many as 175 in each trailer car. A self-contained electric multiple-unit version of the double-deckers has been ordered for the 1980s and the SNCF is also contemplating a long-haul Corail double-deck coach.

The SNCF has an aggreeable fancy for variegated colour schemes these days. A bold mix of the national flag's red and blue with grey will add still more flair to the 100mph electric multiple-units of new design, classified Z2, which are to be outshopped in the early 1980s so that main-line secondary services feeding into the TGV trains will not besmirch the latter's stunning image. The Z2s will have a rakish, upward-tapering cab-end with a single wide and deep driving window in the same contemporary automotive style as the M179 'interconnection' train-sets of Paris.

Still more flashes of colour are the product of governmental devolution of power over rural transport to local authorities since 1972. Previously the choice of local passenger services for investment and the application of operational subsidies was entirely the province of the SNCF and central Government. The only way the SNCF could elude the straitjacket of state surveillance was by persuading local authorities to invest their own money in rail service betterment within their territory. In several areas the SNCF did win support for intensified service with modern equipment, notably: along the Riviera coast between Cannes and Menton under the brand-name 'Metrazur' (employing stainless-steel, sliding-door stock transferred from the Paris suburban network); between Calais and Dunkerque, marketed as 'Metrodunes'; southeast of Nancy, as 'Metro-vosges'; between Nancy, Metz and Thionville, as 'Metrolor'; and between Lyons and its industrial near-neighbour, St Étienne, packaged as 'Stélyrail'

But local councillors would never have put up their own money for the mass of hopelessly deficient rural services. They got the incentive to take a broader view when central Government devolved into the present-day eight Regions and thereby surrendered a good deal of control over the way the state money, available for local public passenger transport, is allocated. Encouraged to rationalize, prune route duplication by different modes and concentrate on what they judged to give the best

social and economic value, some Regions have opted for significant re-invigoration of their local trains and concomitant curtailment of bus operation. The Nord-Pas-de-Calais Region in particular conceived a greatly enhanced role for the railway and put down the cash for 195 new coaches to modernize its services. Here as elsewhere the rolling-stock acquired for the regionally-supported operations is distinctively liveried and branded. Sadly, though, the admini-stration of Prime Minister Barre in the late 1970s appeared to be backtracking on the policy of its predecessors and hankering for a progressive cut in state grants proportionate to the financial savings achieved by Regional rationalization.

A cursory review of the latest SNCF traction resources must open on the electric side. By the late 1950s the French had established the principle of building virtually standard mechanical bodies and chassis which could be completed without problems by either 1.5kV DC, 25kV AC or multi-voltage traction gear, all with comparable outputs. The first twin products of this policy in the late 1950s were the DC

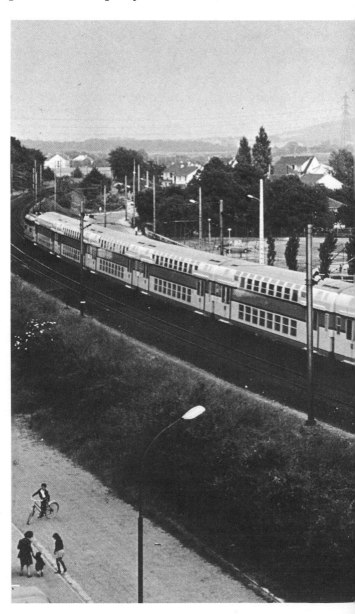

BB9200 and AC BB16000, each with a continuous power rating of more than 5000hp for a total weight of 77.8 and 84 tonnes respectively. They sealed exclusive reliance for the future on locomotives with total weight available for adhesion – that is, with no idle carrying axles. Throughout the 1960s these two 100mph types bore the brunt of the SNCF's inter-city service.

Next to emerge were a mixed traffic pair, the 3000hp DC BB9400 and 3500hp AC BB16500, which embodied another characteristic of latter-day SNCF electric locomotive practice, the monomotor bogie – a single traction motor per bogie, instead of one per axle, with alternative gearing in the final drive to the axles so that the machines can be employed with reduced tractive effort but higher top speed (90mph in the case of the pair under discussion) on passenger work, but with the balance reversed on freight. Other advantages claimed for the monomotor arrangement are that it enhances adhesion and simplifies wiring. Some sub-classes in the SNCF fleet are variants of major types differing chiefly in gearing to meet a local specification, an economical way of catering for the wide range of both physical and traffic conditions encountered in different parts of the SNCF's electrified network.

To date the most numerous of all SNCF electric locomotive types is the mixed traffic family launched in the mid-1960s, the dual-voltage 72.5-tonne 3500hp BB25500, the 70-tonne 3500hp AC BB17000 and the

Left:
The 'Metrolor' operation between Nancy, Metz and Thionville is one of the local stopping passenger operations in which Regional authorities have been persuaded to invest their own money for improved rolling stock and frequency of service.

Increasingly prominent on the SNCF's Paris suburban services are locomotive-powered push-pull sets of these double-deck coaches. A self-powered multiple-unit version of the design was put into production at the start of the 1980s.

3500hp DC BB8500 – this last tipping the scales at a mere 59 tonnes, an extraordinary testimony to the gain in power/weight ratio achieved by the rapid advance in electric traction technology.

Although a small class of four-voltage Co-Cos was built with high power – 4540hp in the first four and 6100hp in the ensuing six – and 150mph capability in the 1960s, that pace has never been exercised in the Paris–Brussels TEE service for which they were primarily conceived. Commanders of the few present-day 125mph TEEs already described and of other heavy, high-speed *rapides* are the handsome 120-tonne 8000hp Co-Cos of Class 6500 which were built for the DC network at the start of the 1970s. These, too, have monomotor bogies with alternative gearing. On the lower ratio, with top speed cut to little more than 60mph, the CC6500 has as much tractive competence to work 600-tonne freights up 1 in 35 gradients on mountain main lines as it has on the higher ratio to whirl the 'Aquitaine' southwards at 125mph. There is no AC version of this type, only a quartet of dual-voltage machines classified CC21000 whose principal assignment has been to work Switzerland-bound freights from Paris to Vallorbe, on the Franco-Swiss frontier, an itinerary which involves a DC-AC catenary change at Dole, en route from Dijon to the border.

In the late 1970s front-line power for the AC *rapides* has been a member of the SNCF's newest four-axle family, the BB15000 type, the first in the SNCF range to employ thyristor control of the power equipment amongst numerous applications of electronics in its design. This book is deliberately eschewing technicality to make space for a rounded picture of contemporary railway problems and practice as well as modern equipment, but since thyristors are the most significant new card to come into the electric traction engineer's hand since semi-

conductor rectifiers, an elementary outline of their function, their pros and their cons is a necessary interpolation.

A DC traction motor at rest cannot withstand immediate application of the supply current at the full voltage for which the machine is rated. In the past the feed had therefore to be built up to the full voltage by progressively switching out resistances that were inserted in the supply circuit, and then by varying the interconnection of an electric traction unit's motors until ultimately each was taking full power. Traditionally this process of 'notching up' in steps has been effected electro-mechanically; in latter-day equipment, commuter multiple-units especially, it is often arranged automatically to achieve an ideal rate of acceleration at an optimal rate of energy consumption. The same process in reverse can brake the vehicle. As power is reduced the motors, driven by the train's momentum, can be made to act as generators, creating energy which the progressively reinstated resistances will absorb and dissipate; alternatively the current can be fed back into the catenary. The first of these braking methods is known as dynamic (or rheostatic) braking, the second as regenerative braking.

The disadvantages of the traditional control method are its progress by palpable steps, which reduces both traction and energy consumption efficiency, and its embodiment of wearing components that are also susceptible to maladjustment. Electronics can now eliminate these handicaps through the use of thyristors, usually arranged in so-called chopper circuitry. Briefly, the thyristor chopper functions like an ultra-high-speed switch, allowing current to flow through it for as little as one-hundredth of a second in one 'on-off' cycle. All that is needed, therefore, is to arrange for the 'off' period of each cycle to be appropriately long, the 'on' relatively short at starting, then for the balance to shift gradually during acceleration until the motors are getting full voltage, and resistances are redundant. So rapid-acting is the device that acceleration is smooth and stepless, enhancing adhesion and tractive efficiency and eliminating the waste of energy through the resistances. Wearing parts are eliminated and the number of electrical contacts greatly reduced. Furthermore, thyristor control vastly simplifies recourse to dynamic braking, a very desirable facility in an electric traction unit because it minimizes use of its mechanical braking system, thereby lengthening the life of braking components and wheel tyres.

There are as yet debits, though. Against thyristor control, apart from long-justified scepticism as to its reliability, are its greater bulk, weight and 30 percent higher cost than that of orthodox electro-magnetic control circuitry, and also its harmonic effect on lineside signalling and telecommunications circuitry, which may need expensive modification for immunization against the interference. The

Class 22200 is the dual-voltage version of latest SNCF four-axle electric locomotive design. Its flexibility is now exploited to run freights from the 1.5kV DC territory of Burgundy and the Rhône valley around Paris to the 25kV AC system of the north without change of locomotive; some locomotives employed this way work expresses from Paris Gare du Nord to Amiens and back before returning to the SNCF's Sudest Region.

A 3600hp diesel-alternator
Class 72000 Co-Co, one of the
SNCF's most powerful series
of diesel locomotives.

second qualification discouraged the Swiss Federal
Railways, in particular, from adopting thyristors
until the end of the 1970s; even then it was impelled
to limit the first of its new thyristor-equipped locomotives to sectors where the signalling and telecommunications had been protectively treated.

The BB15000 is a bigger machine than preceding
families of SNCF Bo-Bos. Styled externally in the
same mould as the 8000hp Co-Cos, it disposes of
5900hp for a total weight of 88 tonnes, and naturally
has 100mph capability. Its relations are the DC
BB7200 and dual-voltage BB22200 types, of which
the former has impressed the Netherlands Railways
to the extent of ordering 30 as the Dutch system's
front-line power of the 1980s; by 1979 the SNCF's
own fleet of BB7200s had already reached 300 in
service or on order.

The SNCF's high-power diesel locomotives are
wedded almost entirely to electric or alternator
AC/DC transmissions; diesel-hydraulic experience has
gone no further than evaluation of prototypes. The

alternator transmission, mentioned in the previous
chapter's discussion of British Rail's latest Class 56
locomotive and its HSTs, became practicable in a
DC-motored diesel locomotive with the perfection of
compact semi-conductor rectifiers. In an orthodox
diesel-electric, transmission problems accumulate
with increase of power, since the transmission is the
rough equivalent of a continuously variable gearbox
that is frequently interposed between a fast-running
motor-generator of DC current and DC motor-driven
axles moving at much slower relative speed. With
semi-conductors and consequent availability of very
compact rectifiers, a diesel locomotive body could
accommodate an alternator-rectifier assembly without weight or size penalty. The output of the diesel-
engine-powered alternator is AC, rectified to DC
before it reaches the traction motors, which conduces
to a higher working voltage and eradicates shortcomings of the traditional electric transmission
scheme.

The SNCF's ranking main-line diesels are

The earliest of the SNCF's present-day range of high-power main-line diesel locomotives is the 2600hp A1A68000.

essentially of three types, within which there are several sub-classes whose variations range from higher power ratings to substitution of alternator for the conventional electric transmissions with which they were first built. Most potent are the 3600hp, 108-ton CC72000s with alternator/rectifier transmission and monomotor bogies, which both fit them for 100mph top-speed haulage of inter-city *rapides* and offer doubled tractive effort at a maximum of 53mph for their assignment to 1500-ton freights over the worst grades in their domain. One of these, No CC72075, is experimentally modified with an SEMT-Pielstick PA6280 engine rated at 4730hp, which makes it the most powerful single-unit diesel locomotive operative in Western Europe at the time of writing.

Insufficient CC72000s have been built to satisfy the remorseless commercial demand for more tightening of inter-city schedules on non-electrified as well as electrified routes, and in several areas – on the non-electrified final stage beyond Amiens of the main line from Paris to the Channel ports, for instance – less powerful designs are consistently operated in multiple-unit pairs. This concerns chiefly the four-axle family in the BB67000 range, an 80-ton type most of which have a 2350hp rating. The third and earliest class in the SNCF's stud of modern high-power machines is the six-axle 2600hp A1A68000, in which, as the designation implies, the centre axle of each bogie is purely weight-spreading and not motored. By far the largest contingent of the SNCF diesel locomotive stud comprises what are four-axle

'hoods' in the American vernacular – that is, with low-bonneted power plant affording panoramic fore-and-aft visibility from a single cab so that they are conveniently reversible for yard as well as line duty. In main-line freight haulage these units are frequently multipled in pairs.

The SNCF has built no new diesel locomotives since 1974, but until 1978 it was still augmenting its fleet of diesel railcars, a motive sector in which the system had the most obsolescence to overtake. In the picturesque mountain-hemmed valleys of the Massif Central, where the railway is a vital winter lifeline but the sparse farming population warrants little more than a skeletal year-round passenger service, renewal money has been saved by a thoroughgoing refurbishment, both mechanically and in internal furnishing, of early 1950s-vintage railcars and manufacture for them of new matching trailers. These twin-sets (the power cars are Type X2800) are distinguished by blue and cream livery instead of the usual SNCF railcar red and cream, to which the other principal exceptions are some sets of the 1950s-era TEE and *rapide* multiple-units bred in the X2700 series known as RGP (for *Rame Grands Parcours*, or 'Long-distance train-set'); a number of the latter on secondary main-line express and semi-fast duty have been confusingly restyled in the cream-and-gold livery of the gas turbine ETG and RTG sets, with which they have a close external resemblance. Latterly SNCF diesel railcar construction has concentrated on a neat-looking twin-set with under-floor-engined power cars produced in

The exercise is pointed at the Iron Curtain, beyond which the Soviets, conveying huge tonnages over a rail network as yet only 30 percent electrified, are eager to cross new horizons of single-unit power; they have themselves built a prototype with an output of 9000hp.

Politically France had, until the end of the 1970s, taken a far more relaxed view of the gap between the national railway's revenue and total costs than Britain. The SNCF was benefiting from about £1600 ($4000) million in state money under a variety of grants and supports and it had been guaranteed a minimum annual rate of investment of £600 ($1500) millions until 1982. Its revenue shortfall on costs was not far short in value of its total income – in other words it was receiving from contracted public authority subsidies and compensations around two-thirds as much as it earned, and recording a further amount roughly equivalent to a third of its income as its officially accounted deficit for the year. Within that framework, naturally, the SNCF could price its freight product more competitively than its British neighbour in comparative terms. And that was a potent factor – though by no means the only one – in the SNCF's ability, in contrast to BR, to stay a predominantly freight railway, drawing 60 percent of its revenue from the goods sector.

In Continental Europe the maximum freight wagon axleload has, since the start of the 1970s, been relaxed to 20 tonnes, even for vehicles operating at up to 75mph, and the SNCF (more than most) has exploited this concession to concentrate its freight-wagon construction almost entirely on bogie vehicles of very generous load capacity. A significant proportion has been custom-designed for the handling of specific traffics – cereals, iron and steel, chemicals, petroleum products, and so on; a third of the wagon fleet, in fact, is special-purpose.

Pursuit of siding-to-siding block train traffic has been assiduous and in the heavy industrial sector the SNCF has some impressive flows of over 2500 tons

three versions and commonly nicknamed the 'Cara-velles': the X4300/4500s are 440hp with mechanical transmission, the X4500/4600s 440hp with hydraulic transmission, and most recently the X4750s which have a top speed of 87.5mph and a 590hp diesel-mechanical power plant.

A very powerful home industry not only supplies all SNCF traction and rolling stock but has built up a 25 percent cornerstone of the world railway market on the solid postwar achievements of French rail technology. Only half its output is for the SNCF. Between 1955 and 1978 it built just under 2000 locomotives for overseas customers. In the dawning years of SNCF postwar modernization the household names were those of single companies like that of the main electric traction supplier Alsthom (a contraction of 'Alsace' and 'Thomson', constituents of the titles of two companies, SACM and Thomson-Houston, which merged to found the concern in 1928). Since the last war, however, alliances to harness traditional skills, rationalize manufacturing resources and thus compete more effectively and on a broader front at home and overseas have familiarized us with new portmanteau titles amongst the industry's front-runners – Alsthom-Atlantique, Francorail-MTE, ANF Industrie and CIMT-Lorraine, for example. One of the most striking projects under development by Alsthom-Atlantique at the close of the 1970s was a diesel-electric locomotive of over 200 tons weight on two four-axle bogies mounting a single 18-cylinder SEMT-Pielstick engine to produce an output of no less than 7200hp.

An X4300/4500 diesel-mechanical railcar twin-set of the range widely used on French stopping services outside electrified territory, seen near Amplepuis.

Above left:
An RO freight headed by a CC6500 electric. Note the amount of container traffic being moved by this wagonload service.
Above right:
Road trailers piggybacked in 'Kangarou' wagons, with the former's road wheels 'pouched' below the rail vehicle's frame level.

One of the SNCF's principal automated marshalling yards.

payload and around 4000 tons gross weight to display, but wagonload business is precious – not least with 11,000 private sidings to serve – and accounts for nearly 60 percent of the system's annual tonnage. Consequently a large part of the freight working has to be focussed on 40 or so key marshalling yards, half-a-dozen of which are sorting over 2000 wagons a day. At some of the biggest, such as Sotteville near Rouen, Woippy near Metz, Sibelin near Lyons and Hourcade near Bordeaux, the sorting operation is automated to the extent of remote radio control of the shunting locomotives from the yard control tower. These key yards and the wagonload freight depots in the country's major production and consumption centres are interlinked by a network of premium-rate merchandise freights guaranteeing 24 or 48-hour transits according to distance, which are designated RA for *Régime Acceléré*.

Some RA trains are components of TEEM – *Trans*

Europ Express Marchandises – the continent-wide network of tightly timed and interconnected express freights, many of them on international itineraries, which complement the passenger TEEs; individual TEEM paths are as far-reaching as from Spain to Sweden. For the vital long-distance flow in season of produce from the Languedoc-Roussillon in the far south to the Paris markets some very smartly-timed RA trains are run to ensure overnight delivery, at speeds up to 87.7mph instead of the usual RA limit of 75mph on suitable trunk route track. The rest of the freight train operation is classified RO, for *Régime Ordinaire*; in the late 1970s a substantial amount of RO traffic was upgraded to RA.

The SNCF was the first European railway to add to its freight armoury what the Americans popularly call 'piggyback', but formally TOFC, for 'Trailer on Flatcar' – the trunk rail movement of road vehicles complete on rail vehicles. The inaugural French

service linked Paris and Lyons in 1958. Other railways–conspicuously the West German, Netherlands, Swiss, Belgian and Italian – subsequently embraced the idea. It has latterly become an important item in their international freight sales portfolio, not only because of rapidly rising road fuel costs but because resort to international piggyback trains is a way for freight forwarders and road hauliers to evade the quotas which Governments impose on the number of foreign road freight vehicles they will allow annually to enter or cross their territory. During the 1970s piggyback traffic between the Netherlands and West Germany on one side and Italy on the other soared from under 400 to well over 12,000 road vehicles a year and the figure still escalates. So promising are the growth prospects of the piggyback business that the Swiss, for instance, have invested in enlargement of tunnel clearances on the Gotthard route to allow acceptance of bulkier rail-hauled road vehicles.

The problem, of course, is to accommodate the modern road trailer's bulk, loaded on a rail vehicle, within the rail loading gauge. The SNCF has favoured what it calls aptly the 'Kangarou' method. As the name implies, this employs a skeletal rail car with a frame of roughly normal height above rail level but embodying pouches into which the wheels of the road trailer are slotted so that the overall height of the loaded rail car is reduced to the minimum practicable. A 'Kangarou' wagon can be loaded by crane lift of the road trailer, or via end-loading ramps over which a tractor can propel it into position. In contrast the Austrians, Germans and Swiss have developed a wagon with unusually small-radius wheels, which permit a fully-floored frame low enough to ease most modern road vehicles within the loading-gauge. Moreover it allows drive-on, drive-off loading and unloading of complete tractor-trailer rigs.

The 1980s may be a period of change for the SNCF. In 1979 it agreed a new contract with the Government which reflected the latter's predeliction for allowing market forces to determine the economy. On the one hand the SNCF was given an unprecedented licence – for France, that is – to fix its own prices in both passenger and wagonload freight sectors, whereas previously it had to work within published tariff scales approved by Government for each freight commodity, to preserve common carrier availability of freight service and also to regulate competition. On the passenger side the SNCF was bidden to keep any passenger rate changes in step with cost-of-living movements, though it was not precluded from pricing its supplementary fares up to whatever level the market would bear.

On the other hand the SNCF had to accept an obligation to cut its nominal deficit by 1982 and additionally some reduction of its subsidies, while to help cut costs French railwaymen were expected to agree to such controversial economies as one-man crewing of freight trains. Single-manning of freight

trains was already practised in some other West European countries, such as Sweden and Switzerland, not always with benefit of the track-to-train radio communication of which West Germany's DB was the only really widespread European practitioner at the end of the 1970s. French crews have now accepted the economy since the SNCF's agreement to install radio links, starting with the Paris–Marseilles trunk route.

To help meet its new commitment to reduced support by 1982 the SNCF has been relieved of financial responsibility for the viability of conurbation passenger services; the responsibility is now shouldered by the Government. The SNCF has also been accorded freedom to abandon totally unremunerative passenger services to an extent not exceeding five percent of its total passenger business, to switch the affected traffic to road, and to restructure its freight operation as demand dictates. Under both these last heads closures on a scale not experienced in France since the last war look highly probable.

A long rake of privately owned, special-purpose hoppers hauled by a dual-voltage, 3500hp Class BB25500 locomotive, one of the mixed-traffic range introduced by the SNCF in the mid-1960s.

A recent SNCF signalling and traffic control centre at Versailles Chantiers.

The three 5150hp Class ET403 inter-city electric multiple-units were conceived in 1973 when the German Federal Railway believed that the only way to obtain high speed without heavy cost in track and vehicle maintenance was to spread the weight of the power plant. All three sets, first-class only, are now relegated to charter work.

3.
THE RESHAPING OF THE GERMAN FEDERAL RAILWAY

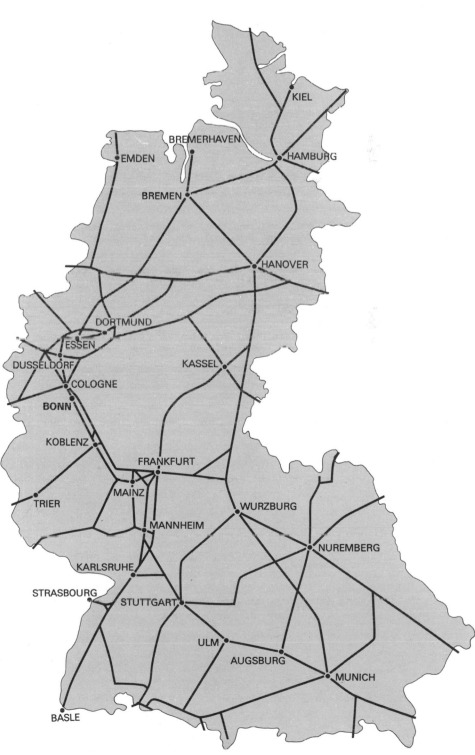

The German Federal Railway, or Deutsche Bundesbahn (DB) of West Germany, had come to a critical phase of its short history in the closing years of the 1970s. The first, significant seeds of its contemporary problems were sown at its 1945 creation in the aftermath of the Allies' post-World War II partition of Hitler's Reich, which sundered the pre-1939 Reichsbahn into the DB and the Deutsche Reichsbahn (DR) of East Germany.

German railways had a daunting enough task to recuperate from wartime devastation, material shortages and make-do-and-mend, but the newly formed DB's difficulties were compounded by the mismatch of their inheritance to the emerging transport requirement of the Federal Republic. Berlin was the focus of the prewar railway system and except for an important axis from Berlin south and southwestwards to Leipzig, Dresden, Stuttgart and Munich, the mainstreams of movement were broadly east-west across the comparatively flat northern half of the country. Partition severed them. Overnight what had been some of Europe's most prestigious and busiest trunk rail routes, such as Berlin to Hamburg and Berlin to Magdeburg and Hannover, were shorn of the bulk of their traffic and reduced to secondary status. For the East German DR, re-orientation to the revised map was not too vexing, since the physical relation of its chief traffic centres to Berlin was unaltered; deprived of access to Hamburg and other ports in Northwest Germany, its main preoccupation was to secure adequate operating capacity between Berlin and the country's only maritime outlet, the Baltic port of Rostock, and to contrive new bypasses around the Allied enclave in West Berlin.

In West Germany, a country stretching roughly three times as long as it is wide, and with political and commercial focuses diffused between Bonn and Frankfurt/Main respectively, the DB, in contrast, confronted a major shift of passenger and freight flows to a north-south alignment. The main burden of the system's trunk traffic was thrust upon – and the DB's prestige, too, had to ride on – lines that were neither engineered (in the 19th century) nor developed (in the earlier years of the 20th) for such an assignment. The author still remembers his astonishment, sitting in the cab of a DB diesel travelling north from Hannover to Hamburg in the 1950s, when he came on more than 20 miles of single track, for the Hamburg-Hannover-Würzburg route and that from Hamburg and Bremen via Münster, the Ruhr and Cologne to the Rhine-Main area had become the two vital north-south rail arteries of the new country (that single-line stretch, needless to say, has long since been doubled). The author has been unable to unearth any data relating present-day freight movement over these routes to that of the 1930s, but the dramatic change in their status shows up clearly enough in a cursory comparison of a 1936 Reichsbahn passenger timetable with the DB's 1979 inter-city

schedules. In 1936, whereas 10 or 11 daytime expresses operated every 24 hours between Berlin, the Ruhr and Cologne, just three linked Hamburg and Frankfurt, two Hamburg and Munich and one Hamburg and Stuttgart. In the West Germany of 1979 the market demands connections between the three latter pairs of cities hourly throughout each working day.

The Germans were always prodigal railway builders – witness the acreage of sidings bestowed on almost every station, some with little more than a village in the vicinity to serve – and it was a plenitude of alternative routes which enabled the railways to avoid total immobilization under the Allied air battering of the 1940s. But the bypasses, the loops, the refuge sidings and the marshalling yards were in all too many instances not pointing the right way after the last war. And another trouble was that in the centre of the country, where ranges of high ground impeded passage of the north-south routes, the Hannover-Würzburg route in particular traces a winding, often steeply graded path through the wooded folds of the beautiful and mercifully unspoiled Mittelgebirge hills that rules out economical multiplication of the running lines. The threading of the deep cleft of the Rhine valley by the other vital north-south route, from Cologne and the Ruhr via Bonn to Mannheim, Frankfurt, Switzerland and Bavaria, is just as curving and as much of a brake on express train speed, but that at least has the benefit of a duplicate double track on the other bank of the river to segregate the bulk of the freight from the inter-city passenger traffic. Another stretch of route curved and graded by its original builders with no conception of its present-day role is that which clambers up to, then down from the plateau between Stuttgart and Ulm en route from Mannheim to Munich.

The DB was the first in Western Europe to run a post-World War II train at 100mph in daily service, beating the French to the three-figure mark by three years with its re-equipped 'Rheingold' of May 1962 – a surprising achievement when one remembers the state of the West German system 15 years earlier. But that level of speed was and still is possible for sustained periods only in the plains of the Ruhr north and northeast of Cologne, at the northern end of the trunk route from Hamburg to the south, and in the broad valley of the Rhine in the south of the country between Mannheim and the Swiss border at Basle. Elsewhere topography is a severe handicap.

Consequently the DB cannot couple its most widely separated cities at the level of end-to-end average speed attained on the prime French routes or on those transformed by Britain's 'Inter-City 125'. The 1979 timetables of the well-aligned stretches of the DB network are studded with a good many short-distance start-to-stop sprints timed at average speeds in the 80mph bracket, of which the most striking example is probably the immaculately

standard booking of 43 minutes for the 61¼ miles from Dortmund to Bielefeld, averaging 85.5mph, set by every one of the hourly expresses from the Ruhr westward to Hannover. But the DB's regular-interval inter-city trains between Hamburg's and Frankfurt's main stations, for instance, cannot better a transit time of four hours 46 minutes for the 329.4 miles inclusive of three intermediate stops (which connotes an end-to-end average speed of only 69.1mph) because of the serpentine course of the railway south of Hannover. With its 'Inter-City 125' HSTs BR runs the 'Flying Scotsman' from London to Edinburgh, almost 63 miles further, in nine minutes' less journey time. The contrast is the more disturbing to the DB because it is operating in the European country where new motorway construction has had the highest priority since the last war, where internal air service competition over the longer inter-city distances is relentless, and where private flying looks to be becoming as much a way of life as it is in the USA. Of the DB's main hope of narrowing the gap, more in a moment.

Like the French, the DB focussed its inter-city attentions on the premium-fare market in the first post-World War II decades. The Class 601 diesel-hydraulic multiple-units which were its contribution to the TEE stock pool in 1957 set standards of comfort, interior appointments and smooth, silent running that outclassed other countries' entrants. In those days there were electrification gaps on some key international trunk routes and, in any event, multi-voltage traction was still in an exploratory stage of development; since several of the TEE

routes touched cities where the main station was a dead-end terminal – Frankfurt, Munich, Lucerne, for instance – the double-ended diesel-powered train-set, affording quick reversal, was the most practical medium for the start of the enterprise. But the drawbacks of the fixed-formation train-set, its incapability of capacity adjustment to traffic fluctuations and its liability to total immobilization by a flaw on just one of its vehicles, gradually discouraged all the TEE participants from persisting with the multiple unit formula as the spread of catenary made haulage by electric traction possible.

The DB was among the most energetic electrifiers. In 1952 only a thousand route-miles or so of its system were under wires, principally in the south of the country, but within 15 years 15kV 16⅔Hz AC catenary had been strung up over 5600 more route-miles. Today the electrified proportion of the DB network is not more than 40 percent, but with all key routes under catenary, 85 percent of its traffic, measured in passenger- and ton-miles, moves behind electric traction.

The image of the present-day electrically powered DB inter-city or IC train was moulded with the 1962 unveiling, already mentioned, of new equipment for the 'Rheingold' and not long afterward for its companion train of those days, the 'Rheinpfeil'. The 'Rheingold', created in 1928 as a Pullman-style train by the prewar German sleeping and restaurant car concern Mitropa to inveigle affluent British tourists to the Harwich, Hook of Holland and Rhine valley route to Switzerland, was the first prestige train the DB revived after the war (but in name and route only,

One of the Class VT601 diesel-hydraulic train-sets which the DB contributed to the start of the 'Trans-Europ Express' service in 1957. All are now confined to charter excursion work, for which they have had their interior layout considerably remodelled.

In its former red livery, now replaced by blue and cream, a Class 216 diesel-hydraulic heads a Cologne–Norddeich train through the north German winter in 1973.

Below left:
A Class 103 electric Co-Co threads the Rhine gorge between Bonn and Mainz with a southbound TEE.
Below right:
In the observation saloon of one of the Vista-dome cars which used to operate in the 'Rheingold' and 'Rheinpfeil', but which have since been sold to a private travel agency operator of charter trains.

not with its Pullman-type cars). While the 'Rheingold' set out in sections from Amsterdam and Hook of Holland (combined before entrance to West Germany) with coaches for Munich, Milan and Swiss destinations, the 'Rheinpfeil' was doing likewise from North Germany; the two converged at Duisburg, where a complex reshuffle of coaches was conducted, after which the 'Rheingold' combined all the cars bound for Switzerland and Italy from both trains, the 'Rheinpfeil' those for Munich. The whole operation is now history, for the 'Rheinpfeil' has been translated to a totally different path while the 'Rheingold' – a TEE – has shed its Hook of Holland link because of evaporated patronage from the source which prompted its 1928 berth. But in the early 1960s these twins were a spectacular cynosure among European rail travellers.

This was because the quality of their fully air-conditioned stock was far in advance of then-prevalent European standards, so much so in fact, that, apart from subsequent development of its already superbly smooth-riding running gear, the design still serves the entire present-day DB inter-city network and is so successfully competitive over other means of travel that it is hard to imagine it being bettered, except at untenable increase in capital and running costs per passenger seat. Accommodation, as it was at the start, is still offered in a choice of roomy compartments or open saloons, the latter furnished with a pattern of semi-reclining and rotatable individual or paired armchairs which the author still rates the most relaxing seats in a European rail vehicle.

Other innovations in the 'Rheingold' and 'Rheinpfeil' which other European systems have since

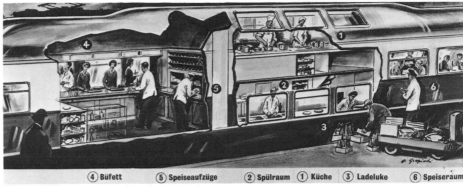

④ Büfett ⑤ Speiseaufzüge ② Spülraum ① Küche ③ Ladeluke ⑥ Speiseraum

Germans often abbreviate it to 'IC'): the DB two-hourly interval service was first-class only. In fact it was indistinguishable from TEEs except in brand logo, since the locomotive-hauled IC trains – all named – were timed at similar pace, used identical coaching stock in TEE red-and-cream livery and rated precisely the same scale of supplementary fares as TEEs. The only odd men out were IC workings covered by the one-time TEE diesel-hydraulic multiple-units of the DB pending construction of more locomotive-hauled equipment, but the diesel sets had been retired for special excursion work well before the end of the 1970s.

The IC timetable was neatly contrived to afford smart cross-platform interchanges between its trains, an essential consideration if every pair of commercially intercommunicating cities in the country was to have the benefit of throughout IC service, since the West German trunk routes do not predominantly radiate from one commercial capital as they do in France or Britain. The DB's main lines

adopted – and some took a long time to follow suit – were the convenience of automatically opening and closing, air-assisted coach vestibule doors, and coach entrance doors that could be closed and locked by the train's conductor from a central control in the train; the second of these two devices is now, by fiat of the International Union of Railways (UIC), *de rigueur* on all coaches built for European international service. From its inception the stock was built and fitted with electro-magnetic track brakes for the 100mph running which, after settling up continuously welded track stretches in the Ruhr and in the south, the DB allowed the two trains to do in 1962; today it runs just as smoothly at 125mph over the few sectors where the DB indulges the higher pace.

Only two features of the original 'Rheingold' and 'Rheinpfeil' equipment have been discarded. One was a kitchen-diner which ingeniously shoehorned a bi-level business area, kitchen upstairs and scullery below, within the European loading gauge, but which gradually incurred upkeep costs that outweighed its economy of coach body area. The other, sadly, was the American-style dome observation cars, a peerless vantage point from which to command the vine-blanketed hillsides, the castles and the incessant rail, road and waterborne traffic threading the Rhine gorge south of Bonn.

At first the 'Rheingold'-type stock was dedicated to a TEE role, but the prompt commercial success of British Rail's regular-interval operation encouraged the DB at the start of the 1970s to create something of the sort between West Germany's main commercial centres. With one essential difference, however, even though the DB borrowed the BR 'Inter-City' brandname untranslated (for logo purposes the

Cross-platform interchange between IC trains in the DB's hourly two-class service inaugurated in 1979.

Left: An air-conditioned first-class saloon with reclining seats of DB Inter-City stock. Right: The 1979 air-conditioned second-class open saloon design for the DB's Inter-City service.

Inter-City train 515, the 'Werdenfels' from Hamburg to Garmisch Partenkirchen, awaits departure from Mainz. Nearest the camera are the train's second-class coaches in today's standard DB blue and cream livery.

form very roughly an inverted 'U', with the North Sea ports at the top and Basle and Munich at the extremity of each fork; within it are enclosed two adjoining squares of which the common horizontal in the centre of the framework extends from Mannheim through Frankfurt/Main to Würzburg and Fulda. Stations like Mannheim in the west and Würzburg in the east were and are pivotal points of interchange between the inverted 'U's' verticals and the Frankfurt transversal. Late running of one IC train scheduled to make a connection at one of them – and the DB boldly timed the meets very tightly – soon had a ripple effect throughout a substantial sector of the IC network, because so much of the service was interdependent.

For its premium fare-paying clientele the first-class-only IC service was at first very appealing, not least because its speed and comfort, even with the

fare surcharge added in, were very competitively priced in the context of West Germany's cost of living. They still are, and have to be, in the DB's view, in a country where Federal investment in roads is annually eight times the outlay on railways, quite apart from what is also spent by provincial and local authorities and where the outcome by the end of the 1970s was some 4500 route-miles of toll-free *autobahnen*: the aim of a West German Transport Minister of the mid-1960s was to bring 85 percent of his electors within 10 kilometres of an *autobahn*.

Besides being toll-free the *autobahnen* are also innocent of speed limits. In the face of the automobile industry's gratification of an inborn German motoring *machismo* with faster cars from year to year, and of intensified internal air services, the enforced stagnation of DB speed began to tell in the first-class market. Traffic growth was further stunted by recession. By the mid-1970s the DB realized that at fare levels that it dared not raise substantially, its TEE and IC trains were, on average, losing about $2\frac{1}{2}$ pence (5 cents) for every passenger-mile they recorded.

Nor were the standard DB expresses, the so-called D-Züge, covering their costs, though in this category the shortfall was not so serious. But even though 90 percent of the DB's long-distance business was second-class, the D-Train plan had never been submitted to a comprehensive redraft. Scarcely anywhere was the service discernibly patterned and average speeds were lacklustre by comparison with what was being done to attract and capture the second-class inter-city customer elsewhere in Europe. End-to-end average speed was stagnant at a beggarly 50mph or so. The D-train's second-class coaches rode as smoothly as the IC trains' firsts, but exterior brightening with a new system-wide DB livery of blue and cream could not mask their lack of air-conditioning, or that decidedly less had been achieved in the betterment of second-class than of first-class compartment comfort since the 1960s. With the continuing spread of *autobahnen* even long-distance coaches were making serious inroads into D-train business. From 1960 to the late 1970s, in fact, the DB's share of the national long-distance passenger travel market had more than halved from over 20 to a mere 8.5 percent.

In brief, seeing that less than 15 percent of all West German business travel was identifiably business-motivated, the DB, while it had valuably burnished its image with its exclusive IC and TEE services, had been neglecting the main chance. The steadily worsening economics of the IC operation was the ultimate goad to change. And when it came it was executed with characteristic German thoroughness. After a field trial between Hamburg and Cologne, in the spring of 1978, the DB redrafted its entire long-distance passenger service for the following spring. Not only the enormous scope of the exercise but the extraordinary precision of its execution made this 1979 revision the most remarkable transformation of a national rail passenger service the world has yet seen.

'Jede Stunde, Jede Klasse' – 'Every hour in each class' was the intensively publicized tag for the change, since the DB overnight rebuilt its entire IC service on the British model. The 33 key towns and cities in the West German network were now interlinked directly or by tightly interwoven cross-platform interchanges every hour of the working day by a daily programme of 152 dual-class IC trains. In the main the latter followed four routes: Line 1, Hamburg–Bremen–Dortmund–Dusseldorf–Cologne Mannheim–Stuttgart–Munich; Line 2, Hannover–Dortmund–Wuppertal–Cologne–Frankfurt–Würzburg–Munich; Line 3, Hamburg–Hannover–Frankfurt–Mannheim–Karlsruhe–Basle; Line 4, Bremen–Hannover–Würzburg–Nuremburg–Munich. Like their one-class predecessors, each train in the considerably enlarged IC network was distinctively named. At a stroke, average journey time between the cities covered was cut by 25 percent for the second-class traveller prepared to pay the modest IC surcharge.

The only blot of consequence on this rejuvenated image of long-distance travel at the start was that, rather strangely, the DB did not anticipate the change early enough to equip every IC train with vehicles of comparable standard in each class. A handsome new air-conditioned 80-seater second-class saloon design came off the drawing board in time only for construction of ten prototypes and a further 30 pre-production samples by the spring of 1979; these the DB was then anxious to evaluate in service before embarking on mass production. Consequently most second-class IC travellers in 1979 were riding in the same type of coach as in D-trains, devoid of air-conditioning and to a 25-year-old design in which visible changes since its conception have been limited to livelier seat and floor coverings and individual seat reading-lamps in examples built from the mid-1970s onward.

The sole first-class-only trains on the DB are now TEEs. The opportunity of the 1979 timetable revision was seized to eliminate, or convert to domestic IC dual-class services, a number of international TEEs which had failed to defend their longer-distance clientele from air competition. In 1978–79 the French and West Germans together motivated a quite drastic clear-out or degradation of long-distance international TEEs. In fact, apart from the indictment that the majority were no longer viable against air competition in the role for which they were cast in 1957, they were more and more of a nuisance as individual systems concentrated their timetable planning on intensively patterned domestic service because the TEEs had to be routed to satisfy commercial requirements in each country they served – and not least because they were prone to import unpunctuality from over the border. At the start of the 1980s the DB hosted only 17 international TEEs, but was running 19 on internal itineraries, the latter at peak business travel periods. All these TEEs supplemented the hourly IC trains.

Since they were introduced by the DB in the 1962 'Rheingold', train telephone and secretarial services have been a standard feature of German-equipped TEEs. The French and Italian Railways have abandoned their limited applications of these ideas, concluding after a while that the demand for them would never compensate for their installation and maintenance costs. But the DB has shrugged off the debit in the conviction that both amenities are as compelling a shop-window attraction in premium-fare trains as a good restaurant. In recent years use of both services has been increasing and now that the telephone is available on IC trains second-class travellers have also taken to using it. The telephone

In 1980 train secretarial services were available in 52 daily TEE and Inter-City trains of the DB. Charge for the use of the service was DM5 per quarter-hour. These trains were also equipped with public telephones for both inward and outward passenger communication with subscribers at home and abroad via the national telephone network.

A Class 221 diesel-hydraulic – the type which spearheaded the DB's main-line dieselization in the 1950s and early 1960s – heads a *Regionaleilzug* in North Germany, where this concept of accelerated, limited-stop local train service with integrated bus connections was pioneered in 1977.

number of each train is listed in DB brochures for the IC service. The secretarial service, however, is now guaranteed only on TEEs; it is provided on IC trains only when there is advance demand for it and room in the train to surrender a compartment to the secretary.

D-trains survive, for the 1979 redraft of the IC service was only the first stage of a reconstruction of the whole passenger timetable. From 1980 onwards D-trains are being gradually restructured on a regular-interval basis – but not necessarily hourly – to achieve the smartest possible connections between IC trains and major centres off the IC map. (This aspect of the D-train restructuring has special significance for first-class travellers in some towns which had to be deprived of their calls from the few IC trains they previously had when the IC service was redesigned to its present strictly patterned framework.) Simultaneously the DB is striving to uplift the average end-to-end speed of D-trains to 60mph. At the end of the day unpatterned long- and medium-haul passenger operation should be confined to the TEEs already mentioned, other international trains, certain domestic expresses conveying

through coach sections that demand extended station stops for remarshalling, special-purpose trains such as the automobile-carrying services, night sleeper trains and main-line stopping trains in rural sectors where demand would not warrant day-long operation.

In the more populous areas between major traffic centres, however, the DB is anxious to cut costs and stimulate business by extension of its *Regionaleilzug* or RE-Train scheme, which was premiered in 1977 in the Hamburg, Oldenburg, Münster and Rheine enclave of North Germany. Briefly, the aim is to end

rail service at many small stations so as to cater more attractively for the larger country towns with a substantially accelerated regular-interval operation running at up to $87\frac{1}{2}$ mph top speed between the more widely spaced stops. The smaller localities bereft of direct trains are linked with the RE operation by connecting bus services from the railheads retained in the larger townships. The extent to which the DB can pursue the RE exercise, though, may be dictated by local politics. The pioneering North German scheme has run the gauntlet of fairly virulent criticism, in the Federal Parliament as well as on its own ground, above all for its inconvenience to schoolchildren; they have always been a privileged category of German rail user, and have benefitted from massively discounted fares for their term-time commuting.

If the residue of the DB's passenger timetable reconstruction is executed with the same attention to meticulous detail as the IC revision, it will be quite a breathtaking achievement. A vital distinction between the DB's regular-interval IC service and that, particularly, of British Rail is that whereas BR (generally speaking) does not attempt to maintain an impeccable time pattern on long-distance routes, DB does. DB has got almost as close to clockwork scheduling as Netherlands Railways, where the goal is a little easier to achieve because of shorter Dutch distances and the restriction of most Dutch freight circulation to the night hours. On not one West German internal IC route (so far as the author's timetable researches can ascertain) do the times of intermediate stops and arrivals at destination vary by more than two or at most three minutes by the clock from train to train, and even such infinitessimal discrepancies as that are rare. This applies even to the longest itineraries intersecting countless traffic flows en route, such as Hamburg to Munich, 508 miles. When one takes into account the juggling of other passenger services and of freight working that will have been involved to secure such precise patterning,

A Class 110 electric locomotive in the type's original livery of dark blue and black at the head of a present-day D-train. The D-train timetable is being steadily restructured on a regular-interval basis.

By 1980 the DB had the most extensive track-to-train radio-telephonic communication system in Western Europe, with over 9000 route-miles of the system and a very high proportion of its total traction fleet equipped to use it.

the planners' job must have been formidable, even with computers at their elbow. Psychologically, though, it is of incalculable value. If a potential passenger has only to memorize one 'minutes-past-the-hour' figure to know when a train is available throughout the day, spur-of-the-moment journey planning is vastly simplified and use of the railway becomes almost as convenient as getting the car out of the garage. On the other side of the fence, moreover, a strictly repetitive operational sequence is much more conducive to punctual working by railwaymen.

But punctual working also depends to some extent on passengers, above all when fulfilment of the fast, every-hour service between so many pairs of towns entails an intermediate change of trains en route. Even where 10–12 minute stops are scheduled at the principal IC interchange stations – and a good many allow only half that time – the actual interval may have to be abbreviated if lost running time needs regaining, so passenger discipline is vital. The DB has done what it can to make that instinctive. (One ought to add that the whole IC operation is deliberately scheduled with a four percent reserve of time in station-to-station allowances – 'recovery margins' in British railway terminology – so that drivers always have that much in hand to recoup lost time without excessive speed.)

The majority of IC trains are of a 10- or 11-car formation – usually three first, a kitchen-restaurant or a 'Quick-Pick' self-service cafeteria car and six or seven second-class cars – which are designated alphabetically in pairs from A to E, the last letter covering three cars if the extra second-class vehicle is run. At the interchanges drivers need to halt their trains with some precision, because each pair of coaches should come to a stand alongside corresponding illuminated A to E signs which have been hung from platform canopies. Furthermore, the *Wagenstandanzeiger* – those invaluable mainland European platform displays which illustrate the marshalling and individual coach class and destination of each

train using the platform concerned – have been modified to suit; each one is now boldly marked 'You-are-here' fashion according to its site on the platform, so that any IC passenger can discover exactly where to stand for whichever group of coaches he is aiming at. With the notable exception of Hannover, where many IC trains heading opposite ways make connections, most likely cross-platform interchanges are between trains running parallel. An even more important benefit of this standardization practice, therefore, is that an IC passenger changing trains knows he has only to head straight across the platform to find exactly the same class of seat and type of coach on the other side.

Invaluable for passenger briefing as well as for its main purpose, tighter control of hour-to-hour working especially when out-of-course running demands extemporization, is the track-to-train radio communication; DB is, so far, the only Western European railway to have standardized this on all main passenger and most freight routes. At the opening of the 1980s over 9000 route-miles, all electric locomotives and multiple-units and a high proportion of the diesel traction fleet had been equipped with it. It is fully selective, so that a control office on the ground can contact any driver individually without being heard by other crews; if necessary the driver can switch the control office straight through to his train's public address system for an announcement direct to passengers. One or two standard instructions or messages have been encapsulated in symbols; a driver or ground controller just presses the appropriately coded button and the corresponding symbol is illuminated on the other's receiver – no words need be exchanged.

The DB rightly put a high premium on effective use of this radio link for prompt passenger briefing in the 1979 re-launch of the IC service. For comparatively minor aberrations from punctuality, what one might call 'Plan B' is pre-prepared for immediate transmission to passengers. Controllers at main traffic centres have, for each IC train calling at their station, a list of every connection, IC or otherwise, it is booked to make, for each connection the amount of lateness by the IC train which will put said connection in jeopardy, and finally the next available substitute on each route which dismounting IC passengers can be offered. Lateness of more than half-an-hour, though, may well entail improvisation, especially late at night, and when that happens – as it did to the author on an IC trip shortly before he undertook this book – one fully appreciates the value of the radio link with the ground. The train's public address system was constantly alive with calls from the driver requesting the conductor to go to his direct train-to-locomotive cab phone to receive instructions and information the driver was passing on from ground controllers. Many of these calls were clearly requests from the controllers for details of the numbers of passengers aiming for (and by now likely to miss) last advertised connections of the day from junctions along the final stages of the IC train's route. Having gone through the train and identified every passenger affected, the conductor had the statistics phoned through to the control office. Soon more 'captain-to-crew' summonses crackled over the public address system, the conductor repaired to his phone, and before long every fretting passenger had firm assurance of a way the controllers had contrived to get him to his destination. In view of the tight connections of the IC service it is supervised throughout the day system-wide by a special IC control room.

The DB has always been prepared to tolerate a wider gulf between train catering costs and revenue than its Western European neighbours, counting comprehensive service in this department a worthwhile loss-leader in the long-haul passenger marketplace. It does not furnish as many trains with catering cars daily as British Rail, but those it does run offer both a more continuous and a much more wide-ranging bill of fare. At the customary main mealtimes the restaurant cars serve fixed-price *table d'hôte* menus in one or two seatings, but at any other stage of the journey – except within half-an-hour or so of the train's destination, naturally – one can order just as sizeable a meal from a voluminous *à la carte* menu invariably running to at least a dozen *entrées* including wiener schnitzels and steaks, five or more soups and almost a score of generously portioned and garnished cold plates. DB passenger management is convinced that in the fiercely competitive German transport market this sort of provision is essential on trains making end-to-end journeys of more than three hours' duration.

Both catering and sleeping cars are now owned by the DB, but the catering itself and the staffing in both sectors remain the exclusive role of the Deutsche Schlafwagen und Speisewagen GmbH (DSG), the wholly owned subsidiary of DB set up to take over the West German sector of Mitropa's business when that prewar company's headquarters was curtained off in East Germany by partition. The only mechanical job retained by the DSG is the upkeep of sleeping cars, for the curious reason that its small workshops at Hamburg and Munich (this one shared with the Wagons-Lits company) can do the job more cheaply than DB's plant. The DSG's other activities include three hotels, a great many West German station bars, kiosks and shops and not least the fine restaurant complexes at 17 key DB stations, the two biggest at Frankfurt and Hamburg main stations. At Frank-

Below:
One of the double-deck kitchen-restaurant cars formerly employed in the 'Rheingold' and 'Rheinpfeil'.
Bottom left:
In the kitchen of a DSG diner.
Bottom right:
Dinner is served in a DSG diner.

DSG's 'Quick-Pick' cafeteria cars – exterior; serving counter; and the attractive menu of hot dishes offered in 1979.

furt alone the DSG's empire embraces three restaurants (one of them rated one of the city's best), a cafeteria, two beerhalls and seven snackbars, the whole provisioned on the station premises by the DSG's own butchery, bakery and pastry cookery. The station's turnover for DSG is near £4 million ($9 million) a year, a healthy component of which is

unsurprisingly generated by the sale of nearly 1¼ million frankfurters, and over 350,000 bottles and around 600,000 glasses of beer!

Full meal service is an imperative item in the DB passenger management's specification for each and every IC and TEE train, but in 1979 the DSG's fleet of 100mph-capability kitchen-restaurant cars was not big enough to cover the intensified IC service as well as other essential commitments. Some IC trains, therefore, are equipped with 'Quick-Pick' cars – the DSG's self-service cafeterias, which I find outstandingly the most attractive and efficient version of the concept so far realized on Europe's railways.

By the start of the 1970s the DSG, like every other train caterer, was agonizing over the sharply escalating overheads of the business and the difficulty of recruiting quality staff to a job in which a considerable amount of unsocial hours of work was inherent. As the decade progressed DSG managers were finding that a conventionally staffed restaurant car needed to pull in as many as 80 percent more customers than a ground establishment each main mealtime to balance its books. This was physically impossible anyway because the seating capacity was lacking in a rail vehicle, so there was no way of escape from deficit working in an orthodox diner. But it clearly had to be confined and since DB was set against degradation to buffet or airline-style catering in the IC network the DSG began cafeteria experiments with converted buffet cars in 1973–75. Satisfied with results, DB and DSG built a production series of 40 new cars brandnamed 'Quick-Pick' which were in service by the end of the decade.

A 'Quick-Pick' need be staffed by no more than two, as against three in 90 half-bodylength kitchen-

diners in the DSG fleet, four in full-length cars and six in many TEEs, which have a supplementary bar. This staff economy coupled with the continuous service character of cafeteria operation, which was touched on in discussion of the SNCF's 'Gril Express' cars, can and does generate a gain of over 40 percent in cash turnover per staff man-hour in DSG experience – and this despite the fact that 'Quick-Pick' wares are generally priced at 20–25 percent less than equivalent items or dishes in DSG restaurant cars.

Within a 90.2ft coach-length – the DB carbuilders are going for longer bodies than anyone else in Europe – the 'Quick-Pick' designers have managed an admirable amalgam of functional efficiency and pleasant environment; it is only a little less relaxing in the 42-seat restaurant area of the car than in a full-scale diner. The remarkable feature of the 'Quick-Pick' is that from such compact equipment and constricted staff area behind the long serving counter and batteries of packaged food and drink displays, it can keep on continuous offer ten or more hot dishes, about half of which are full-blooded *entrées* such as roast pork or braised veal and vegetables. These last, naturally, are ready-prepared deep-frozen dishes rapidly heated to order in microwave ovens, but the author can testify that within those limitations they are exemplary in quality. Nevertheless, discontent rumbled in the first-class market when it was known that 'Quick-Picks' would

serve some IC as well as D-trains and the DB thought it prudent to temper the wind of change: on the 'Quick Picks' in IC employment the catering is standard, but a proportion of the tables in the saloon are kept fully laid for traditional waiter service to order from the cafeteria menu.

After the start of the dual-class IC service in the spring of 1979 one first-class traveller ignited a lively correspondence in the Frankfurt press with outrage at having to share his diner with beer-swilling second-class travellers under the new order, let alone being put at risk of having to eat in a 'Quick-Pick'. The DB anticipated some reaction of that sort from its first-class clientele, who, moreover, had had to put up with some deceleration to accommodate all the extra trains. A 15 percent decline in first class patronage was anticipated, but in the first six months there was a loss of only 2.5 percent to set against a second-class growth of as much as 25 percent (and an 18 percent increase in DSG restaurant-car business on the IC trains). But there were teething problems to resolve. Most serious was the realization that the rerouting of merchandise freight trains to make track-space for the intensified IC service was not only increasing costs but prejudicing the freight services' punctuality and reliability.

Overnight DB train services are slated for 1980s restructure too, in this case primarily to clear more nocturnal space on the trunk routes for desperately

One of DSG's massive 'Universal'-type sleeping cars, each of which includes a shower compartment. Each compartment has its alarm, which can be sounded by the conductor at the waking hour selected by the room's occupant.

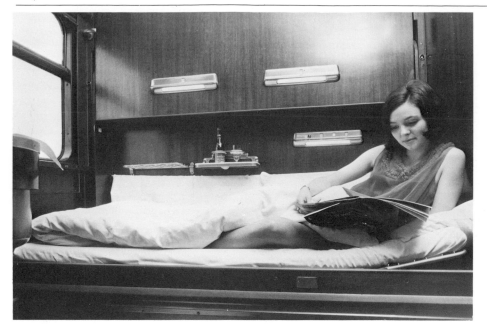

Compartment of a DSG 'Universal' sleeper arranged for single occupation. The fluorescent lights are on the underside of the centre berth, folded out of use against the compartment wall.

needed acceleration of long-haul freight trains. Hitherto, sleeping cars and couchette cars have been dispersed singly or in sections among a considerable number of trains, but the pressure is on DB to concentrate them into fewer workings, each all-sleeper and couchette so far as passenger accommodation is concerned, and to 'flight' these trains French-style in groups over each main route. Inevitably, as with the IC reorganization, the change will deprive some towns of through sleeping-car service.

The DSG sleeper fleet includes some recently built cars to the Wagons-Lits' T2S pattern described in the previous chapter, but the great majority are of the DSG's own 'Universal', class-convertible design. This boasts two frills not indulged in the Wagons-Lits cars: a shower compartment in each coach; and at the head of each berth an alarm buzzer and light operable remotely from the conductor's position in the car, so that every customer can be wakened conveniently at the precise hour of his choice.

A feature of DB holiday season operation deserving mention is the number of international and domestic long-haul trains run to the charter of the country's big travel agencies. Some of these agencies own their own coaches; the ex-'Rheingold' and 'Rheinpfeil' observation domes, for instance, have been acquired by one of the companies, repainted in the brilliant green-and-orange livery which the concern has adopted to match its *Apfelgold* ('Golden Apple') title, and had their dome height slightly trimmed to satisfy clearances on the wide range of routes at home and abroad over which the company runs its land-cruise trains. Generally speaking, though, the accommodation of these German agency trains has been pedestrian set against the make-up of the splendid 'Vacances 2000' cavalcades run for a French agency from Paris to the Riviera coast in summer and to Alpine winter sports Meccas in winter, in both cases overnight. These French equipages mingle the SNCF's latest sleeper and couchette coaches with vintage Pullman cars and, at the rear, one of the SNCF's new cinema cars (internally

perhaps the most brilliantly and elegantly styled coaches manufactured by any European railway in the late 1970s); after dinner, the bar, trainboard disco and cinema stay open most of the night, and the train is amply staffed with hostesses to wash, brush, tuck up and watch over children while their parents live it up until the small hours.

In contrast the DB, though it was courting party charter business by converting existing buffet cars or building new cars as bar-equipped saloons adaptable either for disco-dance or conference purposes, was operating agency trains preponderantly made up of dated couchette and buffet cars, short on toilet rooms and innocent of air-conditioning. Market research proved that this was a prime factor in the 50 percent decline of agency train business between 1962 and the mid-1970s. The DB determined to recapture the loss. Within the standard air-conditioned body, couchette accommodation of really gracious modern style was contrived, with washrooms and two separate WCs per car, and in the same framework a special-purpose car embodying a telephone kiosk, bar, shop, an attractive cafe-type saloon with a number of two-chair tables, and an office and information centre with train public address transmission equipment for the agency's staff. Pre-prepared meals are to be served to passengers in their compartments. The major West German agencies were persuaded to invest in an initial three 'Holiday Express' (*Ferien Express*) train-sets of these striking vehicles – the first in Europe to be custom-built for this sort of traffic – which were commissioned in 1980. They will run some 125,000 miles annually from West Germany to Austria, Switzerland, Italy, Southern France and Northern Yugoslavia.

The DB and the SNCF are the major practitioners of the accompanied car train, the long-haul rail ferrying of automobiles, their drivers and passengers which was the 1955-brainchild of British Rail's Eastern Region and which has subsequently been adopted with gratitude by main-land administrations from the Netherlands to Spain. Each country promotes it under a different title – BR as Motorail, the SNCF as *Trains Auto-Couchettes*, the DB as *Autoreisezüge*, and so on. The DB uniquely ennobles one of its trains with a title, the 'Christoforus Express'. This runs daily, a few public holiday dates excepted, and in the middle of the day not by night like the majority of such trains, from Dusseldorf and Cologne to Munich. It couples the most modern air-conditioned passenger stock including full restaurant car with the DB's long-framed double-deck car-carriers, which can run serenely at up to 100mph. So successful is the 'Christoforus' that demand enforces duplication from time to time – even triplication in one late 1970s pre-Christmas period.

The deficit on the DB's long-haul passenger operation is starkly overshadowed by the real loss on its local working – one says 'real' because a great deal of the shortfall arises from Government fare-

pegging and traditional discounting of fares to selected groups, such as schoolchildren (who pay little more than ten percent of what their travel really costs). The Federal Government closes the gap with compensation sums that amount to as much as 85 percent of the DB's direct local passenger train operating costs in the Hamburg, Frankfurt and Munich conurbations. In total the DB's support under this head alone was bigger than British Rail's entire drawing on public funds in the late 1970s.

Nevertheless in the 1970s stupendous sums of public money were being laid out additionally on the modernization of conurbation railways as an integral component in the creation of a co-ordinated radial and inner-city public transport system to discourage use of private transport. Munich was the first city to have a standard loading-gauge railway driven underground right through its heart to interlink the whole peripheral DB suburban network directly with inner-city public transport at magnificently equipped subsurface interchange stations. In Munich as in other big German cities the prime apparatus of inner-city transport nowadays is a superbly modernized tramway relaid underground in the city centre. Integrated DB conurbation systems of the Munich type are known as *S-Bahnen*, the underground ex-tramways generally but not uniformly as *U-Bahnen*.

The tightly-knit towns and cities of the Ruhr are

Conveyance of private cars is big business for the DB, whether from factory to distributor or in *Autoreisezüge*, the network of services for motorists and their cars operated from the conurbations to the holiday areas and between some main cities. This train of factory-fresh cars in special double-deck carriers is headed by a Class 218 diesel-hydraulic in the DB's formerly standard red-and-black diesel traction livery.

The superb engineering and design of West Germany's *S-Bahnen* is patent in this view of the city-centre sub-surface station of Hauptwache, Frankfurt/Main, with two Class ET420 electric multiple-units at the platform.

embraced by an *S-Bahn* system that is almost entirely above-ground, but the Rhein-Main *S-Bahn*, which takes in the whole industrial and residential area from Frankfurt/Main to Darmstadt, Mainz, Wiesbaden and Friedberg, and that of Stuttgart are being just as grandly projected through the city centres of Frankfurt and Stuttgart as Munich's. A Reeperbahn link similarly integrated the Hamburg *S-Bahn* network in 1979.

The Frankfurt system includes a loop serving a station directly beneath the main terminal of the city's airport, from which a ten-minute interval train service can ferry air travellers to a mid-city interchange at Hauptwache, on the doorstep of the most

prestigious hotels, within half-an-hour. The first stages of the Stuttgart *S-Bahn* funnelled an inlet from the suburban system on three sides of the city beneath the city's prime shopping thoroughfares, there to interconnect with *U-Bahnen* in more remarkable tri-level sub-surface stations with spacious air-conditioned shopping precincts at mezzanine level. At the time of writing this *S-Bahn* is in the midst of extension to the city's fourth suburban quarter, where it too will take in a direct service to and from the city airport. Completion of the Frankfurt and Stuttgart schemes will in each case have DB electric multiple-units converging on the tunnel track through the city centres from different direc-

Standard train-set of the *S-Bahnen* is the Class ET420 electric multiple-unit; the exception is the Rhein–Ruhr network, which has opted for locomotive-powered push-pull equipment. The broad band of colour around the windows of the ET420 is varied for each *S-Bahn*.

tions at 2½-minute intervals in the morning and evening peaks. As at Munich, therefore, the operation of the whole of each *S-Bahn* network, both above ground in the suburbs and below at its hub, is necessarily controlled by a highly sophisticated, computer-based signalling and movement-monitoring apparatus in a central operations room.

To digress briefly, with Dusseldorf airport already connected to the Ruhr *S-Bahn*, Frankfurt to the Rhein-Main *S-Bahn*, Stuttgart all but rail-served and plans under discussion for a rail link to the Cologne-Bonn airport, West Germany leads Europe in this integration of rail and air transport. It may soon go a step further ahead. As this book is written

the adaptation of trains serving Frankfurt airport for airline check-ins of passengers en route to the airport is under trial. The trains involved are three of the longer-haul trains already routed via the underground airport station (there is pressure on the DB to route some IC trains that way, but it cannot be done without some substantial revision of the timetable). A luggage van staffed by airport personnel has been fitted out with check-in apparatus that is linked with the airport's check-in computers by radio, and the only matter still to be resolved in late 1979 seemed to be whether the radio link was foolproof against interference.

At 1979 prices completion of the Frankfurt *S-Bahn* scheme will by the later 1980s have run up a total bill, including train-sets, of certainly no less than £750 million ($1700 million); that of Stuttgart is unlikely to leave any change from £500 million ($1300 million). The DB's share of the cost in each case, however, is limited to the account for the train-sets and the expense of supervising the railway construction. By provisions of the Federal Parliament, 60 percent of the total is put down by the Federal Government; almost all the rest comes from the funds of the city and provincial authorities whose territories are covered by each scheme.

Altogether the Federal Government was supplying over £500 million ($1300 million) a year for DB capital investment at the end of the 1970s. On top of that it was paying out nearly £400 million ($900 million) annually to meet interest charges on the massive sums the DB has been borrowing for years to fund a still bigger annual investment. Add to these amounts (a) the compensation for underpriced local passenger fares noted earlier, (b) subsidies under other heads ranging from provision for railwaymen's pensions to help with maintenance of nearly 10,000 level crossings and their equipment, and finally (c) the DB's official – and substantial – annual deficit after all the grants and subsidies had been excluded from the reckoning, at the end of it all the DB of the

A Class ET420 unit of the Munich network negotiates new flying junction construction for the *S-Bahn* scheme at the approaches to the city.

The heaviest regular freight train operation in Western Europe – two DB 6000hp Class 151 Co-Co electrics at the head of one of the 5000-tonne ore trains of special six-wheel bogie hoppers run from the Hansaport at Hamburg to the Peine & Salzgitter steelworks southeast of Hannover.

late 1970s was absorbing an incredible £4 billion ($9 billion) a year in public money.

Until the mid-1970s an affluent West Germany seemed satisfied that the DB's comprehensive social passenger and common carrier service was value for this kind of money. In addition, though the country was lavishing far more on road modernization, it was ambivalently anxious to have quality rail service to coax traffic off them, heavy lorry freight especially. When the oil crisis braked the German economic juggernaut it was another matter. As the recession's impact on heavy industry seriously eroded the bulk freight mainstays of DB freight revenue and helped depress the railways' financial state still more, DB management, its methods, problems and its prospects, came in for a sequence of in-depth grillings by the Parliamentarians of Bonn. Would they ever see a worthwhile return on the millions poured annually into railway investment?

In many ways it was a rerun of the British situation which Beeching enlisted about 15 years earlier. More desperately than BR the DB needed its high rate of annual investment because of the deficiencies of the infrastructure it inherited, but too much of the money was being spent without tackling critical issues of national transport policy and traditional railway practice. The railway network was too big; it was overstaffed (a problem insoluble except through natural wastage, because of the established civil servant status of well over half the operating staff); it was forced to provide social services without adequate compensation; and in the commercial sectors, shouldering the full cost of maintaining and policing its 'roadway', it was competing under handicaps unknown to its road and waterway rivals. Ten years earlier, under the transport plan of a former Federal Minister, Georg Leber, little-used and profitless lines aggregating about one-fifth of the DB route-mileage were to have been closed and their traffic transferred to road, but only a fraction had been axed. The Federal Government might propose, but the provincial or *Land* administrations have much power in

West Germany; most of the closure plans foundered on their local pride or prejudice.

With the two main political parties on a knife-edge balance and a national election on the horizon, the Government's reaction to the spring 1978 arraignment of the DB in Bonn was predictably wary. The country's need of a modernized railway was reaffirmed and the DB's contention that it could only be made more cost-effective by heavy ongoing investment in labour-saving re-equipment as one of the priorities was accepted. However, a ruthless axing of unprofitable rural service to save staff was not; here the Government did no more than re-endorse the scale of passenger service abandonment hopefully adumbrated a decade earlier. A reappraisal of the terms of public authority support for conurbation passenger transport was promised, also a brake on investment in canals (with a simultaneous look at a quite inequitable fuel tax relief enjoyed by waterway operators) and a moratorium on new trunk road-building parallel to railways.

The most important innovatory item in the Government statement was agreement to study closely suggestions aired during the Bonn enquiry that the state should take over and maintain the DB's infrastructure, whereafter the DB's commercially oriented passenger and freight services should be segregated from the socially costed operations and established as separate, profit-centred companies. The idea that the public authorities should take full responsibility for track and signalling and lease its use to the railway, that way putting railway operators on a similar competitive footing to road operators, is not unique to West Germany. It has been advanced but rejected in Britain and at the time of writing it is being canvassed in the formulation of a new national transport plan for Switzerland, where the previously unthinkable lapse of the Swiss Federal Railway into serious deficit since the onset of the energy crisis recession has knitted many brows. After careful study, however, the Bonn Government decided in the spring of 1979 to reject the concept. And a few months later it impressively reaffirmed its faith in railways by almost doubling their share of the national transport investment budget for the 1980s.

Another high priority in the DB's management book – construction of brand-new high-speed lines bypassing the most constricted sectors of its inherited trunk network – has Government financial support for as much of the massive programme as physical resources can cope with for most of the 1980s. For many years these *Neubaustrecke* were publicized primarily as 150mph passenger railways, but latterly a good deal of emphasis has shifted to their great significance for a redeveloped freight business.

The high-speed passenger promise was held out in the wake of a rather chequered essay in 125mph operation – Europe's first in regular public service –

in 1965–66. The well-aligned sector between Munich and Augsburg was equipped with apparatus to actuate inductively a continuous cab signalling system, also an automatic device on the traction unit that would decelerate it on an ideal curve in face of an adverse signal aspect, and the first of the then-new 8100hp Class 103 Co-Co electric locomotives were fitted to work with it. But a couple of years' experience of consistent 125mph working over this sector had the DB very disconcerted at the cost in wear and tear on track and vehicle running gear, and the 100mph limit was re-imposed while the engineers pondered.

One school of thought insisted that the answer lay in lightweight multiple-units wherein the weight of traction gear would be spread over more axles. This led to design of three prototype four-car streamlined inter city units with automatic body-tilting, Class ET403, which emerged in 1973. Within four years, however, the multiple-unit format was out of favour on the usual grounds of inflexibility in a fluctuating traffic situation (the 1979 inception of dual-class IC service underlined this shortcoming, as the ET403s were built with exclusively first-class accommodation; they are now relegated to special charter work only). It was 1977–78 before the DB felt the wear-and-tear problems had been sufficiently mastered to reinstate the 125mph limit between Munich and Augsburg for IC and TEE trains comprised of suitably braked stock, and to bring into play other 125mph sectors between Augsburg and Donau wörth, Hannover and Uelzen, and Hamburg and Bremen that had been fitted for continuous cab signalling.

But as already implied the sectors where 125 and even 100mph is permissible are too small a proportion of the DB's main IC routes to offset the debilitating effect on end-to-end speed of the unfriendly topography in the heart of the country. This holds true even though the DB intends to have over 300 route-miles – the aggregate of several different sectors – fit for 125mph by 1984. In 1970, therefore, the DB formulated (and three years later the Government accepted in principle) a plan to build seven *Neubaustrecke* totalling 590 route-miles to bypass the worst-aligned sections of the IC route-map. With an eye to the ultimate potential of flanged wheel on rail, the new lines were to be engineered for up to 185mph, which in view of the hilly terrain to be traversed pre-supposed massive bridging, tunnelling and other infrastructure costs. But combined with more heavy expenditure elsewhere to upgrade 775 route-miles for regular 125mph operation, the gain would eventually be a minimum end-to-end average speed of around 90mph between even the furthermost cities in the IC network, such as Hamburg and Munich.

The Hannover–Würzburg *Neubaustrecke* took a step or two southward through the suburbs of Hannover from 1973 and the Mannheim–Stuttgart

line was authorized four years later, but it was 1978 before the Government approved and advanced money for full-hearted progress of the first of these two schemes as far as the Kassel area. On both, progress is sadly halting – ludicrously so in that the DB has been balked from spending the funds the Government has authorized purely because the country's land-use planning processes not only invest a great deal of decision-making power in provincial, municipal and even village authorities but allow individual objectors so much licence. Agreement on a line of route for the *Neubaustrecke* has been an interminable business, protracted in one locality after another by pettifogging objections from tiny communities that must be given full procedural hearing. When the *Neubaustrecke* draft was first published, completion by 1990 was visualized not only for the Mannheim–Stuttgart and the Hannover–Würzburg lines in their entirety, but also of a line cutting through the hills from Cologne to the vicinity of Frankfurt, thus avoiding the Rhine gorge. But the route first projected for the Cologne–Gross Gerau line was rejected almost *in toto*. By the end of the 1970s, only the Mannheim–Stuttgart by-pass looked a surety for completion during the 1980s. However, the investment plan for the 1980s en-visages a start on the Cologne–Frankfurt as far as Koblenz and on a further *Neubaustrecke* from Rastatt through Offenburg to Basle.

Before we leave the subject of 125mph inter-city speed one 1979 development should be mentioned. That is an experiment between Hamburg and Bre-men with radio control of the continuous cab signal-ling and automatic checks on speed of high-speed traction units, instead of the use of track-mounted devices. If the radio control is foolproof it will have several advantages. It will clear the track of appa-ratus that complicates the job of permanent way gangs, but perhaps more importantly it will both simplify the extension of control to several tracks within the range of each transmitter and provide

The driver's console of a DB high-speed electric traction unit – in this case one of the Class ET403 multiple-units – showing immediately above the driver's left hand the display, activated by inductive track-mounted apparatus and trainboard mini-computers, which prescribes the ideal speed at which the train should be running according to the state of the track ahead.

At the start of the 1980s inter-modal freight was the major growth area of the DB's freight operation. The DB has a powerful grip on the movement of deep-sea containers to and from West German ports; in 1978, for instance, it transported inland three-quarters of the total of 327,000 containers with 4½ million tons of freight that were unloaded at Bremerhaven.

By use of bogies with remarkably small diameter wheels a wagon floor can be sunk low enough to 'piggyback' a road trailer without the need to 'pouch' its wheels.

channels which can be used simultaneously for train-control telephonic communication and even the passage of TV images.

Inter-city maximum speed sights have been lowered to 125mph for the *Neubaustrecke* when they are at last commissioned. The new railways are now vital to the improved quality of freight service for high-tariff merchandise which the DB is desperate to develop – and which the Government is spurring it to provide – to close the tonnage and revenue gap opened by the downturn of bulk industrial traffic. As I have already explained in a previous chapter the extremes of the speed band on a mixed traffic railway must not be too far apart for a number of reasons.

The Federal Government, in part for environmental objectives, is anxious for growth of the DB's intermodal freight business – that is, container and piggyback movement. Its 1978 statement of policy set the DB a target of tripling its carryings under these heads by 1985, over which period it was prepared to make the DB a special grant of around £250 million ($560 million) for investment in terminals and equipment, and also to subsidize rates competitive enough to entice new business. One glance at a

map of the DB's heaviest merchandise flows suffices to appreciate that they are at their thickest on the framework of the IC network, except between the Ruhr and Hannover and between Würzburg and Bavaria – hence the great freight significance of the *Neubaustrecke*.

In earlier years the DB was among the wariest of all European systems in its attitude to the British Freightliner model. It was happy to bid for its share of the huge inland movement of deep-sea containers through the North Sea ports of its own country or of the Netherlands, but with so many private sidings it was not prepared to put wagonload business at risk by concentration on block train operation. As a result much of the DB's domestic container traffic has been treated on a wagonload basis, not necessarily originating and terminating at specialized transfer depots and thus subject to transit protraction by proceeding through marshalling yard processing en route. (One ought in fairness to note the corollary: that the DB has thereby been induced into enterprising developments of mobile container lift vehicles, whereas BR has stayed obdurately dedicated to massive high-capacity gantry cranes in costly fixed terminals. Consequently the DB can economically test the potential of any location for establishment of custom-built terminal with high-capacity fixed transfer equipment, which BR as yet cannot – or can only by inefficient improvisation with leased cranage of orthodox type.)

At the end of the 1970s only half DB's container movement was in block trains. The DB's piggyback business, on the other hand, has evolved as a strictly trainload operation between a network of 16 terminals, from which services are projected into Austria, Switzerland, Italy and the Netherlands as well as interlinking West German centres. In the fading 1970s piggyback was by far the fastest-growing sector of Western European rail freight activity. In 1978 all the railways involved in it together carried more than 330,000 road vehicles and DB carryings in early 1979 were reported to be running at a 30 percent higher rate still, with trains booked to capacity a month or more in advance of running. Swiss Federal piggyback trains shuttling between Basle and Lugano via the Gotthard Tunnel, which ferried some 15,000 lorries under the Alps in 1978, were doing as much as 50 percent better in 1979.

The DB employs both basic types of piggyback rail vehicle. The more remarkable are the flatcars marshalled into drive-on, drive-off end-loading trainsets, which are each mounted on a pair of four-axle bogies with diminutive wheels of only 360mm (1ft 2¼in) so that the set makes a continuous platform low enough to shoehorn the generality of Continental tractor-and-trailer rigs complete within the loading gauge. These *Rollende Landstrasse*, or 'Rolling Highway' sets as they are popularly known, were in 1979 operating between Cologne, Stuttgart and Munich, Munich and Italy via the Brenner Pass and Munich

and Yugoslavia via the Tauern route. The other piggyback carriers are skeletal vehicles with pockets into which road trailer wheels can be lowered below wagon frame height. In the next few years the DB is aiming both to increase the number of piggyback terminals to 25 and to equip each of them with high-capacity container transfer apparatus. Located in the country's principal merchandise production and distribution centres, they will form a network offering an option of direct piggyback or container train service over six routes linking most pairs of cities within it.

The size of the DB's wagonload commitment – 60 percent of its total freight traffic in 1979 – naturally accords marshalling yards a key role in the reshaping of the freight operation. Since 1975 the DB has nearly halved the number of its main yards to set up longer and fewer inter-yard runs for wagonload traffic. Further pruning hinges on investment in strategically sited, comprehensively automated yards with the capacity to encompass the sorting work of a wide geographical area. What this entails financially can be gauged from the outlay of nearly £200 million ($450 million) on one installation alone, Maschen, which covers a 692-acre site south of Hamburg and is Europe's biggest. Concentrating the activity of five yards which previously interworked to process the Hamburg area's teeming rail freight at the cost of a great deal of transit-prolonging and expensive inter-

yard freight movement, the two halves of Maschen, one for each direction of traffic, aggregate 34 reception tracks and 150 sorting sidings, the whole interconnected by something like a thousand sets of points.

Computers initiate every phase of train sorting and marshalling at Maschen, fed in advance with every scrap of knowledge about the wagons of an incoming train – size, weight, destination and so on – from input terminals at main originating yards from the Scandinavian borders to the south of the country. Thus a train's sorting programme is ready as soon as it arrives. Simultaneously the computers continuously project forward in time the accumulation of onward traffic by route and destination to assist operators in the efficient tabling of outgoing trains. Entirely computer-controlled, too, are the rail-mounted retarders which brake the wagons rolling off the hump; informed by sensors of the wagons' weight and running characteristics and by track circuitry of the degree of occupation of each sorting siding and hence of the wagons' distance to run before they buffer up with vehicles already occupying the selected track, they adjust the retarders accordingly. Should wagons mislead the sensors and be excessively decelerated, then the computer will automatically call up track-mounted mules to push the offending vehicles the rest of the way.

Maschen's designed through-put is no less than

Europe's biggest marshalling yard takes shape at Maschen, on the outskirts of Hamburg. Covering 692 acres the finished installation has 34 reception tracks and 150 sorting sidings.

A 'Trans-Europ-Express-Marchandises', or TEEM, the international freight equivalent of the 'Trans-Europ Express', heads south up the Rhine gorge. The DB is traversed daily by almost 100 TEEMs, the furthest-running of which has an itinerary of 2036 miles, from Sagunto in Spain to Stockholm; the wagons conveyed throughout by this train have to have their axles changed at the Franco-Spanish border because of the variation of track gauge between the Iberian peninsula and the rest of Western Europe.

11,000 wagons a day from and to all directions, and the outcome of its commissioning is a guarantee of at worst a 36-hour transit for all but five percent of the wagonload traffic that the Hamburg area generates. Overnight service is claimed to destinations as far south as Nuremburg, Stuttgart and Munich. The DB has ambitions to build similar big and highly sophisticated yards in the Ruhr, at Munich and on the Swiss frontier at Basle so as to slim down to an ultimate total of 60 main yards, or *Rangierbahnhofe*.

Within the orbit of each *Rangierbahnhofe* the system is subdivided into areas focussed on a *Knotenpunkt*, or 'nodal station', of which there are just over 400 in the country. Except for ready-made block trains, all freight traffic to or from one of the 400 or more areas passes through the area's *Knotenpunkt*, which alone has through-train service to and from its designated *Rangierbahnhof*. This minimizes the amount of 'rough', unsorted traffic fed into the *Rangierbahnhof* and consequently accelerates its work.

One of the priority objectives in forming this reduction of yards and redefinition of installation roles is to better the economy and reliability of wagonload working by seizing the earliest opportunity in a wagon's transit to associate it with other traffic heading the same way. No trains will need remarshalling between *Knotenpunkt* and *Rangierbahnhof* or vice versa. And they will arrive at the *Rangierbahnhofe* in time and sufficiently part-sorted into sections to make connection with one of the same evening's *Stammerguterzüge*, the nocturnal network of direct freights between *Rangierbahnhofe* which should all average at least 40mph and – like TEEMs –

have a standard maximum speed of 60mph as the wagon fleet is thoroughly modernized.

The most drastic rationalization already completed by the DB in its freight sector repeats one of Beeching's early economies on BR: a curtailment of the railway's role in the so-called sundries or smalls merchandise freight which is less-than-wagonload per consignment. During the 1970s the DB's 1000-plus depots for this traffic were ruthlessly pruned to 400, to secure more block train working between them and extend the territory covered by DB road transport in the local collection and delivery of the packages.

In terms of revenue the DB is still two-thirds a freight railway. And despite a fairly cataclysmic drop in its heavy freight tonnage in the later 1970s industrial bulk traffic remains a major component of the freight business. Like BR, DB operates the greater part of its block trains in this sector (though it is striving to market the same concept for finished products), but with the benefit of the Continental European loading gauge and track layouts indulging greater train lengths than BR can marshall, DB can double the payload per train.

This is exemplified by the most spectacular DB operation, a non-stop haul of imported iron ore from Hansaport at Hamburg to the big Peine & Salzgitter steelworks southeast of Hannover. The four semi-permanently coupled train-sets circulating daily between port and plant are each made up of 40 hoppers with six-wheel bogies with a total payload capacity of 4000 tonnes. Fully laden, each train grosses 5400 tonnes. But on the main line, hauled by a pair of 6000hp Class 151 Co-Co electric locomotives, they bowl along at a steady 50mph, averaging 35mph from start to finish of the ore run. A similar operation employing pairs of Class 151s, but with 37-wagon trains grossing 5000 tonnes, ferries ore from the Rhine port of Duisburg to steelworks in the Saar. This route strikes 1 in 100 gradients in the Moselle valley between Bullay and Urzig, and there even two Class 151s cannot be relied upon to restart 5000 tonnes from rest. Special steps are taken to keep that sector completely clear for the ore trains when they are due, but as a safeguard a banking locomotive is kept on standby with an adaptor wagon that can be attached to the centre coupler standardized on the six-wheel hoppers.

A vital back-up for the revitalized freight service – and a pivotal development in DB's cost and staff-saving programme – is an extraordinarily elaborate computerized management information system which the DB is evolving, again at massive cost. Known as the *Integriertes Transportsteuersystem* (ITS), it will eventually automate all the functions of freight costing and invoicing, passenger train information, reservation and ticketing, and in conjunction with a computerized timetable data system (IFS) serve the same purposes as the TOPS apparatus of British Rail, described in Chapter One. That is, it will continuously trace the movement of individual vehicles throughout the network of depots and yards, thereby monitoring transits to the customer's advantage on the one hand and on the other enabling the railway operators to adjust the timetable as hour-to-hour traffic demand dictates, and most importantly to optimize the utilization of traction, rolling stock and train crews.

The DB and West Germany's signalling and telecommunications industry were post-World War II frontrunners in the contrivance of signalling control centres that could police and regulate traffic over the whole of a complex metropolitan layout with the aid of electronics. As early as 1957 one was erected at Frankfurt/Main where, on the top operating floor, it needed only seven men to signal not only the 24-platform main station (since enlarged by the subsurface *S Bahn* platforms) and the seven different routes converging on its throat, but also the extraordinarily ramified cat's-cradle of inner orbital routes laid down and interconnected over the years to create through routes, primarily for freight, because the station is a dead-end terminal. Five of the operators were signalmen, each seated at a desk displaying diagramatically a section of the layout and studded with signal and point-setting repeater lights, apertures automatically illuminating the timetable number of the train occupying each track section (the numbers moving from aperture to aperture with the trains' progress) and push-buttons to set up or reverse a whole route at one jab. The other two operators were traffic regulators, co-ordinating the whole job from desks fronting a panoramic illuminated display of the entire peripheral layout

and the trains approaching, departing or progressing throughout. In the station area alone these seven men were covering over 5000 train or shunting movements every 24 hours.

It is worth adding, too, that as early as the 1950s the signal engineers had built into the Frankfurt installation provision for trains to signal and set their own route through some junctions on the orbital routes. Automatic route-setting can be actuated by the train describer apparatus, since the digits of a train's working timetable number include one or more indicative of its route. Once the number has been fed into the train describer apparatus through an input keyboard at the signalling point where the train is despatched into the automatic train describer's control area, therefore, the equipment can be arranged to detect the route code at a specific point on the layout and route-set accordingly. Electronically a train's successive passage of track circuits as it threads the layout automatically moves its numerical description in corresponding steps through the train describer equipment.

Equally impressive signalling centres have subsequently been established at other cities such as Munich and Stuttgart, but on the open line the DB has strangely neglected signalling modernization since the 1950s. Whereas on key BR trunk routes the traditional lineside signalbox is increasingly rare as area after area is brought under the remote control of a strategic centre, on the DB it is still a commonplace of lineside furniture almost everywhere. Nor had much been done by the late 1970s to revise signal aspect practice and signalling block section lengths to simplify higher-speed passenger operation on the

A modern DB signalling centre – the room from which the whole of the 'Bird's Flight' line from Lübeck to Puttgarden, 55.3 miles, is remotely operated by Centralized Traffic Control (CTC).

trunk routes heavily occupied by mixed traffic. That is now changing. The DB is budgeting no less than £1.25 billion ($2.80 billion) for far-reaching extension of push-button remote control signalling in the 1980s, not least for its effect in staff reduction.

As the 1970s faded, DB was gradually weeding out the remaining prewar Reichsbahn classes from its electric locomotive stud and concentrating main-line haulage on the range of standard classes initiated with the 4950hp Class 110 Bo-Bo premiered as five prototypes in 1952–53, then committed to series production in 1956. This was essentially an express passenger machine, with a top speed of 93.8mph. In the 1960s a 100mph development, Class 112, externally distinguishable chiefly by its more smoothly rounded cab front, was built in comparatively small quantity – 31 in all – with TEE haulage chiefly in mind; for that reason, after emerging in the now-standard DB blue and cream livery, the Class 112s were subsequently re-styled in TEE red and cream. The 384 Class 110s built are greatly outnumbered by the lower-geared, higher-tractive effort variants of the 1950s design. The production line of the heavy goods version, the Class 140 Bo-Bo with top speed no more than 68.8mph, eventually reached 879 (31 of which, subsequently rebuilt with dynamic braking for assignment to severely graded routes, have become Class 139); and their mixed traffic cousins, the Class 141 with a slightly higher 75mph maximum, were turned out in 451 examples.

The author has already paid tribute to the handsome Class 103 Co-Cos, the 108-tonne, 8100hp machines with 125mph capacity (they can sustain a short-term output of as much as 8750hp at that top speed) which materialized in 1965. Extended to a class total of 148, they command lines 1, 2 and 3 of the DB's IC and TEE network. With gearing specially modified for the purpose one was tested up to a peak of 157.2mph in September 1973. With all forseeable traffic demands for such impressive power and speed combined satisfied by the Class 103s, the DB's latest express passenger design up to the time of writing is

Above:
Two of the principal DB electric locomotive designs of the 1950s in their original colour schemes – on the left, in green, the mixed traffic Class 141 Bo-Bo; and on the right, in blue, the 4950hp express passenger Class 110 Bo-Bo.
Centre left:
The heavy freight Bo-Bo of the 1950s, the Class 140.
Bottom left:
An 8100hp Class 103 Co-Co on TEE duty.
Centre right:
The DB's latest electric power, the remarkable 7500hp Class 120 Bo-Bo with asynchronous three-phase AC motors, which promises both 100mph inter-city passenger and heavy freight haulage capability.
Bottom right:
The 5500hp Class 111 Bo-Bo design of 1974.

cover a high proportion of its trunk haulage, passenger and freight alike, with a single locomotive type, the Class 120, of which five prototypes were ready for exhaustive evaluation from Nuremburg depot in 1979. The 120 is a Bo-Bo of only 84 tonnes weight but with a continuous power rating of 7500hp, and if it fulfils its promise it will be as efficient and comfortable on 100mph, 700 tonne IC expresses as on 75mph 1500-ton merchandise freights or in multiple on 5000-tonne ore trains. Yet to be proved, though, is whether, with gearing variation, the 120 can deputize for the 125mph Class 103 Co-Cos. Maximum versatility is desirable if only because each Class 120 is costing the DB almost £1 million ($2.25 million) per locomotive, as against just over £¾ million ($1.7 million) for a Class 111.

The nub of the 120's attainment of so high a power/weight ratio and the high adhesion factor to go with it is the German electric traction industry's assiduous research into the rail use of AC rather than DC motors. There is no room here to delve into the historic difficulties that have long favoured the DC motor or to unravel the new technology in detail. It must be enough to say that again electronics have come up with the key, here with compact apparatus to mutate the single-phase overhead current supply into the three-phase feed the AC motors need. The latter are smaller and lighter than DC motors and dispense with a number of parts in the DC motor which are subject to wear and demand delicate maintenance.

the 5500hp Class 111 Bo-Bo of late 1974, with a top speed of 93.8mph. These were powering most of the line 4 IC and TEE trains in 1979, despite their less-than ideal top speed, but the DB was then seeking to modify 30 of the class for 100mph.

For the heaviest freight jobs the DB created the 6000hp Class 150 Co-Co to complete its 1950s quartet of standard types and built 194 of them. With a top speed of only 62.5mph, however, the 150s do not satisfy the DB's more stringent freight traffic specification of the 1980s. Consequently they have since 1973 been downgraded by the emergence of an entirely new design of Co-Co, the Class 151, with a very impressive combination of power and top speed – 8400hp and 75mph respectively – which fits the newcomer for TEEM and express merchandise freight haulage as well as the high-tonnage chores.

Another component of the DB electric locomotive fleet in the 1970s which should be mentioned is a small group of multi-current Bo-Bos, the four-voltage Class 184, the dual-voltage Class 182 – the DB's first essay in the genre, a trio derived from the Class 110 design in 1957 for duty between the Saarland and France – and the most numerous and modern, the Class 181, which ply between Germany, Luxembourg and France via the delectable Moselle valley line from Koblenz.

Multi-voltage assignments apart, the DB is optimistic that in the near future it will be able to

The 2700hp Class 220 diesel-hydraulic B-B, the twin-engined type which was front-rank inter-city power in the early 1960s, but the survivors of which were in the 1970s consigned by progressive electrification to North Germany for the conclusion of their careers.

Not only are the AC motors admirably versatile in all conditions of load and speed – their adhesion is excellent even on greasy rail – but their use also simplifies arrangement for dynamic braking. They incur none of the harmonic wave interference difficulties with signalling and telecommunications circuits which is the plague of thyristor-controlled DC motors.

The Class 120's motors are technically described as 'asynchronous three-phase'. In a conventional DC motor the rotor is an electro-magnet which is interlocked with the rotating field and revolves with it – in other words relative movement is 'synchronous'. In the AC motor, on the other hand, the rotating field has to induce currents in the rotor, so that both must revolve out of step to a greater or lesser degree according to the traction unit's track speed. Some technicians describe this kind of machine more prosaically as an 'induction' rather than an 'asynchronous' motor. More inscrutably others have dubbed it a 'squirrel-cage motor'.

The new technique has also been applied to diesel-electric locomotives, incidentally. The Swiss Federal operates six 2500hp heavy yard shunters, Co-Cos of Class Am6/6, German-built by Henschel, with three-phase asynchronous motors as well as ten Class Ee6/6 straight electrics – which also are heavy shunters – employing the same technique.

DB favours push-pull operation with locomotives for a good deal of short-distance passenger working in the conurbations, but for the *S-Bahn* routes that take in city-centre tunnel links the contemporary tool is the three-car ET420 electric multiple-unit. With 3200hp installed power per set, this equipment packs more punch than any other commuter multiple-unit of comparable seating capacity in Europe and the rate at which it glides up to its top speed of 75mph really merits the punning epithet 'electrifying'. Often nicknamed the *'Olympiazüge'* because the first squadron reached the Munich *S-Bahn* in time for the Olympic Games staged there in 1972, the ET420s in *S-Bahn* employment are lined out with a band of different colour for each network. Besides being costly, though, the ET420s' career has not been trouble-free and the treasurers of the Rhine-Ruhr *S-Bahn* scheme have preferred to work with custom-built locomotives and push-pull sets. Early in 1979 the Rhine-Ruhr network acquired ten prototype three-car sets that were eye-catching both for the dashingly raked cab front of the driving trailer and for body floors dropped low over a special design of air-suspension bogie with small-radius wheels, the latter to expedite and ease passenger movement between the trains and the characteristically low platforms of the network (to achieve the same end most platforms have had to be expensively raised in the ET420 multiple-unit-served systems). The Hamburg *S-Bahn* demands a special design of stock because its traction supply system is third-rail and its tunnel loading gauge more cramped.

The Germans were the prime exponents of hydraulic transmission for diesel traction from the latter's cradle years in the 1930s and DB has always been wedded to it for its main-line diesel locomotives. The rapid spread of electrification cut short the evolution of 3000hp DB locomotives, and there has been no need to shape a successor to the twin-engined Class 220 and 221 which were as much a symbol of the system's IC power in the early 1960s as electric locomotives. Traffic demands in non-electrified territory are amply satisfied nowadays by a group of single-engined Bo-Bo diesel-hydraulic classes, of which the most potent is the 2500hp Class 218. The last of these was delivered in 1979, completing the DB's main-line diesel locomotive requirements for the present. The survivors of Classes 220 and 221 were concentrated at Lübeck and Oldenburg in North Germany at the close of the 1970s.

Most prolifically built of the DB's post-World War II diesel railcars were, by a wide margin, the four-wheeled underfloor-engined railbuses developed in various series from a prototype advanced as a thrifty tool for rural byways in the automobile age by the firm of Waggonfabrik Uerdingen in 1949. Almost a thousand were built and complemented by a rather larger quantity of matching four-wheeled trailers. But the lightweight railbuses, though frugal of fuel and tolerant of a minimum standard of track maintenance, still incurred too many unavoidable costs of train-running over a reserved, policed right of way to make the impact on operating expenses their euphoric advocates – notably in Britain – expected of them. Moreover their thrumming engine noise and sometimes boisterous riding vitiated their appeal commercially as road vehicle comfort was steadily improved. Nevertheless though greatly reduced in number the Uerdingen railbuses were still noticeably active in the West German countryside of the late 1970s. One or two elegant-looking new series of DB diesel multiple-units comprising bogie vehicles were introduced in the 1960s and 1970s to supersede pre- and immediate post-World War II equipment, but here again the extent of electrification has limited the need to build in great quantity.

West Germany's railway supply industry is one of the world's largest, and the DB's requirements are supplied entirely by home manufacturers. But the insignia of the leading firms – names such as Thyssen Henschel, Krauss-Maffei, Krupp, MaK, MAN, Maybach and Voith in locomotives, diesel engines and transmissions, AEG and Siemens in electrical equipment, Linke-Hoffmann-Busch, Waggonfabrik Uerdingen and Wegmann in rolling stock – are equally to be found on their export products in many countries abroad.

Numerous independent local railways exist in West Germany outside DB's jurisdiction. Some are industrial and purely freight, but the many which carry passengers include some impressively modernized light railways, or urban rapid transit systems. One such is the Köln-Bonner Stadtbahn. A *Stadtbahn*, incidentally, is not the same as an *S Bahn*. Latter-day German terminology for the country's fast-developing urban rail transport systems has become very confusing and also rather indeterminate, as hinted earlier. The connotation of an *S-Bahn* at least is crystal-clear: it is a standard-gauge

system fully compatible with the rest of DB and DB-operated with DB equipment. But the so-called 'pre-metro' process of fettling street tramways up to light railway standards and relaying them on segregated surface tracks in the suburbs and below ground in city centres has given birth to the uncomfortably similar term of *Stadtbahn*, and at the same time hopelessly blurred the distinction between that and a *U-Bahn*, since the latter no longer denotes a line running wholly underground. That even the natives are muddled was plain when in 1977 Essen, in the Ruhr, publicized its new standard-gauge light railway starting from a subterranean city-centre interchange with its tramways, but then running above ground down the centre of a motorway to Mülheim as a *U-Stadtbahn*!

It looked at one time as though *Stadtbahn* had been coined only for the stage of transition from conventional tramway to *U-Bahn*. This belief is confounded by the firm title of the Köln-Bonner *Stadtbahn*, which is a fusion of three disparate undertakings – a tramway, a *U-Bahn* and a light railway – that in 1978 forged a smart inter-urban railway with a 27½-mile main line interlinking the centres of Cologne and the West German capital with a regular-interval service. Despite 48 intermediate stops the two-car multiple-units of the KBS take only one hour 19 minutes over the end-to-end journey. And in Cologne, by dint of some unusual point-work engineering, they are able to share the tracks of the city's tramways both below and above ground, so that any destination in the heart of the city is immediately accessible to their passengers.

The DB operates some 400 of these 1350hp Class 290 diesel-hydraulic Bo-Bos as heavy yard shunters and short-haul passenger and freight power in non-electrified areas.

Left:
The 2500hp Class 218 diesel-hydraulic, the type with which the DB completed its construction of main-line diesel locomotives in 1979.

A two-car electric multiple-unit of Netherlands Railways' 'Sprinter' type, which went into series production for short-haul services in 1978.

4.
SPRINTING IN
THE LOW COUNTRIES

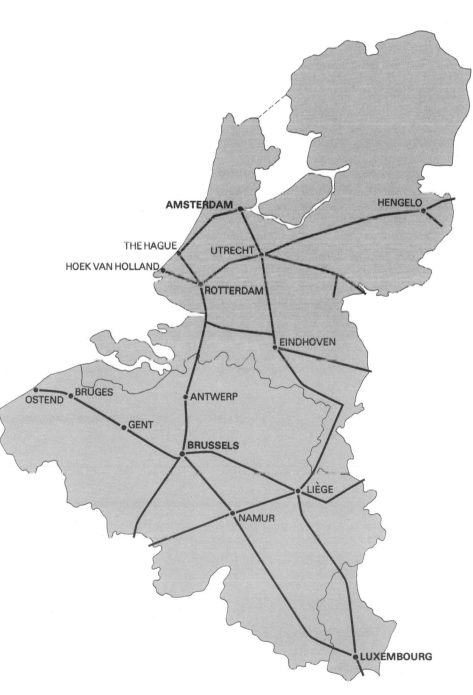

A couple of hours on the platforms of a major Netherlands Railways (NS) station like Amsterdam Central, Rotterdam Central or Utrecht is an education in disciplined railway working. The second hour will still be young when it dawns on you that the first hour's train service pattern is being almost precisely repeated on the ground as well as by the clock. Except that one or two locomotive-hauled international trains will probably interrupt the strict sequence on certain tracks, each platform will be receiving and despatching trains from and to exactly the same towns, at identical intervals, as it did in the earlier working cycle. Practically all of them will be electric multiple-units.

Conspicuous, too, is the railway's full-blooded exploitation of the double-ended, self-propelled multiple-unit's *raison d'être* – the ease with which train formations can be augmented or diminished, in either case with immediate, matching adjustment of traction power, to meet a variety of traffic specifications. In the tight-knit Netherlands, where more than a quarter of the population is concentrated in the 3000-square-mile agglomeration of towns and cities to the southwest known as the Ranstad, or 'necklace of cities', all of them interlinked by an intricate railway network, the requirement is a train service which makes as many direct inter-urban connections as possible, as speedily as possible and at frequent intervals. This specification is ideally satisfied by multiple-units, since they can be started from different originating stations, combined en route for coverage of a key trunk section, then

possibly split to finish at separate destinations; this way interchange between a wide range of towns and cities is set up within the compass of a single train working over the busiest stretches of main line. With powerful traction motors distributed throughout its formation, moreover, the electric multiple-unit also has the acceleration to achieve a smart end-to-end time despite the frequent intermediate stops enforced by the jostling of important stations in the intensively urbanized Ranstad.

Since the 1970 intensification of NS train services (of which more in a moment) train frequency on some Ranstad lines is as taut as every 15 minutes. To cope with such pressure NS makes the most of its main station capacities by dividing their main platforms into two halves, each capable of accommodating a maximum of six cars; then a third track is inserted between each pair of platform lines and interconnected with them by scissors crossings at the mid-point to simplify the berthing or the despatch of trains at each half of the platform. Naturally, that arrangement also expedites the coupling of two units which have arrived from different quarters but will go forward as one train.

Once a unit has backed up to its companion, coupling is almost instantaneous, since a standard fitment of every NS electric multiple-unit is the patent Scharfenburg coupler. At the moment of buffering-up this coupler combines automatic physical attachment with secure face-to-face contact of a number of terminals setting up traction motor, braking, lighting, heating and other essential control lines from the lead driving cab to the rest of the formation. Conversely, it takes only depression of a pedal in one of the driving cabs to disengage one unit from another.

An important factor in punctual operation of the intensive NS passenger service is the installation on the busiest main-line sectors of continuous cab signalling, which the Dutch were the first in Europe to apply to a national railway system on a significant scale. Given the bustle on the tracks (some sectors are carrying 250 trains a day each way daily) and the smart station-to-station speeds of the trains, something better than the intermittent advice of lineside signals is the more essential for Dutch multiple-unit drivers because in winter the coastal belts of their low-lying country are so often cloaked in a dank sea fog. A catastrophic collision in 1962 compelled the NS to shoulder the considerable expense of a continuous driving cab display of signal aspects.

In the territory equipped with the device, inductive receivers on the train-sets are continuously picking up coded currents transmitted through the running rails by the signalling systems. Apparatus on the train-set translates the codes into one of five illuminated signal aspects available in the driving desk display. Four of these aspects prescribe a descending level of maximum speeds, from 140kmph (87.5mph), through 130 and 80 down to 60kmph

Since the last war the NS has set most of Europe a superb example both in the architectural design of new stations and in their interior layout, with systematic use of pictogram directional signs, mechanized train departure indicators on platforms and not least with crystal-clear displays of train service detail.

(37.5mph); the fifth warns that the next signal is at 'danger'. The driver's attention is drawn to a change of aspect by a bell, whereupon he must brake to the freshly ordained speed within a set interval, or else the apparatus will automatically assume control of the train and brake it to a stand.

With just over 60 percent of its route-mileage electrified on the 1.5kV DC system NS stands third in the European electrification league table on a route percentage basis. The bulk of the passenger operation is under catenary, with diesel multiple-units confined mostly to lines or branches in the less-populated tracts of the country. Concentrating its investment resources on EMU development, the NS has been soldiering on with 1950s-vintage DMUs in these areas, but by the late 1970s the latter were getting so costly to keep in working order that a new fleet based on the design of the German Federal Railway VT627 and VT628 diesel-hydraulic railcars had to be commissioned.

The NS had begun to electrify before World War II and the daunting reconstruction that was bequeathed to them – 62 percent of the track, 70 percent of the bridges, 84 percent of the locomotives and well over 90 percent of their passenger and goods vehicles annihilated by Allied bombing or destroyed and looted by the retreating Germans – made faster progress the obvious course from 1950 onwards. The extent to which the passenger element of the electrified service has been entrusted to multiple-units is patent from the statistic that since 1952, NS electric locomotive stud has rested at 107 units, apart from the 1960s addition of six 2400hp Co-Cos bought

second-hand from British Railways when the latter's cessation of passenger service over the 1.5kV DC Woodhead route between Sheffield and Manchester made them redundant in their own country. Freight haulage is the locomotives' main function. In the passenger department they have had until recently only a few domestic chores, such as the service across the country from Zwolle in the northeast to Vlissingen, the southwestern port. Their chief work is handling international trains to and from the Belgian and German borders. Main-line diesel locomotives, employed exclusively on freight, number only 264, of two low-powered diesel electric Bo Bo types.

The Dutch 1.5kV DC system is an island flanked by Belgian 3kV DC and West German 15kV $16\frac{2}{3}$Hz DC. The NS has yet to build any multi-voltage locomotives of its own, so that some international passenger services on which sharp end-to-end time is commercially critical have to be worked into Dutch territory by the neighbours' multi-voltage locomotives to obviate time-wasting engine-changes at the frontier. One is the 'Trans-Europ Express' service from Paris, of which two of the six trains between the French capital and Brussels daily carry on to and from Rotterdam, The Hague and Amsterdam. The French Railways 5000hp CC-40100 quadri-voltage C-Cs, ostensibly designed with their 25kV AC, 50Hz AC, 3kV DC and 1.5kV DC flexibility to power these trains unchanged from Paris to Amsterdam, turned out to be overweight for Dutch track, so it is the latest Belgian Railways (SNCB) quadri-voltage Class 1600 3780hp B-Bs which haul the TEEs be-

Two views of the Scharfenburg coupler, standardized on NS electric multiple-units, which on buffering up automatically combines firm physical attachment with connection of all driving, braking control and train service supply lines via the honeycomb of stud contacts seen in the close-up of one coupler.

tween Brussels and Amsterdam.

TEEs apart, Brussels and Amsterdam are linked by an hourly express service taking three hours or a little under for the 153¾-mile run, intermediate city stops included. It has more than doubled the rail passenger business between the Dutch and Belgian centres since multi-voltage electric traction technology made light of current changeovers in 1959, when dual-voltage EMUs were applied to this operation.

Above:
NS electric multiple-units of the basic 1950s design which dominated the system's Inter-City operation at the end of the 1970s.
Bottom left:
An Amsterdam–Brussels push-pull Inter-City set, showing the driving trailer.
Bottom right:
Amsterdam's new Schipol Airport rail link.

To enable intensification of the service these EMUs were supplemented in 1974 by the world's first international push-pull train-sets, once more using Belgian power, in this instance the earlier SNCB Class 125 multi-voltage B-B. In common with other NS locomotive-hauled coaching stock, the basic livery of these train-sets is dark blue, as opposed to the brilliant yellow with or without grouped diagonal blue bands of NS EMUs, but the so-called 'Benelux' push-pull units are distinguished by broad yellow lining along the base of their coach sides. Their most conspicuous distinction, however, is their end driving trailers which the NS converted from existing coaches and in which the driving cab protrudes like a jetliner cockpit from the main roof; the bodywork proper combines baggage room with a restaurant-buffet.

The dashing livery of contemporary NS passenger equipment dates from the early 1970s, when the railway management was encouraged to re-invigorate and expand its passenger enterprise after various forecasts had convinced the Dutch Government that effective public transport development was essential to stave off strangulation of its highly

urbanized country by private cars. Besides improvement of existing rail services, there was a green light for the construction not only of new stations but of new railways. Thus, for instance, the first and immediately busy half of a new suburban loop line was built to cater for a spreading residential area at Zoetermeer, east of The Hague; and – much more significantly – in late 1978 a line was built from southern Amsterdam to the heart of the city's Schipol Airport and this will have been extended to a junction with the main The Hague-Haarlem line at Leiden by 1981.

Although this 1981 link-up at Leiden will certainly give the Dutch capital much quicker access to the country's main airport, the full potential of this route in relieving pressure on the heavily occupied rail tracks of the Ranstad and opening up a much more direct route between The Hague and Amsterdam itself will not be realized until the Airport line can be projected into the city centre. There NS hopes come up against concern to protect the city's venerable fabric and the problems of its myriad waterways (which has frustrated completion of the planned Amsterdam Metro system). The likeliest

An example of the imagination the NS has applied to so much of its recent station architecture. The device on the fascia of the building is the NS logo.

than ten minutes, at Utrecht and Sittard.

At the same time NS energetically pursued the station improvement programme which, given the early impetus to reconstruct so many from wartime ruins, has long made Holland the European model of modern functional excellence in this department. Apart from the appeal of their neat contemporary architecture, the NS stations immediately impress by the efficiency of their passenger information services, especially their uniform signposting of every facility with pictograms. Co-ordination with other transport is a priority. As anyone familiar with the country would expect, around one-third of rail passengers are reckoned to use their cycle or moped to the station, so capacious cycle standing areas are as characteristic an appendage of most Dutch urban stations as a large car park, the latter sometimes multi-storey; the cycle park at Hoorn, a dormitory town in the Ranstad, has 1020 places, for instance. The fact that NS has a controlling interest in a number of Dutch bus companies has helpfully influenced the convenient siting of many urban bus stations in rail station forecourts.

The most spectacular station reconstruction of recent years has been in the fast-growing city of Utrecht. Here both railway installation and bus stations have been integrated and linked by escalators and elevators with the vast new Hoog Catharijne commercial development, a multi-storey complex of shops, restaurants and car-park covering 60 acres. Incidentally, this shopping centre has since threatened to steer the focus of Utrecht's consumer business away from the narrow and, in some cases, pedestrian-only shopping streets of the picturesque old city, because of the new centre's undercover access from public transport.

Until the late 1970s NS traction and rolling stock were not keeping pace with its environmental development. The system's three main classes of electric locomotive – the Class 1100 French-built (Alsthom) 2580hp B-Bs, the Class 1300 French-built (Alsthom) C-Cs and the Dutch-built but American-influenced Class 1200 3000hp C-Cs – all date from the early 1950s. None is rated for a higher speed than 135kmph (84.4mph), though as yet that is not a serious handicap. The Dutch have thus far been content with a maximum line speed of 140kmph (87.5mph), given the density of their traffic and the frequency of important stops, and also because of the high incidence of level crossings in such a flat country (though in a number of busy urban areas the railway has in recent years been elevated to obviate them). In late 1978 NS, nevertheless, decided to renovate and modify the faithful 1200s for another decade or so of service. The bulbous-nosed four-car EMU embodying a compact 12-seater kitchen-restaurant in one of its trailers is the workhorse of the Inter-City network and is a design which dates as far back as 1954, but which is kept commercially acceptable by interior refurnishing; many

prospect is of a new line from east of Schipol, hopefully to be built by the mid-1980s, which will orbit the western fringe of the city and converge with the route from Haarlem just outside Amsterdam Central at Sloterdijk. That scheme would also open up the putative new The Hague–Leiden–Amsterdam route to the three-track Hem Tunnel which is being driven under the North Sea Canal northwest of Amsterdam with the dual aim of serving another rapidly expanding dormitory area and, further away, industrial complexes on the coast at Ijmuiden and Beverwijk.

Intensive market research in the Netherlands in the late 1960s indicated three clear passenger service priorities: speed, greater frequency, and less subjection to change of trains. Satisfaction of those demands was the primary objective of a sweeping, nationwide timetable redraft in 1970. At the centre of the new framework was an accelerated service (for which NS borrowed British Rail's 'Inter-City' tag), which interconnected 40 key stations carefully picked by NS on calculations that the resultant network would embrace at least half an average day's ordinary ticket purchasers and a sizeable number of season ticketholders as well. No Inter-City service was less than hourly, but in some sectors the regularity was half-hourly and even quarter-hourly over the busiest stretches in the Ranstad where several Inter-City flows converged, such as Rotterdam Central–Amsterdam, Amsterdam–Utrecht and Utrecht–Rotterdam–The Hague. The rest of the semi-fast and stopping service was integrally timed with the Inter-City network, chiefly on at least half-hourly frequency, to establish prompt connections and to make them across or at the other end of a common platform to the maximum operationally practicable extent. At the end of the exercise one could, for instance, make a 232-mile trip from Groningen in the far north to Maastricht in the extreme south – not a particularly popular itinerary – in a very respectable four hours and 24 minutes with only two intermediate changes, neither costing more

short distance EMUs are even longer in the tooth, while the blue-liveried coaches forming the locomotive-hauled international and Inter-City trains in the late 1970s were also of early or mid-1950s vintage.

At last, in the mid-1970s, the NS won approval to begin re-equipment. First to appear, in mid-1975, was a 15-set batch of a smart new two-car interurban EMU design, designated the 'Sprinter'. After a debut between Rotterdam and Hook of Holland, they were applied to the new Zoetermeer line; in 1978 the design was committed to extended series production. The 'Sprinter' was followed early in 1977 by seven prototypes, designated 'Inter-City III', of a three-car EMU designed to run at the 100mph limit to which the new Amsterdam–Schipol–Leiden line was being engineered, though whether and when existing NS trunk routes would be adapted to the three-figure maximum was and remains uncertain.

The 'Inter-City III' EMU's three-car format was adopted, instead of the four- or two-car make-up the NS had favoured since World War II, because the lighter weight made 100mph top speed and smart acceleration to that limit possible with a single power car with every axle motored. Externally the 'Inter-City III' is markedly different in outline from its NS

predecessors because each end's driving cab is raised cockpit-fashion to make body space for a retractable corridor connection between coupled units. The previous streamlined nose of NS EMUs ruled out intercommunication, but it was now essential if only because the NS had decided to do away with restaurants and confine catering to trolley service throughout the entirely saloon accommodation of the unit from a small kitchen at the rear of the power car. The prototypes were introduced to full public service

Refurbishing of the 2580hp French-built Class 1100 electric Bo-Bos for an extended life has included the fitting of a new 'nose' in place of the original flat cab front.

The dashing outline of the new blue-and-yellow-liveried 'Inter-City III' electric multiple-unit.

A 3000hp Class 1200 electric Co-Co of the NS heads an international train of NS coaching stock at Amsterdam. Early in the 1980s this pairing was to be superseded by a new design of locomotive based on the French BB7200 type and new coaching stock built in West Germany to a pattern derived from the NS 'Inter-City III' electric multiple-unit trailers.

between Amsterdam and Nijmegen in April 1979, but series construction was slow to follow.

The centre trailer of the 'Inter-City III' was envisaged as the model for new locomotive-hauled coaches, but by 1977 NS had concluded that competitive pressures would not brook a leisurely evaluation of the new design. The public was impatient with the hybrid push-pull sets and elderly EMUs on the Amsterdam–Brussels run, especially as they were running cheek-by-jowl with brand-new French 'Corail' stock on the ordinary Paris-Amsterdam expresses, and never mind the premium-fare TEEs. On the Amsterdam–Cologne trains, too, the 1950s NS coaches contrasted sharply with the elegant German Federal (DB) 'Inter-City' coaches with which they shared platforms in the Rhineland.

So in 1978, after testing one of French Railways' new internal service Corail coaches, the NS hired more and the following October inaugurated what it branded an 'Inter-City-Plus' operation with locomotive-hauled rakes of these vehicles on certain prime morning and evening business services, such as between Heerlen, near the West German frontier, Rotterdam and The Hague, and between Maastricht, Utrecht and Amsterdam. A supplementary fare of Fl.6 (about £1.50/$3.00) was levied on 'Inter-City-Plus' clients for which, besides fewer intermediate stops and hence a faster end-to-end journey than by 'Inter-City' EMU, they were offered free newspapers, tea or coffee and use of the train telephone facility. As opposed to the cramped restaurant of an EMU they also had benefit of a full kitchen-diner, but that was not an unalloyed blessing, as the only Dutch locomotive-hauled vehicles of that kind were also antiques of the early 1950s (Dutch train catering, one should perhaps mention, is by CIWLT, the International Wagons-Lits Company).

Finally, at the close of 1978 NS did place orders for 186 new locomotive-hauled coaches of their own with the German builders Waggonfabrik Talbot of Aachen. The order was raised to 226 cars a year later. To be delivered from 1980, these vehicles would derive their design largely from the 'Inter-City III' EMU trailer, but would interestingly be mounted on the French Type Y32 bogies sampled under the borrowed Corail coaches. The second-class cars would be entirely open-saloon, but the first partly compartment; catering provision would be confined to kitchens in some of the second-class coaches. At the same time NS also commissioned its first new main-line electric locomotives for more than two decades. Yet again, after testing both German and French products on its own ground, it bought French – 48 6150hp 84-tonne B-Bs classified 1600 with 100mph and even higher speed potential, to be based on French Railways' 1.5kV DC BB7200 type and to be built by the French consortium Alsthom-Atlantique-Francorail-MTE; they will have thyristor chopper control.

Given the constricted land area of the country any

domestic journey can be comfortably accomplished in a day – there and back in a great many cases. For the same reason a well-organized freight operation can achieve overnight merchandise delivery between any pair of main centres in the country: and the Dutch have that, so that few freight trains obstruct the intensive NS daytime passenger service and conversely, a few international overnight trains apart, the nocturnal tracks are monopolized by freight. So far as merchandise is concerned, NS divides the country into 27 regions, each with its own well-equipped railhead depot. The freight trains interlink the 27 depots and the collection from and delivery to the customer within the region served by each depot is performed exclusively by the NS road transport subsidiary, Van Gend & Loos.

As you might expect, despite its efficiency the NS has a tough struggle for freight business, especially minerals and heavy industrial products, with the country's ramified waterways; this competition applies as much to international as to domestic traffic, in view of the easy navigability of the Rhine and the Maas Rivers into Germany (and not least that once inside Germany barge operators have to stump only a fraction of the infrastructure costs their railway rivals have to find). Out of Rotterdam, for instance, no less than 75 percent of the freight heading inland stays on water and a meagre 7 percent is trans-shipped to the railway, with the balance of 19 percent going by road.

Nevertheless, with block train operation of fixed formations of modern high-capacity, automatic-discharge wagons in continuous circuit the NS has amply proved that it can run the waterway operators very close on price and eclipse them in efficiency when it comes, for instance, to maintaining a flow of imported ore from Dutch ports to the Ruhr and Saarland steelworks of West Germany. But the more that kind of exercise develops, the more urgent is NS's need of modern traction underlined; as things are, it takes a quartet of the NS Class 2200 900hp diesels to roll one of the regular 4000-tonne mineral trains out of Rotterdam to the Saar as far as the German border. For a long time NS virtually crushed waterway competition for the movement of maritime containers, the import and export traffic of which through Rotterdam is immense; the bulk of it is to and from Belgium and Germany, but over 20 percent of the trade is with France and Switzerland and a significant element crosses Western Europe to and from Italy. Even here, though, the railway is yielding; between 1977 and 1979 the Rhine operators trebled their container traffic.

SNCB, the Belgian national railway system, has just as firm a grip on the inland forwarding of the Belgian ports' maritime containers, claiming over 50 percent of Antwerp's and nearly 70 percent of Zeebrugge's traffic. Antwerp, where the port's activity has quadrupled since 1950, is one of the most lavishly rail-served harbours in the world, with an incredible 520 single-track miles of railway interlacing its docks, and it generates between one-fifth and one-quarter of all SNCB freight traffic. Heavy industry and mining are a bigger factor in Belgium's economy than in the Netherlands' and consequently SNCB tracks carry considerably more freight than those of NS – in tonnage terms about three times as much, in fact. Like every Western European railway for which heavy industry's inputs and outputs were the mainstay of the freight business – and in the early 1970s the SNCB was reliant on coal and coke, iron and steel, and ore for 70 percent of its tonnage – the Belgian system has been hard hit by the recession since the oil price explosion, but by investing in or leasing specialized wagons it has since mounted a productive compensatory attack on other traffics such as foodstuffs, cereals and petro-chemicals.

By the late 1970s some 2500 route-miles of the SNCB were electrified at 3kV DC, 50 percent more than the NS trackage under catenary, but the SNCB figure was only a third of its total system. Electrification is ongoing, however, and is scheduled to embrace half the SNCB system by 1984; the focus is currently on secondary routes. Under a ten-year plan endorsed by the Belgian Government in 1970 that objective should have been attained much earlier, but subsequent Belgian administrations have never shelled out investment funds to the annual scale predicted by the 1970 plan. This was the more galling to frustrated SNCB managers because at the time the administrations were lavishing three times as much capital on competing waterways as on the railways, let alone spending 15 times as much on the country's roads. Another gripe of SNCB management was – and is – that the railways are inadequately compensated for the Government-imposed sub-standard fares charged to several categories of passenger, such as blue-collar workers and schoolchildren; only one Belgian rail passenger in five is reckoned to be paying full fare.

The delectable but sparsely populated Ardennes hills and forests account for as much as a quarter of Belgium's territory, but elsewhere urbanization is as dense as in the Netherlands. The key cities of Brussels, Louvain, Charleroi, Ghent and Mons are all within 50 miles of each other, so that patronage of the railway for short-distance travel is widespread. That is particularly patent every weekday on one of Europe's busiest multi-track sections, the underground Nord-Midi link in the heart of Brussels.

This six-track connection, with its intermediate sub-surface station at Central in the hub of the capital was completed as recently as October 1952 after more than a century of debate on its necessity. Although they were prescient enough at the very dawn of railways to impose state control and ensure the evolution of a logical trunk route system, the Belgians did shortsightedly allow two separate termini, Nord and Midi, to become firmly established in Brussels. Once railways had joined hands across

The SNCB's latest type of electric multiple-unit at the start of the 1980s, the Class 800, the first of which appeared in 1976.

frontiers these two termini penalized international traffic with reversals and orbits of the Brussels perimeter. Furthermore as Brussels expanded into a thriving metropolis, inability to work commuter trains straight through the city centre cost the railway more and more in turnrounds at Nord and Midi and the public no less in overall journey time and convenience.

Moves for a Nord–Midi link in the 19th century kept foundering on conservationist concerns for the city's fabric; then the first positive scheme of the 20th century, for a surface connection which actually got as far as building a length of viaduct, was overwhelmed by World War I. Finally a 1930 plan of considerable grandeur for a cut-and-cover subsurface link of six tracks from Nord to Midi, with an intermediate station at Central, won Government endorsement in 1935. Again war interrupted, but this time the project was promptly resumed in the rapid recuperation of Belgian railways after 1945, though the protraction of the job accumulated a final bill *13 times* the estimate of 1930. Expectedly one of the previous terminals lost significance with completion of the link; Midi is today Brussels' main SNCB station.

Thus Brussels nowadays is an intermediate call in the itinerary of a train between, for instance, Antwerp in the north and the Charleroi in the south, whereas before 1952 Antwerp trains would terminate at Nord, those from Charleroi at Midi. The Antwerp–Charleroi train will be one of about 50 every off-peak hour, aggregating the services in both directions, which thread the six-track tunnel under the city centre, but in the commuter peaks the figure is more than doubled, to the extent that the busiest of the six lines funnels as many as 21 trains in the critical morning hour, the rest 16–18. In all, just over a thousand passenger trains throng the tunnels in the 24 hours of each working day. They include, incidentally, 35 services each way between Brussels Central and the city's airport at Melsbroeck, run on behalf of the Belgian airline, Sabena.

Some international services apart (principally 'Trans-Europ Express'), the train service through Brussels is repetitive on a regular-interval basis like the Dutch. Short-distance and commuter workings in the metropolitan area are monopolized by electric multiple-units, which have been replenished in the 1970s with a dashing new series of Class 800 five-car units in a striking livery of light brown above the waistline and a broad band of bright scarlet below. But the SNCB does not rely so heavily on multiple-units as the NS because of its greater freight commitment, a proportion of which can be covered by locomotives with day hours to spare for passenger haulage. This, in turn, means the SNCB deploys a good deal more locomotive-hauled coaching stock than the NS; and here the Government's denial of adequate cash to modernize at the pace of the SNCB's competitors is blatantly manifest, since in the late 1970s about half the rail coach fleet was still of pre-1939 build. For inter-city express work, however, the SNCB was starting to get up-to-date with an infusion of the new orange-liveried, air-conditioned

European standard coaches built to TEE comfort parameters, which are discussed more fully in Chapter Six.

On its longer-distance routes the SNCB runs regular-interval expresses at a frequency equal to the best in Europe. Every daytime hour, for instance, an express plies between Ostend and Liège on a near-standard overall time of 2½ hours – a very fair achievement seeing that it has to take account of intermediate stops at Bruges, Ghent and the three Brussels stations, Midi, Central and Nord. Alternate trains are to and from Cologne, West Germany. The

line speed limit is, for the most part, 140kmph (87.5 mph), but in the late 1970s the SNCB readied its first 160kmph (100mph) stretches between Brussels and Liège, Ostend and Ghent, Ghent and Kortrijk, Brussels and Quévy, and Antwerp and Essen; it aims for 200kmph (125mph) in the 1980s.

Most prestigious of all inter-city services on SNCB metals is unquestionably the TEE operation between Brussels and Paris Nord six times each way daily (the vehicles are the French Railways 'Mistral' type). Of these the fastest, the evening 'Brabant' from Brussels Midi, was in the late 1970s timed nonstop between the capitals in two hours 24 minutes for the 193 miles, representing an 80.4mph end-to-end average. Concentration of the European Economic Community bureaucracy in Brussels and the distance between the two city centres correlate to make this route a near-ideal market-place for a premium-fare, all-first-class high-speed service, and the Paris–Brussels TEEs have made the most of it; as a group they are the most remunerative of all TEEs.

A good many loss-making route-miles of SNCB rural passenger service have been turned over to buses since World War II. In the late 1940s the SNCB network exceeded 3000 route-miles, including some ex-German trackage acquired in postwar territorial adjustments, but today it is less than 2500, and a quarter of that runs no passenger trains. Some of the substitute buses were operated by the SNCB, but in 1978 the railway's road passenger services were all handed over to SNCV – Société Nationales des Chemins de Fer Vicinaux – a national light railway or tramway- and bus-operating body dating back to 1885, when it was established to co-ordinate the country's once-extensive metre-gauge railway system. The SNCV was actually the pioneer of Belgian electric rail traction, as early as 1894.

The Paris Brussels TEEs were the genesis of some powerful SNCB electric locomotives, the four-voltage 5870hp C-Cs of Class 18. Inheriting a traction current system incompatible with that of any neighbouring country, the SNCB's latter-day electric traction engineers and their colleagues in the country's railway supply industry were some of the first to refine multi-voltage electric traction units. (Besides being the dominant purveyors of traction and rolling stock to the SNCB, incidentally, Belgian

Above:
The four-voltage SNCB Class 18 was built by Alsthom in 1974 to the French Railways CC40101 design.
Left:
An SNCB Class 800 electric multiple-unit alongside the most powerful electric locomotive type in the Belgian fleet, the 100mph 7000hp Class 20 Co-Co with thyristor control of the traction motors. Built by Belgian industry, the first of this series of 25 locomotives was delivered in 1975.

The SNCB's four-voltage Class 16 Bo-Bo of 1966 was originally conceived for the Paris–Brussels–Amsterdam TEE operation but was subsequently overtaxed by the increasing loads and speeds of the service. It now works chiefly on the ordinary expresses between the Belgian and French capitals.

manufacturers like La Brugeoise et Nivelles, Anglo-Franco-Belge and Cockerill-Ougrée, and electrical equipment firms like ACEC-SEM are powers in world markets.) The SNCB shares the throughout haulage of the Paris–Brussels TEEs with French Railways and in the 1960s contributed two B-B classes, the three-voltage 3600hp Class 15 of 1962 and the four-voltage 3780hp Class 16 of 1966. But four-axle machines of that power were overtaxed when heavy weekend demand compelled reinforcement of the normal TEE formation – still more so when French Railways raised the speed ceiling to 100mph between Paris and Aulnoye and the SNCB planned to do likewise between Quévy and Brussels to accelerate the service end-to-end. To meet the new specification French Railways had produced in 1964 a four-voltage six-axle type, their Class CC40100,

and ten years later SNCB decided for economy to acquire six machines of near-identical design, geared for a maximum of 180kmph (112mph). These Class 18s, built by the French firm Alsthom, are the only SNCB electrics of foreign construction. A broad blue band superimposed on the all-yellow livery which the SNCB adopted for all its locomotives in the late 1970s distinguishes its multi-voltage electrics from the single-voltage 3kV DC types, which wear a green band. The latter are all B-Bs. Their latest members are 30 mixed traffic, 84-tonne machines of Class 27 with thyristor control, capable of 100mph on passenger duty but also of tackling 1900-tonne freight trains on level track.

For a comparatively small system SNCB operates the surprisingly large number of ten different classes of main-line diesel locomotive, all of Belgian design

marketed anew as an Inter-City network. This would interlink 83 stations and urban short-distance trains radiating from the country's 14 chief population centres would serve about 400 more. In sum these two operations would cover 96 percent of the SNCB's existing passenger traffic. The dark side of the plan was a recommendation that the incredible number of 343 other stations which existed for the residual four percent of passenger journeys should be closed.

On the freight side, similarly, the Government advocated that a great deal of wagonload and small-consignment business be discarded. A quarter of the SNCB's wagonload freight depots were said to be dealing in no more than one vehicle a day on average, and the same was alleged of the thousand private sidings served by the railway. Freight depots should therefore be cut from some 440 to fewer than 250 and the system's marshalling yards from 35 to 10, and parcels business should no longer be handled at every staffed station, but focussed on 100 strategically sited depots. Since the plan envisaged an 11 percent cut in staff and a 16 percent closure of SNCB route-mileage open for freight operation, the immediate political reaction to the proposals was understandably fierce. But though the plan may be diluted in detail it seems likely to be adopted in principle at the end of the day.

The SNCB's first multi-current electric type, the three-voltage 3600hp Class 15 of 1962.

One of the special electric multiple-units which maintain one of Europe's two earliest airport rail links, that from the Nord and Central stations in the Belgian capital to Brussels airport (the other pioneer service was in Britain, between London's Victoria station and Gatwick Airport).

origin and hence of distinctive outline. The great majority are diesel-electrics, a few diesel-hydraulics, but in neither range does any type display outstanding characteristics. The most powerful, the diesel-electric Class 51 C-C, for instance, has an output of only 2150hp for a bulk of 117 tons.

By the time this chapter is in print SNCB train services may have undergone some drastic revision. In the summer of 1979 the Belgian Government proposed to attack the SNCB's heavy calls on public money with a Beeching-style rationalization of its activity. Henceforward the railway should concentrate on the bulk transport role to which it is best suited. On the plus side, the country's fast and semi-fast passenger services should be intensified – even extended to revive some links abandoned since World War II – on strict regular-interval bases and

5.
SWITZERLAND'S MOUNTAINEERING RAILWAYS

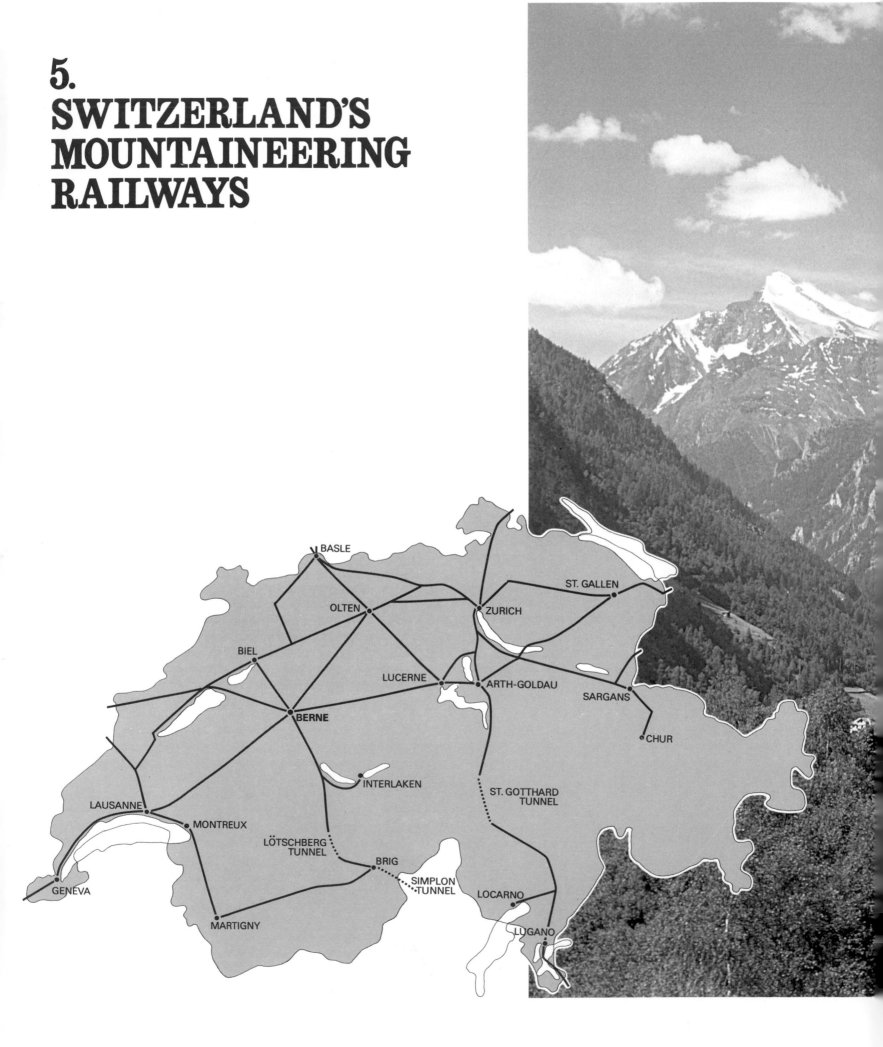

BASLE

ST. GALLEN

OLTEN

ZURICH

BIEL

LUCERNE

ARTH-GOLDAU

SARGANS

BERNE

CHUR

INTERLAKEN

ST. GOTTHARD TUNNEL

LAUSANNE

MONTREUX

LÖTSCHBERG TUNNEL

BRIG

GENEVA

SIMPLON TUNNEL

LOCARNO

MARTIGNY

LUGANO

On the metre-gauge Brig–Visp–Zermatt Railway in the Valais Canton of Switzerland a train clambers up the steep gradient in the Matter–Visp gorge, making for Zermatt from the Rhône Valley. In the background is the Weisshorn mountain.

Compared with the 125mph maximum and 80-to-near-100mph average inter-city speeds of their neighbours' crack trains, Swiss railways' current top speed of 87.5mph and best inter-city average of under 70mph might look pallid. But not if you know the country. If you do, you probably marvel that even mile-a-minute average journeys are attainable.

For perspective take a cursory look at the profile of what the Swiss Federal Railways (SBB or CFF) rate as their *ligne de plaine*, the 179.4-mile trunk route from Geneva to Zurich. The difference in height above sea level between these two cities is only 56ft, yet between them the so-called 'railway of the plain' addresses gradients adding up to a climb of 2755ft!

The start is fairly amiable – a winding, lightly graded 37½ miles from Geneva to Lausanne alongside placid Lake Geneva. This is the second busiest section of the SBB (the most active is Zurich–Winterthur), channelling heavy international Franco-Italian traffic via the Simplon route as well as domestic trains and carrying on average 110 passenger and 30 freight trains every working day. Throughout the 1970s the SBB was rebuilding intermediate stations,

but by the end of the decade it had not made more than 20 route-miles fit for the 87.5mph top speed – a measure of the curvature problem besetting SBB throughout its network. Nevertheless the frequent non-stop expresses between Geneva and Lausanne cover the 37½ miles in 33 minutes.

But beyond Lausanne the route to Bern and Zurich diverges from the Rhône valley main line to Brig, the Simplon Tunnel and Italy, and strikes diagonally up the mountainside bordering the lake. For ten miles the railway climbs at an unremitting 1 in 53½–55, eventually reaching a summit of 2493ft at Vauderens. After that the slope reverses and the route steadily gives up practically all the height it has gained. En route to Bern the railway is not as mountaineering as it was out of Lausanne, but its course is continuously switchback, with a constant succession of speed-restricting curves. Even in the 'plain' between Bern and Zurich the lowland hill contours keep the railway bending to such an extent that the 87.5mph maximum is allowable only over the two miles of the 1975 Heitersberg tunnel bypass, of which more in a moment.

This is the physical background against which

Headed by a Swiss Federal Class Re4/4 electric locomotive, an international train composed of stock from the SBB's batch of Eurofima coaches skirts Lake Geneva at Montreux, with the Schloss Chillon at the lakeside in the background.

Swiss inter-city speeds have to be considered. Modern electric traction makes fairly light work of the long climb out of Lausanne, even with 600 tons of train hanging on its drawbar; it is chiefly the curvature which holds the best Geneva–Zurich schedule at present to 188 minutes for the 179.4 miles inclusive of three intermediate stops, representing an end-to-end average of 57.3mph. In fact, of SBB's total 1783 standard-gauge route-miles only 120 or so are sufficiently curve-free to be passed for the 87.5mph maximum. Half that top-speed mileage is in a continuous stretch of the other main eastbound route out of Lausanne, the Simplon route from the Franco-Swiss frontier in the Jura Mountains at Vallorbe to Italy, which hugs the Geneva lakeshore down to Villeneuve and heads up the Rhône valley floor to the 12¼-mile Simplon Tunnel.

The Simplon route skirts the southwestern corner of Switzerland, but the other SBB international transit route, the Gotthard, cuts diagonally across the country's two main west to east domestic traffic flows, one from Geneva and Lausanne to Bern and Zurich which has already been considered, and the second from Basle and Biel to Zurich, Winterthur and St Gall. The focal intersection of these three streams is in the area around Olten, where over 300 trains a day can converge at a peak traffic period.

Traffic volume in the dying 1970s was not quite what it had been just before the mid-point of the decade. Even though SBB freight tonnage had, by early 1979, recovered from its nadir of a 25 percent downturn in the immediate wake of the oil price explosion and subsequent recession to a 15 percent shortfall on early 1970s performance, the saturation of the main SBB routes which looked imminent in 1970 was a less imminent threat. The problem then was chiefly the upsurging traffic between the North-western members of the European Economic Community, or Common Market, and Italy and South-eastern Europe. By 1979 that trade had regained most of its pre-recession momentum, but the SBB freight movement was below 1972–73 levels for two main reasons: first, desperate price-cutting by road transport to keep its vehicles busy in a diminished overall market; and second, the strength of the Swiss franc, which made other rail routes into Italy cheaper per ton-mile and which had particularly helped to multiply tonnage taking the Mont Cenis Tunnel route from France to Italy eightfold since the EEC Treaty of Rome was signed in 1957. So far as rail freight is concerned, the Mont Cenis route now has to overtake only the Swiss Gotthard Tunnel line to go to the top of the Transalpine league table. And with a Gotthard road tunnel due to open in 1980 the French may yet do it – though as this Chapter was being completed in late 1979 SBB freight traffic was suddenly surging upward again.

With no more reason to foresee an oil crisis and its effects than any other Europeans, the SBB had embarked on a massive programme to enlarge its

operating capacity in the 1960s. A major component was the construction of huge new automated marshalling yards or the extension and modernization of existing ones at Basle Muttenz, Chiasso (the Gotthard route's frontier station with Italy), Lausanne Denges, Olten Dulliken and Zurich Limmattal. Naturally these have so far proved much less productive investments than anticipated.

Whatever happens in the freight sector, though, most of the improvement is vital to the SBB's plan to launch an intensified, system-wide regular-interval passenger service in the 1980s. It was with at least half an eye to bettering its passenger product that the SBB concentrated a heavy investment in layout widenings, new flying junctions and avoiding lines to keep conflicting traffic flows out of each others paths in the critical Olten region. This intricate, interlocking programme, expected to take until the 1990s to finish, is too complex to describe in detail, but one must mention its major components. An important first step was completed in 1975. That was the 12.2-mile Heitersberg cut-off, including a new 3.06-mile tunnel in which the double track is entirely laid on a slab concrete base. It has given Geneva–Zurich expresses a five-mile shorter and largely maximum-speed path between Olten and

A Zurich–Bern–Lausanne–Geneva Inter-City train formed of air-conditioned MkIII stock and headed by an Re4/4II descends the long 1 in 53½–55 gradient from Vauderens to Lake Geneva.

Zurich in place of their previous sharply curved and severely speed-restricted route through the Limmatal via Brugg and Baden. Moreover, Geneva–Bern–Zurich and Basle–Zurich–Chur flows no longer merge in a flat junction at Brugg, but in flying junctions further east; and by 1981 each stream is to have its own pair of double tracks to Zurich. And soon Basle–Lucerne–Gotthard and Geneva–Bern–Zurich flows will no longer intersect on the flat of Olten but will avoid each other entirely on separated sets of double track. Elsewhere on the Gotthard route another valuable move has been the resignalling for two-way operation on each track with crossovers at regular intervals, between Erstfeld and Göschenen, Airolo and Biasca, and Immensee, Arth-Goldau and Schwyz.

The 16-platform main station at Zurich is the busiest and most important in Switzerland, because it is the crossroads of several important international and domestic routes. Over 400 timetabled train connections are made there daily. But it is also a terminus, imposing reversals on all through trains to and from eastern Switzerland apart from a handful for Chur and the Arlberg route to Austria which are allowed to bypass the main station on a mainly freight line. Consequently the station is and always will be an operational headache, but here again a lengthy and massive scheme of new flying and burrowing junctions is underway to mitigate some of the daily problems by eliminating conflicting train paths.

Incidentally Zurich, with its extensive dormitory hinterland, is a hive of the SBB's latest and very impressive commuter multiple-units, the high-power, lightweight Class RABDe8/16 of 1974. Within each of these four-car units each end vehicle is motored on all axles, giving it an accelerative punch that hustles a fully loaded set of 180 tonnes gross up to its top speed of 78mph in just 71 seconds from a standing start. The interior furnishing of the RABDe8/16s is amongst the most distinguished of any European commuter equipment, too, and well worthy of the special livery of deep yellow above the waist and light purple below.

Most spectacular of the many scenically transfixing SBB routes, of course, is the Gotthard. Strictly speaking it starts at Lucerne heading south, but for practical railway purposes nowadays the label pertains to the whole through route from the French and German frontiers at Basle to Chiasso. Its centrepiece comes when the line has passed the southern tip of Lake Lucerne at Flüelen and heads up the deep and narrowing Reuss River valley to the mountain barrier. Erstfeld, base depot of the Gotthard route's motive power, marks the start of an 18-mile grind, almost all of it graded at 1 in 38½–40, which lifts the railway 2080ft to its 3786ft summit deep underground in the 9¼-mile Gotthard Tunnel.

The line climbs rapidly up the eastern wall of the cavernous valley, springing over streams cascading into the Reuss from precipitous gorges on the first of the 101 bridges crossed between Flüelen and Biasca,

Opposite:
Basle Muttenz, the SBB's massive automated marshalling yard at the great rail centre on Switzerland's border with France and West Germany.
Below:
The busy approaches of Zurich main station, with an SBB Class Re6/6 Bo-Bo-Bo heading an express on the right as a Class RABDe12/12 electric multiple-unit formation makes for the platforms on the extreme left. Note the radio transmitter receiver aerial crowning the main signalbox in the right background.

inside Italy. In a pre-cement age, every one was built in metal, but from as early as 1880 the smaller ones were being replaced with graceful concrete arches. By 1952 only the 21 biggest bridges survived in their original metal. Since their structure was deteriorating, the SBB had no option but to face the high cost and operating nuisance of renewing these as well, mostly but not entirely in concrete as the cheapest material; the last reconstruction was due for completion in 1980.

The steep gradient does not keep pace with the sharp rise in the valley floor, so to avoid sharpening it still more fiercely the line corkscrews in and out of the steep mountainsides to gain height without distance. At Wassen three successive spiral tunnels raise the railway over 500ft vertically while it is advancing only three miles horizontally. Many an uninitiated traveller, glimpsing Wassen's little picture-postcard church on its craggy perch three times as his Gotthard train weaves below, then around and finally above it in a figure eight, has entertained suspicions that the Swiss have planted standard prefabricated villages in this nook of the Alps.

Finally at Göschenen the railway is all but locked in by mountains as the valley constricts to the steep ravine of the Schöllenen gorge leading to Andermatt, and the trains burrow into the Gotthard Tunnel. To maximize its $9\frac{1}{4}$-mile track capacity, the tunnel is divided into 13 signalling sections, all controlled from Göschenen, so that a number of consecutive trains can follow each other underground. A double crossover midway allows trains to be switched between the two tracks in an operating emergency.

Creation of this maximum, automatically-signalled track capacity in the tunnel was essential to intersperse amongst the heavy through traffic the intensive shuttle of car-carrying trains between Göschenen and the station at the southern entrance, Airolo. This is a very smart operation with permanently-coupled, push-pull-operated sets of flatcars arranged for side-loading from platforms of rail vehicle floor height at each terminal, so that for motorists, use of the service is a simple matter of drive-on and drive-off. Similar car-carriers shuttle through other Alpine rail tunnels, such as the Lötschberg in Switzerland and the Tauern in Austria, but the Austrians gave up their Arlberg Tunnel service when a parallel road tunnel was opened at the end of 1978 and the SBB is likely to abandon the Gotthard facility when the Gotthard road tunnel is commissioned.

Meanwhile the rail shuttle saves road transport a further climb of 3145ft from Göschenen to the summit of the Gotthard Pass, taxing enough in summer but often impossible in winter and spring because of snow blockage. In the depth of winter, both in Austria and in Switzerland, it is not just the high mountain roads that are sometimes impassable, of course, and then the railways generally are the only secure means of bulk freight or passenger transportation. But they can only be kept working by heavy expenditure on continuous snow protection and clearance.

The keyword is continuous. The modern diesel-powered snowplough (diesel rather than electric, because a heavy snowfall might have interfered with the current supply) can forge through even 3ft drifts at 20 to 25mph with its two vaned lateral wheels at the front end churning up the snow and hosing it up to 100ft clear of the track on either side. Provided snowplough patrol is regular, it takes a phenomenal fall or an avalanche to disrupt service seriously, since the rotary plough hurls the snow far enough away from the line to prevent it sliding or drifting back on to the track. Let it lie and consolidate, though, and the weight of the snow per unit of area will steadily double or even treble without any compression by human or mechanical force.

At the high altitudes where some of Switzerland's independent and mostly narrow-gauge railways operate the effect of persistent rotary ploughing is often the erection of fantastic snow cuttings around the track. In the heights there is little melting in mid-winter, so each ploughing builds up the trackside deposit until eventually trains may be threading a trough between walls of snow anything from 10 to even 20ft high. The tightly packed snow usually holds firm and gives little trouble until the spring thaw.

The chief menace of the thaw – or of the *föhn*, a warm wind from the south – is the avalanche, when a mass of snow that has accumulated on some steep slope high up in the mountains without a really secure foundation gets too heavy for its inadequate adhesion to the rock or ice beneath. Once dislodged, the tumbling snow not only gathers terrifying speed but with every foot it drops more snow and ice are

accumulated and eventually, at lower levels, boulders and whole trees are ripped up by its massive impact. Fortunately the configuration of the mountains is such that avalanches mostly follow well-defined and, by deep scores in the mountainsides, easily discernible tracks. In the mountain sector of the Gotthard route 34 of these have been catalogued. Where their paths threaten the railway the latter is protected by avalanche shelters, usually of reinforced concrete, over the sharply sloping roofs of which the avalanches can thunder on their way to subside harmlessly in the valley below.

Every year, nevertheless, at least one avalanche will take a new course, so the railways still need to be on the *qui vive* for trouble day and night each winter. On the Gotthard it is standard procedure for each station to measure its local snowfall four times a day and to report the depth, the type of snow and wind conditions to the line's central control room. The control room chief is also a meteorologist versed in the local behaviour of snow. The moment he detects a concurrence of conditions prone to set up avalanches he orders railwaymen out on continuous watch at 16 strategic points on the slopes leading up to the tunnel. This sentry-duty is pretty demanding; sometimes the avalanche watchers are standing by their radio-telephone somewhere in the white wilderness peering intently at the crags above for 12 hours at a spell.

But despite all these precautions and many others, such as the obviously essential equipment of all strategic switches in stations and yards with point-heaters remotely controlled from signalboxes, a particularly severe bout of winter can still bring a mountain route like the Gotthard briefly to its knees. Its significance as an international north–south artery as well as the then-threatening strangulation by upsurging traffic was a motive for the mid-1960s

Above left:
An SBB 10,600hp Class Re6/6 Bo-Bo-Bo heads an international freight heading south for the Gotthard Tunnel.
Below left:
Freight bound for Italy enters the north portal of the Gotthard Tunnel at Göschenen. Note that the assisting Re6/6 electric locomotive is marshalled in mid-train to ease the strain on wagon drawgear and improve train stability on the curves and grades of the transalpine route.
Opposite above:

Snow clearance on the Gotthard main line in winter – the rotary vanes of the diesel-powered snowplough eject the snow well beyond the running lines.

discussion of a new Gotthard rail tunnel which would
bypass the mountain section of the route completely.

This so-called Gotthard Base Tunnel would be no
less than 28 miles long. Starting from Amsteg, just
south of Flüelen inside the Reuss valley, it would
emerge in the Ticino valley at Giornico. Not only
would its straight course slice 18½ miles off the present
route's serpentine course between Amsteg and
Giornico, but it would tunnel 2000ft lower beneath
the peaks to maintain gradients no steeper than 1 in
83–100. As a result passenger trains would be saved
35 minutes' journey time and Gotthard freight
timings could be cut by as much as 1–1½ hours.
However, with the downturn of the SBB's traffic
since the mid-1970s and the consequent slide of the
system into deficit – it was the last of the European
national railways to go into the red – the rate of
investment even in the SBB's less ambitious improvement and enlargement schemes has been decelerated by the Bern Government, so the Gotthard
Base Tunnel now looks a highly improbable enterprise until there is a conspicuous regeneration of the
European industrial economy.

To revert to the present-day Gotthard route, the
southern slope is no easier or less spectacular than the
northern. Emerging from the tunnel into the Ticino
valley at Airolo, Italian-bound trains are at once
launched on a descent of 2785ft in the ensuing 28½
miles to Biasca, and here again the original engineers
had recourse to four spiral tunnels to keep pace with
the drop of the rugged Piottino and Biaschina
ravines between Rodi-Fiesso and Giornico. Grades
are more amicable and the track alignment less
restricting along the flatter valley floor from Biasca
to Bellinzona. But when the line is down to 767ft
above sea level at Giubasco trains confront another
long haul at 1 in 38½–40, climbing nearly 800ft to cut
across the mountains between the Ticino valley and
Lake Lugano. At last their mountaineering is over
when at Melide they cut across the lake on a causeway
which the Gotthard builders built from a convenient
glacial morain and head for Chiasso, Como and Milan.

In a beeline Chiasso is only 92 miles from Lucerne,
but the railway's difficult, constantly curving course
through the Alps, in which it has threaded 80 tunnels
aggregating 28½ route-miles, absorbs 140 miles.

Since the curvature imposes a 50mph speed limit almost throughout, it follows that even a comparatively lightweight 'Trans-Europ Express' stopping intermediately only at Lugano and Bellinzona cannot cover the distance in less than two hours 59 minutes for an average of 46.9mph.

Given such route characteristics, SBB traction policy for its totally 15kV $16\frac{2}{3}$Hz electrified system (marshalling yards apart, that is) has obviously concentrated on high tractive effort and adhesion for minimum locomotive weight. The basics of modern Swiss main-line locomotive design were delineated in 1945 by the independent Bern–Lötschberg–Simplon Railway (BLS), when it produced in its Class Ae4/4I the world's first double-bogie design with a 1000hp traction motor on each axle, achieving a 4000hp output for a total weight of only 80 tonnes.

Both BLS and SBB developed the concept into Bo-Bos of insignificantly increased weight but over 50 percent more power in the 1960s. The SBB type was the 6320hp Re4/4II with a power/weight ratio of over 80hp/tonne. It is currently the system's principal passenger power for all but the heaviest

transalpine international expresses; more than 200 are at work, supplemented by a score with different gearing to obtain higher tractive effort at the cost of diminished top speed, which are designated Re4/4III. The new Re4/4IV of the 1980s is to squeeze still more power from each axle by recourse to thyristor-controlled DC motors. Output will be hoisted to 6900hp and yet the locomotives will be capable of

Above:
On its spectacular descent to the floor of the Rhône valley at Brig, a BLS Class Re4/4 Bo-Bo crosses the Luogelkin Viaduct.
Below:
An SBB Class Ae6/6 electric locomotive at the head of a train in the Canton Valais.

Many SBB passenger services are operated push-pull by 2720hp Class RBe4/4 railcars, one of which heads this train of the SBB's familiar low-slung lightweight coaches.

100mph as well as of lugging 650-tonne trailing loads unaided up the Gotthard gradients. Four Re4/4IV prototypes were ordered at the close of 1978, but pending proof of their performance the SBB also ordered 45 more Re4/4IIs to cover the intensified passenger service planned for 1982.

Although the initial Re4/4IVs are to be based at Lausanne for duty across the mountains to Bern and Zurich as well as over the more friendly Simplon route (so far the only one in Switzerland where the Re4/4IVs can exploit their 100mph potential, for a short stretch near Leuk), the SBB recognizes that traction technology has not yet come up with a single all-purpose type to meet passenger and freight traffic demands in mountain and plain alike. Mainstay of the Gotthard route, therefore, are two six-wheeled types, the 5940hp Ae6/6 Co-Co dating from 1952 and the remarkable Re6/6 Bo-Bo-Bos which have been built since 1972. Each Re6/6 generates a virile 10,600hp from its 120-tonne overall weight, for the even and track-sparing spread of which it is mounted on three bogies with every axle motored, so that its wheel arrangement is Bo-Bo-Bo. An Re6/6 can hold the line limit of 50mph all the way up the Gotthard gradients with 800 tonnes of passenger train on its tail.

The SBB has steadily intensified its passenger service since the 1930s, and to such effect that today it is carrying 80 percent more passengers than in 1938 even though the country's automobiles have multiplied no less than 25 times in the same period and nearly 7000 miles of new main road have been laid since 1955 alone. But the additional sales impact elsewhere of a repetitive, easily memorized service pattern has not been lost on the SBB. A massive

redraft of the whole passenger timetable on an interlocking regular-interval frequency was sketched and carefully studied, and it is now to be implemented in the spring of 1982. By that time the still more intensive working – the projected timetable envisages a 17 percent lift of daily train-mileage compared with the schedules of the late 1970s – can take advantage of the completion of several of the infrastructure improvements outlined earlier in this chapter. It will also take into account another important development not yet mentioned, a new loop off the Zurich–Winterthur main line directly serving the heart of Switzerland's key airport, Zurich, which was opened in the spring of 1980; besides hourly local trains, all semi-fasts between Lucerne, Zurich and Romanshorn (on Lake Constance) now travel via the airport loop, which is also served in peak hours by through trains from as far afield as Bern, Interlaken, Brig and the Ticino Canton beyond the Gotthard Tunnel. In 1980 the Federal Government agreed the construction by 1987 of a similar rail link to Geneva's Cointrin Airport, likewise to be served by inter-city trains to and from Bern, Biel and Brig.

The aim of the SBB's national regular-interval passenger timetable is that no line shall have a less frequent service than one inter-city express, one semi-fast (or *train direct*) and one all-stations train every hour. In the most important lines, of course, the frequency will be more intensive, especially where flows merge, as between Geneva and Lausanne. Quite apart from the handicaps of gradient and curvature already described, plus the survival on at least one key route of some single track in locations where even the Swiss boggle at physical problems and cost of doubling, the scheduling of such a timetable is a formidable assignment when it has to be integrated with Switzerland's heavy international rail traffic, freight as well as passenger. The international passenger trains, by and large, have to be accepted from or handed over to neighbours at times which suit their market or operating convenience (and, moreover, international trains are notoriously vulnerable to delay), not when it fits in with domestic travel demand in Switzerland.

Another snag is the inheritance from 19th-century network development of some dead-end stations on what are now through routes, as at Lucerne and Zurich. Even with the most modern signalling controlled from a new central push-button console, it takes prodigies of incredible operating dexterity at Zurich to hold the carefully organized connections between the hourly Geneva–Lausanne–Bern and–Basle inter-city services and other expresses to and from Chur, Lucerne, the Gotthard and Romanshorn, while simultaneously re-engining through trains that have to reverse and also coping with heavy local train services. A train-watcher at Zurich needs to remember, too, that the Gotthard expresses have had to be pathed through that line's heavy international freight flows to make their patterned connections with the domestic regular-interval services.

A particularly irritating trunk route for reversals is Basle–Lausanne–Geneva. It involves two, at Delémont and Lausanne, and hence is still operated on the push-pull principle which the SBB applied to a substantial proportion of its domestic inter-city services in the earlier postwar years. The traction for such trains was the SBB's first adaptation of the BLS lightweight locomotive concept of 1945, its 2500hp Class Re4/4 of only 58 tons weight, which emerged in 1946. So compact was the traction gear that in 1959 the design could be developed into the RBe4/4 electric motor-coach, deploying 2800hp and yet with body room to spare for a 67-seat passenger saloon. In the 1960s the Re4/4s and RBe4/4s were interchangeable power on the inter-city push-pull trains. A new breed of thyristor-controlled motor coaches is in mind to replace older classes of electric locomotive as the national regular-interval service develops.

The RBe4/4's fairly low horsepower sufficed because of the SBB's dedication to lightweight coach design, of which the first manifestation was the SBB's *Leichtschnellzug* – 'light express train' – stock of 1941. Their low-slung bodies and flat roofs made them a rather dwarfish mismatch for most other European mainland coaches in outline, but the significant contrast was in weight: only 25–28 tonnes per car as a result of extensive constructional recourse to aluminium and light steel alloys, compared with a contemporary Continental average of 45 tonnes. Between 1941 and 1974 the SBB progressively renewed three-quarters of its coaching fleet with these vehicles.

Since the mid-1970s the MkIIs have been superseded on the prime inter-city services by the very distinctive MkIIIs, fully air-conditioned and furnished to the highest amenity standards of the neighbours' equipment. Again the Swiss designers have been extraordinarily skilful in weight-saving. Despite the addition of five tonnes per car for the air-conditioning alone, never mind the apparatus for other extras like automatic air-operated vestibule doors, they have limited the all-up weight of an open MkIII saloon to 30 tonnes, 25 percent less than the aggregate of modern French or German air-conditioned cars.

Apart from an exclusive orange and white livery, with which the Re4/4II locomotives assigned to haul them have also been restyled, the MkIII train-sets are distinguished externally by their sharply tapered body-sides. This feature is indicative of their design for adaptation to automatic body-tilting. But only a few MkIIIs have been equipped with the apparatus, which for these vehicles has been devised by their manufacturers, the Swiss car-builders SIG. The SIG mechanism is inoperative unless it is switched on by the driver, whereupon it reacts automatically to a gyroscope mounted in the centre of the car floor, adjusting the distance between coach body and bogie bolsters as the combined effects of speed and track curvature dictate, thus to lean the body up to a maximum angle of six degrees towards the inner rail of the curve. Like most other major railroads the SBB has taken a long time not only to prove the device technically but to weigh up its cost and weight penalties against quantifiable operational benefits. By 1979 it had decided not to proceed with the device and its MkIV inter-city coaching-stock will be of conventional profile and suspension. One reason for the decision is that the SBB reckons its prospects of building some well-aligned new high-speed bypasses grow brighter with every fresh twist of the oil-price screw – maybe even a new transversal

The control centre of Zurich Limmatal marshalling yard. Routes are not set up by switches on the illuminated track diagram at the rear of the room, but on keyed buttons at each operator's desk. Note also the VDUs on which each operator can call up data on the traffic state of any sector of the layout.

Interior of a first-class saloon of the SBB's air-conditioned MkIII coaching stock. Note the tapered side-walls, indicative of the SBB's design with possible automatic body-tilting in mind – a development which is no longer to be pursued.

A piggyback train formed mostly of low-loading, small-wheel SGP flatcars on the northern ascent to the Gotthard Tunnel.

throughout from Lausanne to St Gallen in the north-east.

The MkIII stock is marshalled into semi-permanent 14-car formations each consisting of seven second-class saloons, a restaurant car, five first-class saloons and a brake first with the only compartment accommodation in the set, the main commercial object of which is to offer reservable rooms for business conferences. Like the latest DSG diners in West Germany, the diner has its own pantograph so that it can draw current from the overhead wires for its kitchen equipment when its power lines are not connected to a locomotive – for instance, when it is in sidings and the crew are getting ready for train duty. Swiss train catering on domestic services is run by a separate company, *Cie Suisse des Wagons-Restaurants* (CSWR), which was set up in 1903 when nationalization embraced two of the original Swiss railways with which the International Wagons-Lits Company previously had restaurant-car contracts.

Throughout the last century the only route from Bern, the Swiss capital, to northern Italy was a

circuitous one via Lucerne and the Gotthard Tunnel. But in the 1890s boring of the 12¼-mile Simplon Tunnel was approved to project the then-developing Rhône valley rail route from Geneva into Italy. That prompted the formation of a new private standard-gauge railway, the Bern–Lötschberg–Simplon (BLS) to close the gap between the extremity of the Bernese Oberland standard-gauge system at Frütigen, in the Kander valley, and the Rhône valley route at Brig, below the Simplon pass. It was a formidable enterprise, not completed until 1913.

The BLS parts company with the SBB line to Interlaken at Spiez on Lake Thun, and strikes southward up the Kander valley. The engineering spectacle starts to unfold at Frütigen, beyond which point the floor of the contracting, densely wooded valley rises 1275ft in only five miles. As on the Gotthard, the engineers were forced to spiral in and out of the mountainsides to gain height quickly without incurring a gradient steeper than 1 in 37 and at Mitholz two semi-circles, one just contained within the valley floor by sharp curvature, follow in quick

succession. At Kandersteg, with its majestic back-cloth of the snow-clad Balmhorn and Altels mountains (members of the Blümlisalp group), the railway has climbed 1842ft in 19½ miles from Spiez. Here the line dives into the solid mountain wall rearing up ahead, reaching its 4076ft summit midway through the 9¼-mile Lötschberg Tunnel. When it emerges in the wild alpine valley of the Lötschental at Goppenstein it has passed a significant watershed, for whereas the Kander on the other side of the tunnel flows into the Rhine and ultimately the North Sea, the torrents now tumbling around the railway will drop into the Rhône and end up in the Mediterranean.

An almost unbroken chain of avalanche shelters protects the railway's descent of the Lötschental and Lonza Gorge. Then the train takes to a tunnel beyond which the BLS traveller comes upon one of the most dramatic prospects in main-line European railroading – the busy thoroughfare of the Rhône valley spread out 1500ft below, with the ramparts of the Valais mountains towering behind it. In the remaining 12 miles to Brig the BLS line steadily closes the gap between itself and the SBB Rhône valley main

line in a descent on a ruling gradient of 1 in 37. It is marked by a thrilling succession of tunnels through mountain buttresses and leaps over the gorges between them on striking bridges – none more so than the Bietschtal, with its single steel span of 312ft that floats the railway 255ft above the cascade below.

With the notable exception of the Lötschberg Tunnel most of the BLS route was built as single-track with station passing loops. In the 1960s and early 1970s the Swiss body politic as well as the BLS management was fretting just as much over this severe operational constraint as it was over the threatening strangulation of the Gotthard route by upsurging international traffic. The BLS itself, for which transit traffic is proportionally far bigger business than it is even for the SBB, had already been doubling in the least daunting terrain between Spiez and Frütigen and had laid in a new mile-long loop at Mitholz, but its money would not run to the mammoth job of enlarging the mountain section's capacity; nor would that of the railway's sponsoring Canton, Bern. Came the mid-1970s recession and some speculated that the rest of the job might be shelved alongside the Gotthard base tunnel draft.

However, the Swiss were already concerned at the

A BLS Class Re4/4 locomotive emerges from the north portal of the Lötschberg Tunnel and approaches Kandersteg.

Left:
The BLS main line near the end of its precipitous descent to Rhône valley at Brig, with the river in the foreground. This picture dramatizes the difficulty of the engineering work involved in double-tracking the route, which was under way at this location at the end of the 1970s.

Right:
An SBB Class Ae6/6 emerges
from the Simplon Tunnel's
north portal at Brig.
Below:
A BLS 4000hp Class Ae4/4
locomotive – the pioneer
Swiss high-power, lightweight
Bo-Bo design.
Bottom:
The latter-day successor of
the Ae4/4 – one of the BLS
Class Re4/4 Bo-Bos.

Mont Cenis Tunnel route's sapping of their highly remunerative international freight traffic (such transit business pays, of course, because once marshalled into a train at one frontier it runs intact the breadth of the system). By 1983, they realized, the BLS might be drained of international passenger traffic too if completion of French Railways' 160mph TGV Sud-est line from Paris to Lyons had the ripple effect of making the Mont Cenis route appealingly faster to Italy from northern France.

So in 1976 the Federal Government in Bern – after a hassle with the Italians over contingent agreement to improve freight marshalling installations south of the Simplon tunnel at Domodossola – agreed to put up around £180 million ($405 million) during the ensuing decade for the first stages of doubling the BLS right through to Brig. Apart from the prodigious difficulties of executing such a job in craggy mountain sites, the double-tracking involves reconstructing and widening 168 bridges and rebuilding about $7\frac{1}{2}$ miles of tunnel (apart, of course, from the already double-track Lötschberg Tunnel). Even though the tunnels were hewn with an eye to eventual double-tracking, finishing the job is still a taxing assignment when it has to be done without interrupting normal traffic on the one existing track; naturally the latter cannot be used for work trains, so that every ton of building material and every piece of construction machinery has to be brought to the site by road or cableway.

Since its 1945 pioneering with the Ae4/4 the BLS has pinned its traction faith to the four-axle, total-adhesion electric locomotive concept and its compact fleet nowadays is spearheaded by 29 Re4/4s with a one-hour rating as high as 6780hp. Its most powerful locomotives, however, are its five 8800hp Ae8/8s, which are essentially two permanently coupled Ae4/4s. Still surviving, principally as stand-bys, are eight Class Re6/8 1-Co-Co-1s originally constructed in 1926 which in recent years have been modernized to produce 6000hp.

Despite the ruling 1 in 37 gradient of the BLS main line, coupling strength and length of passing loops are more influential factors in the length of its freight trains than the capability of BLS motive power. An Ae8/8 is comfortable with up to 880 tonnes hanging on its drawbar, a single Re4/4 with 630 tonnes, but a pair of Re4/4s can take no more than 1100 tonnes because that is the limit of trailing load prescribed for coupling integrity. Trains up to 1500 tonnes trailing weight are run, however, with an Ae8/8 or a brace of Re4/4s up front and an Re6/8 inserted in the middle of the train to relieve coupling strain at the rear.

The BLS owns little more than a hundred passenger coaches (a proportion of which, with some electric railcars, operate secondary lines within the BLS group, such as the Bern–Neuchatel), since so much of its main-line traffic is international. The most distinctive BLS passenger sets are those formed of an air-conditioned version of the standard Swiss low-slung saloon which operate inter-city services between Brig and Basle, and Interlaken and Basle, and which are liveried blue and cream instead of the otherwise standard BLS dark green; their Re4/4 traction, however, is in the standard BLS locomotive brown. A component of BLS passenger business which deserves mention is the car-carrier trains which ferry motorists straight from the Bernese Oberland to Italy, shuttling between Kandersteg and Iselle, south of the Simplon Tunnel, with intermediate calls at Goppenstein and Brig.

The BLS is just one of around 80 privately owned Swiss companies which between them operate not far short of half the country's total rail mileage, and most of which are sponsored and aided by their respective Cantons as essential public transport. Some are standard-gauge, some narrow (only one narrow-gauge system, the 46-mile Brünig from Interlaken to Meiringen and Lucerne, is part of the SBB); some are essentially public service lines, others primarily the mountain-climbing funiculars are tourism-oriented. All are electric in day-to-day working (though one or two resurrect steam for special excursions) except for the diesel funicular to Monte Generoso on the shore of Lake Lugano, and the picturesque Brienzer–Rothorn railway, which still cherishes characteristic steam rack-and-pinion engines for its ascent to a 7378ft-high viewpoint in the Bernese Oberland above Lake Brienz. Latterly many of these private concerns have assembled themselves into groups for more economical administration, a trend actively encouraged by the Federal Government since nowadays the majority need financial support from public funds. Most are progressively re-equipping with modern motor-coaches and trailers built largely to standard patterns by the energetic Swiss railway supply industry, but to which the operators apply their own distinctive and often sprightly liveries.

In the space available one can only summarize the extent and character of some of the most striking of these enterprises. Among them is unquestionably the metre-gauge Rhaetian Railway, which runs 244

route-miles in the country's easternmost and most sparsely populated Canton, the Grisons or Graubünden, where the Alps are at their most rugged. Spectacularly engineered all the way, the Rhaetian main line from the Canton's capital (and the narrow-gauge line's junction with the SBB), Chur, grinds up with a final burst of spirals on a ruling gradient of 1 in 29 to its 5982ft summit in the Albula Tunnel before it eases into the famous winter sports resort of St Moritz.

The Rhaetian grades are the steepest encountered

Above:
Cars board one of the BLS drive-on, drive-off shuttle trains at Kandersteg to travel through the Lötschberg Tunnel.
Below:
A 1270hp Class Deh4/6 locomotive heads a train on the SBB's metre-gauge Brunig Railway from Interlaken to Lucerne.
Bottom left and right:
Interior and exterior of the Montreux–Oberland–Bernois Railway's fully air-conditioned 'Panoramic Express'.

on any Swiss line carrying heavy trainload traffic – though not the most severe worked without benefit of rack aids to adhesion. Here the palm is taken by the superbly scenic Montreux–Oberland–Bernois, or MOB, with a long stretch of 1 in $13\frac{3}{4}$ as it clambers up from Lake Geneva to a tunnel under the Col de Jaman on a delightful passage of bucolic mountain valleys to Zweisimmen and the Bernese Oberland. In 1979 the MOB enhanced the enjoyment of its spectacular route from Montreux to Gstaad and Zweisimmen by refurbishing four pre-World War II restaurant cars

Mid-winter on the Swiss narrow gauge – a motor coach and trailer of the Rhaetian Railway.

as fully air-conditioned observation saloons with deep windows raked up to the roof centre and comfortable reclining armchair seating, matching them with two of its 1946-built 600hp motor coaches, decking the whole equipage an attractive blue and white, and running it the length of the route and back daily as the 'Panoramic Express'. The riding of these observation cars is as quiet and smooth as that of many European standard-gauge inter-city vehicles.

The principal Rhaetian Railway passenger services are perfectly scaled-down replicas of

standard-gauge inter-city expresses, including neat restaurant cars (the Rhaetian deploys five of them) in fully vestibuled formations of modern lightweight stock that stands comparison with all but the latest SBB air-conditioned equipment for quality of ride and furnishing. At peak traffic periods trains run to a length of 12 or 13 cars taring 265 tonnes, a load still comfortably within the compass of the Rhaetian's latest traction, a locomotive with an output as high as 2400hp despite the limitations of the gauge; this has been achieved by an ingenious articulated three-motor-bogie running gear layout, which both spreads the power plant weight to spare the comparatively light track and eases its lengthened superstructure round the route's sharp curvature. Incidentally, the Rhaetian also runs a drive-on, drive-off car-carrying shuttle between Thusis and Samedin, which saves motorists to and from St Moritz and the Engadine region the negotiation of the Albula Pass.

At its southwestern extremity, Disentis, the Rhaetian makes an end-on junction with the Furka–Oberalp Railway (FOB), last of the significant Swiss lines to be completed, in 1926. This is a route of vital strategic importance to the Swiss as well as one of gripping tourist appeal, since it threads the Swiss Army's mountain redoubt area around Andermatt. The FOB's 60½-mile course from Disentis to Brig confronts it with the wildest terrain traversed by any Western European railway, purely tourist funiculars apart, as it crosses the totally uninhabited Furka and Oberalp passes between the Rhine and Rhône valleys. Its summit is no less than 7088ft up in the Furka Tunnel; to attain this, engineers had to resort to gradients as steep as 1 in 9 and hence to rack-and-pinion sections. Even so the FOB manages to run a buffet car on its principal summer train (of which more shortly).

But the FOB cannot compete with the elements in winter. Depth of snowfall at that height is perhaps less of a problem than the vulnerability of practically the entire pass section to avalanches. At one notorious avalanche site, where the railway crosses the Steffenbach gorge just below the Furka Tunnel, the FOB has a neatly sectioned bridge which is dismantled each winter; it can be re-erected in a day. Consequently the Furka section of the line between Oberwald and Realp is shut down every winter from October to April inclusive. In 1971, however, the Federal Government accepted that this was a risky severance of its strategic communications and agreed to finance the boring of a 9.6-mile tunnel between Oberwald, in the Rhône valley, and Realp, in the Reuss valley. This tunnel would cut out the stiff climb to the exposed region around the Furka Tunnel, allow adhesion working all the way from Andermatt to Oberwald and beyond, and scissor some 30 minutes off journey times. The job was begun in 1973 and should be finished in the early 1980s, much later than originally forecast – and at a cost of around £70 million ($160 million), over three times the early

1970s estimate, partly because of geological miscalculations. Revelation of this gross excess set off a political tempest in Bern and the appointment of a board of enquiry which eventually caused some heads to roll. When the new tunnel is eventually complete its traffic will include regular automobile-carrying services, hauled by some striking new Type Ge4/4III thyristor-controlled electric locomotives of only 50 tonnes weight but a one-hour output of 2280hp; that will give them the muscle to haul the trains up 1 in 11 grades by pure adhesion.

At Brig the FOB in turn converges head on with another smart and scenically delectable metre-gauge system, the Brig–Visp–Zermatt (BVZ), whose sophistications include control of the colour-light signalling on its entire 27½-mile single-track route from one CTC centre at Brig. This installation also features automatic programming of trains through the line's passing loops at stations. The BVZ, which runs up to 50 trains a day in the tourist season peak, likewise needs rack sections to contend with gradients as steep as 1 in 8 on its ascent of the narrow, abruptly shelving clefts from the Rhône valley to its Zermatt terminus, 3150ft higher than its start at Brig and nestling at the foot of the Matterhorn.

In summer the BVZ, FOB and Rhaetian combine to offer what must be Europe's most consistently spectacular rail journey, running the 'Glacier Express' as a through train from Zermatt to St Moritz via Brig, Andermatt, Disentis and Chur. It is a trip of nearly 8½ hours for just 187 miles, but on a fine day who counts the hours with such a panorama continuously unfolding through the windows ? Moreover, the FOB keeps passengers plied with light refreshment between Brig and Andermatt, where a Rhaetian restaurant car – unique in Europe in its service of a full lunch menu while the train copes with

The superb Langwies Viaduct on the Rhaetian Railway line from Chur to Arosa. Its reinforced concrete span across the Plessur valley is 315ft long.

One of the smart push-pull, buffet-car-equipped train-sets of the standard-gauge Bodensee–Toggenburg Railway seen between Nesslau and Wattwil, with the serrated Churfirsten mountains in the background.

rack-equipped 1 in 9 slopes – is added for the early afternoon sector to Chur.

In the past few years other private railways have elaborated their services with catering cars, in some cases as a standard amenity, in others as a promotional device. The standard-gauge Südostbahn (SOB) and Bodensee–Toggenburg (BTB), which combine their own routes and exploitation of running powers over the SBB to put on an important through service from Lucerne to St Gallen and Romanshorn on the shore of Lake Constance, effect it with very elegant five-car train-sets each featuring a well-appointed buffet-restaurant-car. The Südostbahn–BTB route is one of the most expensively studded with civil engineering works in all Switzerland. As much as $12\frac{1}{2}$ percent of its route-mileage is in tunnel, compared with a national public railway average of 6.4 percent, and its 86 bridges and viaducts aggregate all but two miles in length. The impressive Sitter viaduct west of St Gallen, with its huge near-1000-

ton iron span soaring 328ft above the ground and its full length including approach arches of 1197ft, is the loftiest European standard-gauge railway viaduct of mixed iron-and-stonework construction. The start of a Südostbahn journey from the route's junction with the SBB Gotthard line at Arth-Goldau is one of the Swiss standard gauge's memorable experiences, for its single line sails away on a ruling gradient of 1 in 20 to climb 1384ft in the first eight miles, while a superb panorama unfolds away to the Gotthard mountains.

The BTB was also the first in Switzerland to exploit the salability and public relations value of vintage steam operation. It went on to gild the enterprise by converting the interior of a veteran passenger vehicle into a sensuously exotic lounge with bar and adjoining boudoir, then marketing it, with steam haulage, as just the equipage to carry away the bridal party in an extravagant finale to local weddings. Other companies have since elaborated the period theme. The standard-gauge Emmental–Burgdorf–Thun–Bahn, a substantial group with 100 miles of route touching three Cantons – Bern, Solothurn and Lucerne – operates a fairly antique ex-SBB car refurbished as a country restaurant and named the *Emmentalstübe*; and the short Onsingen–Balsthal–Bahn has resurrected a Prague-built, wooden-bodied Wagons-Lits diner of 1907 which once saw 'Orient Express' service.

As you might expect, it is a Swiss line which attains the highest point of any railway in Europe. That is the Jungfrau Railway, a member of the Berner–

A Berner Oberland train leaves Grindelwald for Interlaken. In the background is the notorious North Wall of the Eiger mountain, in front of which another line of the BOB (not visible in this picture) climbs from Grindelwald to Kleine Scheidegg.

Above:
In mid winter a train begins
the descent from Kleine
Scheidegg to Grindelwald.
Below:
Jungfraujoch, tunnel
terminus at 11,333ft.

Oberland–Bahnen (BOB) group of narrow gauge railways based at Interlaken. The main BOB artery is the metre-gauge line from Interlaken, which at Zweilütschinen forks into branches to Grindelwald and Lauterbrunnen, each of which has gradients steep enough to compel rack assistance. Through

running between Interlaken and the Jungfrau Railway is impossible because the builders of the intervening link, the Wengernalp Railway, elected for an unusual 0.80m gauge to ease the formidable problems of lifting their line out of the deep, steep-walled cleft of the Lauterbrunnen valley to Wengen, the charming resort – still totally inaccessible, thank heaven, by motor vehicle – 4291ft up on the wooded slopes that roll away from the great Oberland mountain trio of the Eiger, Mönch and Jungfrau. The gradient is 1 in $5\frac{1}{2}$ and the prospect breathtaking as the 600hp motor-coach – again rack-assisted, naturally – propels its two trailers steadily up the steep valley wall. Meanwhile another Wengernalp arm is climbing away from Grindelwald, finishing up even more awesomely on a 1 in 4 slope at the base of the stupendous 6000ft precipice that is the Eiger's dreaded North Wall. Reaching upward beyond Wengen the line from Lauterbrunnen, having ascended 4147ft in $6\frac{1}{8}$ miles, converges with that from Grindelwald 6762ft up on the Kleine Scheidegg ridge, where the metre-gauge Jungfrau Railway takes over.

The Jungfrau Railway is only $5\frac{3}{4}$ miles long, but it took 16 years to build, such were the rigours of tunnelling through the exceptionally hard rock within the Jungfrau range and of working in the rarefied atmosphere and temperatures at such an altitude in the first decade of this century without benefit of modern aids to survival. The railway approaches the foot of the snow-cloaked range on $1\frac{1}{4}$ miles of shelter-protected open track, but the rest of the route is entirely within the mountain. Winter and summer alike the two-car train-sets need continuous heating to keep passengers comfortable in the Arctic climate of the tunnel, which slants upwards just inside the north face of the Eiger, then U-turns to climb on beneath the Mönch, the central peak of the trio. The train stops twice inside the mountain: first at Eigerwand, where windows have been carved out of the Eiger's North Wall and passengers are given five minutes to detrain and peer out over the sheer precipice to Grindelwald, huddling 6000ft on the valley floor below; then at Eismeer, under the Mönch, inside the further wall of the range, where the windows open straight on to the Aletsch glacier.

The terminus is inside the tunnel, 11,333ft up at Jungfraujoch on the ridge between the Mönch and Jungfrau, and its underground exit leads directly to a substantial hotel (ravaged by fire a few years back but since reconstructed) which is set into the rock. The *Berghaus*'s rooms and balconies command an unforgettably dazzling view of the vast peak-fringed glacier which slopes away for a distance of about 16 miles to tail off above the Rhône valley near Brig. The ice-cap of the Jungfraujoch ridge is innocent of crevasses, so anyone can walk out over the snow to the crest and, with the Jungfrau looming above them on one side and the Mönch on the other, take in too the fabulous prospect extending as far (on a fine day) as the Jura mountains on the Franco-Swiss border.

An Austrian Federal Railway class 4010 electric inter city multiple unit train on the Vienna–Salzberg main line near Rekawinkel in the Wienerwald.

6.
AUSTRIAN RAILWAYS: THE EAST-WEST LAND BRIDGE

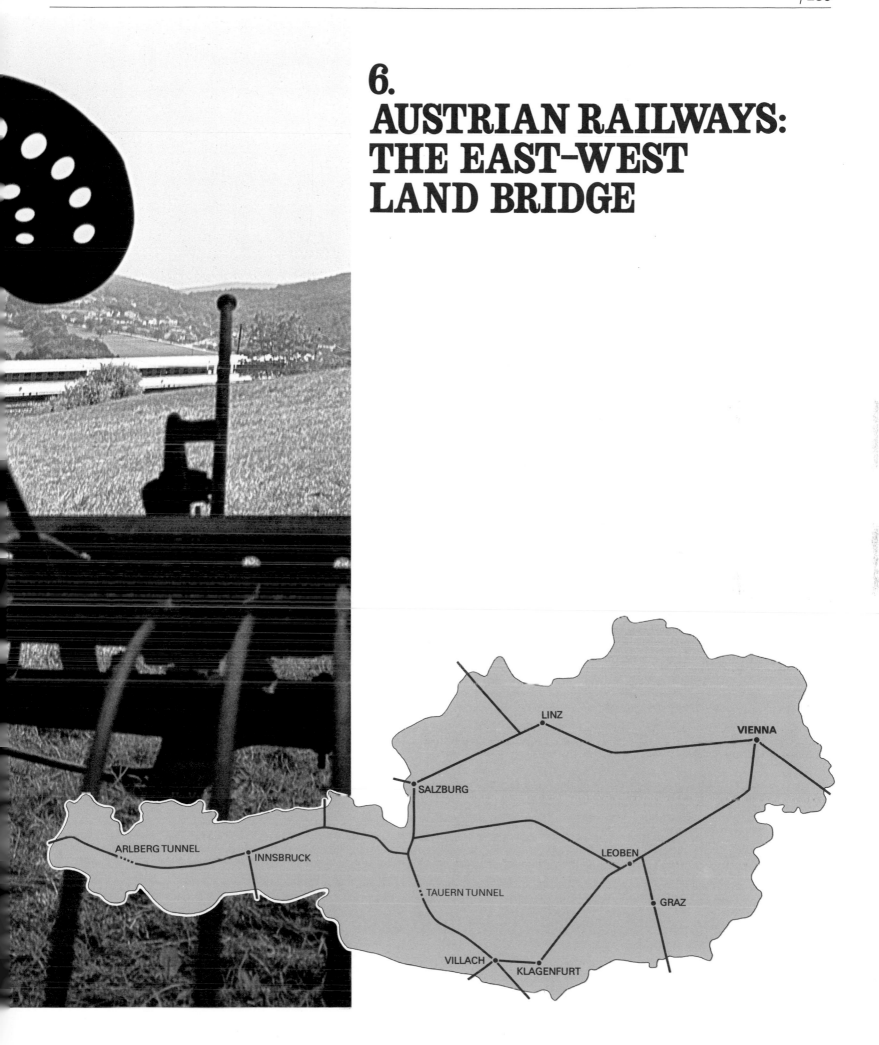

Below:
An OBB Class 1042 and two
of the OBB's Eurofima
coaches on the Lindischgraben
bridge, one of the three new
mountainside viaducts built
during the double-tracking
and realignment of parts of
the southern ascent to the
Tauern Tunnel.
Bottom:
A Class 1042 and train of
'Schlieren'- type OBB coaches.

Like the trunk routes of Switzerland, the main lines of the Austrian Federal Railway, the OBB, have taken on still more international significance with the growth of European trade since the 1950s. But the OBB's role is perhaps more crucial, since besides linking West Germany and Italy via the Brenner Pass it is a land bridge for much of the sharply increased traffic between the European Common Market countries and Eastern or South-eastern Europe. Measured in ton-miles as much as 60 percent of the OBB's freight traffic is international

and 28 percent of it is transit business, moving between countries beyond the Austrian borders. The bulk of this transit movement, no less than 60 percent of it, is overwhelmingly Italo-German, which generates mounting concern over the capacity of the Brenner route. As yet transit traffic to and from the East is way below that level, but Austria's own trade with the Eastern Bloc countries has now reached 40 percent of its total imports; and because of the underdevelopment of road transport in the East the OBB has to shoulder more than half Austria's import-export trade with the Comecon countries.

Since the dismantling of the old Austro-Hungarian empire the OBB has had to grapple with two dominant problems. Like West Germany's DB it has had to re-orient a railway system built on a different socio-economic axis: the former empire's ran from northwest to southeast through Prague, Vienna and Budapest, whereas modern Austria's is west to east from Innsbruck through Salzburg and Linz to Vienna. That apart, latter-day Austria has never been affluent. The OBB came to mid-century less well-equipped than its neighbours, and although it has sagely spent the annual investment funds budgeted by its Government, the cash allocated has fallen well short of what is needed to update the system and enlarge its trunk-route capacity for today's traffic and the service quality the market demands.

The shoe pinches tightest on the transalpine routes, only one of which, the Brenner, was laid from the outset as double track throughout [that is to discount the Semmering, which despite its difficult course does not rate transalpine status in my book]. Today key international routes like the Arlberg, from Bregenz (on Lake Constance, where the Austrian, Swiss and German frontiers converge) to Innsbruck and the Austrian Tyrol, and the Tauern, from Salzburg to southern Austria and the Yugoslav border, are coping with up to 130 trains a day over mainly single track with passing loops – and single track, moreover, that is an aggravated operational handicap because it is so continuously curved and graded. The ruling slope on the western slope of the Arlberg line up to its 4297ft summit in the 6.4-mile Arlberg Tunnel is as steep as 1 in $32\frac{1}{4}$ and the eastern ramp grinds uphill at 1 in 38 for 17 miles on end. At least both the Arlberg – highest of all the transalpine routes, by the way – and the 5.3-mile Tauern Tunnel were built as double track bores.

By the end of the 1970s nearly half of the OBB's route-mileage was electrified at 15kV $16\frac{2}{3}$Hz AC, the same overhead system as that of the Swiss and Germans. All key main lines were under catenary, so that around 90 percent of the OBB's traffic is already electrically powered; contemporary plans for additional secondary-route electrification aim to have 60 percent of the route-mileage and 95 percent of train movement electrified by 1986. But while

A Class 4010 Inter-City electric train-set on Salzburg–Klagenfurt service crosses the Falkenstein bridge, another of the impressive new double-track viaducts at high altitude on the southern slope of the Tauern route. Note the avalanche shelter on the far side of the viaduct.

modern electric traction has significantly increased the speed and weight of freight trains that can be operated over the Arlberg route or up the consistently steep slope – it averages 1 in 50 and is 1 in 40 at its steepest – which lifts the Tauern line 2175ft in only $17\frac{1}{2}$ miles from near Spittal-Millstättersee, south of the mountains, to Mallnitz at the mouth of tunnel under the High Tauern range, it cannot iron out the speed-restricting curves or spirit up a passing loop to accommodate opposing traffic. Obviously the time table aims to schedule meets so that priority traffic will get a clear road through loops, but a high proportion of the trains on the Tauern and Arlberg routes are international: and international services, passenger as well as freight, are notoriously prone to stray from their timetables. At peak traffic periods, inevitably, Tauern route expresses are liable to kick their heels in at least one loop on their way from Carinthia to Salzburg or vice versa.

All this explains why the prime morning train from the Carinthian provincial capital, Klagenfurt, to the north has to be allowed as much as 173 minutes (in the timetable current as this is written) to run the 117.5 miles from Villach, focal junction for traffic to and from Yugoslavia, to Salzburg inclusive of seven intermediate stops. The overall average of just under 41mph that this schedule represents looks commercially etiolated now that an *autobahn* tunnels through the Tauern mountains east of the railway.

The OBB is laying a second track and smoothing out curves where this is topographically feasible on both Arlberg and Tauern routes, but in a ten-year programme the sights cannot be set higher than a total of 175 miles covering both lines, because the rugged environment makes every mile of realignment so costly and physically demanding. The easing of some particularly cramping curves and the laying of a mile or two of new double track on the Tauern's southern slope which was finished in 1978,

for example, entailed erection of three superbly soaring viaducts in vertiginous sites high up the mountainsides above the Möll valley: one was 1236ft long and 394ft high, the second 1037ft long and 246ft high, the third 925ft long and 394ft high. This was the only way to procure a straight alignment and eliminate the sharp curves round the mountain buttresses enclosing chasmic gorges to which, for economy's sake, the Tauern's builders resigned themselves in the first decade of this century. On the other side of Villach, the Austrians and Yugoslavs have recently combined to double the track through the Karawanken Tunnel, on the vital route to Jesenice in Yugoslavia. A signalling block post is to be set up in the tunnel to make two sections within the bore and that will raise its operating capacity to about 100 trains each way daily, four times what was possible in the mid-1970s when the 4.96-mile tunnel was still single-track.

The new locomotive-hauled Vienna–Basle 'Transalpin' on the Arlberg route's Trissanna bridge. Located on the eastern slope to the Arlberg Tunnel five miles west of Landeck, the bridge is seen with the steel bowstring arch that was erected in place of its original truss span in 1964 to ease a severe speed restriction. The 394ft-long span carries the railway 287ft above the ground.

The Brenner route, which leads from Innsbruck into the Italian Tyrol and eventually debouches into the Italian State Railways' (FS) trunk network at Verona on the Milan–Venice main line, is the OBB's busiest international thoroughfare. It is the channel for passenger traffic between West Germany, Italy's inland cities and her popular Adriatic coastline as well as for a heavy tonnage of freight. This is another stiffly graded line, more so on the Austrian side of the frontier, where the railway climbs 2405ft on a ruling grade of 1 in 40 in the 23 miles from Innsbruck – through magnificent mountain scenery, one should interpolate – to the Brenner border station in the pass.

Equally, the Brenner is yet another main line engineered with all-consuming anxiety for economy, avoiding earthworks by curvature wherever possible, so that it concedes no higher speed than the Tauern. Consequently its daily TEE, the Munich–Milan 'Mediolanum', takes three hours 35 minutes over the $171\frac{1}{4}$ miles from Innsbruck to Verona even though it stops on the way only at the Brenner, Bolzano and Trento and is held for no more than 13 minutes at the frontier, not the 25–30 minutes of frustration inflicted on other trains while the border bureacracy goes through its leisurely routines. As on all TEEs, 'Mediolanum' passengers are scrutinized and catechized on the move, but a pause at Brenner is inevitable to change locomotives, since the Italian electrification is 3kV DC.

The 1970s completion of a Brenner autobahn/autostrada the whole way from Innsbruck to Italy's Po Valley has not alleviated worry at the Brenner railway's inadequacy in the transport market conditions of the 1980s and 1990s. Anxiety is almost as acute in Bavaria, the nearest West German territory, as it is in Austria. The Austrians' intensifying concern to limit the international road freight exploiting

their country as a corridor is shared to a considerable degree by the Bavarians now that West Germany's prodigal investment in motorways has yielded autobahnen the whole way from Hamburg to Bavaria's border with Austria.

Consequently the Bavarian provincial Government has been as vociferous as many Austrians in calling for action on the concept of a new Brenner base tunnel. This tunnel figures in the long-range plan of the International Union of Railways (UIC) to upgrade for higher speed a key network of international routes in Europe. In mind is a well-aligned and easily graded base tunnel 35 miles long, going underground at Innsbruck and emerging in Italy at Brixen, north of the Italian Tyrol 'capital', Bozen, though the Italians would prefer a shorter, less expensive tunnel eliminating just the crown of the present route. To go with it super-optimists would like to see a new 150mph railway built from Munich to Innsbruck and something similar from Brixen to the Po plain, to supersede the present serpentine main line of the FS down the Trento valley from Bozen to Verona. But since the tunnel alone would cost at least £1 billion ($2 billion), it needs sanguine faith in a world economic revival to envisage execution of any part of the scheme. The same goes for other base-tunnel plans cherished by the OBB and the UIC, which include one of 45 miles obviating almost the whole of the present Tauern main line and another of 13 miles to bypass the worst of the Semmering pass grades on the main line southwestwards from Vienna to Graz.

The OBB's more immediate, practical objective so far as inter-city passenger business is concerned is the modest one of adding to the route-mileage fit for its present maximum speed limit of 140kmph (87mph); it is not ambitious of anything higher at the moment. As yet the only route where this maximum is permissible quite consistently is the east–west transversal from Vienna to Salzburg, which has some well-aligned stretches of considerable length. Consequently the prestige westbound morning train from Vienna, the 'Transalpin' to Basle, just edges into the mile-a-minute bracket with an overall time of three hours 12 minutes for the 198 miles to Salzburg, a single intermediate call at Linz included. It might do better still if inter-city trains did not have to contest track space with such a weight of freight traffic, for which loops off the double-track main line are comparatively infrequent. The OBB mitigates this difficulty by extensive signalling of the double track for reversible working on each line and then by exploiting gaps in the timetable one way to loop faster trains around slower in the opposite direction; one can easily get bemused as to which is the theoretical rule of the road on the OBB, left or right (it is, in fact, right), so protracted sometimes are a fast passenger train's sojourns on the wrong line.

West of Salzburg, incidentally, the 'Transalpin' becomes one of the peculiarities of the OBB inter-

The Vienna–Basle 'Transalpin' at Kufstein, on the Austro-German border. Between here and Freilassing it crosses a finger of West German territory as a sealed 'Corridor train'. The new Eurofima train-sets of the 'Transalpin' were the first on the OBB to be equipped with passenger telephone service, a facility which quickly proved so popular that at the start of the 1980s the OBB was extending it to some Class 4010 electric multiple-units on the Vienna–Salzburg–Innsbruck trunk route.

Exterior and first-class saloon interior of one of the Class 4010 electric multiple-units which covered the bulk of the OBB's internal inter-city services at the start of the 1980s.

city timetable on its spinal east-west main line – a *Korridorzug*, or 'Corridor train'. The delineation of Austria's frontiers protruded a finger of West German territory between Salzburg and Innsbruck, and to move all traffic between the two cities entirely on OBB metals would not only choke the double track between Salzburg and Schwarzach St Veit (the Tauern traffic's exit from Salzburg) but inflict an intolerable speed penalty on passenger trains even if there were spare capacity, because of the tortuous character of the route through the narrow, steep-walled Pass Lueg and the clefts of Pongau to Zell-am-See. Consequently through OBB trains between Salzburg, Innsbruck, Buchs and Bregenz at the western tip of Austria take the easier route across the West German extrusion, sharing German Federal (DB) tracks to Rosenheim, where they join the DB main line from Munich, then re-enter their own territory at Kufstein. During their passage of West German territory the OBB *Korridorzüge* are 'bonded' – that is, passengers are theoretically sealed in their coaches and no business is transacted on DB ground. (A similar arrangement is applied to some workings over the Karwendel line, which meanders in and out of the two territories on its deliciously scenic route from Innsbruck to southern Germany via Garmisch

Partenkirchen, catering for some popular Austrian winter sports centres on the way.) So vital to the OBB's arterial operation is the DB sector from the outskirts of Salzburg to Kufstein that in 1979 the OBB reached agreement with the DB whereby the latter's construction of a spur on its own ground at Rosenheim, to give OBB trains a through run and obviate the reversal in Rosenheim station dictated by the junction's historic layout, would be financed by Austrian payments of £200 to £325 ($450–730) for each and every OBB train movement taking advantage of the new curve.

The reversals entailed in a number of itineraries influenced the OBB to adopt the double-ended multiple-unit format when it renewed its inter-city equipment from the 1950s onward. The bulk of its inter-city timetable at the start of the 1980s was furnished by six-car, fully air-conditioned electric train-sets to a design of the mid-1960s (but multiplied as recently as 1976) which are classified 4010. Developed from a four-car unit (Class 4030) conceived in 1956 to pioneer the 'Transalpin' service, the 4010 is essentially a compact 3350hp locomotive and five cars, including a restaurant, permanently coupled. Its sparkling livery of overall ivory with a broad, window-enclosing band of ultramarine and lining

Exterior and interior of the OBB's latest type of restaurant car. Until recently most of the system's restaurants were embodied in the Class 4010 multiple-unit formations, but with the trend to locomotive-hauled formations the OBB uniquely had a series of kitchen-restaurant cars built within the standard Eurofima body-shell, like this one. Some of these new cars have a smaller kitchen-restaurant and use part of the body for ordinary compartments.

flourishes of bright red is a hallmark of unexceptionable ride quality on the OBB's prevalently long-welded rail and of seating comfort that, despite the 4010's mounting years, does not surrender many points to Europe's latest models, especially in the generously spaced reclining seats of the first-class saloons. The diners, which are catered by the International Wagons-Lits Company, offer, besides set lunches and dinners, a journey-long *á la carte* service from a menu almost as compendious as that of neighbouring West Germany's DSG. The OBB's inter-city trains are all named and nowadays are run to a consistent pattern in the regular-interval time-tables which the OBB has been progressively applying to its whole passenger network as a component of the energetic marketing programme launched following a reshuffle of the OBB's top management in 1974.

The window-dressing of that marketing offensive has included an abrupt departure from the drab green which used to merge all locomotive-hauled OBB trains into the landscape. Every locomotive, shunters included, is now taking on an overall bright scarlet, lined with cream; and the low-slung Swiss-type coaches of which the OBB has acquired a large fleet for its internal services (the Austrians categorize them as 'Schlieren coaches', after the Swiss builders who originated them) stand out in overall ivory with a band of scarlet enclosing their windows. All electric multiple-units are donning the same livery as the Class 4010 sets, partly because the OBB regards a tri-tone, light-dark-light colour scheme as a good compromise between aesthetics and premonitory conspicuousness to men working on the track.

Still more colour has been splashed over the domestic OBB fleet since the railway became one of the major customers for the so-called European standard coach in its distinctive – and supposedly universal – livery of bright orange-red with grey waistband.

To digress from the OBB briefly, this project should have opened a significant new chapter in the rationalization of European mainland railway in-

vestment. Since the last war railway managements have co-operated to an unprecedented extent in mutual exchange of technical information within the International Union of Railways (the UIC, head-quartered in Brussels), but not in pooling research, design and production. While the same models of Ford automobile, for instance, throng every road in the Continent and the same Boeing airliner types fly under practically every national airline insignia, product standardization on the railways has been minimal. It has been largely limited to components, such as bogies and suspension systems, apart from mass production of at least one wagon design and of basically French and West German passenger coach designs of the 1950s. Most ludicrously and uneconomically of all, of course, each major railway has pursued an entirely independent line of research and development into high-speed passenger railways and rolling-stock.

In the 1960s the mainland European railways grasped the fact that to counter the steady betterment of air and automobile comfort and convenience the exclusive 'Trans-Europ Express' amenity standards of the 1960s must become the non-supplementary fare inter-city rail norm of the 1980s, at the latest. If the inter-city concept demanded upgrading internationally, urged the UIC, then here was a prime case for standard equipment from a marketing as well as an economic angle.

The principal administrations agreed and committees set about hammering out a specification that would pass universal muster. They eventually gave laborious birth early in 1974 and a total of 500 standard coaches were ordered from builders in four countries – Linke-Hofmann-Busch of West Germany, la Brugeoise et Nivelles of Belgium, Alsthom of France and Fiat of Italy – for delivery in varying quantities to the national systems of Italy (FS), France (SNCF), Belgium (SNCB), Switzerland (SBB), West Germany (DB) and Austria (OBB). Construction was financed by Eurofima, the Swiss-based company set up by the European railways after the last war to raise capital for new rolling stock and remunerate its subscribers through leasing.

These air-conditioned Eurofima coaches began filtering into service in 1977. They integrate components and design detail from various national sources – most importantly, perhaps, their bogie design originates with Fiat in Italy – but in outline they are predominantly DB. In fact, it needs a keen eye to distinguish them externally from the DB's majestic TEE and IC vehicles – not least because the DB has had its Eurofima coaches painted in its standard TEE and IC livery of red and cream!

Incomprehensibly, since a general European trend to an open saloon configuration for second-class accommodation was patent, the committeemen voted for a compartment layout seating three a side in the Eurofima second-class coach design. Within the then-standard 26.4m length of European mainland coaches on the international circuit that afforded a total of 66 seats in 11 compartments per coach as against 72 in existing DB Inter-City seconds with 12 less roomy compartments and as many as 88 in the latest SNCF Corail stock open saloon seconds. Through inflation and refinements, notably air-conditioning, the first cost of a Eurofima compartment second would anyway be a hefty 80 percent more than the accounting book figure for one of its existing compartment seconds, according to the DB, but per passenger seat the price increase was alleged to be 100 percent more, because of the capacity reduction; on a passenger-mile basis a switch to the Eurofima seconds would therefore inflate the total inter-city operating costs in that class by 16 percent overnight. The DB consequently confined its Eurofima purchases to compartment firsts, opting – as already described – to build its own air-conditioned 80-seater open-saloon seconds for its reshaped 'Inter-city' operation and to study a 12-compartment concept in a longer, 27.5m vehicle. The French have likewise spurned the Eurofima compartment second, though they are retaining that configuration as well as the open saloon in their Corail coach fleet. The SNCF is securing the high capacity per compartment coach to cover the cost of air-conditioning not by length but by enlarged body width, which the French claim is possible because their latest Type Y32 bogie constricts lateral body movement and thus wins them a bit more breadth from the leading gauge. By complementary slimming of interior partitions and a fractional narrowing of the lateral corridor they claim to have gained enough room for four-a-side seating in tolerable comfort, so that they will achieve an 88-seat total in 11 compartments, exactly the same as in a Corail open saloon.

The DB has subsequently detached its Eurofima first-class cars from every 'Inter-City' train-set timed at the line limit over its 125mph sectors (a maximum for which the Eurofima stock was supposed to be engineered), complaining that consistent service at 100mph-plus had the coaches side-tracked over-

An outstanding feature of the Eurofima compartment coach design is the width of its side vestibule. Air-conditioning is standard.

frequently for reprofiling of bogie tyres. Perhaps implicitly supporting the DB, both SBB and OBB announced almost simultaneously that their second batch of orders for Eurofima-patterned coaches, besides incorporating other changes of detail, would be mounted on bogies evolved by their own national supply industries, Simmering-Graz-Pauker in the case of the OBB and Schindler for the SBB coaches.

Agreement on the Eurofima livery was only reached after a lengthy hassle, with the French and Germans arguing volubly for their own styles of Corail, and blue and beige respectively. The other four participants have adhered faithfully to the final choice of orange and light grey proposed by the Swiss. But the French have made, if anything, more nonsense of the Eurofima livery than the Germans. A substantial proportion of the SNCF's Eurofima coaches have been marshalled into formations of their latest Corail stock (see Chapter 2) on domestic routes and these have been painted in Corail livery to match; but conversely, where other Eurofima vehicles have been associated with earlier classes of SNCF air-conditioned coach on the chief non-TEE services between Paris, Brussels and Amsterdam, they have been left in the Eurofima livery, and it is the French coaches which have been repainted – in Eurofima style! The Dutch, one will observe, have steered clear of the whole business.

To return to Austria, the OBB was particularly hungry for a project of this kind because of its dearth of coaches fulfilling the stringent specifications the UIC now imposes on equipment in international service. From the start of 1980, amongst other things, the UIC has been insisting that all coach doors in a scheduled international train be capable of being locked by train staff from a single remote control point: that means, of course, that they must also be capable of closure by remote control before a train is flagged away from a station.

Lack of coaching stock meeting such requirements as this and, in addition, passed to run at the line speeds in excess of 140kmph permissible on inter-

The 'Transalpin', its coaches in the generally standard Eurofima livery of orange-red with white lining, pulls out of Vienna West for Salzburg, Innsbruck and Basle.

national routes in France and Germany has been costing the OBB money, because the vast proportion of international trains between Austria and her western neighbours consequently have to be formed of other administrations' stock. Given the gaily mixed palette from which the OBB draws its own liveries nowadays, that makes for some vivid contrasts of colour on Austrian main lines and at some key traffic centres, Vienna especially.

Preponderant is the coaching stock of the DB, in both red-and-cream and blue-and-cream, a great deal of which penetrates deep into Austria in complete train-sets, DSG restaurant cars or 'Quick-Pick' cafeteria cars included. The OBB relies quite substantially on the DB and DSG for diner service in locomotive-hauled trains since so much of its own restaurant-car resources are locked up in the permanently-coupled Class 4010 electric multiple-units, though its small fleet of independent kitchen-diners has at last been replenished by the inclusion in its Eurofima order of new diners, some with a layout unique to the OBB: three second-class compartments at one end of the body and the rest occupied by a kitchen and restaurant saloon. OBB Class 1042 electric locomotives have through workings to

Munich and Frankfurt-am-Main in West Germany, but they do not range as freely over DB metals as DB machines do over Austrian track. DB units from Munich, chiefly Class E111s, are a commonplace of the railway landscape at Villach, the Carinthian junction for Yugoslavia, at the Brenner pass change-over to Italian 3kV DC traction and as far east as Vienna (which, after Hitler's Austrian Anschlüss of 1937, was regularly host to the Reichsbahn's stream-lined Class 03.10 Pacifics in the last prewar years of steam).

The OBB desperately needs the new Eurofima coaches for some of its domestic inter-city routes, too, because the Class 4010 multiple-units, besides looking progressively more dated in their second-class accommodation, are an inflexible tool for the easily convenient service the OBB is now eagerly promoting. When a fixed-interval timetable is as intensive as, say, British Rail's 'Inter-City 125' the operators can argue – but even then not very convincingly – that passengers crowded out of one over-loaded train have not irritatingly long to wait for the next. When the frequency is two-hourly, as it generally is on the OBB, that apologia is quite un-acceptable. Peak demand must be met by strengthen-

ing the train's consist; and on OBB services implemented by 4010s, in which neither power car nor driving cab at the opposite end of the unit is vestibuled, this means either expensively doubling up with a whole second unit of six cars and a second restaurant car crew to ensure train catering for every passenger, or else hanging one or two of the Schlieren-type coaches on one unit's tail, in which event the extra vehicles' occupants are, of course, denied the restaurant service promised them by the timetable.

First of the hitherto regular 4010 multiple-unit workings to be transmuted to a locomotive-hauled operation with Eurofima coaches, in the spring of 1978, was the Vienna–Basle 'Transalpin'. At the same time the 'Transalpin' became the first scheduled OBB inter-city service to offer coin-in-the-slot telephone connections with the national network to its passengers. This was done by a radio link between train and the system established the length of Austria's *autobahnen* by the Posts & Telecommunications Ministry for the benefit of motorists with telephone-equipped cars; consequently the train's telephone kiosk, located in a corner of its diner, is operational only where the railway parallels an *autobahn* in close proximity, that is between Vienna and Salzburg and Innsbruck and Kufstein. This amenity has proved so popular that it is to be added to other OBB inter-city train-sets.

Vienna relies heavily for passenger movement on its intricate tramway network, which records nearly 70 percent of all short-distance passenger journeys within the metropolitan area. Bit by bit the tram tracks are being lowered underground in a pre-Metro operation to establish a *U-Bahn* system based on the German city pattern. Another component of the city's rail transport is the most antedeluvian (unquestionably) of all Western European city railways, the third-rail *Stadtbahn*; the strings of creaking four-wheelers which trundle the *Stadtbahn* loop, alternately burrowing underground and grumbling past the rooftops on elevated sections, are mostly relics of the 1920s.

Political and railway history bequeathed the OBB several terminals in Vienna, but some have lost a great deal of status since the Iron Curtain was brought down. In the splendid days of the Austro-Hungarian Empire the Franz-Joseph station, for example, ushered out Pullman and other *trains de luxe* to Imperial society's spas at Karlsbad, Marienbad and Franzenbad. Today, its platforms lately submerged under a glass-fronted confection of avant-garde commercial development, the terminus deals with only two trains a day to and from Prague and otherwise contents itself chiefly with a busy and newly electrified commuter service along the southern bank of the Danube on the Austrian rump of the Franz-Joseph Railway, which is now single track on the Czech side of the frontier station of Gmünd. Interesting, by the way, is one of the Franz-Joseph station's daily Prague services, the 'Vindo-

bona' to and from Berlin, which has run a fascinating gamut of equipment since its inauguration in January 1957 – first one of the prewar Reichsbahn Class VT137 'Flying Hamburger'-type diesel multiple-units then operated by the East German Reichsbahn (DR) in its original purple-and-cream livery; then from 1960 to 1962 a Czech multiple-unit; from 1962 to 1964 an OBB multiple-unit of the now obsolescent 5045 or 'Blue Lightning' series; from 1964 to 1972 Czech and East German diesel multiple-units in turn; from 1972 an East German Type 173 or 'Görlitz' type diesel multiple-unit with a flashy streamlined outline; and finally from spring 1979 a locomotive-hauled rake of OBB coaches and Czech diner.

Sparse nowadays are the through coaches between Western and Eastern Europe which need manoeuvring between Vienna's key termini – the handsomely modern Westbahnhof, which enfolds the main line from Salzburg and West Germany; and the Süd-bahnhof, principally the starting-point for Graz and southern Austria via the Semmering, but also for Budapest and, via one of the inner-city orbital routes of the OBB, for Moscow in a sleeper travelling via Czechoslovakia. In days of old the inter-station traffic was an absorbing facet of rail working in Vienna.

The one OBB line which cuts across Vienna close

The façade of Vienna West station, the Austrian capital's rail starting point for Linz, Salzburg, Innsbruck, West Germany and Switzerland.

Rennweg, a typical station on the Vienna *Schnellbahn*, the northeast to southwest railway traversing the capital which the OBB operates as a rapid transit system.

Schwarzach-St Veit, junction of the main lines from the Tauern and from Innsbruck via Zell am See to Salzburg, is a fine example of recent OBB station modernization in admirable stylistic keeping with the environment.

to its heart is probably the system's operational showpiece. This is primarily the route of the *Schnellbahn*, a rapid transit operation which has been progressively extended until it now stretches some 60 route-miles from Gänsendorf, northeast of the city, to Bernhardsthal in the southwest. Its regular-interval frequency is quarter-hourly in the off-peak, but at least twice as intensive in the rush-hour.

However, *Schnellbahn* trains have no segregated right-of-way in the metropolitan area. Their route has five vital points of contact with the main-line system and is therefore the key to a great deal of cross-city freight movement, which is the more intensive because of Vienna's innocence of one large-scale, automated marshalling yard – a crucial handicap to OBB's freight performance (of which more shortly). The *Schnellbahn* route is automatically signalled for close-headway working throughout, but even with all-electric operation it needs astute traffic regulators at each of the five junctions, in continuous telephonic touch with a central control room, to judge the respective gaits of freight and smartly accelerating multiple-units finely enough so that the two categories are interwoven without signal checks to either. Incidentally Vienna Mitte station on the *Schnellbahn* route is the starting-point of another recent rail acquisition in the Austrian capital, a direct link with its airport at Schwechat.

The Vienna *Schnellbahn* is subsidized both by the city authority and the Federal Government. The OBB is statutorily obliged to operate basic local passenger services with heavily discounted fares:

scholars and students even travel *free* between home and academic centre in term time. The Federal Government compensates the OBB for the shortfall on the mandatory cheap fares and also separates the financial provision for these local services on the one hand and the rest of the OBB on the other in its annual allocation of investment funds. Anxious to furnish more than a basic service, the OBB has lately been pressing the Vienna model successfully on city and provincial authorities elsewhere in the country, coaxing them into contracts to put up extra money of their own to finance station modernization, new car parks, enlargement of track capacity, etc, and then to underwrite a more intensive regular-interval train-service. (One might add that one of these authorities is a substantial railway operator in its own right: Styria runs both standard and 760mm-gauge lines under the banner of the Steiermärkische Landbahnen – the longest of them is the 48-mile narrow-gauge Murtalbahn from Unzmarkt to Mauterndorf.)

The OBB moves about half Austria's domestic freight, but that healthy global statistic masks the fact that too much of the rail share is unremunerative business which common carrier status obliges the railway to handle, while high-rated merchandise goes by road because of the railway's comparative inefficiency. At the start of the 1980s the OBB admitted that on average its goods wagons were over five days in transit.

The crippling factor, given the mainland European railways' dedication to wagonload freight, has been Austria's dearth of modern marshalling yards. At the end of the 1970s Salzburg–Gnigl, with a daily through-put capacity of 2000 wagons, was the OBB's only installation matching up to modern specifications. Operations were hobbled above all in Vienna, which still had to disperse its freight-train sorting and assembly over six flat yards so antiquated that their points were partly hand-worked and not one was blessed even with a hump. Too hemmed in for expansion, in sum, they could not cope with the city's freight peaks, when up to 18 additional yards further away might have to help out. At last, however, the

A late 1970s addition to Vienna's rail facilities was a direct link with the city's Schwechat airport, where a Class 4030 electric multiple-unit stands in the sub-surface station. Note the Vienna *Schnellbahn* logo just above the train-set's number on the lower front of the driving cab.

OBB has been granted the funds to invest in a big new automated yard with a potential daily through-put of 6000 wagons to fulfil the city's entire demand at Kledering; another has been started for Villach, the key freight junction for Yugoslavia; and a third is planned near Bregenz.

Meanwhile, the OBB is just about holding its own competitively by dint of aggressive marketing and a drive for the most disciplined working possible with its existing resources. Amongst other measures, the score of overnight fast merchandise freights which interlink all the country's main commercial centres, fed by and feeding into alertly monitored connecting local services, have been named to enhance their status psychologically with both railway operating staff and customers.

Practically all the OBB's present-day traction is Austrian built, with the name of Simmering-Graz-Pauker the most prominent in the construction credits. In the fading 1970s a number of pre-World War II types still survived, including some of the 'Crocodile' configuration nowadays venerated by afiocionados of electric traction history. The Swiss Federal adopted this layout of centre-cab 1-Co-Co-1 with long bonnets at each end as a mountain haulier for the Gotthard route in its early days and the Austrians followed suit with two types, Classes 1089 and 1189, in 1923–26, which in 1978 were still on freight duty in the Attnang-Puchheim area.

Under the tutelage of the German Reichsbahn in 1940 the Austrians bought its first Co-Cos, Class 1020, and in the mid-1950s ordered two more Co-Co types, the 5400hp Classes 1010 and 1110. Since then, unlike the Swiss, the OBB has opted exclusively for Bo-Bos, content to double-head the heaviest loads over its mountain trunk routes. The closely related Classes 1040, 1041 and 1141 of the 1950s, ranging from 3200 to 3400hp and devised originally for general mixed duty, have been relegated for the most part to freight and secondary passenger work since the 1963 debut of Class 1042. The first 60 of this type were rated at 4770hp, but in the second batch of 197, sub-classified 1042.5, the output was upped to 5360hp and a maximum speed of 93.8mph made permissible for an overall weight of 84 tonnes, only a fraction more than that of the SGP Bo-Bo designs of the 1950s.

The 1042s more or less probed the limits of orthodox electric Bo-Bo locomotive design. So, in 1969–70, the OBB borrowed thyristor-control Bo-Bos for trials on the long climbs of the Semmering route from Vienna to Graz, which are on a ruling gradient of 1 in 40 for 17.5 miles of the northeastern slope from Gloggnitz to the summit and for eight miles of the southwestern descent to Mürzzuschlag. The first loan was the experimentally thyristor-equipped Re4/4 No 161 of Switzerland's BLS Railway, the second one of Swedish Railways' ASEA-built Class Rc2s. The outcome was an order to ASEA for ten 4830hp thyristor-equipped Bo-Bos, delivered in 1971 and classified 1043 by the OBB; the 1043s are

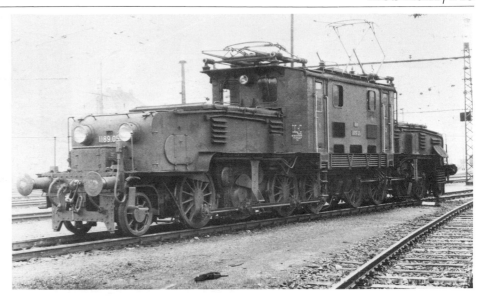

all based at Villach and employed chiefly on heavy freight haulage over the mountain routes.

Building on experience with the 1043s, the OBB has called for thyristor control in its latest SGP-built type, the Class 1044 with a very impressive peak output of 7250hp and 100mph capability. The first of a 50-unit order was delivered at the end of 1977. The 1044s can take all but the heaviest trains over any of the mountain main lines single-handed, since their load limits over the Semmering, Arlberg and Tauern routes are 500, 550 and 580 tonnes respectively.

The OBB's secondary passenger equipment gets more urgently in need of comprehensive renewal by the year. On rural lines and even on the main lines away from the conurbations many short-distance stopping trains, the *Personenzüge*, were still a mix of decrepit 1930s-vintage bogie and rigid-axle vehicles at the end of the 1970s. The Vienna *Schnellbahn* and other conurbation services were better served by Class 4030 and 4130 electric multiple-units, but even these are of mid-1950s design, disguised to a degree by the interior refurbishing which the OBB is apply-

A Class 1089, one of the few historic 'Crocodile'-type electric locomotives to a design derived from the Swiss which the OBB was still operating at the end of the 1970s.

The ten 4830hp Class 1043 Bo-Bos with thyristor control of the OBB were built by ASEA in Sweden. As a result of its experience with these machines the OBB ordered thyristor control in its latest type, the Austrian-built Class 1044.

evaluating one of the German Federal's ET420 electric multiple-units in Vienna commuter traffic. Finally, one ought not to complete this cursory review of the OBB's most recent electric traction without mention of the useful Class 4061, a 2200hp unit of the mid-1950s for secondary passenger work which yields about one-third of its body area to a capacious baggage compartment; the 4061s are, in fact, designated as motor brake-vans.

The OBB's sizable diesel locomotive stud displays a marked preference for hydraulic transmissions and, as with the electrics, for local industry. Only two recent types, the 1000hp Class 2045 and 1520hp Class 2050, are diesel-electric and the latter are the only significant main-line machines of foreign build, by Henschel. The rest, distinctively Austrian in outline, are the products of SGP or Jenbacher Werke, with Voith hydraulic transmissions from West Germany; none but a single prototype, Class 2020, has a rated output higher than 1500hp. One should add that the OBB deploys both diesel and electric locomotives for its 760mm-gauge lines.

The OBB cleared the final remnants of steam from its adhesion-worked standard gauge in late 1976, but one steam bastion survived, a Mecca for the steam buff – the rack-assisted Eisenerz–Vordernberg line in Styria, which clambers up 1 in 14 grades to the ore faces in the extraordinary 2400ft Iron Mountain. The line's passenger traffic had long since been entrusted to some of the Class 5081 Uerdingen four-wheeled railbuses of German manufacture which the OBB operates along with bogie diesel railcars of Austrian build, but the freight was left in the charge of the Erzberg line's specialized steam. Steam power included some remarkable rack-and-adhesion 0-12-0 tanks with driving wheels of only 3ft 5½in diameter and Herculean tractive effort that were designed by the renowned Austrian master of steam, Karl Gölsdorf, in 1913. Steam was not dismissed until the

Above:
The OBB's latest electric locomotive type, the 7250hp Class 1044 Bo-Bo.
Below:
Predecessor of the Class 1044 was the 5360hp Class 1042.5
Bottom:
A Class 4030 EMU.

ing pending ability to finance general replacement.

At least the forerunners of the next-generation electric multiple-units had taken the tracks by 1979, 40 three-car units of Class 4020 with thyristor control and enhanced power by comparison with the 4030; they were assigned to the Vienna area. The OBB elected to develop its own design after borrowing and

spring of 1978, when tests convinced the Austrian Transport Ministry that the freight trains could be safely managed by a pair of standard 1500hp Class 2043 diesel-hydraulics relying on simple adhesion, provided they were specially equipped with electro-

magnetic track brakes and devices ensuring automatic brake application should the line speed limit of 20mph be exceeded. For the present the Abt rack remains *in situ* and some of the line's idiosyncratic steam is mothballed for possible special train work.

Above:
The OBB's Eisenerz–Vordernberg line.
Below, left to right:
Class 4020 interior and exterior.

7.
RAILWAYS AROUND THE MEDITERRANEAN AND THE ADRIATIC

Manarola – between Genoa and La Spezia – an express of Ale601 electric power cars and multiple-unit trailers heading for Genoa.

A Class E444 Bo-Bo heads one of the FS system's domestic TEEs, the Milan–Bologne–Ancona–Bari 'Adriatico'. For internal service the Fiat-built coaches are liveried dark blue and white with red lining.

The Italian State Railways (FS) confronted as formidable a repair and reconstruction job as anyone after World War II. They made a splendid job of it – with one qualification. The system was restored almost precisely to its physical state of the 1930s (with some notable exceptions: in particular, the magnificently styled and furnished new central station in the country's capital, Rome Termini, which was constructed with the benefit of Marshall Aid rehabilitation dollars from the USA). On the one hand this respect for the status quo conserved all the rural branches which quickly became grossly un-economic anachronisms in the postwar motor trans-port age, but which local political pressures made it exasperatingly difficult to close. On the other it did nothing to enlarge the operating capacity of key trunk routes, some of them still partly single-track as they had been originally built for economy; and the evolving postwar concentration of industry would pile progressively more FS traffic on to these main lines.

Today very nearly half the FS business is chan-nelled over one-eighth of its total route mileage and about 30 percent of its traffic is crowded on to the 865-mile spinal chord stretching from the Swiss border at Chiasso through Milan, Bologna, Florence, Rome and Naples to the train ferry port for Sicily on the Straits of Messina at Reggio Calabria. The FS

capacity problem has been aggravated, too, by the upsurge of European international trade since the creation of the European Economic Community, the EEC or Common Market. The post-oil crisis recession of the later 1970s has kept the total volume in check, but the strength of the Swiss currency has diverted a huge tonnage of rail freight to the Mont Cenis trans-alpine tunnel route between France and Italy, some of it bound for Eastern Bloc countries and the Middle East, as discussed in an earlier chapter. Yet this line's most steeply graded (and scenically superb) final sector from Turin up to the tunnel was built mainly as single track. Mention of the Mont Cenis route's gradients is a reminder, too, that much of the FS trunk network is snagged by curves and inclines enforced on its original main-line builders by the Apennine mountains' dominance of so much central Italian land area.

The priority for the FS directors since the 1950s, consequently, has been to enlarge key trunk route capacity by eliminating single-track wherever traffic density exceeds 70 trains daily; by electrifying and upgrading subsidiary lines which, linked up new connections, can be integrated as a relief route; or in one vital instance, by building an entirely new main line. The FS began bypasses of two of its most con-stricting main-line sectors soon after its creation as a national system in 1905 – it was the first in Europe, in fact, to plan supercession of 19th-century routes that were no match for 20th-century transport market demand. Initially progress was halting, but under Mussolini's Fascist regime, with its chauvinistic anxiety that Italian technology should dazzle the world, both were given fresh impetus.

The first new *direttissima* taking a well-aligned and easily graded coastal route from Rome to Naples was opened in late 1927 and by 1939 was running electric multiple-units between the two cities at an average of 72.5mph, start to stop. The more titanic enterprise, however, was the second *direttissima* finished in 1934, which drove the 11.5-mile Apennine tunnel through the mountains to obviate the pioneer route from Bologna to Florence that had wound and clambered up to a 2021ft summit at Pracchia on inclines as fierce as 1 in 45. On this second *direttissima*, the Italians staged a phenomenal demonstration of their electric traction technology on 20 July 1939, flighting a three-car Type ETR201 electric multiple-unit the whole 195.8 miles from Florence to Milan at a start-to-stop average of 102mph – and that despite the fact that the new *direttissima*, though much more comfortably curved than the old line, had to approach the Apennine tunnel on all but 11 miles of sustained 1 in 106 gradient. The restraint this imposed was offset by an average of 109mph for 124 miles across the plains of the great Po valley between Bologna and Milan, one of the few long-established FS racetracks, where the ETR201 touched a maximum of 126mph.

Postwar Italian governments have not been as generous with investment allowances as the latter-day FS desperately needs to redevelop its trunk routes (one brake on strategic investment in the railways for system-wide benefit is Rome's political anxiety to disburse a steady capital flow to the impoverished, underdeveloped south of the country). Nevertheless critical improvements have already been achieved, several of them financially and structurally daunting. Along the Levantine Riviera coast, where the mountains loom almost straight up from the sea between the outskirts of Genoa and La Spezia and the main line from France, Turin and Genoa to Rome is tunnelling through rock buttresses for over half the distance or else leaping over gullies on 14 major viaducts, the operationally crippling single track is at last double throughout. Similarly difficult widening has eliminated some of the single track on the important coastal route between Genoa and the French Riviera border at Ventimiglia, and is doubling that bottleneck on the upper reaches of the Mont Cenis track already mentioned. In the south the trunk route from Naples to the Sicilian ferries on the Straits of Messina has been doubled throughout and had many of its once cramped curves realigned to allow significant betterment of train times; a great deal of the Adriatic coast main line from Ancona to San Severo and the south is newly doubled, too. An outstanding instance of capacity enlargement by the integration and electrification of previously in-coherent secondary lines is the creation of a double-track Naples bypass for through north-south freight; it leaves the original inland Rome–Naples main line via Cassino at Cancello, veers inland of Mount Vesuvius and rejoins the Naples–Sicily trunk route at Salerno.

This last enterprise is a component of the biggest FS scheme of all: the effective quadrupling of that spinal chord route all the way from Milan to the south of Naples at Salerno. Extra tracks have already been laid at the Milan and Florence ends of the sector across the Po plain, in the centre of which, between Piacenza and Bologna, the FS dreams of laying down a long stretch aligned for 150mph. That is already possible – but in theory only, as I will explain in a moment – on the completed stretches of Italy's third *direttissima*, the massively expensive new double-track railway which the Italians have been slowly and rather painfully building from the outskirts of Rome to Florence since the start of the 1970s. Further south, the old Rome–Naples line via Cassino has lately been electrified to keep north-south freight clear of the coastal *direttissima*.

The traditional Rome–Florence main line pursues such a serpentine course around the hills and mountains flanking the Tiber valley that for the first 90 miles or so out of Rome the line speed limit is obligatorily 110kmph (68mph). Thus 63–64mph was the best average speed at which a Rome–Milan express could be timed over the first 196.3 miles of its itinerary to Florence, in sharp contrast to the 84–85mph timings feasible across the Po valley in the 135.5 miles from Bologna to Milan. The case for a new Rome–Florence railway to enlarge operating capacity was reinforced by the urgent need of a more speed-conducive alignment if the FS was to stay in credible contention for premium Rome–Milan passenger traffic with the north-south *Autostrada del Sol* and the airlines.

A Class E656 Bo-Bo-Bo hurries an express over the completed section of the new Rome–Florence *direttissima*, which has been engineered for 180mph, although at the start of the 1980s a limit of 112.5mph was imposed on all its trains apart from the automatic tilt-body 'Pendolino', which was permitted 125mph.

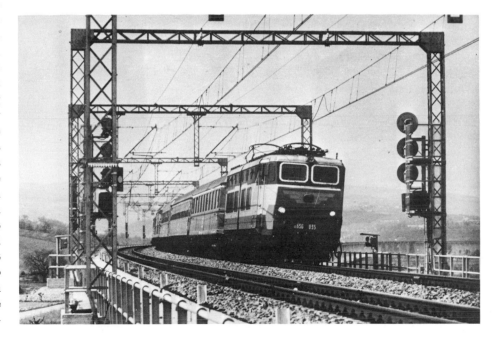

Two views of the 3.3 mile-long Allerona viaduct over the Paglia valley on the new Rome–Florence *direttissima*. This is one of the longest stonework structures in the world.

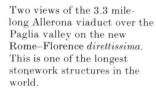

The start of one of the complex bi-directional arrangements of flying and burrowing junctions between the new Rome–Florence *direttissima*, seen here in the centre, and the old route between the two cities, which allows the parallel lines to be operated to all intents and purposes as a four-track trunk route.

The priority requirement, however, was extra tracks to share the old route's near choking peak load of 100 trains each way daily, among them a few passenger expresses running to as many as 20 coaches. With mixed traffic use seemingly an objective from the start, and flexibility to switch trains from old route to new or vice versa (provided for the operators by eight very elaborate complexes of bi-directional burrowing and flying junctions at intervals in the planned 145-mile length of new line), one is baffled that the Italians incurred the enormous cost – in such terrain – of engineering the Rome–Florence *direttissma* for a potential top speed as high as 185mph. It is the more stupefying because they have installed a traction current supply system which could cope with the simultaneous demands in a single feeder section only of very lightweight and infrequent trains running at more than 125mph.

What that speed ambition and the resultant compulsion to restrain curvature and grading very strictly has entailed in engineering cost can be imagined from the statistics: 34 percent of the first 76 miles of *direttissima* north of Rome is in tunnel and 15 percent is on bridges or viaducts. Of the 17 separate tunnels in this distance, Orte is 5.8 miles long and Monte Sorate 3.5 miles. Further north the railway sweeps across the Paglia River valley on one of the world's longest stonework viaducts to date, the 3.3-mile Allerona. And more extensive tunnelling, including one bore of nine miles and another of 6.8 miles, will be needed to bring the *direttissima* into Florence. The Italians were hopelessly optimistic in their first completion date forecasts, which have been negated by a combination of Government tardiness in funding successive stages of the exercise (especially since the mid-1970s recession – for a period it looked as though the *direttissima* might be stalled unfinished), environmental argument (over the approach to Florence above all) and plain underestimation of engineering problems. The southern half of the new line is already operational, but arrival in Florence now looks unlikely before 1983.

Up to the end of the 1970s availability of a substantial section of the *direttissima* had made little of

the anticipated impact on FS Rome–Florence express schedules since, inexplicably, a 180kmph (112.5mph) limit was clamped on its tracks, even for electric traction units with a designed 125mph capability. As long ago as the early 1960s the FS set itself a 125mph operational target on its principal trunk routes wherever the topography permitted. To this end it began equipping its main lines for the transmission through the signalling system's track circuitry of coded impulses, to be picked up by inductive receivers beneath traction units and converted into a continuous display of signalling aspects on the driver's control console. But so far this driving aid has not been held to justify more than a modest lift of the maximum to 100mph from the 93mph (150kmph) which is the prevalent FS trunk route limit. A handful of exceptions includes some 50 miles of the Rome–Naples *direttissima*, where a fourth, advance warning aspect has been added to the signalling to allow a speed limit of 112.5mph. In the earlier 1970s this was the fastest FS inter-city route, with the two cities linked daily by a pair of *rapidi* making the 130.5 miles non-stop in $1\frac{1}{2}$ hours flat at an average of 87mph, but latterly the timings have been relaxed by five minutes.

At the time of writing these Rome–Naples *rapidi*

are furnished by multiple-unit train-sets drawn from the final series of Type Ale601 motor coaches and their range of companion trailers, which includes kitchen-restaurant and restaurant-bar cars as well as pure seating vehicles. Premiered in 1961, these light-weight vehicles still fulfil many FS inter-city duties. They are not maintained as semi-permanent formations, but marshalled in whatever mix of catering and seating cars of either class suits the traffic demand of a specific service – always, of course, with sufficient power cars inserted to match the total tonnage of the rake. Only five of the initial series of Ale601 power cars, which were subsequently modified for higher speed (and proved themselves at up to 155mph in tests over the Rome–Naples *direttissima*, incidentally), plus the final 1970 series have 100mph-plus capability, however.

The FS entered the 1980s with about 150 electric locomotives and multiple-units powered, geared and passed for 125mph operation, but only one was exploiting this potential. The 125mph locomotives are the 80-tonne, 5600hp Class E444 Bo-Bos dating from 1967 which the FS, with ponderous wit, designated the *Tartaruga*, or 'Tortoise'. In the 1970s the FS talked seriously of 'stretching' the E444 into an 8500hp, six-axle E666 as a tool for 1½-hour Rome–Florence scheduling over the new *direttissima*, which for the distance of 157.8 miles would represent an average of 105mph. Designs were published, too, of a new high-speed Ale541 inter-city electric multiple-unit power car, but since then neither project has left the drawing-board.

The E444s are staple power for the FS 'Trans-Europ Express' and flagship inter-city services on Italy's domestic trunk routes which are locomotive hauled. As on West Germany's DB, these two train categories are distinguishable only by livery, since the FS has applied to both the handsome air-conditioned vehicles which Fiat was commissioned to design and build primarily for the FS-equipped TEE services in 1972. The TEE coaches are liveried in the international scheme's red and cream, the others in dark blue and light grey with broad horizontal red lining, a style which also characterizes the E444s. A number of these FS *rapidi* are equipped with telephone booths from which passengers can make national and international calls.

Striking nonconformists in the FS inter-city fleet are the three Type ETR300 seven-car electric multiple-units which are dedicated exclusively to the Rome–Milan 'Settebello' service, nowadays branded a TEE. Now more than a quarter of a century old the ETR300s do not ride as sweetly as later equipment embodying the major advances in ride and suspension technology of the 1960s and 1970s, but nothing built since has been more sumptuously furnished. Glumly realizing that it would be decades, not years, before they could rehabilitate their war-ravaged system to make their stunning speed stunts of 1939 daily operational practice, the Italians decided in

Close-up of a Class Ale601 electric power car fronting an inter-city multiple-unit formation.

1953 to offer the Rome–Milan inter-city market unexampled luxury as next best. The passenger space of the all-first-class, air-conditioned ETR300s was laid out entirely as elegant ten-seater lounges, with settees against each lateral wall and free-standing armchairs in the centre of the room. The restaurant and bar of each set, an aesthetic delight in the contemporary Italian decor, were just as impressive, but most eye-catching of all was the nose-end layout, with each driving cab raised like a plane cockpit to clear the floor below for a panoramic passenger observation saloon. The FS at first planned a whole series of ETR300s, but pulled in their horns and built only two in 1953, adding a third six years later. A four-coach variant, the ETR250, emerged in 1960, but only four were constructed. The ETR300s, too, have been equipped to operate at 125mph, but are not run at that pace, even over the Florence–Rome *direttissima*.

Until the ETR300s the FS livery was a uniform,

First-class saloon in the Fiat-built stock employed on the internal TEEs and other front rank inter-city services of the FS.

Top:
A Class E444 Bo-Bo
approaches Rome Termini
with the 06.18 express from
Turin in June 1978.
Above:
An ETR300 'Settebello'
electric train-set and one of
its lounge compartments.

drab brown, insignificantly relieved by the use of two shades. This is still the style of all the older and menial classes of electric locomotive, but to the ETR300s the FS applied a refreshing new style of pastel grey and brilliant green which was subsequently applied to all inter-city electric multiple-unit vehicles and to the E646 electric locomotives, of which more shortly.

Before long, happily, a two-tone green and khaki brown livery brightened all main-line diesel locomotives and a variety of other two-tone styles was applied to new classes of secondary service electric and diesel multiple-unit. The bulk of the FS locomotive-hauled coaching stock, on the other hand, looks as lacklustre as ever it did, whatever its vintage; true, the colour has changed, but to an overall, mechanically-sprayed dark grey, from which the only relief is the Fiat luxury coaches already mentioned and the FS quota of Eurofima standard inter-city coaches (see Chapter 6).

The present-day FS 3000V DC electric locomotive fleet is dominated by well over a thousand machines of a distinctive articulated Bo-Bo-Bo layout. The FS pioneered it way back in 1928, when the first Class E626s were built for the mountainous Benevento–Foggia line in the south of the country, following 1926 trials of a prototype Class E625. Spread of the electrical equipment over two body halves articulated across a centre bogie looked a sound way of packing more power into a locomotive without the penalties of a wheelbase too long or individual axle-weights too ponderous for the many sharply curved main lines of the FS network. The E626 was succeeded from 1940 by the E636 with improved speed potential; then in the mid-1950s came the E645 and E646 classes in which the power was doubled to 4670hp by the unusual device of fitting every axle with two traction motors, for a total of 12 per locomotive. The E645s were geared for lower top speed and higher tractive effort to fit them for mixed traffic duty on the mountainous routes, but the E646s, arranged for

90mph maximum, became the system's primary heavy express passenger power.

The next version of this Bo-Bo-Bo breed, introduced in 1976, was the 120-tonne E656 in which the peak output was hoisted to 5630hp and the maximum pace to 100mph; to mark this event the

Above:
Restaurant in a 'Settebello'.
Below:
A recent addition to the FS family of Bo-Bo-Bo electric locomotive types is the 5630hp Class E656.

One of the green-and-grey liveried Class E646 Bo-Bo-Bos heads a morning *rapido* to Rome and Milan out of Naples.

Close-up of a 5600hp Class E444 Bo-Bo – the class officially nicknamed *Tartaruga* ('Tortoise') in ponderous comment on its 125mph top speed.

class was ennobled with the same blue and pastel grey livery as the E444s. With more elephantine humour the E656s have been christened the *Caimano* or 'Crocodile'. Yet another variant, rather less powerful and lighter at 102 tonnes, appeared early in 1980. This, the E633, features chopper electronic control of current supply to the traction motors, of which there is only one per bogie, for these locomotives will employ the monomotor bogie with variable gearing perfected by the French. On the higher gearing the E633 is a 100mph machine for passenger duty, on the lower a freight haulier with enhanced tractive effort. It has been named the 'Tiger' Class. The Italians intend to evaluate the type at up to 125mph and if it passes the examination, then the big E666 design mentioned earlier will certainly become a dead letter. Next on the FS production line will be a heavy freight Bo-Bo-Bo,

Class E844, with a peak output of 8000hp.

The FS is anxious to weed out its veteran electric locomotive classes and standardize rapidly on E444s, E646s, E656s and possibly E633s (only five prototypes of this type were ordered initially) and E844s because the unsophisticated bulk of the veterans is far too punishing on the track by today's stringent criteria. The 100mph E656 demonstrated that FS policy has veered away from the multiple-unit concept so long preferred for Italian inter-city operation. Despite the ease with which the Ale541 power cars and their various types of trailer can be manipulated into individually market-oriented formations, the FS is now convinced that in general its substantial seasonal fluctuations of traffic demand the still greater flexibility afforded by locomotive haulage.

A good many experts are mystified by the Italians' obsession with refinement of the Bo-Bo-Bo layout for 100mph passenger duty. Granted, they will be deriving some economic benefit from standardization of mechanical components, but an alternative development of the E444 Bo-Bo, though it might be higher in first cost, would secure a decidedly superior power/weight ratio and commensurate saving in energy costs on high-speed haulage. In the state of the high-power electric traction art in the 1980s there is no reason why a Bo-Bo of comparable output should be any more damaging to the track.

At the start of the 1980s there was a solitary train licensed for 125mph over the finished stretches of the Rome–Florence *direttissima*. This was the 'Pendolino,' a prototype four-car electric set with a gyroscope-actuated automatic body-tilting mechanism which was built by Fiat as a private venture in 1975 and accepted by the FS for scheduled public service between Rome and Ancona (later Rimini) the following spring. The 'Pendolino' begins its journey on the *direttissima* but soon turns off to head for the Adriatic coast on a serpentine trans-Apennine route via Foligno which optimizes its ability to negotiate curves 25 percent faster than orthodox coaches. As a result it can be timed a whole three-quarters-of-an-hour faster over the 185.5 miles from Rome to Ancona than conventional equipment.

The 'Pendolino' has run the gauntlet of political harassment – from railwaymen, incredibly – which is another factor hobbling FS attainment of its inter-city passenger speed objectives. Quite reasonably, the FS levied a supplementary fare on the train. There was nothing new about that; in common with practically all its Western European railway neighbours the FS had long charged extra to ride its domestic front-rank *rapidi* on grounds of superior speed and comfort, and TEE trains, of course, had been extra-fare since their 1957 inception. Nevertheless, the radically left-leaning Italian railwaymen's unions volubly objected that putting a premium on superior speed outraged every canon of egalitarian theory. But it is primarily FS determination to concentrate its resources on increasing operating

capacity and renewing heavily dated short-distance passenger equipment that has stalled mass-production of the 'Pendolino,' which would seem a godsend for the more difficult FS mountain main lines. Such teething troubles of the prototype as were reported seem to have been put right – including one that must give the progenitors of BR's tilt-body APT pause: 15 percent of passengers quizzed on their opinion of the 'Pendolino' complained of travel sickness in rearward facing seats. As a result all seats thereafter had to be made rotatable to face the direction of travel whenever the set reversed.

Just over half the FS route-mileage was electrified at the start of the 1980s. Conversion in the 1980s of the Ferrara–Rimini, Vicenza–Treviso, Carnate–Seregno and Bari–Taranto routes will see catenary strung over all key main lines, so the FS has no need of high-power diesel traction. It took up diesel railcars on a substantial scale in the 1930s and because of the heavy postwar calls on its investment resources for electrification and trunk-route improvement has lacked the means to keep the fleet fully up-to-date; little more than half the total of more than 1000 railcars is of the modern Fiat-engined Aln668 type. The FS persisted with steam longer than most Western European systems and did not embark on its mainline diesel locomotive production until 1957. All Italian-built, mostly by Fiat and with Fiat engines, the present-day FS locomotive types are mostly diesel-electric and designed primarily for mixed traffic work on secondary routes. Highest powered are the 2120hp diesel-alternator Class D445 B-Bs. In diesel as in electric territory the FS is inclining to locomotive haulage of passenger trains rather than perpetuation of railcars, not least because passenger services on many rural lines are so sparse that railcars spend far too much time idle, whereas locomotives can be switched to freight work during lulls in the passenger timetable.

A postwar phenomenon in Italy is the dormitory spread to the periphery of the country's major cities. In the 1930s most people lived close to their job, but

in the past two decades the FS has had to cope with and cater for a commuter business rapidly dilating to dimensions unimaginable before World War II. This compelled the FS to soldier on for many years with a large fleet of dingy, life-expired coaches while it pleaded for resources to fund modern high-capacity commuter equipment. One venture in this category was a 100-seater of a quaint-looking configuration – a bi-level (but not a double-decker) vehicle of which the long body's floor level is sunk close to rail level between the bogies so as to speed up passenger loading and unloading at the customarily low Italian platforms. After testing some of French Railways' Paris suburban double-deck coaches proper, how-

Driving desk and exterior of the automatic tilt-body 'Pendolino' electric train-set.

A latter-day FS push button signalling control centre at Genoa.

A pair of Fiat-built Class Aln668 diesel railcars stand at Rome Termini in April 1978.

A Fiat-built, diesel-powered TAF train-set of RENFE near Calatayud on the main line from Madrid to Zaragoza, which was undergoing electrification at the end of the 1970s.

ever, the FS in 1979 ordered 150 to this design from an Italian builder; they will be operated push-pull like the Paris sets. Although FS also took delivery in 1979 of the first of a smart-looking new series of four-car electric commuter multiple-units by Breda it is tending to wider use of the locomotive-worked push-pull method in its commuter and secondary passenger services.

The 5ft 6in-gauge main-line system of Spain was nationalized by the Franco regime as Spanish National Railways (RENFE) as recently as 1943. The socio-economic character of the country and its generally inimical terrain inhibited the early railway builders from planning for an ambitious quality of service even by the late 19th-century standards, but adaptation to the far more rigorous competitive conditions of the mid- and late 20th century was additionally handicapped by the Spanish Civil War as well as the side-effects of World War II and Spain's restricted economic resources. Accompanied by Portugal, Spain had to soldier on with steam on a considerable scale much longer than most in Western Europe; the last fires were not dropped until 1975.

Steam had been going quite rapidly to the wall from the mid-1960s, however, after the regime itself recognized the urgent need of modernization and released more capital. The rationalization and re-equipment begun then was intensified from 1974 into what, considering the size of the RENFE network, was one of the most energetic rail modernization programmes in the world when the Spaniards took fright at the oil crisis and ordered heavy investment in electrification. Up to that point just over 2000 route-miles, or one-quarter of RENFE route-mileage, had been electrified, mostly at 3000V DC overhead but in part at 1500V DC as a result of differing practice in pre-RENFE days. Apart from standardization of existing catenary at 3000V DC a further 1700 route-miles were to be electrified by the 1980s, whereafter more than 40 percent of the system would be wired and over three-quarters of RENFE's traffic electrically powered. At the close of the 1970s most of the *red basica* was electrified.

RENFE classifies its network into three categories. The main arteries are the *red basica*, or basic routes, which are chiefly in the northern half and the southeast of the country. Pre-eminent among them are the main-lines from Madrid northwest to Palencia, Leon, Oviedo and Vigo on the Atlantic coast, from Madrid to Santander, Bilbao and the French frontier at Hendaye, from Madrid northeastwards to Barcelona, the cross-country line from Zaragoza to Bilbao and San Sebastian, from Madrid to the southern coastal belt running from Sevilla through Cadiz and Malaga to Almeria, and the Mediterranean east coastal route from near the French border at Port Bou through Barcelona to Valencia. This basic network aggregates about a third of the system. Less significant main lines form the *red complementaria* and the rest of the system the *red secundaria*. Naturally, the electrification programme was conceived to convert most of the *red basica* as a priority, leaving the more lightly-trafficked lines in the western half of the country diesel-operated for some time to come.

Substantial stretches even of the *red basica* remain single-track, but apart from doubling some troublesome bottlenecks in these sectors RENFE is content that electrification and efficient regulation of movement over long route-mileages by Centralized Traffic Control (CTC) will satisfy their forseeable demands for extra operating capacity. (CTC is one of the methods of remote control from one strategically-sited operating room of switch and signal operations over 100 miles and more of basically single-track route.) RENFE can afford this modest attitude because, even with its substantial growth of traffic since mid-century, operations on its trunk routes lack the intensity of those in Northwestern Europe. From Madrid south to Cordoba, for instance, there is no express passenger departure between 09.35 and 14.30, and Malaga has only two daytime and two overnight expresses from the capital; even Barcelona, the country's second biggest city, has only three daytime express departures from Madrid.

It is the very considerable inter-city distances of Spain and the rail journey times enforced by the rail routes' unhelpful alignments (and RENFE's 9000 level crossings, over 7000 of which are unstaffed) which limit the demand and dictate the pattern of service. Barcelona is 430.6 miles from Madrid's modernized Chamartin station and the fastest daytime train takes eight hours five minutes with only four intermediate stops; Cordoba is only 276.3 miles from the capital, just a little further than Newcastle from London Kings Cross, yet the crack morning service from Madrid absorbs $5\frac{1}{4}$ hours over the journey.

RENFE is only too conscious that this is no pace

to set against private road transport, which probably generates five times as much passenger mileage in Spain as RENFE's trains. Still less does it compete against the airlines, whose fares have risen much less steeply than RENFE's since the railways were given some freedom in 1973 to adjust their tariffs in relation to rising costs. At the end of the 1970s it was substantially cheaper to fly the air shuttle from Barcelona to Madrid than to take the train, while overnight sleeper travel on RENFE was 50 percent more expensive than flying.

RENFE had been cherishing fully worked-out plans for a brand-new 455-mile, 4ft $8\frac{1}{2}$in-gauge, 150mph-or-more railway on the French TGV model from Madrid through Zaragoza to Barcelona and up the coast via Port Bou to a connection with French Railways. Like the French TGV it would have been an exclusively passenger railway, with intermediate stations only at Zaragoza, Barcelona and Port Bou, and electrified at 25kV AC instead of the 3000V DC standardized on RENFE's 5ft 6in-gauge system. This seems unlikely of achievement now, though in the spring of 1979 the Spanish government paid a handsome first instalment on its new contract with

One of RENFE's 3345hp Class 333 diesel locomotives, built in Spain by Macosa to designs licensed by the Scandinavian firm, Nohab, and General Motors, heads a passenger train near Avila.

General view of Madrid Chamartin station.

RENFE – outlined later in this chapter – by authorizing an immense expenditure on the trunk route south from Madrid to Andalusia, which is not only to be double-tracked all the way to Cordoba and electrified beyond there to Malaga, but very expensively re-aligned at the cost of considerable tunnelling in the mountains of the Sierra Morena to create 100mph trackage. Meanwhile RENFE is taking other steps to help achieve the 75mph inter-city average speeds it recognizes are commercially essential in the 1980s.

It has plumped for a new refinement of that uniquely Spanish device, the TALGO train, which currently furnishes the top category of Spanish inter-city service. The structure of RENFE express trains is quite complex. The basic supplementary-fare train, the *rapido*, is either (and mostly) a locomotive-hauled rake of orthodox day or night coaches, but it can also be provided by a three-car TAF (*Tren Automotor Fiat*), the designation of the first postwar build of diesel railcars for RENFE by Fiat; yet the latter are second-class only – a curious limitation for supplementary-fare equipment. Higher charges are levied on the more sophisticated and more recently built inter-city multiple-units, the two-car, 850hp diesel-hydraulic TER (*Tren Espanol Rapido*), also Fiat-built, and their counterpart on electrified routes, the ELT (*Electrotren*). Most highly-priced of all and categorized as luxury are the TALGO trains.

The TALGO system of lightweight vehicle suspension and wheel guidance was conceived in 1942 by two Spaniards as a means to higher speed over the country's tortuous and often insubstantial or poorly maintained permanent way without passenger discomfort, or insupportable wear and tear of the track. Its two inventors are commemorated in the final initials of the acronym, which stands for *Tren Articulado Ligero Goicoechea y Oriol* – the 'Lightweight Articulated Train of Goicoechea and Oriol'. A prototype TALGO train was put to work between Madrid and Irun in 1949 and in the 1960s RENFE invested in a fleet of TALGO vehicles with matching low-slung 2400hp diesel-hydraulic locomotives by Krauss-Maffei of Germany.

The TALGO has the characteristics of a gargantuan caterpillar. Each of the very short cars, only $34\frac{1}{2}$ft in body length, is single-axled and rides piggy-back at one end on a pivot above the axle of the next vehicle ahead. The floors of adjoining cars overlap and are connected by a simple arrangement of pins; an acoustic blanket deadens noise within the car and zip-fastened flexible diaphragms link the roofs and sides of neighbouring cars to enclose the whole train. To achieve the lowest possible centre of gravity, the car floor is sunk to within $2\frac{1}{4}$ft of rail level – below wheel-centre level, in fact, so that the axles have to be U-shaped to allow inter-car communication. This low-slung layout and extreme economy in weight – each car weighs no more than ten tons – are vital features of the TALGO formula, the principal element of which is the patented suspension and mounting of the single axles so that the independently rotating wheels are effectively steered into and through curves.

Like the TER and ELT multiple-units the TALGO equipment is fully air-conditioned and exemplary comfort has been shoehorned into the confined body space. First-class seats are not only adjustable for semi-reclining but rotatable to face the window, and each train-set offers a cafeteria-bar as well as full meal service at every seat from a central kitchen; for the latter a decent-sized table, vastly superior to any in an airliner, is clipped onto your seat (RENFE's train caterers, by the way, are the International Sleeping Car Company, CIWLT). As an instance of TALGO's superior speed over conventional equipment, take the day services from Madrid to Cadiz, 454.4 miles apart; the ordinary *rapido* pulling out of Madrid's Atocha station at 09.35 does not make Cadiz until 21.22, where it is followed little more than an hour later, at 22.30, by a TALGO that has left Madrid at 14.30 and which has made only six fewer intermediate stops.

TALGO equipment covers two of the four daily passenger services which eliminate the nuisance of passenger trans-shipment at the Franco-Spanish border break of gauge. The one orthodox Paris–Madrid train which crosses the border intact, except for its restaurant car and one or two day coaches, is the 'Puerta del Sol', which offers sleeping-car or couchette departure from Paris or Madrid in the early evening and arrival in the other capital immediately after breakfast the following morning. At the border

Bar cars of this attractive design feature in both the 'Catalan–Talgo' and the 'Barcelona–Talgo' train-sets.

station of Hendaye the 'Puerta del Sol's' night cars are threaded through an avenue of hydraulic jacks which gently hoist their bodies off the bogies; these are then rolled away and their place taken by bogies of the other gauge, onto which the bodies are eased back and connected. The whole operation takes about an hour, during which the cars' occupants are left undisturbed – or hopefully so: the sensations of jacking up and down are reasonable nerveless, but they can never be noiseless. Inter-capital travel by the 'Puerta del Sol' is sensibly marketed as a package, by the way, with one ticket buying dinner, breakfast and a berth or couchette as well as mileage (the same applies to the crack Paris–Rome overnight train, the 'Palatino'); RENFE provides the dining car in Spain, the SNCF a diner in France. Worth recording too, is that RENFE at one time attached a cinema car to the 'Puerta del Sol' between Madrid and Irun to entertain passengers in the early evening. Distinguished by a fast Paris–Bordeaux timing as well as its dismissal of the break-of-gauge handicap the 'Puerta del Sol' naturally skimmed the cream of the Paris–Madrid traffic from the historic and one-time luxury Pullman train between the two capitals, the 'Sud Express', after its June 1969 debut. The 'Sud Express' has since been reshaped primarily for Franco-Portuguese business and since the summer of 1973 it has been equipped with second-class couchette cars mounted on interchangeable bogies; two of these run through between Paris and Lisbon, three between Paris and Oporto and one between Paris and Vigo.

In the late 1960s Patentes Talgo SA, the TALGO concern, devised a means of altering the wheel gauge of their equipment's axles with the latter *in situ*. It involved adjusting the spacing of sliding stub axles in a special installation of tapered track, which was set up at the other key Franco-Spanish border rail crossing, Port Bou. Thereafter, in 1969, appropriately equipped TALGO stock, all first class, was introduced on a through service between Barcelona and Geneva, Switzerland, via Narbonne, Nîmes, Avignon and Lyons in France. Named 'Catalan-Talgo', the train was subsequently dignified with TEE status. At first the 'Catalan-Talgo' was routed via Grenoble, not Lyons, which took it over unelectrified French trackage, and at that date the RENFE line was not electrified throughout from Barcelona to Port Bou. Two of the special TALGO Krauss-Maffei diesel-hydraulics of RENFE, therefore, were also modified with axles adjustable for gauge and briefly worked over the border, the only RENFE locomotives ever to have travelled French track, let alone that of Switzerland. Nowadays the 'Catalan-Talgo' has RENFE electric power to Port Bou, French diesel traction over the as-yet-unelectrified sector thence to Narbonne, and French multi-voltage electric locomotive traction on to Geneva.

In 1974 Patentes Talgo SA partnered the 'Catalan-Talgo' with an overnight train-set featuring adjust-

Talgo train

able stub axles that went into service between Barcelona and Paris as the 'Barcelona-Talgo'. The constricted cross-section of the TALGO body, essential to secure the low centre of gravity that is a cardinal virtue of the concept, ruled out the usual lateral layout of berths; this way there was insufficient width both for beds of normal length or for a side-corridor in which passengers could pass each other comfortably. Instead each two-bed or four-bed compartment was angled at 25–30 degrees from the lateral, which not only made room for the usual size of bed but, on the corridor side, created a saw-tooth profile of angled recesses at the junction of each compartment where passengers could take refuge to allow contra-flow traffic down the corridor. Like the day trains, the fully air-conditioned 'Barcelona-Talgo' incorporates both a kitchen and a bar, and originally featured a very attractive 24-seater restaurant as well, but that has lately been discarded. Now one can only have a tray meal served in one's berth.

The 'Barcelona-Talgo' units have been passed for a maximum speed of 112.5mph (on test one has been run at up to 138.8mph on RENFE track), so they can be operated at the line speed limit on French metals. Plans are now complete for the 1981 introduction of a companion service between Madrid and Paris which will relegate the 'Puerta del Sol' to a secondary role because the TALGO equipment's gauge change can be accomplished on the move. The new train will shave three hours from the conventional train's Paris–Madrid time.

The Madrid–Paris train will be formed of the latest TALGO variant, committed by RENFE to series production of 132 day and 56 sleeping cars at the end of 1978. It made its debut in 1980. In this an automatic pendular body-tilting mechanism complements the company's patent suspension and wheel guidance system. In two years' testing of four prototype cars a comfortable ride was proved at speeds up to a peak of 143.8mph and the new vehicles are designed for operation at up to 125mph. Their advent has substantially cut inter-city times on the

A TER train-set of RENFE.

Below left:
RENFE's most modern
electric locomotive design at
the end of the 1970s was the
4160hp Class 269 Bo-Bo, built
to designs by the Japanese
firm Mitsubishi.
Below right:
The earlier Class 8600 electric
locomotives were to the
designs of the French traction
builders, Alsthom.

gear. Whereas other tilt-body devices begin to react as the sensors detect the preparation of the track for a curve, the TALGO system is not motivated until the precise start of the curve itself. As a result, the manufacturers claim, it does not tilt the body so far as other methods: the degree of tilt is exactly proportioned to the centrifugal forces which are being exerted and consequently it should not provoke the complaints of passenger sea-sickness some other tilt-body cars have aroused, especially from people in rearward-facing seats.

In recent decades RENFE has been shopping around the world for its traction designs, but latterly committing them to Spanish industry for manufacture under licence. For its major postwar class of 3000hp electric Co-Co, for instance, RENFE took an English Electric design from Britain, the 7700 type, and a more numerous breed from Alsthom, the French manufacturers, which form the 7600 and 8600 classes. Its most modern class, the 4160hp Class 269 Bo-Bo dating from 1973, is to a pattern by the Japanese firm, Mitsubishi, which is also the originator of the smart-looking three-car electric multiple-units of Class 440 that RENFE has standardized for commuter service in the country's major cities, a high-ranking area of development in the Spanish system's contemporary modernization programme.

Early in 1979 RENFE ordered its first thyristor-controlled locomotives, 30 Class 250 6100hp monomotor-bogie Co-Cos of Krauss-Maffei mechanical design with Brown Boveri electrical equipment. The German firm, Krauss Maffei, is assembling the first five, due for delivery in late 1980, but the rest will be constructed in Spain. These locomotives will have 100mph capability.

In its diesel territory RENFE is now deploying some of the most powerful single-unit locomotives in Western Europe. Here again the provenance of designs is polyglot. Two major classes of 1960s origin, the 2000hp Class 1900 and 2180hp Class 2100, both

prime Spanish inter-city routes, thanks to faster negotiation of curvature. The mass production order implies that RENFE has preferred the native body-tilting development to a facsimile of the Italian Fiat-built 'Pendolino' (mentioned earlier in this chapter), the *Tren Basculante*, which the Spanish builders CAF constructed to the Fiat design and which RENFE had under protracted and somewhat chequered evaluation in the late 1970s. For the time being the new TALGO tilt-body trains will be limited to 112.5mph on RENFE metals.

One attraction of the TALGO tilt-body concept is that the makers are charging no more for cars fitted with it than for stock with the basic TALGO running

A Class 333 diesel locomotive poses in Madrid Chamartin station.

Below:
The 2000hp Class 1900 diesel locomotives of RENFE are of General Motors origin.
Bottom left:
Spanish produce is loaded into Transfesa-owned wagons for export to Britain; the wagons have their axles changed for standard-gauge sets at the French border and cross the English Channel by train ferry.
Bottom right:
Merchandise freight on the move in RENFE's electrified territory.

diesel-electric Co-Cos, are US creations with American engines, the former a General Motors design, the latter ALCO. Subsequently RENFE bought some German 3000hp diesel-hydraulics, but its latest high-power type to be built in quantity, the 3345hp Class 333 diesel-electric, is a product of the important Swedish manufacturers, Nohab, in collaboration with General Motors of the USA.

One ought not to leave Spain without mention of just two components of RENFE's freight operation, which also looms large in the system's redevelopment schemes under three main headings: abandonment of a host of loss-making rural depots; investment in modern high-capacity and special-purpose wagons; and evolution of block train workings to the maximum extent and distance that is commercially marketable (these account for 60 percent of RENFE's total freight traffic). Bracketing all three objectives is the container train network set up in the mid-1970s under the brandname *Trenes Expresos de*

Contenedores, or TECO. It is the only one in Western Europe immaculately reproducing the British Rail Freightliner system of dedicated, semi-permanently-coupled trains shuttling exclusively between a complex of strategically sited and comprehensively

A Class 1350 diesel-electric Bo-Bo, a 1350hp machine built by English Electric, on rural service for the Portuguese Railways (CP).

Alsthom built this two-car diesel-electric train-set for the metre-gauge network of CP; it is at work on the suburban Lisbon–Sintra line.

mechanized rail-road trans-shipment depots. Other railways run all-container trains, but a substantial proportion of their container business is moved as individual wagonloads whose transits are protracted by marshalling-yard processing from train to train. British Rail's consultancy subsidiary, Transmark, was instrumental in the drafting of the TECO scheme, which connects 25 key centres in all quarters of Spain. As on British Rail, several 'company trains' are operated exclusively to the order of major firms as well as the scheduled services available to all customers. The other freight operation deserving mention is the export of Spanish fruit and vegetables in Transfesa-owned vans fitted with axles interchangeable at the frontier, so that they can and do eventually bring Spanish produce to British markets in considerable quantity, crossing the Channel from France to England by train ferry.

A new and more encouraging chapter in RENFE's history may have opened in 1979 with the conclusion of a contract with the Spanish Government that provides for long-term development and separates the losses on services operated at sub-standard fares to the Government's social policy requirements from the rest of the RENFE balance sheet. In effect, the Government has shouldered the financial responsibility for these social services by allowing RENFE to reduce its tariffs where it is in commercial competition with other forms of transport. RENFE's investment allowance has been doubled, but at the

same time it has had to give an undertaking to keep its deficits in check. The result will be rural economy and inter-urban expansion of services. As 1979 unfolded RENFE was formulating plans for closure of 500 miles of *red secundaria* and the application of simplified operating methods to some 475 miles of the *red complementaria*, including conversion of 100 stations to unstaffed halts. On the other hand it was aiming long-term for a 75 percent increase in inter-urban passenger services, with an average overall acceleration of 40 percent. Another objective is to build more radial short-distance railways in the area of Madrid, where the outward spread of the population is persistent.

Neighbouring Portuguese Railways (CP) are the most underdeveloped in Western Europe. Their state reflects that of a large part of the country, the unfriendly geo-physical hinterland which has confined the preponderance of Portugal's economic development to a coastal belt along the Atlantic shore from Oporto and Braga in the north down to Lisbon. The basic CP gauge is 5ft 6in, but in the north of Portugal beyond the Douro River and, apart from the lateral main line from Oporto to Madrid this gauge is represented only by the coastal route from Oporto to Braga and across the Spanish border to Vigo. The rest in this area – including, most inconveniently, a busy Oporto commuter line – is metre gauge, which accounts in total for nearly one-fifth of CP route-mileage. The reason is the mountainous northern terrain, which enforces very tight curvature and consistent grading as steep as 1 in 40 on this picturesque system. It was the last major Western European redoubt of nationally-operated steam power in the late 1970s, when a few of the spectacular articulated Mallet compound tank engines were still active (it was early 1977 before the last 5ft 6in-gauge steam was retired).

The metre-gauge network is almost entirely single-line; and so, very largely, is the 5ft 6in-gauge system. Double track is sparse away from the Lisbon–Oporto main line and the suburban networks of these two principal cities. The single-line handicap is exacerbated by the primitive character of CP signalling over so much of the country, with the conspicuous exception of the Lisbon–Oporto trunk route and urban commuter complexes. Numerous main lines in the agrarian areas of Portugal are still operated without benefit of block signalling, but by what is in essence the historic American method of control by train despatcher and *ad hoc* train order. At all too many rural stations on single-track trunk routes points are still hand-operated, and both opposing trains staging a meet in a passing loop are compelled to stop, even if one is a supplementary-fare *rapido*, the other a menial pick-up freight. What finally cripples the pace of CP passenger trains – and CP has the highest passenger-to-freight traffic ratio of any Western European railway: the proportion is roughly two to one – is that the sparsely populated

inland areas of the country and their patterns of socio-economic life cannot support a frequent service, so that the majority of express trains have to double as local pick-ups and make an excess of intermediate stops.

The CP comes bottom of the Western European electrification table with only 15 percent or so of its route-mileage electrified at the close of the 1970s. Before World War II the only electrified line in the country was the short-haul Estoril line from Lisbon, converted at 1.5kV DC; main-line electrification, starting with the key route from Lisbon to Oporto and its tributaries in the vicinity of both cities, was not launched until 1953, under a National Development Plan which unbuttoned the Government purse for transport modernization.

For its main-line scheme and all future electrification CP plumped for a 25kV 50Hz AC system on the French pattern. The first CP main-line electric locomotives were 2750hp Bo-Bos of Class 2500 embodying mechanical and electrical equipment from a consortium of French and German manufacturers, but CP's latest acquisitions, the 77-tonne 4000hp Class 2600, are French-built by Alsthom – unmistakeably so in outline. The design is an adaptation of French Railways' Class 15000 and 17000 Bo-Bos and the bodywork has the distinctive reversed-Z cab-front raking of modern French types. It embodies the French style of monomotor bogie with double-reduction gearing which varies tractive effort and maximum speed characteristics to suit passenger and freight working. The 2600s are ambitiously arranged for a top pace of 100mph on passenger duty, but until 1979 CP nowhere aspired to a line speed limit higher than 100kmph (62mph).

Portugal has one significant traction and rolling stock manufacturer, the Lisbon-based Sorefame, which has built both diesel and electric multiple-units with imported traction gear for CP and also some of the system's road diesel locomotives, which are exclusively diesel-electric. For the latest and, by a wide margin, its most powerful diesel traction units the CP has been shopping in Canada. Following an early 1970s purchase of some 2000hp 'hood'-outline

locomotives, CP returned to the Canadian firm, Bombardier-MLW, at the end of the decade for 43 massive-looking 120-tonne Co-Cos of 3300hp output.

Not until January 1979 could CP boast a single express train averaging a mile a minute from end to end. That month saw an unprecedented fifth addition to four named *rapidi* dominating the service of seven expresses each way daily over the 210.6-mile electrified route between Lisbon and Oporto – a train non-stop between the two cities apart from a virtually obligatory halt in Oporto's outskirts at Vila Nova de Gaia. The 'halt' is as good as compulsory because Eiffel's century-old rail bridge over the Douro between this suburban station and central Oporto is single track and heavily speed-restricted. The Douro and the Tagus at Lisbon are yet more physical barriers to CP's operational efficiency, since they effectively cut the western coastal half of the system into three separate zones; the first rail bridge over the Tagus inland from Lisbon is 35.6 miles northeast of the city and though there is some through running from Oporto to the south of the country the quickest and the recognized course for a through journey is to transfer between Santa Apolonia and Barreiro, Lisbon's northern and southern rail terminals, by Tagus ferry.

Above left:
The 2750hp Class 2500 Bo-Bo was CP's first main-line electric locomotive. At the start of 1980 CP's further electrification was making little progress because of the railway's serious cash flow problems.

Above:
The French parentage of CP's Class 2600 electric locomotives is obvious; the 4000hp machines were imported from Alsthom.

CP's most powerful diesel locomotives are the 120-tonne 3300hp Co-Cos, of which the first 13 were designed and built by Bombardier-MLW of Canada and the remainder assembled by Sorefame in Portugal.

Eiffel's single-track bridge over the Douro at Oporto is a severe handicap to operation of the main CP trunk route between this city and Lisbon. Its replacement has been long promised but is still far from achievement.

Below left:
The diesel train-set which furnishes the 'Sotavento' service between Lisbon and the Algarve has lately accelerated to run the 213.8 miles to Faro in four hours 21 minutes.
Below right:
Existing coaches were gutted and rebuilt as lounge cars for the accelerated Lisbon–Oporto *rapidi*.

Until the start of 1979 the best Oporto–Lisbon overall time was 3¾ hours, inclusive of three intermediate stops, by one of the three *rapidi* each way daily brandnamed *Foguete* ('Comet'). Their new companions, named 'Miragaia' after an area of Oporto in the north-bound direction and 'San Jorge' after a Lisbon castle southbound, have slashed the journey time to 3 hours 12 minutes. In part this reduction is possible because they hitch one of the Alsthom-built 4000hp electric Bo-Bos to a rake of just four cars totalling a mere 180 tonnes, but more significantly because the vehicles are air-braked (both RENFE and CP embarked on a gradual changeover from vacuum to air braking in the 1970s) and on that account the Alsthom Bo-Bos have had the line speed limit relaxed to 87.5mph for a useful, reasonably well-aligned proportion of the route and to 75mph over other sectors. The cars are all of the American firm Budd's stainless steel design which Sorefame has built under licence to form the core of CP's inter-city day coach fleet. One is a bar-restaurant and another in each set (two of which are needed, as the trains are on identical 10.45 departure paths from each city) has been specially furnished to recreate what one had thought was an extinct species

in Western Europe – the luxury lounge car, with genuine loose and ponderous armchairs, the whole presided over by a hostess; its use entails a surcharge on the usual *rapido* supplementary fare, however. Incidentally, CP is unique among major European railways in entrusting its train catering to local private enterprise.

Conjointly with the launch of these two mile-a-minute trains the other Lisbon–Oporto *rapidi* were commensurately quickened. In particular the morning and evening *Foguetas* each way, now renamed 'Sete Colinas' (the seven hills of Lisbon) and 'Cidade Invicta' (Oporto's historic name) and re-equipped with similar air-braked stock, were accelerated to a three hours 20 minutes overall time inclusive of three stops en route. The timetable was simultaneously re-drafted to establish a near-regular-interval *rapido* operation every three hours of the day in each direction. Amongst a number of other early 1979 passenger timetable improvements the Tagus ferry service was reinvigorated with the primary objective of making rail journeys more appealing the whole length of the north-south coastal axis from Brago to Faro, the principal city of the booming tourist area in the Algarve, lining the southern tip of Portugal. The CP faces a long haul in fettling up the single-track route south of Lisbon for really competitive express service, however; Faro is only 213.8 miles from Lisbon, but as much as 5 hours 25 minutes distant in time by the only *rapido* in the book, the 'Sotavento' – and that runs only three times a week each way.

Yugoslav Railways (JZ) has recorded the most rapid electrification rate, proportionately to the size of its network, of any European country outside the Eastern Bloc in the past decade or so. Since 1968 the electrified sector of its route mileage has jumped from just over five to around 30 percent. By an accident of political history the Italian 3000V DC system was introduced for the first conversions in the north-western area of the country between Zagreb and the Italian and Austrian borders, but for the energetic extension of the catenary southeastwards from Zagreb to Belgrade and Skopje, and from Belgrade through Sarajevo and Mostar to the Adriatic coast

pursued under a wide-ranging modernization programme launched in the early 1960s, the 25kV AC method has been preferred. In 1979–80 alone JZ was tackling over 400 miles of electrification on this system.

The high-voltage AC system has been applied *ab initio* to the most impressive of all JZ's latter-day modernization projects, a new trunk route of no less than 321 miles from Belgrade to Bar on the lower Adriatic coast close to the Albanian border. Until the enterprise was finished in 1977 this rugged quarter of the country was scarcely penetrated by JZ standard gauge, only by JZ 760mm narrow-gauge lines, which total about 650 route-miles. The Belgrade–Bar line is no racetrack – the best train of the day takes nearly nine hours over the end-to-end journey, because of the severe speed limits imposed by the route's serpentine alignment – but the wild, mountainous landscape it traverses with the aid of 46 substantial tunnels aggregating more than 70 route-miles and numerous spectacular viaducts and earthworks is among the most memorable one can experience from a European train.

The spine of the JZ system is the main line from the Austrian border at Jesenice through Ljubljana and Zagreb to Belgrade and the southeast, nowadays a key Balkan land-bridge for rail-transported trade between northwest and southeast Europe. This, expectedly, is the track of the country's swiftest train, the electric multiple-unit 'Emona Express', which covers the 258 miles between Zagreb and Belgrade in four hours 44 minutes inclusive of two stops en route. A substantial proportion of the expresses negotiating this busy thoroughfare are international, of course, feeding through coaches from Germany and Austria to Greece, Bulgaria and Turkey on trains like the 'Akropolis Express', 'Hellas Express' and 'Tauern-Orient Express' as well as to Yugoslav destinations. The through vehicles in these fascinatingly cosmopolitan equipages are preponderantly West German, among them the majestic, domed-roof sleepers of West Germany's DSG which originate from as far to the northwest as Hamburg and Dortmund. But JZ's own sleepers penetrate deep into West Germany and even a Bulgarian sleeper functions nightly between Istanbul and Dortmund in the 'Istanbul Express'.

Infrastructure improvements, such as doubling of single track and junction reconstruction with the adjunct of modern electronic signalling to enlarge operating capacity, are a salient feature of JZ's contemporary modernization. Outstanding under this head is the comprehensive reformation of the Belgrade city network, begun in 1976 and to be completed early in the 1980s. A main objective was to supersede the old main station dating from 1884, an unroofed and primaevally signalled terminus in which trains from the northeast to the southeast, Bulgaria and Greece had to reverse. The old station was approached from Zagreb by a route that orbited

the southwest of the city and entered it facing north. That is now the main route for through freight, which via a new marshalling yard (at Zeleznik) and connection can be funnelled straight into the main line to Nis and the southeast without touching the city centre and the new fully-roofed through city station. Passenger trains from the Zagreb direction now approach the city centre in a beeline, soaring over the Sava River on a graceful suspension bridge which, including its approach viaducts, is 1.2 miles long. Creation of exits in the Nis and Rumanian border directions from the new station (and also from the new marshalling yard) involved a great deal of tunnelling under the city. Three new stations have been constructed within the tunnels.

Top:
A Class 441 5550hp electric Bo-Bo of Yugoslav Railways (JZ). The design of these locomotives for the 25kV 50Hz AC area of JZ was Austrian.
Above:
Steam survival on the JZ – a Class 33 2-10-0 of the famous German wartime design.

8.
THE RAILWAYS OF SCANDINAVIA

The 'Henrik' express of the Norwegian State Railways (NSB) links Bergen and Oslo, a trunk route which is above the tree line for 62½ miles in its passage of the country's central mountains. More than 45 miles of this bleak sector are shrouded in tunnels or snowsheds.

In the summer of 1979, as the oil-exporting countries jacked up their prices more menacingly still, most Governments in the West responded with little more than pious hope that their motorist voters would try the train now and then. Not so the Swedes. Overnight, in June that year, the Swedish Transport Minister better than halved the price of most passenger journeys on the Swedish State Railways (SJ) – or to be more accurate, slashed the cost by about 50 percent for Swedes prepared to make a modest commitment to use of the railway, since the cut was ingeniously framed. Basic fare levels were reduced by up to 30 percent, but to realize the most attractive discounts one had to buy a rebate card (the second-class price of which was just over £50/$110 at the time) good for a whole year's use and applicable to an unlimited number of journeys every day except Fridays and Sundays, the country's peak travel days. Within a year the volume of inter-city business rose by 50 percent.

This move was the culmination of a *volte-face* in political attitudes to the SJ, which were previously a little irrational. The country has contentedly tolerated a route-mileage of railway greater per head of population than anywhere else in Europe because of its value as an all-weather standby, during the hard winters in Sweden's more northerly latitudes above all. An admirable philosophy, but, in Sweden, indulged to the extreme of maintaining a 467-mile open line from Gällivare to Ostersund – to cite a particularly egregious example – simply to run one train a day each way through an area where the sparse habitation averages no more than one person per square kilometre. Even before the oil price explosion Swedish Governments consistently re-sisted SJ management pleas for all lines like this to be closed and for their meagre traffic to be transferred to road (though over 2000 route-miles, it must be conceded, have been shut since 1950). They preferred to subsidize irretrievably loss-making lines totalling more than half the SJ system, but at the same time required them to be run as rudimentarily as possible. One consequence is that just over one-third of the SJ's stations are unstaffed.

In the commercial sector of its system, on the other hand, the SJ was allowed nothing like the financial leeway of, say, France's SNCF or West Germany's DB. Until the late 1970s' change of front it was constricted almost as severely as British Rail – curbed as to its rate of investment and driven into a rapid succession of passenger and freight price increases in a vain chase of escalating costs, but with the inevitable result that passengers were lost to road or to upsurging and keenly priced domestic air services, and that the ensuing decline in business kept the annual deficit spiralling upward.

Now the Swedish Government seems to have changed tack completely. Along with the 1979 summer's revolutionary fare cuts it warned that it would be seeking closure of about one-third of the SJ's total route-mileage, currently standing at just over 7100. If the Swedish electorate will stand for it – and that is no foregone conclusion – the SJ will contract to a virtually all-electric system.

The residual two-thirds is the core network of the SJ, moving 90 percent of its traffic, and this is almost entirely electrified at 15kV $16\frac{3}{4}$ Hz AC. With their lack of indigenous coal but plentiful hydro-electric resources Swedish railways were among the earliest electrifiers; at the end of World War II, in fact, only

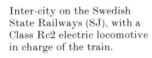

Inter-city on the Swedish State Railways (SJ), with a Class Rc2 electric locomotive in charge of the train.

Italy surpassed them for extent of railway electrification. One important outcome of this pioneering is that the Swedish firm of ASEA has world status for its advanced electric traction technology, most notably in the application of thyristor control. The many overseas customers for its complete locomotives, components or know-how include Amtrak, the passenger service operators of the USA, Scandinavian neighbours, Eastern European countries, Austria, Rumania, Yugoslavia and British Rail. Of these, BR startled its own countrymen by equipping the vaunted crown of latter-day British rail technology, the first trio of pre-production Advanced Passenger Trains (see Chapter One), not with British-made but with ASEA electric traction control and motors.

Recast on a regular-interval pattern in recent years the SJ's inter-city passenger service, mostly locomotive-hauled but also featuring some multiple-unit operation, attains hourly frequency on key routes in the populous south of the country, such as Stockholm to Göteborg or Malmö. Speed is severely circumscribed, however, for two reasons: only about ten percent of SJ route-mileage is double-track; and the incidence of level crossings – roughly two for every route-kilometre on average – is one of the highest in Western Europe. Modern SJ coaching stock is sensibly designed for 100mph, but until the SJ can afford the civil and signal engineering to exploit it, the limit even on tangent track is 81.3mph (130kmph). Against that the SJ's fastest end-to-end timing of three hours 59 minutes for the 285-mile non-stop run from Stockholm to Göteborg, which predicates a 71.5mph average, is extraordinarily creditable, the faster-still 77.3mph timing of one train each way daily over the 70.8 miles from Halls-borg to Skvode almost incredible.

A Government promise to raise the investment ceiling as back-up for the new passenger fares policy has encouraged SJ hopes of ordering series equipment based on the prototype three-car electric multiple-unit with automatic body-tilting, designated X15, which it evolved with ASEA in the mid-1970s and which has been encouragingly tested at up to 150mph. With automatic body-tilting the SJ could persevere with today's speed limit and yet achieve the same cuts in journey time as a lift to 100mph would enable with orthodox trains. Any ambition of 100 or even more mph with the X15, of course, is presently just as thwarted by the single-track and level crossing constraints as it is with conventional rolling stock. Nevertheless, late in 1979 SJ announced that it was about to order three prototype 100mph train-sets for delivery in 1982.

The interior style and comfort of SJ long-haul

Above left:
Control room of a modern CTC installation. The breadth of the illuminated track diagram on the rear wall is indicative of the length of route covered by this centre.

Above right:
One of the operator's desks in SJ's computer-based signalling centre at Göteborg. The operator sets his selected route by picking out its reference code on the keyboard in front of him. The left-hand VDU pictures the area of the layout in his charge; on the right-hand VDU he can call up an enlarged picture of a specific sector of his area.

passenger coaches has long been impressive, particularly in the open saloons, where the latest first-class seating justifies the description of 'armchair', especially when the three-a-side layout gains width per seat by alignment of the gangway against one wall instead of its more usual placement between bays of one and two seats. An admirable characteristic of recent SJ second-class stock is the provision in some of a compartment appropriately equipped for nursing mothers, with normal seating for them, a bank of push-chair/stroller-type seats for their offspring and every basic tool for infant care to hand, from washbasin and pot to a milk-heater. An increasingly high proportion of SJ inter-city trains has restaurant or cafeteria service.

The SJ's conurbation passenger transport role is restrained by the model co-ordination of public transport in the capital, Stockholm. When the city's Metro, the *T-Bana* (for 'Tunnel Railway' – as much a misnomer as *U-Bahn* in West Germany, since two-thirds of the Stockholm system is above ground) was built in the 1950s it was prudently routed through the radial gaps left by SJ lines, not alongside them. Then the Stockholm Transport Authority grasped the unique opportunity of Sweden's 1967 switch from a left to right-hand rule of the road to reorganize its entire bus operation as a feed of *T-Bana* stations in the suburbs and city centre, making every conceivable commuter journey from the inner and middle suburbs a bus-Metro-bus sequence under a zonal ticketing system that disregarded the number of modes employed to complete the trip. That left the SJ primarily an outer suburban carrier.

The whole of the SJ's Stockholm suburban network as well as its main station layout is signalled from one centre. With its vast mileage of single track and the pressures to operate the sparse train service in so much of the country as cheaply as possible, the railway and the country's signalling and telecommunications industry were spurred to exploit remote control earlier than most. The technique mostly employed predated the developments in electronics which today allow such vast, intricate and busy layouts to be supervised from one centre,

as described in Chapter 1. Known as Centralized Traffic Control (CTC) it was pioneered in the 1920s by railroads with long threads of single-track transcontinental main line across the plains and mountains of America's Middle West and West.

CTC's *modus operandi* was and is akin to that of early automatic telephone dialing. Each point or signal-setting switch on the operator's console, when moved, transmitted its individual coded current down a circuit of one, two or three wires extending the length of the area under control; the code was detected by the relevant piece of apparatus on the ground, which moved or changed aspect as directed, then returned a code up the wire to the operator's console to alter his illuminated route diagram appropriately as proof that the function required by the operator was completed. The limitation of pre-electronics CTC was that transmission and return of each code took at least three seconds, generally more; and therefore, since only one code could be transmitted at a time, a CTC installation could only cope simultaneously with two or three trains. But with the light traffic of so many remote SJ single lines – and of one of Sweden's two chief privately-owned standard-gauge systems, the Grängesberg–Oxelösund – it still enabled one CTC panel to cover not only all signalling and point-seating over 150 miles and more, but also level-crossing barrier operation, the switching on and off of point heaters in winter, and in the case of the private railway mentioned, the opening and shutting of three swing bridges.

Transistorized remote control transformed the possibilities by accelerating the transmission of codes and the response a hundredfold and more. It was enhanced by the development of systems permitting simultaneous transmission of several commands or responses – either what is known as Time Division Multiplex (TDM), wherein synchronized scanning devices at each end of the control-apparatus circuit test several times every second for lack of correspondence (ie, that an operating button has been activated and that the apparatus needs to respond, or conversely that it has and the fact must be reported to the operator's console); or Frequency

Division Multiple (FDM), wherein coded signals of different frequencies are carried over the same circuit.

For its size the SJ makes as impressive use of computers and electronics as any Western European railway. Its latest computer-based signalling centre at Göteborg, focus of five routes and a busy port served by two marshalling yards and a network of freight lines to goods terminals, is especially novel in that it dispenses with the usual panoramic track and signal diagram covering the whole layout, on which illuminated displays continuously indicate the lie of points, the setting of signals and the occupation of individual track circuit sections. The bigger the operating areas brought within control of one centre by miniaturization and electronics, the more un-wieldy these illuminated diagrams are tending to get. So far as the signalmen's route-setting controls are concerned, one method of making those more com-pact which has been adopted in some mainland Euro-pean installations is to replace push-buttons located at the appropriate geographical spot on the track diagram with a typewriter-like keyboard on which the signalman picks out, by its reference number, the specific route he wants to actuate, then depresses an 'execute' button; this way he can control a sub-stantial track area without leaving his seat.

In the Göteborg centre a sedentary job is made still easier. Each of the signalmen sits at a keyboard flanked by two Visual Display Units, or VDUs, which display in colour. The left-hand VDU screen shows the whole sector of the layout controlled by the signalman concerned, the routes set up and the circuits with trains in occupation, plus the latter's timetable description numbers. On the right-hand screen the signalman can call up an enlarged picture of the area of his sector with which he is dealing at any moment; this will show him in detail the individual setting of each point and signal. The computer will store any route-setting he orders which cannot be executed until a previous movement has been completed.

All SJ main-line passengers are served by a centrally computer-based system that can issue a combined travel and seat or berth reservation within 20 seconds – and for international as well as domestic journeys, since the SJ installation is interlinked with those of Danish, Norwegian and West German rail-ways. An SJ operations control and planning appa-ratus similar to British Rail's TOPS (see Chapter 1) is taking shape for the 1980s. So is a fairly sophisticated Automatic Train Control under which each traction unit will be equipped with a microcomputer to monitor observance of speed limits and the correct-ness of a driver's braking at sight of a cautionary signal as well as basically applying an emergency brake if a danger aspect is ignored. Also in mind is application to the whole electrified network of selective two-way track-to-train radio communica-tion, a development limited up to the end of the 1970s

to the Greater Stockholm area and the iron ore line between Lulea and Narvik because of investment restraints.

The iron hauls to Lulea and Narvik are the most spectacular SJ freight operations. Well over 80 per-cent of the SJ's freight tonnage consists of the country's three main natural resources – ore, iron and wood, of which the first is mined principally in Lapland, north of the Arctic Circle. The richest deposits lie around Kiruna, which is served by a sometimes steeply graded, 294-mile single line run-ning northwest to the ice-free port of Narvik, in Norway, and southeast to the Swedish port of Lulea, on the Gulf of Bothnia. The Swedish sector of this route was the first line in the country to be electrified, in 1915; the Norwegians electrified their end in 1923. CTC controls the working throughout.

The railway functions all year round even though mid-winter temperatures are bitter enough to con-geal the ore and entail special apparatus to vibrate and warm the wagons at terminals before they can be unloaded. In the late 1970s demand for the ore was badly depressed compared with that of pre-recession years, when the line was moving up to 32 loaded trains and the same number of return empties every 24 hours, and individual workings would gross up to 5200 tons, locomotive weight excluded, of which the payload factor was as high as 4000 tons, carried in 50 purpose-built bottom-door discharge bogie hopper wagons with automatic centre couplers. To lift this tonnage up slopes as steep in one part as 1 in 100 with a single power unit, the SJ commissioned one of Europe's most powerful electric locomotives to date. In 1960 some existing 1-D+D 1 twin units built by a consortium of Swedish firms headed by the loco-motive builders Nohab and the electrical giant ASEA had a third unit spliced into their format to create a

A 9750hp Class Dm3a 1-D+D+D-1 electric of the SJ heads a Kiruna–Lulea ore train. The annual production of mines in the Kiruna and Gällivare areas, both served by the line stretching from Narvik to Lulea, is 25–30 million tonnes, or about five percent of total world production, and it moves to the ports entirely by rail. In October 1979 one day's movement from Kiruna to Narvik reached a record 100,174 tonnes, transported in 27 trains. The line's fleet of ore wagons totals 4200.

The 5900hp Class El-16 Bo-Bo, ASEA's version of the Swedish Rc4 for the NSB.

Below left: SJ's Class T44 diesel-electrics, built by Nohab, have General Motors engines.
Below right:
An SJ Class Rc4 electric at work.

trio of 258-ton, permanently articulated, 1-D+D+D-1s (a wheel arrangement signifying three sets of four powered and coupled axles) with a 7740hp output. Three of these Class Dm3s were built; seven years later the design was elaborated into the mighty 9750hp Class Dm3a.

Since then, however, the recession in tonnage and ASEA's advancing technology have combined to bring the Kiruna–Narvik line within the potential of SJ's renowned range of Bo-Bo electrics with ASEA thyristor control which are designated Rc. Launched

with the Rcl series in 1967, the type's latest manifestation at the time of writing is the 4900hp, 78-tonne Rc4 premiered in 1975; examples of this class have been enthusiastically borrowed for trial not only by other European railways but by the US passenger train corporation, Amtrak, which subsequently adopted the design in essentials as the basis for a US-built series of locomotives to operate its forthcoming Boston–New York–Washington high-speed passenger service. Six Rc derivatives, Class Rm, built for Kiruna–Narvik line duty are

specially modified 4800hp units with rheostatic braking which incorporate a so-called 'creep control' device (first installed in the ten ASEA Bo-Bos for the Austrian Federal Railways – see Chapter 6) that substantially enhances their adhesive efficiency in all weathers

Long-haul inter-city trains on the main SJ routes are locomotive-powered, but for some secondary routes SJ deploys extremely attractive four-car electric multiple-units. Officially classified X9, they are popularly dubbed the 'Paprika' trains by reason of their vivid red livery, though it is also worn nowadays by the Rc locomotives.

With all its 'core' network electrified the SJ has no call for high-power diesel locomotives and its most modern classes are essentially heavy yard shunters and freight types. The latest is the 1650hp 'hood'-type Class T44 diesel-electric, one of the range evolved by Nohab in collaboration with the Electromotive Division of General Motors, whose diesel engines are the prime movers. Ironically SJ took delivery almost concurrently with the 1979 closure threat to its diesel-powered territory of the first of 100 new 400hp railcars ordered in 1977 to re-equip many of the one-man-operated rural passenger services in the threatened regions. The newcomers are Italian-built by Fiat to the basic Class Aln668 design used by the Italian State Railways, which has been perhaps the most successful diesel railcar concept of the 1970s; by the end of the decade almost 1000 had been constructed, half for domestic employment in Italy, the remainder for export to no fewer than 15 other countries in Europe, North Africa, Asia and Latin America.

The neighbouring Norwegian State Railways (NSB) is another of the foreign customers for the Swedish Rc4 electric locomotive. NSB's version, the Class El-16, has a 5900hp rating and differs externally from the home product in the dramatically raked outline of its cab. The El-16 is not the NSB's most powerful electric unit. That palm goes in a walk-over to three twin units built in 1966 as the NSB's contribution to the Narvik Kiruna ore operation by the Norwegian firm of Thunes with ASEA traction apparatus. The NSB's 12-axle, 260-ton Co-Co-Co-Co twin-units far surpass their Swedish colleagues in the Arctic for power, since each of them has the formidable rating of 14,700hp. Behind them in the NSB power league rank the 46 6900hp Co-Cos of Class El-14, an extrapolation of the Swiss Federal Railway's Ae6/6 design which the Norwegian firm of Thunes built in the late 1960s under licence from the Swiss electric traction manufacturers, SLM.

The El-16s are assigned to what is arguably the most taxing inter-city route in Europe and possibly the world, that from Oslo to Bergen. The Swiss and Austrian transalpine routes discussed in earlier chapters climb slightly higher, some North American transcontinentals vastly higher, but not in latitudes so inhospitable for so much of the year. The Oslo–Bergen line, lying between 60 and 61 degrees latitude, is the world's most northerly mountain main line rising to 4000ft above sea level; in this area the tree line is passed at only 2000ft or so and the Oslo–Bergen line is above it for 62½ miles, reaching a summit of 4336ft west of Finse. The bleakness of the environment can be deduced from the fact that the parallel motor road is certain to be free of snow or ice

The SJ's Class X9 electric multiple-units are popularly known as the 'Paprika' trains.

After iron and ore, wood is the principal component of SJ's freight traffic. The timber industry is mainly located in the coastal area of northern Sweden, so that it generates quite lengthy freight-train hauls to the south of the country.

Below:
An NSB Class E1-14 electric locomotive pulls into Finse, not far from the 4336ft-high summit of the Oslo–Bergen line.
Bottom:
The NSB's 1900hp Class Di3 diesel-electric, Nohab-built with General Motors engines.

and open for no more than ten weeks in late summer. More than 45 miles of the route are in tunnel or protected by snowsheds.

Testimony to the unique character of the Oslo–Bergen line was amply forthcoming in the 1970s from Canadian Pacific. Canadian Pacific (CP) used it as a laboratory for tests of an SJ Type Rc2 electric with ASEA thyristor control to assemble data proving that, were the Canadians to electrify their trans-continental route over the Rockies, a thyristor-control machine could in all imaginable weathers shift 50 percent more tonnage than a comparable four-axle diesel-electric. It was subsequent trials of a similar character with an SJ Rc4, which demon-strated that it had a better tonnage-hauling capacity than the E1-14 Co-Cos of theoretically greater power output and which persuaded the NSB to invest in the ASEA design.

An Oslo–Bergen journey is one for absorbing barren but breathtaking mountain scenery, not for speed, since like NSB main lines in general it is largely single-track, sharply and incessantly serpen-tine and studded with gradients as steep as 1 in 40 or 50. Another handicap of the NSB in more populated areas, as with the SJ, is the prevalence of level cross-ings – no fewer than 7000 in the whole network at the end of the 1970s. To reduce the present best time of $6\frac{3}{4}$ hours for the $294\frac{1}{4}$-mile journey by the limited-stop 'Henrik' express, the NSB has ambitions to invest in a small fleet of automatic tilt-body multiple-units, but though Norway's national Planning Commission for Transportation professes anxiety to see more traffic switch from road to rail – freight especially – the legislature has so far witheld the full financial means needed to update the NSB com-petitively. Similar self-contained train-sets are sought to eliminate an hour from the seven-hour transit between Oslo and Trondheim (350 miles) dictated by a line speed limit of only 75mph.

The 60 percent of the NSB system that is electrified at 15kV $16\frac{2}{3}$Hz AC caters for 80 percent of the traffic and embraces all trunk routes in the southern half of the country. The most important non-electrified route is the Northland line which was driven up to the Arctic Circle from Trondheim and saw its last stage, from Fauske to the Arctic port of Bodö, finished as recently as 1962. Still unsettled is whether this line will be pushed still further north to Narvik, where the existing Norwegian track is totally cut off from the rest of the NSB; it is accessible only from Sweden over the ore line from Kiruna (and thus, quaintly, receives its daily named train, the 'Lapplandspilen', from Sweden with a sleeper from Malmö, and another train bearing a through sleeper from Copenhagen,

but nothing from its own country). A beeline extension from Bodö to Narvik would entail resorting to train ferries to negotiate several fjords biting deep into the coastline. A scheme of the kind has been on the table since 1923, but seems of late to have been firmly jettisoned in favour of a single-track route bent inland and very expensively tunnelled through hard rock to achieve a 100mph alignment most of the way, not only to Narvik but still further north to Tromsö. The traffic potential was held to justify the cost by a commission appointed to appraise the project in the 1970s, but its authorization looks remote in the contemporary economic climate.

The paucity of traffic beyond catenary limits is patent from the NSB's need of only 35 main-line diesel locomotives and fewer than 50 diesel railcar units. The locomotives are all of the Class Di3 1900hp diesel-electric type, a design of mid-1950s vintage built by Nohab with American GM engines which is now regarded as obsolescent; it is slated for replacement in the 1980s by a new Class Di4 from a West German consortium which includes Henschel among its constituents.

A marginal upward trend in passenger revenue heartened the NSB as the 1970s ebbed, but the railway was still locked in serious deficit by the drift of its freight to road and the irredeemable losses of its remote branches. In 1978 a Government commission advocated closure of almost one-fifth of its route-mileage. Among the lines fingered were some built as recently as 1934 and electrified, such as that to Hardanger – though from the look of the latter's antique stock one would guess it has never once generated sufficient business to warrant updating re-investment since its opening! Up to the time of writing, however, the Norwegian Parliament has stomached very little of the closure plan.

Despite its problems the NSB is modernizing to the hilt of its resources – for instance, in the steady application of CTC to half its system by the late 1970s, CTC will govern the entire Oslo–Bergen line by 1984. The biggest enterprise of the late 1970s was the boring of a new double-track tunnel beneath Oslo to end the NSB's inherited handicap of two main-line terminals, West and East, in the city and nothing but a single-track freight line through the harbour area to link the two halves of the NSB network converging on the capital. The tunnel connection will serve a new Central station with 12 through and seven terminal platforms, due for completion in the mid-1980s, wherein Oslo's entire main-line and commuter passenger operation will eventually be concentrated.

There is less going for a railway in Denmark, perhaps, than in any other Western European country. Scarcely any heavy industry generates the bulk freight that is one *raison d'être* of the modern railway and the close proximity and littoral situation of the country's chief population centres limits the passenger traffic potential. Worst of all, a substantial proportion of the country's land area is on four islands on one of which stands the capital, Copenhagen, which is inaccessible overland from either Germany or the rest of Scandinavia. Even the main peninsula of Jutland has a coastline so serrated that its railways are forced into irksome detours.

The most intensively trafficked route in the country, the transversal from Copenhagen westward through the cities of Aarhus and Aalborg to the Jutland port of Esbjerg, is an island hop that confronts two wide waterways. The westernmost, from the central island of Fünen to Jutland over the Little Belt, has been bridged by a structure carrying a main road and a single rail track which is well over a mile long; the approach spans total of 3865ft and the spans which soar 108ft above water another 270ft. But the Great Belt between Fünen and Zeeland, Copenhagen's island, is nearly 16 miles wide. So here as elsewhere in its network the Danish State Railways (DSB) has to resort to train ferries (it is the country's major passenger-carrying ferry operator). This handicap is exacerbated by the Great Belt waterway's winter vulnerability to icing and at any time to fog, which redoubles pressure for construction of a Great Belt Bridge as the pace of commercial life tightens from year to year At the end of the 1970s, the authorities seemed about to seek bridge-building tenders and the scheme was at last looking more of a realistic possibility than a mirage, but it has been deferred to the next century.

The Oresund waterway between Zeeland and Sweden, crossed by ferries plying between Helsingör in Denmark and Hälsingborg in Sweden, is another irritant on a key rail route. Here the Swedes and Danes seemed of one mind to finance an underwater tunnel in 1970, but since then the project has gone cold largely because the Danes have decided that the Great Belt bridge has priority and that improved ferry services area more sensible investment. Another factor is the Swedes' improvement of the direct ferry route from their port of Trelleborg to Sassnitz in West Germany. This reduces the value to Sweden of the new direct overland rail route between West Germany and Sweden which was established after the post-World War II partition of the Third Reich. The latter cut the original route to Germany by

Inland movement of deep-sea containers is an expanding element of the NSB's freight traffic.

A Class MX diesel-electric shows off the latest DSB livery, a striking combination of the traditional DSB house colours of bright red, black and white.

One of the *Lyntog* diesel-hydraulic train-sets based on the German Federal Railways' first TEE equipment which were built for the DSB's front-rank internal express services in the 1960s.

allocating its southern port, Warnemünde, to East Germany. West Germany therefore laid new line over the Fehmarnsound to the small Fehmarn island east of Kiel and there built a handsome new ferry port at Puttgarden. Across the water in their territory of Lolland, 11½ miles away, the Danes, too, laid out a new ferry port at Rödby, and from it projected 23 miles of new railway to connect with the prewar international route. This gains Zeeland with a leap from Falster island over another spectacular bridge – the Störstrom, finished in 1937 and at 10,535ft overall the third longest in Europe. The Danes know the Puttgarden–Rödby route as the 'Beeline', but the Germans dub it more romantically the 'Bird's Flight'. Its through passenger trains are ennobled by a number of titled services conveying sleeping cars heading for a gamut of European cities ranging from Paris and Amsterdam to Munich, Rome and Vienna.

Against all its geographical odds the DSB has since 1974 operated an immaculate hourly-interval inter-city service on the vital transversal from Copenhagen over Fünen island to the Jutland peninsula, and rebuilt the rest of its main-line passenger operation on a similar timetable basis around this spine. Testimony to the smartness of

ferry loading, unloading and operation the DSB has had to make instinctive is the fact that the inter-city trains are allowed no more than a standard one hour 16 minutes from arrival at one Great Belt ferry terminal to departure from its counterpart across the water. As a result – and even though the DSB line speed limit on dry land is currently 87.5mph – the standard transit time for the 158¾ miles from Copenhagen to Fredericia, the first important centre reached in Jutland, is no more than three hours 36 minutes inclusive of four intermediate stops other than those at the ferry ports. This time should be significantly reduced after the 1980–81 delivery of three new wide-beam, four-track Great Belt ferries with 50 percent increase of rail vehicle capacity and completion of new double-track ferry ramps at the ports. In conjunction these developments are expected to halve the time of the Great Belt crossing.

Until the end of the 1970s electrification – at 1.5kV DC – was confined to the suburban network of Copenhagen, though the DSB should now step smartly up the European electrified mileage table for early in 1979 the Danish Parliament approved a 15-year 25kV AC 50Hz electrification plan. Starting with the link between Copenhagen and Helsingör, the train-ferry terminal for Sweden, the electrifiers will reach out from the capital to the other ferry ports in Zeeland, cross into Fünen and start the spread of catenary in Jutland from around 1986 onwards. For the present, therefore, the inter-city service is still entrusted exclusively to diesel traction.

The fastest journeys between Denmark's main centres are offered by the limited-stop *Lyntog* – 'Lightning Trains', a brandname coined in 1935 to dramatize the very substantial cuts in end-to-end express passenger schedules which followed completion of the Little Belt bridge and the simultaneous debut of self-contained diesel-electric train-sets which could roll on and roll off the Great Belt train ferries, whereas the previous locomotive-hauled equipment had to be shunted on and off. In 1963–66 those early sets were superseded by 13 diesel-hydraulic four-car units of German build based very closely on the Deutsche Bundesbahn's design for its first TEE equipment contribution. Other reasons for the DSB's adoption of a multiple-unit format were the reversals enforced on through trains by the junction layouts at the key centres of Aarhus and Fredericia. However, the multiple-unit format had one disadvantage: the need to carry idle power plant across the Great Belt, wasting train ferry space. The complexity of the traction control and other circuitry between cars ruled out uncoupling en route to discard the power units for the ferry crossing.

Fully air-conditioned, these German-built sets are still creditably comfortable but technically obsolescent. To supersede them the DSB was unveiling in 1981 two prototype train-sets of new *Lyntog* equipment, built by Scandia in Denmark. Electrification has compelled a switch to locomotive power

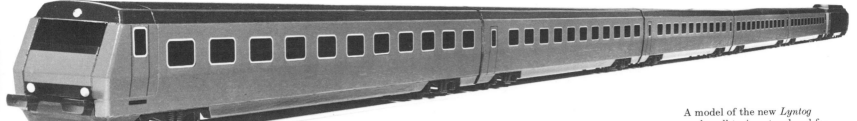

A model of the new *Lyntog* push-pull train-set ordered for the 1980s by the DSB. Note that each car has only one entrance door, to increase seating space.

and the new equipment is in five-car push-pull sets, with coaches of the customary European mainland 26.4m length instead of the short bodies of the previous multiple-units. The new and bigger ferries applied to the Great Belt at the start of the 1980s can accommodate one of these sets complete. The previous ferries had track length only for one of the German-built units, so that when two were operated in multiple they had to be uncoupled and berthed separately on the ferry. Two novelties of the new *Lyntog* equipment deserve attention. The central 'service car' in each set embodies a conference room as well as a buffet and a public telephone kiosk. And to make more room for seats the DSB has boldly dispensed with entrance doors and vestibules in the two saloons, which can only be reached through the entrance doors of the adjoining compartment coaches.

The DSB hopes before long for more economy through a lift of maximum line speed over favourable stretches to 100mph – possibly 125mph. This had been planned for the later 1970s but realization was frustrated by circumscribed investment resources. Had there been a thoroughly proven automatic body-tilting system on the world market the DSB might have bought it for the new *Lyntog*, but the Danes are not disposed to spend any of their limited funds on devising a system of their own.

The *Lyntog* of the 1980s will be the second new train-set design styled *ab initio* by the Design Group which the DSB established in the early 1970s. Their mandate was to impress a new corporate image of modernity on the whole undertaking and to ensure that it was co-ordinated and rationalized in its application to fixed assets – station architecture, furniture and signposting, for example – and to all printed material as well as to rolling stock. So far as the exterior of passenger trains is concerned, the conspicuous outcome has been a bold new livery combination of traditional DSB house colours – bright red, black and white. On coaches, hauled or multiple-unit, the red predominates, but on locomotives the red is confined to the lower cab areas and the engine body-space amidships is black, offset by the plain white of the unassuming new DSB logo in simple sans-serif capitals. Practically speaking the Design Group's work is more gratifying in its transformation of the attractiveness and convenience of many stations and their amenities, especially those that are interchanges with road transport, and in its thoughful refurbishing of existing coach interiors, both short-haul and inter-city, where its work has embraced the 1960s *Lyntog* sets.

The DSB's first new rolling-stock acquisitions after the Design Group's enthronement allowed it little scope, as the DSB bought virtually off the shelf for local service in Fünen and Jutland the two-car diesel multiple-unit design by Uerdingen which is

At the end of the 1970s the Copenhagen suburban system was the only electrified section of the DSB, but in 1979 the Danish Parliament approved progressive mainline electrification at 25kV 50Hz AC.

One of DSB's majestic 3900hp Class MZ diesel-electric Co-Cos, Nohab-built with GM engines, on freight duty.

the West German DB's Type 628. Nevertheless the DSB units were fitted with superior seating for their medium-distance role and had their cabs slightly reshaped by comparison with the DB 628s, to conform with the front-end look the designers were keen to standardize on all DSB multiple-units. These German imports, classified MR, are virile performers – necessarily so, as their stopping duties are partly along routes shared with hourly inter-city services; each car of the pair is motored with two 270hp engines, which punch the unit very rapidly up to its maximum speed of 75mph.

The first train-sets wholly representative of Design Group thought were four prototype multiple-units of four cars apiece with thyristor control (two with

ASEA equipment, two with traction equipment from Britain's GEC) which were delivered to Copenhagen's electrified *S-Bane* early in 1979. Since the spring of 1978 the *S-Bane*, though still the operational responsibility of DSB, has been integrated into the co-ordinated public transport enterprise and intermodal zonal fare scheme of the Greater Copenhagen Council's subsidiary, Greater Copenhagen Transport. The latter now shoulders the financing of all DSB local passenger service in the territory it administers, which takes in the whole of North Zeeland.

As in Norway, the economic squeeze of the later 1970s threatened a number of the DSB's heavily lossmaking rural services with abandonment, most of them in Jutland. But the Danes, too, quailed at the political repercussions. Not only were closure proposals quashed, but the services concerned are being given a blood transfusion by purchase of more Class MR multiple-units, but for this more relaxed work with only one car of each pair motored.

With no heavy industry to tap and in face of a taxation system which, DSB management protests, is far too indulgent to the road haulier in the context of his highway wear and tear, the railway has a thin time of it in the freight business. Less than a third of its revenue comes from that sector and more than half of what it does earn is generated by international traffic; the DSB share of the home freight market is a meagre 13 percent. To arrest and reverse the decline the DSB has been investing heavily in apparatus to deal mainly in unitized freight – that is, in containerized and palletized consignments handled through private sidings or a reduced number of purpose-equipped rail depots.

A Danish State Railways (DSB) train is taken on board one of the Great Belt ferries. Replacement of these ferries by a bridge has now been deferred indefinitely.

The DSB's main-line diesel-electric locomotives are Nohab-built with American GM engines. The now elderly MX and MY classes of 1960 and 1956 respectively are of A1A-A1A wheel arrangement – that is, only two axled of each six-wheel bogie are motored – and neither is very high-powered; output of the MX is 1425hp, of the MY 1950hp. The subsequent standard design, the MZ, on the other hand is a Co-Co with all axles powered and an impressive 3900hp rating in the second and third series constructed, as opposed to 3300hp in the first. Amongst refinements in the third series is provision for push-pull operation on the intensive regular-interval Zeeland passenger services between Copenhagen and Helsingör.

The Finnish State Railways (VR) is another national system beavering away at electrification. At the end of 1975 only 250 route-miles or less than seven percent of its route-mileage was under 25kV 50Hz AC catenary, but a target of as much as 50 percent conversion by 1985 has been set. About two-thirds of the 425-mile trunk route northward from Helsinki through Tampere to Oulu was already under wires by the end of the 1970s, plus the eastward transversal from the capital to the Soviet border at Vainikkala (VR is on the same 5ft track gauge as Soviet railways, but Soviet electrification in this area is DC, which

enforces a traction change to a Soviet dual-voltage locomotive at the approach to the frontier). The first class of VR electric locomotive, the 4460hp Type Srl 84-ton Bo-Bo, is a thyristor-controlled machine built by the USSR's Novocherkassk works but embodying electrical equipment by the Finnish

VR freight headed by one of the Soviet-built Class Sr 1 electric locomotives.
Below:
Two Class Dm9 diesel-hydraulic multiple-units of the Finnish State Railways.

Top:
A VR Class Sm2 EMU.
Above:
VR car-carriers attached to
an overnight express.
Below:
A VR Class Dr13 diesel-
electric Co-Co.

firm of Strömberg. This may well be the pattern of future construction, since early in 1978 the Finnish and Soviet Governments signed a partnership agreement for the development of designs for Soviet construction with Finnish traction gear, though the objective in view was primarily export trade to the Third World. The VR's only other electric rolling stock up to the end of the 1970s was a considerable number of Type Sm1 and Sm2 electric two-car multiple-units, used indiscriminately on Helsinki commuter lines and medium-distance stopping services within 25kV AC territory.

On its trunk routes the VR presents and polishes an image of quite dashing modernity. It is not merely a case of attractive exterior styling of locomotives and multiple-units blending stylishly with well-chosen liveries – red and cream for locomotives, lightish blue and white for inter-city coaches, red and polished metal for the inter-city diesel multiple-units. Nor just that the coaching stock on the principal inter-city services is modern (though elsewhere over 200 wooden-bodied coaches were still active in 1979) and features such up-to-date amenities as a ten-seater first-class lounge, self-service cafeteria cars of mid-1970s build and in all named, supplementary-fare expresses a telephone facility for passenger communication with any subscriber on the national network. A few are tailed by double-deck automobile-carriers in which, uniquely, the lower floor is fully enclosed in windowed bodywork.

On key main lines the service is gradually assuming a regular-interval pattern, even if the intervals are longer than in neighbouring Scandinavian countries and on some routes there are yawning gaps at times other European systems would treasure as a peak travel period – for example, around breakfast time. At present the line speed limit is 75mph, which coupled with the handicap of over 7500 level crossings – a ratio of two per route-mile on average for the whole system – keeps end-to-end averages rather pedestrian by European standards further south. But despite climactic conditions which demand special precautions to prevent track distortion by incessant frost the VR has a 100mph ceiling in view for some main-line stretches in a widespread track strengthening programme.

VR's rolling stock and traction requirements can nowadays be met almost entirely by Finnish industry, though in most cases the products embody foreign design or components. The modern locomotive-hauled main-line coaches, for instance, have the same basic bodywork as the system's first batch of all-steel coaches constructed by a German firm, Esslingen, at the start of the 1960s. VR's most power-ful main-line diesel-electric, though constructed by the principal Finnish manufacturers, Lokomo Oy and Valmet Oy, is intrinsically a French design by Alsthom with Alsthom monomotor double-gear bogies and a pair of French MGO 16-cylinder engines also built in Finland under licence by Tampella. This is the 93½-ton 2800hp Class Dr13 Co-Co, which has a theoretical top speed of 87½mph. Apart from another Co-Co type, the 1900hp Class Dr12, which has Tampella-built engines to the pattern of the German firm MAN, VR has preferred hydraulic transmission in the rest of its recent diesel traction, including the elegant three-car multiple-units of Class Dm8 with 1000hp output which undertake some express work.

The outstanding area of VR traffic growth is the freight flow across the Soviet border, which nearly doubled in the 1970s and is likely to accumulate more tonnage still as the USSR uses Finland as a land-bridge for exports to other countries. At the close of the 1970s VR's international freight traffic, which amounts to just over a quarter of its total business in goods, was a massive 20 times heavier across the Soviet frontier than over the western borders to Finland's Scandinavian neighbours.

A VR unit coal train hauled by a pair of 1360hp Class Dv12 diesel-hydraulic B-Bs. VR operates 148 of these mixed traffic locomotives, construction of which was shared by the Finnish builders Lokomo Oy and Valmet Oy.

A standard 16-car Shinkansen train-set of the Japanese National Railways (JNR) threads through Hiroshima on the New Tokaido Line, the first of Japan's custom-built, high speed, standard-gauge passenger railways.

9.
THE TWO FACES OF JAPAN'S RAILWAYS

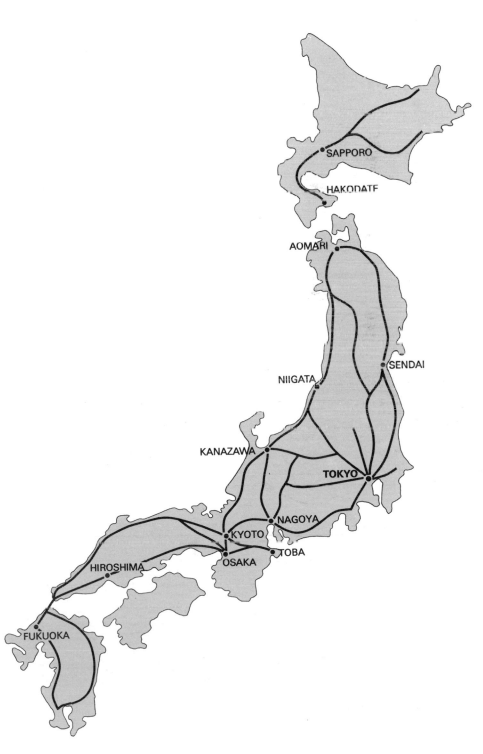

Favourite Shinkansen setting of Japanese photographers is the neighbourhood of Mt Fuji, the backcloth for this impression of a 'Hikari' limited-stop train speeding from Tokyo to Osaka.

Japanese National Railways (JNR) has two sharply contrasted facets. The glossy side, promoted worldwide and symbolic of the whole system so far as the Western man-in-the-street is aware, is the 'Bullet Train' – the 130mph electric multiple-units of the standard-gauge Shinkansen, or 'New High-Speed Railways', which were inaugurated with the October 1964 opening of the New Tokaido Line from Tokyo to Osaka. Despite its colossal initial cost the New Tokaido Line's pace and intensive regular-interval service straightaway pulled in such a weight of business that by 1970 it was showing a financial surplus even after coverage of depreciation and interest on the cash borrowed to build it.

The other and rather less assiduously reported or publicized facet of JNR is the bulk of its network, the historic Japanese railway built on the 3ft 6in gauge. Since the 1950s that has been losing traffic to other modes at one of the most depressing rates in the industrialized world and accumulating losses which submerge all the Shinkansen gains, although there was the first sign that the downward trend had been halted in early 1979.

For years past the annual JNR deficit has been around £1¾ billion ($4 billion) overall and the direct running costs of the system's trains have exceeded the latter's intake of revenue by one-third to one-half. Since the late 1950s JNR's share of the country's total freight market has collapsed from 50 to barely 12 percent; and even though Shinkansen carryings have helped to double passenger business in terms of annual passenger-mileage on trains, JNR's hold on the country's total passenger market has slipped during the same period from 55 to about 30 percent. Outside the Shinkansen system there is only one single JNR passenger service which is financially in the black (Tokyo's Yamanote commuter loop line), in sharp contrast to the Shinkansen, where in the late 1970s the original Tokyo–Osaka stretch was still costing only 46 percent of its annual ticket revenue to run. The Shinkansen network's overall operating ratio was 57 percent. The outcome is that at the end of the 1970s JNR had run up cumulative deficits of just over £7 billion ($16 billion) and that its annual subsidy from the Government was £1.3 billion ($2.8 billion).

History and Japanese tradition have combined to lock the JNR in a fairly intractable situation. The 3ft 6in gauge is totally unsuited to a railway catering for a population and an industrial economy of Japan's magnitude. It was laid with no vision of the country's growth needs, so that even in the coastal belts of comparatively flat terrain curvature can be severe and gradients quite significant. But the central mountains of the Japanese island chain and their foothills cover well over three-quarters of the

since World War II has heightened the dominance of passengers in JNR traffic. The proportion of passenger-miles recorded per annum to freight ton-miles is roughly five to one, compared with a ratio of only 1.5 to one on British Rail, even though the British system stands well down the table of European railways for volume of freight activity in relation to its size. Measured in passenger-miles JNR is burdened with almost seven times the passenger traffic of British Rail, yet the difference in system size is a narrow one: 13,200 route-miles for the Japanese network against BR's 11,100. The commuter traffic of London and every other European city pales against rush-hour rail movement in Tokyo. British Rail's London termini handle under $1\frac{1}{2}$ million people a day, accounting incoming and outgoing passengers separately, whereas in the Tokyo area the JNR alone is dealing with ten million each working day and many more are riding on the independently owned local railways in the capital's metropolitan area.

JNR's all-sleeper 'Asakaze' express on the 3ft 6in gauge, headed by a Class EF65 electric locomotive.

Below left:
Rush-hour in Tokyo.
Below:
Tokyo's Central station in the evening. In the centre of the picture, on the 3ft 6in gauge, the 'Hayabusa' overnight train leaves for Kyushu island, while in the foreground a standard-gauge 'Hikari' enters the Shinkansen annex.

country's land area. Inland travellers can encounter climbs as stiff as the 25 miles of continuous 1 in 30 on the electrified Fukubei branch of the main line from Tokyo to Aomori, at the northern tip of Honshu island. The unfriendly character of so much of Japan's land space has packed industrial and population growth into the littoral areas of the island, aggravating the difficulties of the narrow-gauge system. One consequence is that the 345 miles of the 3ft 6in-gauge line from Tokyo to Osaka, the first rail trunk route in the country, is now intersected by about 1000 level crossings – just one factor in the constraints which limit maximum speed throughout the bulk of JNR to 75mph.

The surging growth of the Japanese population

A Class KIHA 23 diesel multiple-unit for short-haul service on one of the rural passenger lines that the JNR is socially obliged to operate, but which lose money heavily.

A major influence on the state of JNR's balance sheet has been an obligation to carry practically all these passengers at uneconomic fares. Many groups of rail-users such as commuters and students were and still are benefitted by the Japanese Government's massively discounted fares (up to as much as 90 percent) as a matter of social policy, but until 1976 the basic fares against which the privileged groups' rates were proportioned were lagging far behind inflation's effect on costs. Not only did JNR have no liberty to fix its own prices but any application for higher fares had to go through the rigmarole of debate and vote in the Japanese Diet.

That was changed in 1976–77. With the railways' accumulated deficit threatening to take off into infinity the Government staggered its electors by pushing through a 50 percent uplift of fares and freight rates at a stroke. Later the Diet was persuaded to relinquish its power of veto in a second Bill which allowed JNR much more flexibility to adjust its fares and tariffs, though any fare rise still has to be approved by the country's Transport Ministry, and neither passenger nor freight tariffs are allowed to get ahead of the inflation rate in wages and com-

modity prices. So JNR has no hope of resolving its financial crisis by edging its prices up to the limit the traffics will bear.

Another millstone around JNR's neck is the rural 40 percent of its system which contributes no more than four percent of the railway's total revenue but runs up one-quarter of the annual loss. For a nation whose name is synonymous with efficiency in almost any industrial process one cares to think of, the Japanese attitude to these heavily loss-making lines is unfathomable. It is not merely that the JNR earmarked some 1600 or more route-miles of them for closure as long ago as 1968, but as yet has been prevented from shutting down more than 125 route-miles. So sensitive is central Government to local political pressures that the same regional interests which have hamstrung the closure programme have been and still are managing to procure the continuous construction of brand-new local railways.

At the start of 1979 as many as 47 new lines aggregating about 1250 route-miles were underway. Some of them, granted, were justified inducements to population resettlement away from the overcrowded areas or response to a real need of new public transport, but a good many sounded more like what the Americans would scornfully call 'pork-barrel' sops to importunate local politicians. The JNR has no conclusive say in the decision to build such lines and equally no option but to operate them once they have been completed by the Japan Railway Construction Corporation, an agency set up to take the financial weight of new railway projects undertaken as state policy off the JNR's back. On the other hand, the Government has flatly refused to adopt some form of separate contract for the operation of such lines, so that the lossmakers – and many are patently going

A Class EF58 electric locomotive on the original 3ft 6in-gauge main line from Tokyo to Osaka, the first railway to be laid in Japan.

into irretrievable deficit from the day they open – simply swell JNR's overall debit.

JNR's other grave problem is its inability to trim its labour force in step with its modernization and rationalization. The frequently-used but crude measure of railwaymen's productivity which relates the annual sum of a system's recorded passenger-miles and freight ton-miles to the number of staff employed produces a statistic to shame most Western railways. On that basis JNR has registered a near-90 percent improvement in productivity since 1957. But that figure results almost entirely from the sensational growth in passenger traffic. Almost half the additional passenger movement has been generated by the Shinkansen, to which every conceivable labour-saving device of modern rail technology has been applied. Much of the remainder is on the short-distance commuter railways, where the Japanese tolerate travelling conditions which would have Western cities in a ferment. Western media has by now made most people familiar with the 'pushers' employed at Tokyo stations to shove the last knots of rush-hour commuters like cattle into already jam-packed trains, and of the quite sober Japanese calculation that individual train capacity is that much higher in summer because less space is occupied by standees' overcoats and winter underwear.

The reality is that since the late 1950s JNR has been able to reduce its staff by no more than three percent. The tradition which enshrines Japanese industry as a family to which one dedicates one's life and which in return virtually guarantees one lifelong employment is so ingrained that JNR has far more difficulty in shedding staff than any railway in an industrialized Western country, no matter whether many of the latter's employees have an entrenched civil servant status, as they do in West Germany, or the railway trades unions are powerfully protective. For that matter the Japanese railway unions are themselves as militant as most: a few days' stoppage of work is practically an annual ritual over the period of negotiating the following year's rates of pay.

All in all, the JNR is largely dependent on attrition – retirement through age or voluntarily on other grounds – to slim down its workforce. In the interim the crucial problem is that since the 1950s Japanese railwaymen's wages have climbed twice as fast as the rate at which JNR was allowed to increase its tariffs, at least until 1976. This has swamped the effect of modernization savings to the extent that whereas wages accounted for only 40 percent of JNR's running costs as recently as 1974, they now absorb as much as 80 percent of all passenger and freight income. In an ideal world – from the management's standpoint – JNR could slash its manpower by one-quarter overnight through a technically practical switch to one-man operation of its manifold commuter trains. But needless to say the unions will have none of that.

JNR's outstanding need is to win more freight traffic, for which there will be increasing 3ft 6in-gauge trunk route capacity as the Shinkansen standard-gauge system expands and relieves the narrow gauge of more long-haul passenger movement. Like more than one Western European railway, JNR has so far been unable to pull in merchandise traffic in sufficient volume to offset lost bulk industrial freight. JNR's problem is the depletion of the country's natural resources by its phenomenal industrial activity. The outstanding case is that of coal; rail movement from Japanese pits today is only one-seventh of the tonnage carried as recently as the early 1960s. Because all the country's post-World War II industrial development has been in the coastal belts, the only areas of reasonably flat terrain, imported raw materials can too often make the short distance from port to plant most conveniently by road. Another immensely strong competitor of JNR is coastal shipping, which actually holds a slightly bigger share of the Japanese domestic freight market than road and rail put together. Nevertheless JNR has developed a promising network of block train services in such commodities as oil, limestone, cement, iron and steel, paper and motorcars besides what survives of its coal traffic; about one-third of its freight tonnage is covered by these commodities.

In the merchandise business the JNR effort is spearheaded by a Freightliner service of fixed-formation container trains on the British Rail pattern interlinking around 150 road-rail transfer depots. The JNR Freightliner wagons are of even more sophisticated design than BR's, boasting electromagnetic track brakes as well as conventional air-braking systems on their air-sprung bogies, but the Freightliner trains are limited to a maximum of 62.5mph on the road. Like BR, the Japanese have developed a computer-based data system for effective control of container distribution and transits, but in addition JNR has evolved computerized control of the depot container transfer gantry cranes to reduce labour usage. The Freightliner operation was badly hit by the sharp rate increases of 1976, which lost traffic and led to a 25 percent reduction in the number of daily trains two years later; a substantial amount of block train business in commodities was forfeited too. Substantial new cuts of

JNR is one of the few systems in the world to have adopted the British Freightliner model and build up a network of dedicated container train services between strategic trans-shipment depots. In charge of this 3ft 6in-gauge Tohoku line train is a Class EF81 triple-voltage B-B-B electric locomotive.

A Class EF60 electric locomotive heads freight on the 3ft 6in-gauge Old Tokaido Line. Over 70 percent of JNR's goods traffic is handled in wagonloads.

routing of wagons to their appointed sidings and automatic control of the track-mounted retarders which brake the wagons as they come off the hump, but also for automatic routing of incoming and outgoing trains. At several yards JNR has installed in each siding, between its running rails, a linear induction motor-powered mule which automatically detects a wagon's entrance into the siding it serves, starts moving with the vehicle, then grasps its wheel flanges; as soon as the mule detects that it is about 200ft from the end of the siding or from other wagons already occupying it, it slows the wagon it is holding down to walking pace, releases it, then returns automatically to its normal sentry post near the mouth of the siding to await the next entrant.

But automation only reduces the cost of shunting; it does not eliminate it. Nor does automation of yards remove all the risks of delay in transit or achieve much quicker delivery from consignor to consignee unless there is an effective overall train-working plan. In Japan road freight transport is still virtually unregulated either in scope or in the prices it charges. To compete with it in the merchandise market JNR has an imperative need of cheaper, quicker and more reliable wagonload operation. How far it has to go can be guessed from the fact that the average speed of a JNR wagonload consignment from despatcher to recipient in the early 1970s was a beggarly 7mph!

In the late 1950s JNR was still a very substantial steam operator, but electrification of all trunk routes was already policy. In the next two decades steam was rapidly withdrawn and the last fires were dropped in 1975. Today 40 percent of the system is under catenary and that accounts for more than two-thirds of all passenger and over three-quarters of all freight movement. The system is mixed. The earliest main-line electrification, of the Old Tokaido and Sanyo lines from Tokyo down the east coast of Honshu island from Tokyo through Osaka and Hiroshima, was at 1.5kV DC, but in the early 1960s JNR switched to high-voltage AC drawn from the industrial grid. In Japan the latter system runs up against the complexity that commercial current is generated at 50Hz in some zones, 60Hz in others, so that the railway's 20kV AC supply varies in frequency from area to area. There are trunk routes, such as that from Maibara to Aoimori on the west coast, which feature stretches of DC and both AC systems, with the result that one of JNR's most numerous freight locomotive types, the 3200hp Class EF81 B-B-B, is a triple-current machine to allow uninterrupted through running. At the end of 1979 the JNR announced a fresh electrification programme of 3000 route miles to cut down oil consumption.

passenger as well as freight services were ordered in 1980 to conserve energy.

JNR cannot now make its Freightliner operation competitive with road over trunk distances of less than 350–400 miles and consequently half its container business is handled by the wagonload. Over 70 percent of JNR's total freight, in fact, is wagonload traffic, which means that JNR is dealing in roughly 12 times as much freight of that sort as, for instance, British Rail. At the end of the rationalization in progress in the late 1970s JNR will still be processing this traffic through some 150 marshalling yards and serving around 1500 freight depots, twice the number of yards to which the West German DB, for example, is reshaping its system.

JNR has been investing huge sums in automation of its bigger yards, of which the equipment has no superior in the world for sophistication. At the Musashino terminal yard which is a terminal for the whole Tokyo metropolitan area, for instance, 4400 wagons can be processed daily by computer-based apparatus that provides not only for automatic drafting of train marshalling orders, automatic control of hump shunting locomotives, automatic

The great majority of JNR electric locomotive types created since the early 1950s have been either four-axle B-Bs of 2550hp (Class ED70–75 inclusive), of which the most numerous Class is ED75, found at work throughout the AC network, or six-axle B-B-Bs with outputs ranging from the 3400hp of the DC

Another freight on the Old Tokaido Line, but in this case headed by the most powerful electric type in JNR's 3ft 6in-gauge fleet, the 5200hp Class EF66.

Classes EF63–65 to the impressive 5200hp of the 101-tonne DC Class EF66, which with its 75mph maximum speed is the DC system's first choice for heavy locomotive-hauled express trains. The AC Class ED76–78 2550hp machines, have the novel B-2-B arrangement, signifying that the centre bogie is unpowered; this idle bogie is equipped with adjustable air springing so that the driver can vary the load bearing on its axles — and as a corollary that on the motored bogies' axles – to control the weight transfer inevitable during periods of maximum power output, as at starting or when climbing, and thereby avoid wheel-slip.

JNR's electric locomotives are primarily freight hauliers. Well over 80 percent of all JNR's passenger services under wires are covered by reversible multiple-units and JNR is intent on increasing the percentage because of the format's operational economy. The electric multiple-unit fleet features not only sets of all types for commuter, medium- and long-distance service but even complete all-sleeping car units. One batch of units, Class 381, incorporates automatic body-tilting apparatus and since the series is now over 160 cars strong JNR is, at the time of writing, the most energetic practitioner of this technique in the world. Introduced to the mountainous 157.5-mile route from Nagoya to Nagano in 1973, the Class 381's ability to take its curves up to 15mph faster than orthodox equipment allowed an early cut of the best journey time for the distance from three hours 57 minutes to just three hours 20 minutes. More recently Class 381 sets have been applied to the Kisei line from Osaka to the Kii peninsula holiday resorts.

Express service on the narrow-gauge trunk routes yet to be superseded by Shinkansen is intensive. On the Tohoku line from Tokyo to the north, for instance, there are three departures from the capital's Ueno station almost every hour of the working day from 07.00 to 20.00, the majority travelling the 220 miles to Sendai, but only six continuing beyond to Aomori in the far north, 462 miles from Tokyo; a few branch off before Sendai to take the Akita line from Fukushima. Every one of these Tohoku line trains is shown as purveying a restaurant car service. As for speed, the standard time from Tokyo to Sendai inclusive of three intermediate stops is $4\frac{1}{4}$ hours, which represents an end-to-end average of just under a mile a minute.

The standard electric type of the 20kV AC electrified sector of JNR's 3ft 6in-gauge network is the 2550hp Class ED75, one of which heads the 'Yazuru' limited express on the Tohoku line.

One of JNR's numerous Class 381 automatic tilt-body electric multiple-units on the Hanwa line.

Before 1981 is out the narrow-gauge Tohoku line will have surrendered its long-haul passenger traffic to one of the two new Shinkansen which were being pressed to a belated conclusion at the end of the 1970s. Belated because, although they were once scheduled for completion in 1977, these two projects fell foul of a combined assault from inflation, environmental agitation, somewhat unexpected technical hiccups and sheer bloody-mindedness on the part of some local politicians which has unbelievably blurred Japan's own image of the Shinkansen since the spectacular early triumph of the New Tokaido line.

Even before World War II the Japanese had recognized that duplication of the overcrowded 3ft 6in-gauge main line from Tokyo to Osaka was inescapable sooner or later, but the decision to throw off the narrow-gauge shackles and develop a new broad-gauge, high-speed technology was not taken until the 1950s. At first the new railway was to combine daytime passenger service with a night-time Freightliner operation, but the latter was discarded during the planning of the new railway, when it became clear that in view of the planned intensive

daylong passenger timetable the tracks would have to be surrendered completely to the civil and electrical engineers in the small hours for routine maintenance.

The daring of the Shinkansen concept at the time of its formulation ought never to be forgotten. Although the French had just raised the horizon of possible rail speed to 200mph no one was yet essaying intensive regular operation at even 100mph. The Japanese proposed to jump straight to 160mph as standard practice, though at the end of the day they lowered their sights to 130mph. The leap required the evolution and perfection in cast-iron reliability of an entirely new technology integrating every element of the railway – track design, traction, vehicle dynamics, braking systems, overhead current collection, signalling and traffic control. This took six years, one year more than the actual building of the 320-mile New Tokaido Line – and construction of that in only five years was remarkable enough, considering the work involved in clearing paths through the Tokaido belt's teeming cities for its elevated viaducts, in boring tunnels that included

A New Tokaido Shinkansen
train at speed near Atami,
some 50 miles out from Tokyo.

three of 5500 to 8580 yards' length, and in erecting numerous other viaducts.

The New Tokaido Line was the first JNR line to be electrified at 25kV AC. It was the first railway in the world to standardize continuous display of signalling aspects on drivers' control desks and to dispense with intermittent lineside signals entirely. And it was the first trunk railway anywhere on which route-setting as well as the operation of signals was entirely automatic when trains were running to schedule.

This was facilitated by the simplicity of the layout. The line's exclusively inter-city passenger purpose required only ten intermediate stations, each with a standard plan of a loop enclosing an island platform in each direction, so that in the whole railway, including the Tokyo and Osaka terminals with their ancillary depot installations, there were only 230 sets of points. The whole route could be supervised from one central control panel in Tokyo, but in everyday operation the controllers there only interrupt the automatic functions and vary commands to the trains if the service lapses from schedule.

The Tokyo controllers have a continuous panoramic view of the traffic situation on an illuminated track diagram to which each train reports its position by service number through an electronic code it transmits to track-mounted receivers studding the length of the route. Conversely, commands from Tokyo and impulses to actuate the cab-signalling display are in the form of coded frequencies imparted through the track circuiting, which are picked up and decoded into driving-desk displays by apparatus on the train-set. This automatic liaison between controls and train is supplemented by a radio-telephone system which embodies controller-to-train, train-to-controller and train to train channels as well as connection between passenger booths within the train and the national telephone network. Each train also transmits to lineside receivers an electronic code signifying whether it is due to pass or stop at the next station; this automatically sets the points for the loop or the straight road past the island platform. The controls of the first New Tokaido Line train-sets were arranged for fully automatic graduation of acceleration, deceleration and braking in response to the signalling impulses with a view to total automation of driving, but this was never implemented and the apparatus serves only as an aid to drivers, a check on their responses and a safeguard

against extravagant consumption of energy.

The Shinkansen train-sets pack the most formidable power of any in the world. Each pair of cars is a self-contained traction unit, with or without driving cab, and every axle is motored, so that when the inaugural 12-car formations of the New Tokaido Line were extended to 16 cars to cope with the huge volume of traffic the aggregate power of each set was 15,875hp for a total train weight of 880 tonnes. Even that output was eclipsed in the Series 961 equipment built to expand the fleet to over a thousand twin-sets when the New Sanyo Line was added to the New Tokaido route in 1975 to establish a continuous 664-mile Shinkansen route from Tokyo to Hakata on Kyushu island, via a new 11.6-mile tunnel under Kanmon Strait between Honshu and Kyushu islands which only Switzerland's Simplon beats for length. The continuous power rating of a 16-car 961 set is a massive 23,600hp for a tare train weight of 930 tonnes. In 1972 what was then a prototype 961 six-car unit was tested up to a Japanese speed record of 178mph.

Especially since JNR abolished first-class in the late 1960s (though a form of discrimination survives: former first-class cars are now designated 'Green' and in them advance seat reservation is obligatory) seating comfort in Shinkansen trains has not matched Europe's modern best. A three-and-two arrangement athwart a central aisle shoehorns as many as 110 seats into each 82ft-long car, compared with 88 in the slightly longer body of the Deutsche Bundesbahn's latest second-class saloon design for its dual-class IC operation. Shinkansen train-sets are fully air-conditioned and are furthermore fitted with an ingenious compressed-air device which, automatically activated at the run-up to a tunnel, seals all entrance and vestibule doors tightly in their frames so as to shield passengers from the uncomfortable effects of trains passing each other at top speed underground. The first Shinkansen train-sets had only buffet catering, supplemented by trolley service, but for the longer hauls created by the opening of the New Sanyo Line the Series 961 units were built with both restaurant and buffet amenities.

In speed JNR's Shinkansen were still supreme at the end of the 1970s, though run close by some of British Rail's 'Inter-City 125' diesel timings and certain to be surpassed by French Railways' new Paris–Lyons TGV early in the 1980s. The zenith of

On board a Shinkansen train in one of the former first-class cars, now designated 'green cars' and carrying obligatory seat reservation charges; in standard class cars the seating arrangement is three-and-two, as against two-and-two in the 'green' accommodation.

On the Sanin line, one of the Class KIHA 58 diesel multiple-units which provide express service on secondary 3ft 6in-gauge routes.

Shinkansen service so far was late 1975 and early 1976, after the New Sanyo opening, when passenger carryings topped a million in one 24-hour period and on a normal working day over 100 trains were scheduled each way over all or part of the 664-mile route from Tokyo to Hakata, with many extras on public holidays. From the start of a day's service at 06.00 to the nightly shutdown for maintenance around midnight the regular-interval timetable offered six trains each way between Tokyo and Osaka in almost every hour (more in the peak), three or four of them in the superior 'Hikari' category which called en route only at Nagoya and Kyoto, the remainder in the 'Kodama' category which served all stations. Each day's timetable showed a staggering total of almost 450 inter-station runs scheduled at start-to-stop average speeds in excess of 90mph. The savage fare increase of late 1976 abruptly halted traffic growth – for a time business receded quite significantly, in fact – and in 1979 some of the 'Kodama' trains were annulled as an economy. But the standard 'Hikari' Tokyo–Osaka time is still three

hours ten minutes for the 320 miles, which constitutes an end-to-end average speed of 101.1mph, two stops en route notwithstanding. Numerous 'Hikari' station-to-station allowances represent higher averages, up to a peak of 110.3mph for the 108.5 miles between Nagoya and Shizuoka by one working. Average speeds over the New Sanyo extension are considerably slower, because it is subject to numerous 100mph speed restrictions in mining areas which are prey to subsidence. Even so some 'Hikari' complete the 664-mile journey from Tokyo to Hakata in only six hours 56 minutes for an end-to-end average speed throughout the 664 miles, stops on the way included, of 95.8mph.

The classic, toy-railway-like simplicity of the Shinkansen track layout, its patterned operation with standard train-sets and its high degree of automation made the New Tokaido line a paragon of efficiency. In the late 1960s the Japanese were estimation made the New Tokaido Line a paragon of generating nine times as much revenue as the rest of JNR staff.

Why, then, the delay in building the six further Shinkansen which in 1970 the Japanese Government affirmed were an essential first step, let alone the dozen more it advocated as desirable to establish a 4350 route-mile high-speed railway system which would help coax population and industry away from the crowded coastal belts?

The first deterrent was the particularly severe impact on Japan of the oil price crisis. It stunted economic growth and set off a rate of inflation which by the mid-1970s had trebled the per-mile building cost of Shinkansen. Then there was the worsening financial state of JNR, which had railway management itself wary of the primarily social intent of some of the Shinkansen routes proposed. They feared the incubus of yet more lines on which revenue would never cover operating costs. Developing Japanese

road transport, too, was eroding the Shinkansen case and soon it was further jeopardized by the advent of the wide-body jetliner.

As unpredictable as the oil price explosion was a sudden eruption of environmental objection to Shinkansen. The appalling pollution of Japan's industrial areas had suddenly, after years of tolerance, become a political issue and the Shinkansen were an easy target. In part or in whole the additional routes projected became hotly controversial. Not only that, but the Government enacted stringent new noise-abatement measures which forced JNR to spend millions on erection of sound-baffling walls and parapets alongside existing Shinkansen tracks and modification of bridges to reduce vibration wherever the 'Bullet Trains' ran close to dwellings.

Meanwhile JNR had been discovering that all their research had underestimated the effects of sustained operation of an intensive train service at 130mph. Track wear leading to over-frequent rail breakages was the first problem. As a result of the first few years of New Tokaido Line experience the JNR changed to a much more costly concrete slab foundation for the continuous welded rail for the New Sanyo Line (except for the third of that route affected by mining subsidence) and any Shinkansen to come, and steeled themselves to a complete reconstruction of the New Tokaido Line track. Both this and installation of heavier catenary throughout were ordered for completion by 1984 after a disastrous four months in the 1974 summer when Shinkansen punctuality was in shreds through a welter of track, vehicle and automatic signalling equipment failures. It has also been found that the nightly six-hour closure of the high-speed lines affords inadequate time for all the essential maintenance tasks to be completed, especially on pointwork, and in consequence the Tokyo–Osaka stretch now shuts for a whole day seven or eight times a year – advertised in advance – to allow the engineers longer possessions of the track.

Nevertheless, though the grandiose draft of a 4000 route-mile Shinkansen network is almost certainly scrap paper, two of the projected additional high-speed lines made headway in the late 1970s against the economic constraints and – much more laboriously – against chronic environmental niggling that was often politically motivated. One or two more routes have since been resurrected for serious reconsideration.

The two fresh Shinkansen which will be completed in the early 1980s are the Tohoku northwards from Tokyo to Morioka and the Joetsu northwestwards from the capital Niigata on the west coast of Honshu, overlooking the Sea of Japan. The full Shinkansen plan of the early 1970s envisaged continuing the Tohoku line by another Shinkansen through Aomori and into the northernmost island, Hokkaido. This entailed crossing the Tsuguru Strait between Honshu and Hokkaido in by far the world's longest rail tunnel to date. This, the 33½-mile Seikan Tunnel, was well on

the way to completion at the end of the 1970s, but at the time of writing there remains uncertainty whether the finished bore will carry a Hokkaido Shinkansen or simply a narrow-gauge link between the 3ft 6in-gauge systems of the two islands. It may even be laid with mixed-gauge track.

The Joetsu is on some counts the most remarkable Shinkansen project yet. The New Sanyo Line, unlike the New Tokaido, came up against formidable mountain massifs at the southern tip of Honshu and had to negotiate 138 of the 247 route-miles from Okayama to Hakata in 111 tunnels (one of which, as mentioned earlier, was the 11.6-mile crossing of Kanmon Strait). But the Joetsu Shinkansen cuts straight across Honshu's Mikumi mountain spine at a summit of some 1500ft in a latitude where winter snow depths of up to 8ft are common. Most of the mountain passage is in tunnels, of which the line will have 23 aggregating 65.9 of its total 171 route miles (longest of the principal mountain tunnels is Dai-Shimizu, extending for 13.8 miles), but in the open the Shinkansen has to be protected by snowsheds

Mt Fuji dominates this view of the Old Tokaido Line; the 'Mizuho' express is heading for Tokyo.

The 33½ mile Seikan Tunnel under construction; on the right is the main tunnel, on the left the service tunnel for movement of men, equipment and excavated spoil, which has a connection to the main bore every 600 metres.

A 3ft 6in-gauge Class DD51 B-2-B diesel-hydraulic locomotive with 2200hp output.

The world's only electric multiple-units with sleeping cars are the dual-voltage Class 581 train-sets of JNR's 3ft 6in-gauge network.

and in the foothills it will be flanked by a series of trackside water-sprinklers which will prevent falling snow from settling and freezing. The original New Tokaido line train-sets were troubled by snow damage to their electrical gear, which had to be more fully enclosed in subsequent Shinkansen train-sets, and this protection will have to be reinforced in the Joetsu and Tohoku equipment. Almost all the open mileage of the new Shinkansen has had to be built on viaducts 20 to 30ft above the ground, partly because of the many roads and waterways to be bridged, partly to meet the stringent noise-abatement specifications foisted on the JNR since the first Shinkansen was commissioned.

Both Joetsu and Tohoku Shinkansen are engineered for the 160mph top speed of the first high-speed lines, but until almost the end of the 1970s JNR still seemed content with a 130mph limit, both to check wear and tear and also to control noise. This limit seemed implicit in the 1978 order of a prototype Series 962 unit of potential Joetsu and Tohoku equipment with less powerful motors than the 961 and a firm 130mph maximum speed rating. But its delivery and evaluation in 1979 was not followed by a production order and in the autumn of that year JNR started a fresh series of tests with the 1972 series 961 prototype on a completed stretch of the Tohoku line. These culminated in a new JNR speed record of

198.3mph. Early in 1980 JNR made known that it had changed its mind and was going for 160mph as the normal operating speed on both Joetsu and Tohoku Shinkansen.

One theory advanced for this backtracking was that the Japanese had finally grasped that 160mph was no longer just test vehicle performance in France but fast approaching standard daily performance on the Paris–Lyons TGV. It is a plausible explanation because of the massive export business which the Japanese built on the pioneer Shinkansen work of JNR's own highly respected Railway Technical Research Centre and the eager collaborative effort of Japanese industry. The French, already one of the strongest export competitors in world railway markets, will undoubtedly reap similar benefit from successful TGV operation.

The foremost name in Japanese locomotive construction is Mitsubishi, which is shared by two separate concerns. In the traction sector of its output, Mitsubishi Heavy Industries is primarily a diesel locomotive builder. It deals in all three main types of transmission – New Zealand Railways, for instance, have been a steady customer for an MHI design of 1050hp diesel-electric – but JNR has preferred diesel-hydraulics almost exclusively for its 3ft 6in-gauge system. Most numerous JNR types are: the 2200hp Class DD51 B-2-B, an 81-tonne centre-cab, low-bonnet machine; the 740hp Class DD13 B-B; and the 1350hp Class DE10 with an idiosyncratic AAA-B wheel arrangement, signifying that the three leading axles are independently motored. Japanese railway equipment manufacturers are tightly integrated under the aegis of their industrial association and long-run orders, whether for home or overseas customers, are frequently shared among several firms other than the one which created the design.

Mitsubishi Electric Corporation is primarily occupied with electric locomotives and railcars, a field in which Hitachi is also prominent (Hitachi is equally active in diesel locomotive and railcar design and manufacture). Mitsubishi has been employing thyristor control in its electric traction designs since 1970 and it is a feature of the most recent JNR locomotive types.

As one would expect from JNR's predelicition for multiple-unit railcar operation, powered and non-powered coaches dominated the Japanese industry's output at the end of the 1970s. Production lines were the busier for JNR's decision to renew the entire first-generation fleet of Shinkansen train-sets after a career of only 13 years, which was being accomplished at the rate of some 150 new cars a year. The biggest firm in the coach-building business is Kawasaki Heavy Industries, creator, amongst other things, of the Series 381 automatic tilt-body electric train-sets for 'Limited' express service. Kawasaki is also a locomotive manufacturer, its products in this sector including the JNR Class EF62 C-C and EF65 B-B-B electrics. The other major railcar builders are

Tokyo Car Corporation and Nippon Sharyo Seizo Kaisha, though the latter plays a proportionately larger role in construction of JNR's freight stock.

Japan's industry's market is enlarged by the country's very important corps of independent railways. Most of them are short-haul railways in the great metropolitan areas, but not all. An outstanding exception is the Kinki Nippon Railway, which owns a 581-route-mile network in the Osaka Kyoto-Nagoya region and runs two score of locomotives and almost 900 railcar vehicles of modern design. Like almost all the independent companies, Kinki Nippon is fully electrified on the overhead DC system; and like roughly half of them it is standard-gauge, not 3ft 6in. One company, the Kei-Sei on the eastern side of Tokyo, is inscrutably 4ft 6in.

In sum these private railways shift only 25 percent fewer passengers than JNR on an average day, a ratio which holds good for the metropolitan area of Tokyo itself. If one adds to the traffic of the independent surface railways the passenger volume of the country's six city Metros – in Tokyo, Osaka, Nagoya, Sapporo, Yokohama and Kobe – then the daily passenger business of JNR is just about equalled. Moreover new independent railways are still emerging. As recently as 1979, for example, the numerous Tokyo group was supplemented by the Hokuso Rapid Railway, constructed to cater for a new development to the northeast of the capital.

A number of the independent railways are distinguished by the very latest refinements in traffic control. A notable example is the Keio Teito Railway of metropolitan Tokyo, which runs a two-minute headway service on its main line to Hachioji. The route has four branches completing a network of about 40 route-miles, all supervised from one control centre where a computer complex not only routes all trains automatically in accordance with timetable data banked in its memory, but instantaneously recommends the best course of improvisation to the controllers if the working gets out of phase. Since the line operates six different categories of train the apparatus has a considerable range of options to ponder before it offers its split-second advice – which might be to vary the point at which fast trains overtake slower, to revise platforming, to change train categories en route, or perhaps to turn round late-

Top left.
Commuter travel in Osaka.
Top right:
A Kinki-Nippon Railway electric multiple-unit.
Above:
Rush-hour on the Kinki-Nippon system.
Left:
On the Keio Teito Railway, an independent electric system serving the western suburbs of Tokyo.

running trains short of scheduled destinations. If its recommended decisions entail no special complications the apparatus will automatically implement its optimum choice unless the controller overrides the computer.

In recent years South African Railways (SAR) have achieved outstanding advances in the operation of unit freight trains on their 3ft 6in gauge. This coal haul is crossing

the White Umfolugi Bridge behind electric power in Natal.

10.
THE 20,000-TONNE FREIGHT TRAINS OF SOUTH AFRICA'S NARROW GAUGE

With a dynamometer car sandwiched between the first pair, seven of the 4000hp Class 7E Co-Co electrics built for SAR's first 25kV 50Hz AC electrification, from the Transvaal to Richards Bay, are tested on a huge block coal train grossing almost 10,000 tonnes.

The present-day performance of South African Railways (SAR) as a freight carrier has rewritten as many historic conceptions of a narrow-gauge system's potential as that of Japan's 3ft 6in-gauge city commuter lines has in the passenger sector. No standard-gauge railway in Western Europe matches the maximum trainload tonnages regularly shifted in some areas of the SAR. Trains of 6000 tonnes gross are now common practice even where gradients are as steep as 1 in 70.

It is not European standards, however, but North American which are challenged as SAR aims higher still. Trials with loads of as much as 14,800 tonnes have been conducted on a ruling gradient of 1 in 80, while on the new Sishen–Saldanha ore line in the southwest of the country, where inclines are no stiffer than 1 in 250, trainloads of 20,000 tonnes are being

operated as a norm and experimental train loading has been taken up to a peak of just over 23,000 tonnes.

SAR has learned to live with and make the best of its inheritance of a 3ft 6in gauge from pioneers preoccupied with economy in construction, as a result of which they also bequeathed their successors steep gradients and a great deal of speed-restrictive curvature wherever the terrain was unfriendly. Well over 90 percent of SAR's passenger traffic is local, the greater part of it focussed on the suburban networks of Durban, Cape Town and Reef around Johannesburg. Thus there is no pressure for quicker inter-city rail passenger movement (or national socio-economic need to provide it) of the intensity which compelled Japan to throw off some of its narrow-gauge shackles and build standard-gauge Shinkansen.

On the other hand South Africa, unlike Japan, is still rich in fossil fuels and other indigenous raw materials. Limitations imposed on long-haul road freight transport in the 1930s to safeguard the railways when the latter were relied upon to underpin national economic development are still substantially in force, though in recent years they have been relaxed in particulars that have made the competition for high-value merchandise goods much more severe and have crowded SAR out of the shorthaul market. Consequently SAR's main technological thrust has been directed at the improvement of long-haul bulk transport efficiency. And here South African advances have been quite striking in

The Class 6E 3340hp Bo-Bo electric specially streamlined for the trials under 3kV DC catenary near Johannesburg in late 1978 when a world narrow-gauge speed record of 152mph was set.

the past decade or two.

South African steam power always looked unbelievably majestic in bulk for its narrow gauge. But its most modern and still active examples are lighter in maximum axleload by 15 percent or so than each fully laden wagon of many contemporary SAR mineral trains. This is indicative of the attention paid to track and vehicle running gear as a basic priority of SAR modernization.

SAR undoubtedly has more track-mileage of continuous welded rail laid on concrete sleepers than any other narrow-gauge system in the world, proportionately to its size. A good deal of main-line curvature has been eased and some steep gradients relaxed by realignment but since 1976 SAR has been obtaining better line speed more economically through a development of its Test Section which has excited keen interest outside South Africa, in the USA especially.

This is the High Stability or HS bogie, sometimes known as the Scheffel cross-anchor bogie in honour of the SAR Test Section chief who devised it and to denote an essential feature of its construction. In brief, the bogie allows each wheel-set a measure of self-steering so that the profile of the wheel is better matched to that of the railhead whatever the configuration of the track. This reduces any tendency of the wheel-set to 'hunt' – that is, to yaw from side to side. It also limits wear and tear of track and running gear and allows sharp curvature to be taken faster than is advisable with bogies of previously orthodox design. All new SAR freight vehicles have been built with this type of bogie since the end of 1976; they have included vehicles with as much as 26 tonnes' permissible maximum axleload for the Sishen–Saldanha Bay ore line.

More interestingly a coach experimentally fitted with cross-anchor HS bogies has been run up to speeds of 152mph. In a trial of late 1978 this pace was held for almost two miles over straight track between Midway and Westonaria, near Johannesburg, behind a Class 6E electric locomotive specially prepared with a streamlined bullet nose and altered gearing. A few months earlier SAR had hustled a party of Parliamentarians including South Africa's Transport Minister up to 146mph in the same vehicle.

Another crucial factor in the rapidly advancing efficiency of SAR's block mineral trains has been the switch from the previously standard SAR vacuum to air braking in the latest equipment. Air brakes not only allow a 30 percent increase in per-axle gross loaded weight of a wagon but also a greater length of train.

Two lines in particular demonstrate some spectacular consequences. One is the direct route recently completed by a combination of new construction and upgrading of existing infrastructure to ferry export coal (principally for Japan) from Transvaal mines in the area of Johannesburg southeastwards to the port of Richards Bay, up the coast from Durban. This was

the first SAR line to undergo 25kV AC 50Hz electrification (of which more in a moment) but even before the catenary was commissioned in 1978 SAR had successfully experimented with 160-wagon trains on the Richards Bay haul. For traction no fewer than 11 diesel locomotives had to be mobilized, five at the head end and the remainder spliced into the formation between the 100th and 101st wagon under radio control from the crew of the front-end quintet. With electric traction and the flow from the mines at its peak SAR aims to run 180-wagon trains of 9540 tonnes gross as regular practice.

The other setting for phenomenal trainloads is the 534-mile line built by ISCOR, the South African Iron and Steel Corporation, to convey export ore from mines at Sishen, west of Johannesburg, to the deepwater port of Saldanha Bay on the coast northwest of Cape Town, which SAR took over in April 1977. ISCOR had embarked on electrification before the takeover and complicated life for the SAR by selecting a 50kV 50Hz AC system, because of its economic suitability to the semi-desert character of the scrub country which the route traverses. At that high voltage even 500+ miles of route can be fed satisfactorily with no more than six sub-stations, because there is such a wide margin for transmission loss over distance; at worst the power falls no lower than 25kV and the locomotives have been designed to cope with that, if at reduced speed. One penalty of excessively high catenary voltage is the extra clearance essential for the overhead wires, but on this single-track line

Block trains of 200 wagons grossing more than 20,000 tonnes are regular operating practice on the new line built to move export ore from Sishen, west of Johannesburg, to the port of Saldanha Bay.

The 5070hp thyristor-controlled Class 9E Co-Co locomotives for the Sishen–Saldanha Bay line, electrified on a highly unusual 50kV 50Hz AC system, were British-built by GEC Traction. Three of them are the normal power for a 20,000-tonne train.

A trio of Class 5E electric locomotives head one of SAR's network of Freightliner-type trains dedicated solely to container movement near Newcastle in Natal.

The last of the world's true luxury trains – SAR's celebrated 'Blue Train' from Cape Town nears Johannesburg behind a pair of the 3340hp Class 6E 3kV DC electric locomotives maintained in blue livery to haul it.

there are no overbridges to make it a nuisance. The 25 5070hp thyristor-controlled Co-Co locomotives which power the ore line were British-built by GEC Traction. Normally they work in multiple-unit trios hauling trains of up to 200 four-axle wagons grossing just over 20,000 tonnes, which they run the length of the route in about 18 hours, pausing only to change crews halfway, at an average overall speed of 29mph.

In contrast to its strength in minerals transport SAR has been losing ground to partially derestricted road transport in the markets for manufactured goods such as iron, steel, machinery and chemicals, and in timber. One line of counterattack is exploitation of the rise in permissible axleloads and exploration of the extreme SAR loading-gauge limits to raise individual wagon capacity and thereby justify more competitive tariffs. All new wagons are now bogie and in recent years the average loading-space volume of SAR freight vehicles has been almost doubled.

In many of these freight sectors the obvious need is door-to-door transport capability, for which the prime tool nowadays is the container. But although

SAR moved into containerized freight as long ago as 1950 the country's industry was slow to adapt to modern international containerization. It was 1974 before SAR, as South Africa's national harbour as well as railway authority, was deputed by the Government to set up terminals in all major ports and at City Deep, Johannesburg, and 1977 before the installations were complete. With some 4000 container flat wagons now in its fleet SAR has since made promotion and expansion of a Freightliner train network one of its priorities.

Despite international economic depression SAR freight tonnage climbed almost 50 percent in the 1970s thanks to the drive for exploitation of the country's mineral resources. Tonnage was already rising in earlier postwar years and some of SAR's predominantly single-track trunk routes would now be choked had not SAR prudently applied itself to in the 1950s. Since then nearly 2000 route-miles of the system have been fitted with modern CTC, the latest examples of which are computer-based to relieve operators of many routine chores.

On one 185-mile section of the Richards Bay coal line, for instance, the control centre's computer can take over the routing of trains through passing loops and store instructions from the operator for future action; this one centre at Vryheid, manned by five operators, embraces 1199 track-circuit sections, 398 sets of points and 747 signals. The whole of the 546-mile Sishen–Saldanha Bay ore line is supervised from one computer-based centre at Saldanha, from which the commands to the distant interlockings in the desert and the responses from these to the apparatus and visual displays on the operators' panel are transmitted by microwave. A CTC installation in a very different traffic environment, that at Clairwood covering the four-track route from Booth to Reunion in Natal, which carries one of SAR's busiest commuter services, features automatic junction route-

The lounge and dining car of the 'Blue Train'. The elegant styling in semi-alcoves is enhanced by the bowl teeming with fresh fruit placed in each bay of tables.

setting, actuated by the equipment's detection of a train's destination through its reporting number as it progresses through the train describer from one track-circuited section to the next. SAR is also busily extending track-to-train radio communications systems.

The high-speed probes with a cross-anchor bogie coach mentioned earlier manifest that 100mph passenger-train speed would be attainable on SAR tangent track without much technical difficulty if the commercial case for it were overwhelming. But long-haul passenger traffic is not a money-maker for SAR; and even if there were enough extended lengths of potential 100mph trackage to secure really worthwhile cuts in transit time from sustained bursts of three-figure speed, some probably intractable problems of carving train-path room for it amongst the rising numbers of much slower-moving freight trains would persist. So the general SAR passenger train speed limit is still only 55mph at the time of writing, though intermittent relaxations to 70mph are permitted for the prestige 'Blue Train'.

The 'Blue Train' is SAR's shop-window display in its worldwide tourist travel marketing – and understandably so, since apart from Australia's transcontinental 'Indian-Pacific' it is the last of the classic 'hotels on wheels' in the world and certainly the most luxurious train left on earth in the range of its amenities. Born in 1903 as the 'Union Limited', a quality overland link between Cape Town and inland Pretoria for passengers off the Union-Castle liners from England, and renamed the 'Blue Train' in 1946 when it was re-equipped with air-conditioned stock built by Metro-Cammell in Britain, the present 'Blue Train' is formed of coaches built in 1972 by the South African firm, Union Carriage & Wagon. These superb vehicles offer eight different types of overnight accommodation for the 26-hour journey of almost exactly 1000 miles from Cape Town to Pretoria.

The lowest category of accommodation is the equivalent in comfort and fitments of a European Tourist-class sleeper berth, but in the two so-called 'Demi-luxe' cars (each of which is designed for a payload of only nine passengers at most!) all three double/treble-berth rooms and the one single-berth

compartment each has its own private shower and WC, as well as armchairs and a table to complement the bench settee into which the lower berth converts during the day. The summit of luxury is a car laid out for just six passengers, in which the centrepiece is a three-room suite for two with separate twin-bedded room fully fitted with wardrobe and dressing table, full-scale bathroom, and lounge with settee, armchairs and refrigerated drinks cabinet. The other two suites in the car also have their own fully equipped bathrooms, but only a combined bed-sitting room as living accommodation. Elsewhere in the 'Blue Train's' 16-car formation is an elegant bar-lounge car and a diner which besides being a model of gracious interior design nobly preserves the finest menu and service traditions of the *train de luxe* golden age in Europe and North America.

That is not the only way the 'Blue Train' keeps the true Pullman model burnished. Since the touch of a button in one's accommodation instantly summons steward attention for anything from drinks service to clothes valeting, it is not surprising that including the locomotive men 27 train crew have to be deployed for each 'Blue Train' trip, which is an extraordinarily prodigal ratio of one employee for every four passengers. Needless to say, one imagines, the 'Blue Train' loses money on every trip, but so long as SAR manages to keep in the black in the rest of its activity the luxury train seems in no danger of withdrawal: it is too valuable an image-builder, not only for SAR but for South African industry and for the country as a whole.

However SAR recently decided that there was a limit to the shop-window loss-leaders it could afford. In the spring of 1978 the first-class-only 'Drakensberg', the system's other passenger service flagship which operates superseded 1946 'Blue Train' equipment, had its route curtailed and its frequency halved. Instead of running twice a week between Johannesburg and Durban, then making a once-a-week trip from Durban via Kimberley to Cape Town and back, the 'Drakensberg' is now turned out for just one weekly Johannesburg–Durban return trip.

Incidentally, the 'Drakensberg' is, despite its luxury status, lumped with other SAR overnight

Above:
The Johannesburg–Durban 'Drakensberg', made up of the 1946 'Blue Train' cars, and its diner.
Centre:
Mixed SAR freight with a Class 5E electric in charge.

One of Johannesburg's suburban electric multiple-units.

trains in one idiosyncratic particular: its passengers do not get mattress, sheets and blankets in their berths as a matter of course but have to book and pay for bedding materials as an extra. Only the 'Blue Train' is exempt from this practice, which seems incredibly anachronistic in a railway system so advanced in other sectors of its business – and one which, moreover, is imaginative enough to package all the amenities of a 'Blue Train' journey, dining car meals not excepted, in a single fare that is varied only by one's choice of accommodation.

SAR began 3kV DC electrification as long ago as

1923, starting in Natal to simplify the movement of coal from the province's pits at the 4000ft contour to the coast at Durban. The initial electrification of suburban lines in the Cape Town area four years later was at 1.5kV DC, but in time this was modified to the 3kV system which was steadily extended along SAR main lines. But as yet less than one-quarter of the system's total route-mileage is under catenary and on some important trunk lines it is not continuous – the 'Blue Train' route from Cape Town to Johannesburg is a conspicuous example.

The change to 25kV AC 50Hz for the Richards Bay line was dictated by the DC system's inadequacy for the massive train loadings planned in that project. SAR has not yet ordered any dual-voltage locomotives and the extent to which AC extensions may be tacked on to lines already part-electrified at 3kV DC is unclear at the time of writing because SAR is anxiously reappraising its future traction policy.

The oil price explosion prompted a determination to electrify as rapidly as possible and a long-range SAR plan was promulgated in 1974. But since then SAR has been staggered to find the price of its traction current rising almost as rapidly as that of diesel fuel, thanks to an apparent determination of the Government and the supply industry to amortise in short order the cost of grid extensions to serve the railway. By the end of 1978, for instance, the bill for traction current on the Sishen–Saldanha line was almost two-and-a-half times the estimated figure when the project was costed in 1974 and SAR's General Manager was hinting that if that escalation could have been foreseen the line might have been left to diesel traction (almost certainly it would not have been electrified at such phenomenally high voltage if SAR had had charge of the enterprise from the start). So, contrary to expectations, SAR was shopping for 75 more of its American-type Class 34 1980hp Co-Co diesel-electrics at the end of 1978. These locomotives, incidentally, are built by a General Motors' South African subsidiary.

Meanwhile, conveniently fed from South Africa's ample coal reserves, steam soldiers on in quantities which have made SAR a Mecca for countless buffs from all corners of the globe in recent years – and SAR itself, one might add, has encouraged their pilgrimages quite energetically. Some South African steam centres, such as De Aar, which caters for the stretch of the Cape Town–Johannesburg trunk route from that point northward the 175 miles to Kimberley, have latterly become as renowned across the world as were Britain's Crewe and Swindon in the steam age of a century ago. At the start of 1979 the active SAR 3ft 6in-gauge steam locomotive fleet was still almost 1500 strong.

As I write nearly a hundred burly 194-tonne Class GMA 4-8-2+2-8-4 Beyer-Garratt articulateds, the most numerous breed of Garratts still alive, are active in the Cape, Natal and Eastern Transvaal on both passenger and freight haulage.

Class 25 4-8-2s, the 119-tonne apotheosis of South African steam which was built by Henschel and the former North British Locomotive Company in 1953–55, were still magnetizing steam enthusiasts to the Orange Free State's Bethlehem–Bloemfontein–Kimberley line. Originally 100 of this class were built with a complicated apparatus for condensing their exhaust in their tenders so as to conserve water when they were working the Townsriver–De Aar line, which negotiates extremely arid terrain. Over the years these machines were gradually rebuilt as conventional Class 25s because of the exorbitant cost of keeping the condensing device in order, thereby depriving the steam world of an exhaust sound without railway parallel. In action a condensing Class 25 sounded more like a jet plane than a locomotive. A few remain in their original state to keep alive the memory of one of the late steam era's more unusual concepts, but all are on menial work and none is still working as a condensing steam locomotive.

SAR 2750hp Class 34 diesel-electric Co-Co, a product of General Motors (S Africa).

The energy crisis has reprieved a good deal of steam power in South Africa and Rhodesia (now Zimbabwe), such as these two Rhodesia Railways Class 14A 2-6-2+2-6-2 Beyer-Garratts, but SAR's decision at the start of 1980 to renew electric traction orders with a call for 25 locomotives from a European consortium may have revived the threat to the South African survivors.

11.
AUSTRALIA'S RAILWAYS OVERHAUL YEARS OF NEGLECT

CAIRNS

FORSAYTH

TOWNSVILLE

MOUNT ISA • CLONCURRY

WINTON

ROCKHAMPTON

ALICE SPRINGS

CHARLEVILLE

BRISBANE

BROKEN HILL

KALGOORLIE

NEWCASTLE

PERTH

PORT AUGUSTA

BUNBURY

PORT PIRIE

MILDURA

SYDNEY

ADELAIDE

CANBERRA

ALBANY

MELBOURNE

PORTLAND

Heavy block train operation in Australia – on the privately owned 265-mile line of the Mt Newman Mining Company to Port Hedland on the Western Australian coast, a trio of 3600hp diesels heads a 138-car train of iron ore in wagons that are each of 95 tonnes' payload capacity.

Amongst the world's developed countries scarcely any railway system has more arrears of modernization to overtake than Australia's. Some large-scale projects of recent years to tackle the crippling heritage of mixed gauge, to improve access to remote mineral resources or to enlarge the capacity of city commuter networks cannot mask the consequences of fairly parsimonious investment in railways overall since World War II.

These consequences were patent in the hectic slide of every Government-owned railway bar one from a working surplus – or very near it – into heavy deficit between the mid-1960s and mid-1970s. The red ink was not the result of dwindling traffic. On the contrary, in the boom years immediately preceding OPEC's inflation of oil prices some Australian railways were recording unprecedented freight tonnages. The trouble was that the extra traffic cost more to carry than it paid because so much of it had to be moved in antiquated low-capacity rolling stock.

Outside North America, Australia is the only industrialized country in the world where railways do not confront the competition of modern air and road transport as a unified national system. But at least the private enterprise railroads of America have standard gauge in common. Australia still wrestles with the effects of the muddles of sheer bloody-minded independence which had their pioneering forefathers build New South Wales and Queensland main-line railways on the standard gauge, South

Australian and Victorian railways on 5ft 3in gauge, and Western Australia's railways on the 3ft 6in gauge. As late as the early 1960s it was still impossible to complete an east-west transcontinental transit, whether passenger or freight, without break-of-gauge trans-shipment.

That handicap at least was eliminated before the 1960s were out. The stimulus came from Western Australia, where the railways show the best financial results of any of the state systems. Persuaded that the flow of bauxite from vast inland deposits on the western outskirts of Kalgoorlie to the Indian Ocean port of Kwinana, south of Perth, was beyond economical handling on narrow gauge, Western Australia voted to reconstruct its end of the transcontinental line on standard gauge. Previously Kalgoorlie was one of the route's break-of-gauge points, the western extremity of the extraordinary 1051-mile trans-Australian standard-gauge line of the then Commonwealth Railways from Port Augusta in South Australia – extraordinary because it traverses one of the most inhospitable railway environments in the whole world, the lunar-like and desperately arid Nullarbor Plain, where scarcely any vegetation survives in the climatic extremes of 50°C in summer and sub-zero temperatures in winter, and where 297 continuous miles of dead straight track are still a world's record.

The Western Australian initiative prompted action at the other end of the country to get rid of the remaining gauge-breaks in the through route from New South Wales. That entailed reducing to 4ft 8½in gauge 216 miles of South Australian main line between the New South Wales border at Cockburn and Port Augusta. At the same time the existing standard-gauge sectors of the transcontinental line, the desert stretch alone excepted, were effectively improved. These various enterprises were finished in 1969 and in February of the following year the achievement was crowned by the rebirth of the prime transcontinental passenger service, the 'Indian-Pacific', a superb air-conditioned standard-gauge train of stainless-steel-bodied luxury stock running the entire 2462 miles between Sydney and Perth on a

Below:
The first 'Indian-Pacific' makes a ceremonial departure from Perth, Western Australia, on 30 August 1974.
Bottom left:
The 'Indian-Pacific' en route through Western Australia behind two of Westrail's Class L2386 2900hp diesel-electric Co-Cos. Early in 1980 Western Australia's Premier announced electrification of the Kwinana–Kalgoorlie stretch of the trans-Australian route as a first step to conversion of all Westrail's main lines.
Bottom right:
First-class suite in the 'Indian-Pacific'.

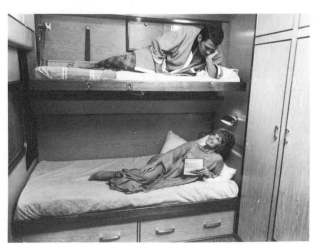

schedule of just over 2¾ days. More significantly the trans-Australian's freight traffic has trebled in volume, swollen in part by maritime containers for the east offloaded at Perth and by new transcontinental piggyback services.

The range of accommodation in the 'Indian-Pacific' is a little less opulent than in South Africa's 'Blue Train' yet still impressive. The deluxe grade first-class rooms for two do not have the delightful twin beds of the top-category 'Blue Train' rooms but orthodox sleeper berths, the lower of which as usual converts into a daytime settee. But the rooms are attractively spacious, affording a wardrobe,

occasional armchair and table as well as the convertible settee, and each has its own enclosed shower and toilet. As on the 'Blue Train', every room of whatever class has iced drinking water on tap, its own radio and adjustable power operated venetian blinds enclosed within the windows' double-glazing. Besides a diner the 'Indian-Pacific' conveys a cafeteria-club car which caters for the whole train plus an exclusive bar-lounge car for first-class customers. This last cherishes a long-established tradition of trans-Australian rail travel by including a piano among its enticements.

At some peak periods the 'Indian-Pacific' runs in

Top:
A 20,000 tonne ore train on another of the privately owned railways in Western Australia, the Hammersley Iron Railway
Above:
An Australian National Railways train in the arid desert of the Nullarbor Plain, where the trans-Australian line is dead straight for a world-record length of 297 miles.

duplicate. When that happens it earns another entry in the record books, since the usual practice is to couple the two trains west of Broken Hill, once the climb out of Sydney across the Blue Mountains is past. The normal double formation is 26 cars.

Australian timetables feature one or two other inter-city passenger trains with high-quality accommodation. Following a re-gauging which preceded the trans-Australian, that of Victoria's line from Melbourne to the New South Wales border at Albury in 1962, the Victorian and New South Wales railway administrations went into partnership with the 'Southern Aurora', an exclusively first-class air-conditioned all-sleeper train which links Melbourne and Sydney overnight. This train also offers a private shower and toilet with every twin room and a club bar as well as a diner.

But in general the medium-haul Australian passenger train has been losing out to the airlines and the automobile because of the obsolescence of so much of the coaching stock and the unappealing speed of train travel. The lack of pace is not a deterrent when major cities are still within the transit compass of a convenient overnight journey in a comfortable berth with diner and club car close at hand. So far as Melbourne is concerned, for instance, overnight trips include journeys to Adelaide as well as Sydney. The prime overnight train for Adelaide is the air-conditioned 'Overland', on which passengers can also transport their automobiles.

Over shorter distances capable of halfday travel, however, Australian schedules were innocent even of mile-a-minute point-to-point timings at the start of the 1980s. The liveliest journeys in the country appeared to be by the diesel railcars of Western Australia – or Westrail, as the state's railway system now promotes itself – plying the western end of the trans-Australian line between Perth and Kalgoorlie. Westrail's 'Prospector' was managing the 408-mile run between these two cities in $7\frac{3}{4}$ hours inclusive of four intermediate stops.

At the turn of the decade the maximum permissible speed on Australian railways was 75mph, though generally speaking the ceiling was under 70mph because of the indifferent quality of the track and the incidence of severe curvature. But New

South Wales at least has serious ambitions to go faster and make Australian inter-city rail travel more attractive overall. How much faster that will be is none too clear. NSW politicians have talked euphemistically of three-figure speed, but that is fantasy without thoroughgoing track reconstruction. A lift to 90mph on the straight may be possible with running gear which can tolerate Australian track standards: NSW's Public Transport Commission seems satisfied it has found this feature in the power cars of British Rail's diesel HST.

At the end of 1979 the New South Wales Transport Commission announced its intention to place the first Australian order of any size for new inter-city passenger equipment since the 'Indian-Pacific' trains were commissioned at the end of 1960. For an operation brandnamed 'Inter-City XPT' it planned to acquire 26 power cars based very closely on those of the British HST and, to operate with them, eight driving trailers, nine buffet cars and 57 other vehicles. The non-powered coaches were to be of the American manufacturer Budd's stainless-steel-bodied pattern which Commonwealth Engineering builds under licence. This Australian firm will also construct the power cars, but the latter will have the same power plant as the British HSTs.

With this equipment the NSW administration is intent on revitalizing all so-called 'country', or inter-city services out of Sydney with air-conditioned stock and gradually accelerated trains. It will take time to upgrade the track and modify the signalling so that the speed potential of the new trains can be decently exploited, but in due course NSW expects to supersede a number of overnight mail trains with 'Inter-City XPT' units completing the same itinerary between the late afternoon and midnight. On main routes the 'Inter-City XPT' trains, like the British HSTs, will be operated with power cars at each end, but driving trailers are included in the plan so that

formations can be divided en route and each part despatched to a different destination with one power car. Incidentally, the NSW management has also promised to back this rejuvenation of the inter-city service with a computer-based reservation system.

The two-tier structure of federal and state government is not conducive to rationalization and integration of the Australian railway system. For instance, in the freight market, railways do not compete on the same terms in neighbouring states. When inter-state road haulage was nationally freed from control in 1954 as the result of successful legal action establishing it as unconstitutional, some states proceeded quite quickly to de-regulate road freight transport within their borders as well, but others acted less precipitately. On the other side of the fence some states kept their railways' freight tariffs pegged well below the general inflation rate in the 1970s for nakedly political ends.

In 1972 the Labour Government of Gough Whitlam, alarmed at the low rate of investment in railways, their reddening balance sheets and the implicit threat to some of their rural services, launched a determined effort to reorganize them as a federal system. Each state was invited to hand over its railways to the Australian Government, which would thereafter shoulder both the deficits and the responsibility for capital investment. But only Tasmania and South Australia responded – and South Australia transferred only the non-metropolitan area of its network, retaining control in the Adelaide area to simplify operation of the city's metropolitan passenger transport as a co-ordinated network. Consequently the Australian National Railways formed on 1 July 1975 out of the former Commonwealth Railways (the main constituents of which are the Port Augusta–Kalgoorlie trans-Australian line and its branches, and the isolated Northern Territory line), Tasmanian Railways and part of South Australian

Many so-called 'country' services operated between cities in New South Wales by locomotive-hauled air-conditioned train-sets such as this will soon be taken over by 'Inter-City XPT' units based on British Rail's HST design.

One of the first series (above) and one of the latest design (below) of air-conditioned, double-deck electric multiple-units operated by the NSW Public Transport Commission on Sydney's electrified suburban system.

Railways has scant operational coherence.

The Whitlam Government's successors have been disinclined to pursue the effort to integrate the railways. And ironically, despite South Australia's accession to ANR, Adelaide seems no nearer an end to its invidious distinction as the only major Australian city without direct access to the standard-gauge system. An ANR plan to lay a single standard-gauge line from Adelaide's main station and freight depot to the 4ft 8½in-gauge Sydney–Perth main line at either Port Pirie or Crystal Brook was pigeonholed as devoid of economic justification after a 1977 federal investigation. At this writing the best Adelaide can hope for seems to be refinement of the mechanized bogie-changing apparatus which caters for interchange of 5ft 3in and 4ft 8½in gauge freight vehicles at such frontier points as Melbourne, Peterborough and Port Pirie.

Nevertheless a good deal of federal money has been disbursed for significant railway improvement schemes. Within a year or so of ANR's establishment a programme of new high-capacity freight wagon construction was set in motion. The aim was primarily to serve ANR, but the new vehicles were made available to state systems on a rental basis, hopefully as a lever that would initiate a nationwide drive for rolling stock renewal on up-to-date lines.

The biggest project of the 1970s – in fact, the largest single Australian railway enterprise since the trans-Australian line was painfully laid through the desert in 1912–17 – has been the construction of a new standard-gauge line 516 miles long from Tarcoola on the trans-Australian route, north to Alice Springs. Until now this important community in the heart of Australia has suffered from a break of gauge in its only rail link. Just over 200 miles out of Port Augusta standard gauge yielded at Marree to the 540-mile 3ft 6in gauge of the Central Australian line, which with no overhead structures to cramp the depth of its loading gauge operated some of the most unlikely narrow-gauge freight trains in the world, mingling piggyback conveyance of full-size road freight vehicles on ordinary flat wagons with that of passenger automobiles and with more orthodox freight. It was surely unique, too, in running air-conditioned mixed trains; freight was admitted to its twice-weekly passenger train, named the 'Ghan' after the territory's one-time Afghan camel teamsters, the coaches of which were perforce air-conditioned because of the area's extremes of climate. But apart from the break-of-gauge embarrassment there was

one sector west of Lake Eyre where the historic route was prone to dislocation by flash floods. Early in 1974 they stopped all trains to and from Alice Springs for nine weeks on end. The new standard-gauge line completed in late 1980 has been started further west, from Tarcoola, and steers clear of the vulnerable area.

A new phase of Australian rail modernization is about to begin with the Federal Government's approval in late 1979 of the electrification throughout of the 600-mile standard-gauge line between Sydney and Melbourne, the busiest inter-state route in the country. Almost simultaneously Queensland decided to electrify the same amount of route in its own state.

One of the most conspicuous areas of Australian railway re-equipment is the metropolitan systems of the biggest cities, which was generously financed from Canberra under the Whitlam regime. In 1970 New South Wales took delivery from Commonwealth Engineering of a stainless-steel-bodied double-decker electric multiple-unit prototype, fully air-conditioned, with Mitsubishi electric gear. Since then it has been steadily superseding the antique single-deck train-sets (some dating from the late 1920s) of Sydney's 1.5kV DC overhead suburban network with these elegant train-sets. The final objective is a fleet of 800.

At last, too, Sydney has the benefit of the largely underground Eastern Suburbs railway, a link between Erskineville and Bondi Junction which, though a mere 6¼ miles long, has been a 'work in progress' since 1947. The initial work was slow enough, but the job lapsed completely between 1952 and 1967 for lack of funds, so that practically all the Sydney office-workers who happily imagined themselves sneaking a midday dip at Bondi Beach when the job was begun must now be retired or too venerable to join the younger generation's lunch-hour rush to the sea. The NSW's Sydney area catenary extends 97 miles as far as Lithgow on the main line westward to the South Australian border. This takes in the famous climb of the Blue Mountains where the railway rises from 89ft above sea level at Penrith to a 3336ft summit at Katoomba, 34 miles further on, and 20 miles are graded at an average of 1 in 47 with stretches as steep as 1 in 33. Then comes the precipitous descent to Lithgow on the deviation which replaces the two sets of 'zig-zag' inclines with intermediate reversing stations whereby the original builders forced the railway virtually straight up the faces of escarpments. One three-mile section of this descent which threads in quick succession ten tunnels where permanent way maintenance was appallingly difficult has lately been rebuilt with a paved concrete trackbed, which has also been lowered to extend the range of double-deck EMU service.

NSW has lately been quadrupling the main line out to Penrith and extending the 1.5kV DC catenary elsewhere in the Sydney suburban area. It had a mind to embark on main-line electrification at 25kV AC before the Federal decision to back electrification of the whole route to Melbourne. This is almost certain to be at 25kV AC, but its execution is several years distant. For the present, therefore, NSW is still ordering DC traction. In 1978 Commonwealth Engineering, the manufacturers who dominate the Australian railway locomotive and rolling stock industry, were commissioned to build, for NSW, the first electric locomotives erected in Australia. NSW's previous front-rank type, the Class 46 3780hp Co-Co, was constructed by Metropolitan-Vickers in Britain. The new 3600hp Class 85 Co-Cos will nevertheless have foreign traction motors, from Mitsubishi.

Contemplating the rising weight of its mineral traffic, especially of export coal through Sydney, the NSW is ambitious for more powerful diesel locomotives than Australia has yet seen. The privately-owned Hammersley Iron Railway has some 3600hp units with Alco engines, but otherwise Australia's most powerful diesel machines are the 3300hp Class Co-Co hood units assembled in 1977–78 by Australia's Clyde Engineering to a General Motors USA design for VicRail, the new brandname of Victorian Railways. In 1979 NSW's fleet was headed by Co-Cos of no more than 2200hp, built by Commonwealth Engineering in 1978, and the earlier 1800hp Class 421 Co-Cos from Clyde Engineering; but for the

Standard locomotive of NSW's 1.5kV DC electrified area has been this 3780hp Class 46 Co-Co, British-built in the mid-1950s, but in the 1980s they were to be superseded by the first Australian-built electric locomotives.

One of South Australia's 2200/2400hp diesel-electrics of Class 80, built by Commonwealth Engineering with Alco engines.

Australia's first 25kV 50Hz AC electrification is inaugurated in the Brisbane suburbs on 17 November 1979. Queensland now plans to electrify all its main lines, starting with a 586-mile programme on the Brisbane–Gladstone route.

Close-up of one of Brisbane's new AC electric multiple-units, prototypes of an aborted scheme for standard Australian urban passenger train-sets. The air-conditioned units have a 75mph top speed.

future the NSW administration has its sights on diesel-electric locomotives with an output of as much as 6000hp.

Australia's first 25kV AC 50Hz electrification is in Brisbane, where 1.5kV DC suburban electrification began in 1950, made halting progress and was abandoned for lack of cash in 1960 – but only after 112 new stainless-steel multiple-unit coaches had been built, if not to the final stage of installing their traction equipment. Since then these cars have been operated as push-pull trailer sets with diesel traction. They have been the only stock in Brisbane's commuter network that is not wooden-bodied and heavy with years.

In the 1960s Brisbane electrification had a low priority because of Queensland Railways' dominant role as a bulk mineral, grain and livestock haulier. But the project was revived in the early 1970s, together with another aborted plan for a new rail crossing of the Mayne River to link the city's downtown on the north bank with its big dormitory area on the south side and allow local trains from the

southeast to terminate in Brisbane's central Roma Street station. The plan got a boost under the Whitlam Labour administration's Urban Passenger Transport Programme of 1973, which offered to put up two-thirds of the capital cost. It was at this juncture that QR plumped for 25kV AC catenary. The Whitlam scheme has since been abandoned by the Fraser Government, which has refused to pay a cent of the bill for the Brisbane AC multiple-units.

These air-conditioned sets are Australian-built by the Queensland firm of Walkers with ASEA thyristor-control traction gear and are arranged for 75mph top speed, though for the present they are limited to 62mph. They are in essence the prototypes of another Whitlam regime concept, the standard Australian Urban Passenger Train (AUPT), but Queensland apart the whole concept has become pretty much a chimera because of bickering over detail alterations to suit their own fancies by the various state transport authorities.

QR's ultimate objective was always to create a Brisbane electric system of nearly 100 route-miles, possibly combined with electrification of the Queensland Railways main line northward from Brisbane to Rockhampton and westward to Toowoomba. The first stage, finished in 1979, converted a 21-mile route from the northwest to the southern suburbs of Brisbane and completed the new crossing of the Mayne River. Now, as mentioned earlier, full electrification of the QR state policy to save oil.

The Brisbane electrification leaves only Perth and Adelaide of Australia's major cities still totally reliant on diesel traction for commuter services. However South Australia's State Transport Authority has prudently had its latest batch of Adelaide diesel-electric railcar sets designed for straightforward conversion to pure electric traction should the money become available. These new units, the power cars of which have a pair of underfloor MAN 500hp high rpm engines, emmanate from Commonwealth Engineering; fully air-conditioned, they are also equipped for UHF radio communication between driver and Adelaide control centre.

Biggest of all Australian city commuter service improvement projects in the 1970s was the mammoth reorientation of the Melbourne network through construction of an underground circuit which, when complete in the 1980s, will reorganize the layout as four independent single-track loops making a circuit of the city centre. The primary aim is to substitute continuous running for the reversals at Flinders Street which absorb all existing operational capacity and rule out any intensification of service. Allied to the infrastructure work is one of the biggest-scale signal concentration schemes yet seen in the world; the ultimate objective is to supervise the whole of the city's central and suburban rail system from a single computer-based centre, which will also have radio contact with all suburban trains. Trains fitly complementing this development, un-

happily, are another matter. In the early 1980s more new stainless-steel air-conditioned electric multiple-units were due to roll off Commonwealth Engineering's production lines at the rate of ten a year, but the quantity involved would go only part-way to renewing a fleet of which nearly half were wooden-bodied veterans up to 50 years old at the end of the 1970s.

Some of the most spectacular operations in present-day Australia stands to the credit of a privately owned railway, one of four constructed in Western Australia to shift export shipment ore from the huge Pilbara deposits to coastal ports. Most of these loads, like those of Australia's coal, are destined for Japan. In Britain the Hammersley Iron Railway is best known because its owners acquired the Great Western 4-6-0 *Pendennis Castle* as a steam diversion, but it earns distinction in this book for its seven-days-a-week traffic in gigantic triple-headed trains grossing well over 20,000 tonnes. The Hammersley line runs 244 miles from the ore mines to the coast at Dampier and is controlled throughout by track-to-train radio and CTC from a single control centre.

The greater part of its motive power fleet comprises 3600hp American-type Class 636 Co-Co diesel-electrics, a trio of which has to cope with trains formed of up to 180 bogie hoppers of 100 tonnes' load capacity and 30 tonnes' tare weight apiece, despite adverse gradients of 1 in 330 en route to the port. The wagons operate in permanently coupled pairs, each of which can be unloaded as a pair by rotary tippler.

Above:
Power car of one of the handsome new diesel multiple-units acquired by South Australia's State Transport Authority from Commonwealth Engineering for the Adelaide suburban services. Its livery calls for a dashing orange band superimposed on the stainless steel.

Left:
Track upgrading for heavier axleloads was a major Australian railway activity in the late 1970s; here Westrail work proceeds on the Brunswick–Collie branch.

Below:
A unit coal train headed by two of NSW's diesels.

'Piggyback' or TOFC ('Trailer-on-Flatcar') was the US railroads' major freight growth area in the 1960s and 1970s, to the extent that it is now second only to coal in terms of volume. It figures prominently in this transcontinental Union Pacific freight threading Cajon Pass in California.

12.
DIFFICULT DAYS FOR NORTH AMERICA'S RAILROADS

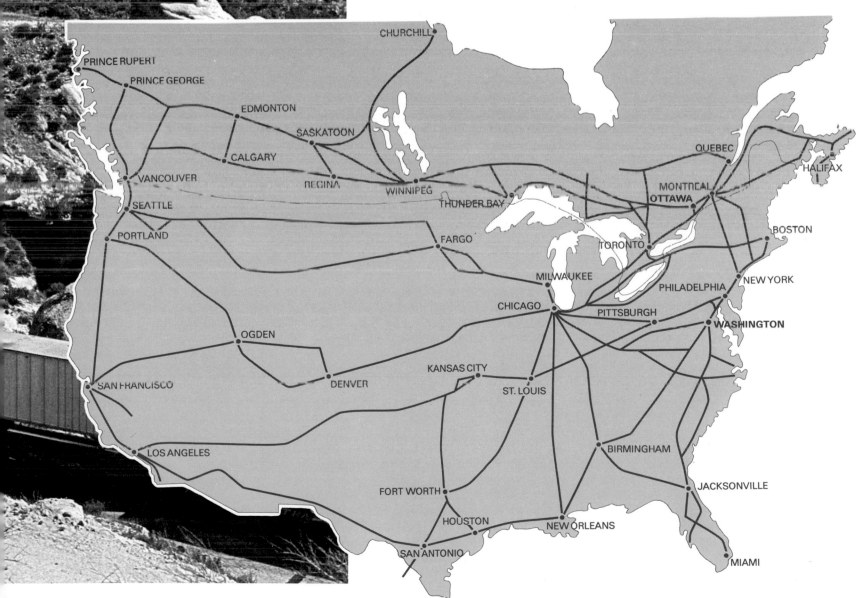

North America is the last redoubt of the private-enterprise main-line railway. But many would be reluctant to bet a substantial sum that it will stay that way into the 21st century. An uncomfortable number of US railroads are finding it progressively harder to generate the money for adequate re-investment in traction and rolling stock, or even to keep the track in basic order.

As this chapter is being written statistics just issued outline a sharp upturn in the major US rail-roads' financial performances during 1979 as a result of the country's road transport fuel crisis during that period and also of tariff increases. But it will need more than the overall five percent growth of freight traffic and ten percent rise in receipts reported at the end of 1979 to relieve the pressure which was mounting in the immediately preceding years.

In 1977 the major or Class I railroads of the country were averaging a return of only 1.39 percent on investment in them and a year later the figure was no better than 1.62 percent. As a group the railroads of the Eastern US were in operating deficit, while those in the South were failing to hold the level of their modest operating profit, let alone keep it riding in step with inflation. Only the railroads of the West were advancing their operating surplus quite healthily. Even in 1979 the average rate of return rose only to 2.53 percent.

It is the big companies of the West alone which, with their transcontinental main lines, still demon-strate that efficient and profitable private-enter-prise railroading is possible. The 9431 route-mile network of Union Pacific is probably the outstanding proof.

UP runs its trains over continuously welded rail which is kept as well-aligned and maintained as any in Europe, and effectively controlled by modern CTC. As a result its merchandise freight trains make up to 70mph on the open road and – in part thanks to smart management of UP's marshalling yards – average nearly 35mph from end to end of their journeys, whereas most Class I railroads cannot boast even 20mph. To some extent that disparity reflects other railroads' obsession with the heaviest practicable tonnage per train and their inclination to power the huge consists that result with less diesel traction horsepower than theory holds to be adequate for the loads. UP tends to run more com-pact trains and power them generously. That way, too, it can run them longer distances without time- and money-wasting halts for re-marshalling. In the late 1970s UP was chalking up an average length of freight train haul – 661 miles – which was all but twice the national Class I railroad average and a marked improvement even on the performance of the USA's most far-flung system, Burlington Northern, operat-ing more than double UP's track mileage.

As a result of all this UP returned well over nine percent net operating profit in 1978, the sort of performance which has for years enabled it to keep its equipment properly updated. In 1979, for in-stance, over half its fleet of diesel locomotives was under 15 years of age and in that year it was to spend a record amount on renewals including, amongst other things, 127 new diesel locomotives and 2225 freight cars.

The authorization of such heavy expenditure on a US railroad in the recessionary late 1970s was the more significant testimony to UP's efficiency be-cause UP is one of several big American systems which is no longer just a railroad. As the rate of return on railroading slumped below three percent in the 1960s (compared with the airlines' average of over five percent and road transport's mean of over

Close-up of a UP 6600hp EMD DD40-X at Omaha. Known as the 'Centennial' type because it was built to special UP order at the time of the 1969 centenary of the golden spike ceremony which completed the USA's first transcontinental, the design was a high-point of the late 1960s period when some US railroads were captivated by very high horsepower diesel units.

12 percent) more than a dozen companies sought to diversify into other, more profitable activity to keep themselves afloat. The major railroads to take this course were Union Pacific, Chicago & North Western, Penn Central, Santa Fe, Southern Pacific, Seaboard Coast Line and Illinois Central. Some sought to move into multi-modal transportation with the objective of an integrated system but they tended to fall foul of the Interstate Commerce Commission, which brandished archaic regulations that had been enacted in the previous century as a safeguard against monopolistic abuse and had never been repealed. Subsequently these constraints were relaxed a little,

but the successful diversifications were those which took companies into areas not related to transportation.

Here the ICC had little pretext for regulatory action. Obvious avenues for a railroad's diversification were property management and energy, but Illinois Central, for instance, branched out not only into engineering but into the consumer goods industry – cola bottling and hosiery manufacture amongst other things. UP, on the other hand, was content with oil, gas, coal and land. Together these enterprises generate half the revenue and half the annual profit of Union Pacific Corporation, the

This UP formation of 5000hp EMD Type DD35 multipled with two cabless 5000hp DD35-B units also dates from the late 1960s high-power era. All three units are D-Ds on two four-wheel bogies. The freight passes a track maintenance gang at Neals, Utah.

Two of UP's 6600hp EMD Type DD40X diesels and an EMD 3000hp Type SD40-2 lean into Sherman curve in Wyoming with an all-TOFC train.

A massive Burlington Northern freight headed by a quintet of EMD 2000hp GP38 diesels.

holding company which, as on other diversifying railroads, has been established to run the whole group of businesses. The UP railroad is now just one company in the UP conglomerate: hence the holding company's willingness to spend so much on UP in 1979 attested significant faith in at least one US railroad's private enterprise future.

Some diversification, on the other hand, has been at the expense of the railroad concerned. Revenue which should have been ploughed back into the railroad has been diverted to more promising speculations. The most egregious example of this practice occurred on the once great Pennsylvania RR, which aggravated the traumatic Eastern US railroad crisis at the start of the 1970s and led to the first injection into US railroading of nationalization.

In the east of the country the 19th century railroad promotors and barons built duplicate and triplicate routes to harass their rivals with even more recklessness than their British counterparts. From 1950 onwards the excess of capacity created a century earlier was more starkly obvious by the year as competition killed off the long-haul passenger streamliners and badly dented freight carryings, while wage demands spurred cost inflation. One company after another eyed its neighbour as a potential bedfellow and many began the protracted rigmarole of seeking Interstate Commerce Commission blessing on a merger to rationalize route systems and cut costs. Even now a third of the country's route-mileage generates only two percent of traffic and loses around £75 ($175) million a year.

Some of the biggest amalgamations eventually approved were: the Norfolk & Western's takeover of the Virginian, which rationalized two of the great hauliers from the eastern coalfields to the coast, and N & W's subsequent takeover of the Nickel Plate and the Wabash; the merger of Erie & Delaware and the

Lackawanna & Western as the Erie-Lackawanna; and Chesapeake & Ohio's takeover of the Baltimore & Ohio. A few years later the enlarged C & O and the N & W were all but pledged to each other and had the ICC's nod for a scheme that might also have absorbed in the combine the Reading, the Central of New Jersey and the Boston & Maine; but as a result of the crisis on other eastern railroads (described below) and the Federal reaction to it the parties broke off the engagement by mutual consent in the spring of 1971.

Sensible mergers were not confined to the east side of the country. In March 1970 what is currently the country's biggest railroad, Burlington Northern, with some 23,000 route- and nearly 34,000 track-miles was forged between the Great Lakes and the west coast by a merger of the Chicago, Burlington & Quincy (popularly abbreviated as 'the Burlington'), the Great Northern, the Northern Pacific and the Spokane, Portland & Seattle. And in the south the Seaboard Air Line merged in 1967 with the Atlantic Coast Line to create the Seaboard Coast Line, which in 1972 took over the Louisville & Nashville as a wholly-owned subsidiary and subsequently leased four other southern railroads to create a network which is now corporately marketed as 'The Family Lines'.

The most improbable marriage of all united the arch-rivals of over half-a-century, the New York Central and the Pennsylvania, who had so often seemed to pursue a different practical course to each other as a dictate of competitive policy. They had started talking in 1961 when the bankruptcy of the New York, New Haven & Hartford RR appeared an ominous indication of worse to come. However, the potential effects of an NYC-PRR merger and of any drastic rationalization of facilities which might ensue on customers and on the competitive railroad situation in the ramified railway network of the northeast were so serious it took seven years of hearing, petition, litigation and ultimately an appeal to the US Supreme Court to quash opposition so that the alliance could be sealed in 1968.

The merger never achieved its forecast economy. Even if the harmonization of so many conflicting practices had not been such a formidable job (the inability to tackle the problems resulted in some appalling operational muddles that drove away a host of freight customers), the whole operation was bedevilled from board-room to shop-floor by animosity between ex-NYC and ex-PRR men. Some of it was desperate seniority-seeking in the new set-up; a lot of it was trivial niggling over detail: for example, the issue of whether NYC or PRR freight vehicle jargon should be standardized is said to have been fought all the way up to Board level, where it almost broke up a meeting in factious acrimony.

Most serious of all, the ex-PRR Chairman of the Board and his intimates, who had been trying to diversify the Pennsylvania out of its worsening deficit before the merger – and borrowing heavily to accelerate the diversification – carried on as before. Such savings as the merger did secure, plus most of the cash from the stock in other railroads NYC was statutorily required to sell off as a condition of the merger, was re-invested not in the railroad but in diversification. The new Penn-Central looked one of the country's wealthiest conglomerates, sitting on nearly $6 billion (£3 billion) worth of assets, but the facade was deceptive.

The US economy was reversing into recession and the PC property investments in particular did not pay off. The redundancy payments cost of the merger was quite crippling, inflation was sharply escalating other expenses and the losses on passenger services – PC was the last major long-haul operator in this sector, with three-quarters of the surviving US services – were soaring. PC was compelled to borrow heavily at rising rates of interest (the product of the recession) just to cover its basic wages bill and Wall Street's antennae twitched apprehensively. Eventually in the spring of 1970 the banking world became so wary that it shut its money-bags.

A desperate PC Chairman sought loans from Washington, where the Nixon administration was amenable because a liquidity crisis was brewing simultaneously at Lockheed and if two pillars of US big business were left to founder the spectre of the 1929 crash could take on flesh and bones. However, a Congress where several influential members were deeply suspicious of companies which looked as if they might be trying to dump railroads for more shareholder-satisfying diversification blocked immediate Federal aid. PC had no option but to file a bankruptcy petition, but under a special provision of US law which grants railroads a moratorium on their debts while they reorganize.

That opened up the whole can of financial worms in the northeast. At the time, the Administration and the Legislature in Washington were just finalizing their protracted difference over salvation of the US long-haul passenger trains and giving birth to the new nationwide Rail Passenger Corporation, soon to be retitled Amtrak, of which more shortly. By the time the legislators got to grips with the crisis in the northeast six more systems operating together about 17,000 miles of track – the Ann Arbor, Boston & Maine, Erie-Lackawanna, Lehigh Valley, Central of New Jersey and Reading – had joined PC in the bankruptcy courts. A total shutdown of railroads over a wide area of the northeast was a very real possibility.

It was forestalled by the Rail Reorganization Act of 1973. With the objective of providing the eastern US with a 'financially self-sustaining rail service', it established first the United States Railroad Association (USRA), a body representative of the Government, railroad management and unions, and customers, to plan a rationalized rail network; and second, Consolidated Rail Corporation – Conrail for short – to run it. The final arrangements were enshrined in the Rail Revitalization & Reform Act of 1975, or the '4R Act' which tidied up a lot of loose ends affecting the rehabilitation of ailing US railroads in general, including an offer of Federal money for the restoration of delapidated track. The cost schedule attached to the 4R Act ended up at around $6 billion (£3 billion) of Federal money and as a result both Administration and Congress choked on it for a time – in fact President Ford threatened a veto at one stage.

One-third of the 4R Act's money was loans to get Conrail started. The rest of its money Conrail had to raise in the market. Washington shied from any idea of wholly funding Conrail; it had done that for Amtrak, (except for the passenger corporation's intake of cash or equipment from the railroads who handed Amtrak their passenger trains to operate) and as a result had appalled some sectors of public opinion. Moreover, the Amtrak concept was a good deal too close to the anathema of railroad nationalization for some politicians' comfort. Conrail must be above suspicion as at worst a 'quango' – a 'quasi-non-

A trio of EMD 1750hp GP9 diesels – the popular road-switchers of the second half of the 1950s when more than 3400 were built – in the livery of Conrail, the corporation which took over from the bankrupt railroads in the northeastern USA.

governmental-organization'.

At the start of its operational career on 1 April 1976 Conrail jumped into second place behind Burlington Northern in the league table of the USA's biggest railroads, with a 19,200 route-mile system, over 4600 locomotives, more than 151,000 freight cars, a daily catalogue of some 1500 freight trains (but also a substantial amount of short-haul passenger service in the heavily populated northeast, the deficits of which it was at first unable wholly to escape as its creators intended) and 15 major marshalling yards. But by the end of 1979 Conrail had spent all its initial loans, had had to go back to Congress for more and was still heavily in the operating red. Conrail was promising it could be self-supporting by 1984 given pricing freedom and the ability to abandon 2200 route-miles and discard one in ten of its employees under the reform of railroad regulation promised by the Carter administration.

Conrail inherited a sheaf of troubles. Most serious was the decrepitude of so much of the track, the traction and the freight vehicles it took over from the bankrupt companies; the amount of repair and renewal which was essential had been seriously underestimated. Union agreement to the Conrail concept was not won without heavy concessions on job protection, as a result of which the new organization was unable to rationalize staff to the extent anticipated; a year and a half after its operational start, for instance, it was still employing nearly three times as many men per route-mile of its network as Burlington Northern. Nor did Conrail make anything like the speed anticipated in trimming its ramified route network. In part this was because when it came to the crunch political opposition frustrated some of

the planned elimination of lightly trafficked branches, but also Conrail itself was slow to abandon duplicate routes and excess yard capacity by rethinking traditional operating practice or applying new technology. On top of all this Conrail's operation was savaged as severely as anyone's by the unprecedented North American winter of 1976–77 and the little less ferocious one of 1978–79, and its fundamental coal traffic was reduced by recession's impact on heavy industrial output – though here at least the worsening oil situation of early 1979 lightened Conrail's outlook, reviving the demand for coal and contributing to a substantial cut of Conrail's operating deficit by comparison with 1978. Some railroads such as Burlington Northern, Santa Fe and Missouri Pacific were confidently expecting at that time to double their coal tonnage in the 1980s, but as the year progressed expectations dimmed a little.

The 'gas-hungry motorists' line-ups of the 1979 spring also saved Amtrak from a really severe network truncation. Like Conrail, Amtrak only got life after barely evading a Presidential veto, in this case from Nixon, following painful conclusion by Congress that the devastation of the US railroad passenger timetable which had seen the 15,000 or so daily trains of the late 1930s dwindle to around 500 inter-city services three decades later could not be allowed to go as far as total extinction of the long-haul train. Even so 300 more were eliminated on the eve of Amtrak's birth on May Day 1971, for the new corporation was handed by the Government a system of just 184 daily trains on 21 routes with which to open its account. As remarked earlier, some of Amtrak's initial funding came from the Federal Government, the rest in the locomotives, passenger cars or

A pair of Conrail's 2000hp EMD Type GP38-2 diesels of the 1970s front a mixed freight at one of the best-known locations on the former Pennsylvania RR – the Horseshoe Curve at Altoona, Pennsylvania.

cash which the railroads previously operating long-haul passenger trains had to pay to have their services taken over by Amtrak. Their compulsory alternative was to go on running the trains themselves for two years at least, losses notwithstanding. This course was preferred notably by the Denver & Rio Grande Western, the Rock Island and the Southern, of which the latter proudly kept its Washington–Atlanta–New Orleans 'Southern Crescent' running to the US streamliner standards of old until early 1979, when it finally gave annual losses of nearly $7 millions and worn-out equipment and the train to Amtrak.

Amtrak set out with similar problems to Conrail's—nothing but the often obsolescent and in many cases fault-prone coaches, diners and sleepers of the previous passenger railroads plus their ageing cab-body diesel locomotives with which to fulfil the timetable, and in too many areas ill-maintained track on which to run the trains. Amtrak had no control over the infrastructure it used. It leased track room from the railroads which owned the routes and paid them to operate its trains. In that situation, quite apart from the quality of the track, a lot depended on the goodwill of the hosts and some were openly hostile to the survival of the long-haul passenger train: it was a nuisance that interfered with the profitable business of freight haulage – and why should the railroads spend money to make their track fit for fast passenger trains which paid them as landlords a fixed return however much traffic higher speed might capture?

Nevertheless, Amtrak began to revive some public enthusiasm for the passenger train, especially among young Americans. Congress not only assured its future, gave it more freedom to modify and expand its network as its own commercial judgement dictated and legislated to ensure it better treatment from its few malcontent hosts, but massively increased its annual operational subsidy. Now Amtrak could start to renew its elderly and ever more fallible equipment.

Here Amtrak was up against a fresh handicap. Ten years and more of a moribund American rail passenger service had called a halt to any ongoing research in the American long-haul car-building industry and Amtrak itself had no readymade design staff. It could only adapt the last new design to be built for US inter-city operation. That was the Budd-built New York–Washington 'Metroliner', which

The Chicago–Seattle 'Empire Builder' heads west from Minneapolis behind a brace of Amtrak's EMD-built Type SPD40F diesels. Since this picture was taken the train's make-up of pre-Amtrak streamliner cars, including Vista-domes, has been superseded by Amtrak's new bi-level Superliner cars.

An Amtrak SPD40F approaches Alexandria, Vermont, with the Chicago–Washington 'James Whitcomb Riley'.

rode acceptably at speeds up to 125mph in the North east Corridor. A so-called 'Amfleet' of nearly 500 cars was purchased from Budd in various internal configurations which were inelegantly dubbed 'Amcoach', 'Amcafe', 'Amlounge', 'Amdinette' and even 'Ampad' in the case of some cars experimentally rebuilt to test a new design of overnight accommodation.

The 'Metroliners' were the product of the first moves in the 1960s to stave off the threatening genocide of the US long-haul passenger train. In 1965 President Johnson was persuaded by prophets of dangerously crowded skies above the country's most populous inter-city corridors and choked highways within them to sign a High Speed Ground Transportation Act. This Bill was more significant for its affirmation in principle of Federal interest in a rail revival than for the amount of cash it laid on the table, but the funding was enough to sponsor what was termed a demonstration project in the Northeast Corridor between Boston, New York, Philadelphia and Washington.

Between New York and Boston the tool was the United Aircraft Turbotrain first accepted for trial by Canadian National on its Montreal–Toronto run. UAC was one of several aerospace firms tempted by the Johnson Act to dabble in rail vehicles, optimistic that this was going to be an expanding market to offset contraction in military hardware expenditure, and it had adventurously packaged a mass of innovatory technology in its Turbotrain. Very short, low-slung bodies of steel-strengthened aluminium, extremely light in weight, were articulated by a single-axle bogie embodying a patent steering device and with pendular suspension, to allow higher speed through curves without excessive wear and tear or deterioration of passenger comfort. Particularly complex was the design of the two-axle power bogies, one at each end of the unit, and the drive to them from the group of Pratt & Whitney aircraft-type gas

turbines.

Sadly, the Turbotrains added practically a chapter to the volume of evidence which states that technology, proven in other applications, is not *ipso facto* foolproof in a rugged railroad operating environment. This dictum has proved true of a whole range of equipment from train-heating boilers, microwave ovens and automat food dispensers to diesel engines. The prudent builder does not sketch one innovation after another into a single rail vehicle design until each component has been separately submitted to rigorous road as well as bench tests. Canadian National's Turbotrains were intended to celebrate Canada's centennial in the 1967 summer, but were not available until late 1969. For a few weeks they sparkled, clipping the Montreal–Toronto schedule to four hours flat for an end-to-end average of 83.8mph, but then a rash of failures had them taken off the track until the following spring. In February 1971 all five CN sets had to be withdrawn yet again and this time they were out for all but three years, during which they were substantially modified. When they did resume service, reformed as three nine-car sets, it was on a considerably decelerated schedule.

Then at the end of May 1979 three cars of one unit on a Montreal–Toronto run were totally destroyed when a fuel supply pipe fractured, sprayed oil over a turbine and set the power car ablaze. Passengers and

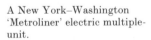
A New York–Washington 'Metroliner' electric multiple-unit.

engineers with men of the newly formed Federal Office of High Speed Ground Transportation. The results here again were train-sets employing a lot of technology untested in service, and also most absurdly designed for a standard of performance that was out of the question without expensive reconstruction of the New York–Washington infrastructure as well. These electric multiple-units, the 'Metroliners', were built to a specification demanding acceleration from rest to 150mph within only three minutes on level track and maximum speed capability of 160mph. Consequently each car was fitted on every axle with a traction motor continuously rated at 300hp but capable of delivering a short-term 640hp at 100mph – and that for an individual car weight of only 75 tonnes, so that a six-car 'Metroliner' could call up as much as 15,360hp to accelerate no more than 450 tonnes of train.

The cars hit so much trouble before they even carried a fare-paying passenger that it was early 1969 before any were entrusted with public service, and 1971 before enough of the 61-car order was pronounced fit to launch a seven-train service each way daily between New York and Washington and the 'demonstration' could be endorsed as officially under way. At that time the New York–Washington 'Metroliner' schedule was two hours 59 minutes

One of the 'Turboliners' built to the basic French turbine powered RTG train set design by Rohr in California, following Amtrak's successful experience with RTG sets imported from France. In 1980 the French were still winning export business for the RTG concept with the sale of two sets to Egypt for the Cairo-Alexandria route.

crew escaped, but the Canadian Transport Commission ordered immediate grounding of the other two train-sets until their fire safeguards had been reinforced. At the close of the 1970s, therefore, only two Turbotrains survived in Canada.

The two three-car Turbotrains operated between Boston and New York were also derelict. They were applied to a much less demanding schedule than the Canadian sets and were less trouble-prone, but when the original economy of gas turbine traction was nullified by the escalation of oil prices they were less appealing to Amtrak than the conventionally designed French Type RTG sets – categorized as 'Turboliners' by Amtrak – which the Americans imported from France in 1973 and then supplemented with units built in California by Rohr in 1975–76.

Over the electrified 226-mile, former Pennsylvania main line between New York and Washington President Johnson had euphorically promised 125mph operation within little more than a year of his signature of the High Speed Ground Transportation Act. Not only was there no native US experience in designing rail vehicles and traction for 125mph, but the project was given the sure kiss of infection, if not actual death – it was entrusted to a committee combining railroad and consulting

Inside one of the Amfleet range of cars which Budd built for Amtrak on the 'Metroliner' car model. This is an Amcafe.

northbound and two hours 50 minutes southbound, inclusive of five intermediate stops. The running between those stops was among the most tightly timed in the world, notably over the 68.4 miles from Baltimore to Wilmington, where the standard booking demanded an average speed of 95.4mph start to stop one way and 93.3mph the other.

Another year and the 'Metroliners' had built up a clientele solid enough to warrant expansion of the service to 14 trains each way daily. By now they were Amtrak-run and just about the only operation on Amtrak's books that was covering its running costs with something to spare. Not only that, but over half Amtrak's total revenue was being generated in the Northeast Corridor, so Amtrak naturally lobbied for a thoroughgoing effort to realize the Johnson Act's objective by creating an infrastructure fit for 150mph trains. Instead it was slapped in the face by the Penn-Central bankruptcy, which dried up the money for proper track maintenance in the Corridor and within a year or so clamped a 100mph limit on the 'Metroliners'.

Conrail's creation to resolve the northeast railroads' insolvency crisis raised any number of questions concerning the area's passenger services, above all those for commuters. Set up essentially as a rail freight operator, Conrail incongruously found itself the country's biggest passenger train operator as well.

In the late 1950s the country's major cities one by one faced up to the reality that if metropolitan rail services were left to the play of market forces they would be extinct by the end of the century. The trend-setter was Philadelphia in 1958, closely

followed by New York a year later. From small beginnings area transportation authorities such as those of southeastern Pennsylvania (SEPTA) and Massachusetts (MBTA) were established to finance and administer co-ordinated road and rail public services. In 1964 the movement was blessed by the Johnson administration's Urban Mass Transportation Act, which offered two-thirds cash grants towards the cost of approved urban public transport improvements. The money that Act put at the disposal of the newly formed Urban Mass Transit Administration (UMTA) was greatly increased by the Nixon administration's Urban Mass Transportation Assistance Act of 1970, which also guaranteed the scheme's existence for ten years to facilitate authorities' long-term planning.

In and around Boston, New York and Philadelphia alone Conrail found that it had taken over from its predecessor railroads, contracts to operate trains over its tracks on behalf of five different authorities: MBTA in the Boston area; SEPTA in the Philadelphia area; the New Jersey Department of Transportation; the Connecticut Department of Transportation; and New York's Metropolitan Transportation Authority. The latter is the largest single people-moving organization in US surface transportation; it handles some seven million passengers a day on the New York subway, on New York's inner city and suburban buses, on the Long Island Railroad – an exclusively commuter system which MTA purchased complete in 1966 when the LIR was disintegrating both physically and financially – and on the metropolitan tracks of the former Class I railroads. One ought perhaps to add that New York is also served by the rails of the Port Authority Trans-Hudson Commission (PATH), formed jointly by the states of New York and New Jersey in 1962 to rehabilitate a destitute 14-mile line from Manhattan to Hoboken and Newark, which now operates one of the USA's smartest, fully air-conditioned rapid transit services from a brand-new terminal beneath lower Manhattan's towering World Trade Center.

Conrail did not take kindly to its passenger charge and soon announced that it intended to unload the responsibility when the contracts with these authorities expired in the later 1970s. Some of the threatened authorities had already taken the precaution of buying or taking out a long-term lease on the Conrail tracks used by the trains they financed, as well as purchasing the locomotives to haul them, while the MBTA had rejected Conrail's terms and handed over operation of the ex-Penn-Central services it sponsored to the Boston & Maine. But it was a New Jersey Senator who urged Congress in late 1977 to put through an amendment to the Conrail legislation which compelled that body thereafter to operate suburban passenger trains for any agency willing to foot a reasonable bill for the service. A year later, nevertheless, New Jersey followed the example of New York and Connecticut and doubled its insurance by buying up the track of its commuter trains, except for a 58-mile stretch of the New York–Philadelphia–Washington main line they employed.

This main line was now the property of Amtrak all the way from Boston to Washington. Since its passenger traffic was so significant, the '4R Act's' draughtsmen proposed a reversal of roles: here Amtrak should be the landlord and Conrail's freight trains the tenants. The Ford administration and especially its Amtrak-disdaining Secretary of Transportation doggedly opposed the idea, but Congress won the struggle and Amtrak was allowed to acquire 107 stations and the track and maintenance facilities to go with them for a knockdown price that had Penn-Central's creditors and stockholders apoplectic. However, President Ford did demolish any idea of thoroughly realigning the route as a super-speed railway. Amtrak was handed funds only to rebuild the track and structures for 125mph where the alignment allowed, to resignal, to electrify from Boston south to the frontier of the route's existing electrification at New Haven, and to renew the latter as 25kV 60Hz AC. The Corridor's traction of the future has got to be triple-voltage, though, because New York's MTA fought successfully for a 12.5kV 60Hz supply in its territory and in addition inflation has so seriously outrun the project's funding that conversion of the Pennsylvania 12kV 25Hz AC between New York and Washington to 25kV 60Hz AC has been deferred *sine die*.

In parenthesis it is worth remark that the sale of the Northeast Corridor trunk route to Amtrak has made the interweave of Federal, Federally-sponsored and local agencies in some of the area's short-haul

passenger working almost impenetrable to the outsider. The 103-mile Philadelphia–Harrisburg service, for instance, uses Amtrak infrastructure, is furnished by SEPTA-owned rolling stock (but vehicles bought with benefit of an 80 percent Federal grant) and crewed by Conrail men! Much the same applies to the local passenger operation between Philadelphia and Trenton.

Because the Northeast Corridor route has been starved of infrastructure re-investment for so long, a huge sum of money was and is needed just for reconstruction of life-expired structures such as bridges and tunnels. What is left for positive route upgrading, therefore, is not going to lift the Northeast Corridor route into the world's highest rail speed bracket. At the end of it all target time for the New York–Washington time, inclusive of stops, is as much as two hours 40 minutes for the 224.6 miles and a very unimpressive three hours 40 minutes for the 231.8 miles from New York to Boston. Still, the New York–Washington schedule will at least be a relief after the 3½-hour transit to which that service had relapsed in 1979 because of speed restrictions and stopgap use of conventional locomotive-hauled trains (plus some 'Jersey Arrow' multiple-units borrowed from the NJ authority) to cover for 'Metroliner' sets undergoing a comprehensive technical refurbishing.

To prove that the 'Metroliners' were intrinsically sound the Department of Transportation had in 1973 footed the bill for four cars to undergo a long schedule of almost a hundred modifications with the two firms which shared their original electrical equipment contract, General Electric and Westinghouse. The rebuilds were shown to the press in an impeccable demonstration run of July 1954 during which a peak speed of 152mph was touched. The only drawback was that each car's revamping had cost more than $500,000 (£250,000). Unsurprisingly it took Amtrak four years to make up its mind that the rest of the fleet should be successively modified in the same way, seeing that by the end of the 1970s the 'Metroliners' would be about halfway through the

A Budd RDC-1 diesel railcar in Boston & Maine service at Reading, Massachusetts, 12 miles north of Boston on what was once a main line to Dover, New Hampshire and Portland, Maine.

The Swedish ASEA-built Rc4 electric locomotive during its trials on the New York–Washington route. Amtrak's new Type AEM-7 electric locomotive design is derived from pleasant experience with what became known in the US as the 'little Volvo'.

One of Amtrak's Class E60CP electric locomotives by General Electric heads a train of Amfleet cars between New York and Washington.

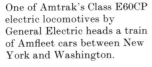

normal life expectancy of rail traction in intensive high-speed use.

The 'Metroliners' will not be the Northeast Corridor's only high-speed passenger equipment, for General Motors is building for Amtrak a series of Type AEM-7 6100hp Bo-Bo locomotives based on the Swedish manufacturer ASEA's widely purchased Type Rc4 with thyristor control (ASEA is supplying all the electrical equipment and overseeing the mechanical design of the Amtrak machines). This resort to European technology was the outcome of Amtrak's very chequered experience in buying American. Here again the reasons were fundamentally the previous lack of domestic demand, so that ongoing research and development work had lapsed. Various North American railroads dealing in heavy

freight flows over difficult terrain, such as Canadian Pacific, Southern Pacific and Union Pacific, have, since the last war, pondered adoption of high-voltage AC traction on the European model, but the only concrete project to date has been that of a purely industrial line, the 78-mile Black Mesa & Lake Powell in the southwestern USA, which was designed for fully automated coal haulage but has yet to achieve it. When Amtrak needed replacements for the revered but elderly ex-Pennsylvania Class GG1 electric locomotives of the Northeast Corridor, therefore, the 3000hp Type P30CH Co-Cos supplied by General Electric were almost inevitably an adaptation of the Black Mesa locomotives, which were essentially designed as heavy freight power.

By the end of the 1970s a disenchanted Amtrak

An Empire Builder
approaches East Glacier
Park Station.

had got rid of more than half its P30CHs on hire to other operators. It has fared little better with its subsequent Type E60 6000 Co-Cos from General Electric; specified as 125mph machines, these have had to be pegged to 85mph because of their running gear's chronic disagreements with the track. So after importing for a trial a French Railways multi-voltage Co-Co No CC21003 (which was very ill at ease on US track and quickly retired to France) and a Swedish Railways Rc4 Bo-Bo (which took little time to endear itself to Amtrak operators, who cherished it as their 'little Volvo'), Amtrak decided the best electric traction buys were on display overseas.

Amtrak's traumas with new equipment have not been confined to electric traction. Its first diesel locomotive acquisitions to supersede the ageing E and F type cab-body models it took over from the railroads were basically off-the-shelf General Motors freight haulers shrouded in passenger-style bodywork. The six-wheel bogies of these 3000hp Type SPD40F Co-Cos soon demonstrated in a sequence of derailments that they were unsuited to reasonable passenger train speed over curves as minimally maintained as many of Amtrak's cash-hungry host railroads were tolerating. Journey times, already dismally protracted compared with the best timecards of the US streamliner heyday, had to be further padded as the railroads clamped harsh speed limits on the Co-Cos: the Chicago–Pacific Coast 'North Coast Hiawatha', for instance, was decelerated by seven hours at a stroke. Amtrak had little option but to order a progressive and very expensive reconstruction of these locomotives to the four-axle 3000hp Type F40PH model it had sub-

sequently commissioned General Motors to custom-build for passenger duty.

Ill-starred, too, was Amtrak's 1975 order for 284 bi-level cars to an entirely new design, drafted in conjunction with builders Pullman Standard, to succeed the ex-streamliner day cars, dome cars, lounges, diners and sleepers on the really long hauls such as Chicago to the West Coast and New Orleans to California. Beloved of the buffs as the elegant pre-Amtrak cars were, their air-conditioning and other apparatus were becoming more and more fallible with age, occasioning a good deal of passenger discomfort that was disastrous for Amtrak's image and aggravated the vehicles' debit of mounting upkeep costs.

Mounted on German-type air-sprung bogies and with 125mph designed capability, the new bi-levels – christened 'Superliners' – were ordered in various configurations, from diners and sleepers to day cars and a variant of the Vista-dome, the Sightseer-Lounge, with a 26-seater cafe on the ground floor and a 46-seater bar-lounge beneath a fully glazed roof on the upper storey. The Superliner's auxiliary equipment was to be all-electric, supplied by train line from generators on the locomotives, whereas much of the obsolescent streamliner stock was steam-heated. With that in mind the FP40H diesels were built for head-end electrical feed only of train auxiliaries. Consequently when a prolonged labour dispute at Pullman-Standard shut down the Superliner production line, Amtrak found itself still forced to run a considerable fleet of cars which could not take power from the new locomotives. In desperation it had to spend money on modifying some of the vehicles to accept head-end electrical power for their auxiliaries

– an absurdity considering that the cars were all but life-expired. When peace was eventually signed at Pullman-Standard the first Superliners were inevitably dogged by the teething troubles of any entirely new design, so that it was 1979 before the first few of them at last took up public service on the Chicago–Seattle 'Empire Builder'.

Earlier in 1979 Amtrak was champing at the non-arrival of the Superliners as it was forced to refuse space reservations on some trains overcrowded by motorists impotent through the sudden spring-1979 shortage of petrol. This influx of passengers was the first fresh glimmer in an Amtrak outlook which had grown more and more sombre in the later 1970s.

Once it assured Amtrak an indefinite future Washington had taken it for granted that Amtrak operation would have to be subsidized. But not limitlessly. By the start of 1979, however, Amtrak was not only losing annually three-and-a-half times as many dollars as the sum with which Congress launched it, but pressing for bigger and bigger annual capital allowances to execute the complete renewal of its outdated equipment that was inescapable as soon as its survival had been guaranteed. Over the whole of its network only the 'Metroliners' and the popular New York–Florida vacationers' trains were covering even their direct operating costs, let alone generating any surplus for re-investment.

Although some Amtrak routes had registered an encouraging resurgence of passengers, too many were not holding their own because of fault-prone and old-fashioned equipment, awkward or too infrequent timetabling, gross unpunctuality and schedules which were dismally uncompetitive – largely because of the constraints of poor track – even if they were approximately observed. The best Amtrak Chicago–New Orleans time, for instance, was 18¼ hours as against 15 hours 55 minutes in 1947; the best New York–Chicago time was 20 hours 40 minutes via Buffalo or 19 hours 5 minutes via Pitts-

burgh as against 15½ hours by each route in 1947 and 1954 respectively; and the best Chicago–Minneapolis time was 8¾ hours as against 6½ hours in 1940. To hold the traffic it had, Amtrak could not overprice against the fierce competition of the country's cheap domestic air travel and what it could charge in that context lagged behind the rate of inflation and the soaring price of fuel. Compound all this with the money drained away by enforced rebuilding of defective equipment and its late deliveries, and with the revenue forfeited when services disintegrated in the phenomenal winters of 1976–77 and 1978–79, then the depressing trend of Amtrak's balance sheet was a foregone conclusion. One more cross Amtrak had to shoulder was that the rejuvenation of the Northeast Corridor main line, originally forecast to be complete by 1981, had been so retarded by bureaucratic infighting and inflation that realization had receded to the mid-1980s at the earliest.

The Carter administration had reaffirmed a commitment to the Northeast Corridor project, but Amtrak was an appealing target for crusaders against unwarranted public expenditure. In January 1979 the White House urged Congress: that the Amtrak network be trimmed by 43 percent, chiefly by paring the really long-haul services to a barely skeletal framework; that Amtrak fares be adjusted so that every passenger paid at least half his direct movement costs; and that sleepers, lounges and full meal service be offered only where demand for them was really healthy. Fortunately for Amtrak the Carter proposals came before Congress just as the 1979 petrol shortage was biting hard, Amtrak's telephone lines were choked with space reservation bids and at least one Amtrak operation, Los Angeles–San Diego, was moving more passengers than its equivalent trains did during World War II. Adopting a favourite procedural ploy, Congress let the deadline for voting down the Administration's measure pass without dissent; but then it hammered out a special appropriations measure of its own which limited the service cuts to about five trains, reprieving such routes as Washington–New Orleans, Chicago–Los Angeles via the Santa Fe, Portland–Salt Lake City and trains into Canada and even authorizing a brand-new 'Desert Wind' service from Ogden to Los Angeles via Las Vegas. Not only that, but Congress substantially increased Amtrak's operating subsidy and all but doubled its annual investment grant! Train after train was restored as influential Congressmen staked their vote on agreement to reprieve threatened trains that catered for their particular constituency.

Many of the latter-day inflation factors which have harassed Amtrak have made their impact on the private-enterprise Class I railroads, too, spreading insolvency to the Midwest and inducing discussion of fresh mergers to cut costs by rationalization. The Chicago, Rock Island & Pacific – more familiarly the Rock Island Line or just the 'Rock' – trod the

Former streamliner car in Amtrak livery on the 'Coast Starlight' operating between Seattle, Oakland and Los Angeles. The train's name perpetuates the memory of the famous pre-Amtrak 'Starlights' of the Southern Pacific.

The first transcontinental freight operated under the Burlington Northern banner after the system's creation by merger crosses North Dakota en route from Chicago and the Twin Cities to Seattle. The six EMD 2000hp GP-38 diesels in charge wear the new BN livery of green, white and black

steps into the bankruptcy courts for the third time in 1975. It had collapsed first in 1915, then again in 1933 and had succumbed once more after the Interstate Commerce Commission took 12 years, no less, to ponder a proposal to merge the 7350-mile road with Union Pacific, during which period UP understandably lost interest in the idea. Frozen out of an attempt to merge with the neighbouring Chicago & North Western and barred from 'absorption in the giant Burlington Northern combine, the Chicago, Milwaukee St Paul & Pacific — the 9800-mile Milwaukee Road which once ran the world-famed 'Hiawatha' streamliners and which was one of the USA's smartest merchandise freight operators — also filed for bankruptcy in 1977, unable to compete with road hauliers exploiting a parallel interstate highway system on one side and Burlington Northern's integrated and thus much quicker rail freight route from Chicago to the northwestern USA on the other.

A reported statement of a Milwaukee Road executive at the time the bankruptcy was officially recorded, starkly outlines the condition into which the infrastructure of the more financially beleaguered US railroads had been allowed to lapse by the late 1970s. Of 152 miles of route between Montevideo, Minnesota and Aberdeen, S Dakota, he advised that 'we will have considerable 10mph territory and in fact some very marginal track. . . . By fall it is expected that the track will be out of service to coal trains' — over this stretch the Milwaukee was moving an important 60,000 tons weekly to a power plant — 'and increased running time would be approximately seven hours for other trains. The track in the entire area from Twin Brooks to Aberdeen (88 miles), with

the exception of the welded rail and upgraded track, is expected to be 10mph. The present transit time is six hours'. Besides its infrastructure deficiencies, moreover, the Milwaukee had a high percentage of its diesel traction out of action awaiting the resources for repair.

One solution floated was that the ailing Midwest railroads should be integrated under Government sponsorship as some sort of 'Conrail West'. But the idea got little more than a Bronx cheer not merely in Washington but from one or two prospective railroad components of the association. The Carter administration made it clear in the summer of 1979 that the Milwaukee would not be kept intact with Federal money; and in the autumn both it and the Rock Island ran out of cash as the Federal Railroad Administration cut off further grants. As an interim measure operation of the 'Rock' was taken over by the Kansas City Terminal Railway on behalf of a dozen systems with which the 'Rock' interlinks. By the spring of 1980 the 'Rock' network was up for sale to interested neighbours and two thirds of the Milwaukee looked certain of closure.

When the final crash came one proposition awaiting an Interstate Commerce Commission verdict was a Southern Pacific bid for the 992 miles of Rock Island trunk route from the southwestern extremity of the latter's system at Santa Rosa, New Mexico, to Kansas City and St Louis, an acquisition which would shorten Southern Pacific's existing route for traffic from the Pacific Coast to St Louis (via interchange with the Cotton Belt railroad) by some 400 miles. The main vocal opponent of the deal was the Santa Fe, but others were moving behind the scenes

to counter it. In January 1980 Union Pacific and Missouri Pacific startled the railroad world with the news that they were planning a corporate merger, and then Union Pacific announced a bid for Western Pacific. In prospect was the creation of the USA's third largest railroad, with a total route-mileage of almost 23,000.

Santa Fe had been getting more than a little apprehensive at Southern Pacific's efforts to expand eastward by alliance. Southern Pacific had strongly courted Seaboard Coast Line in an effort to mould a coast-to-coast system of some 30,000 route-miles, but SCL broke off the engagement in the spring of 1978. Instead SCL (and the Family Lines System of which it is a component) later that year took the first steps to a merger with the Chessie System – as the C & O's holding company has titled itself since 1973 – under the banner of a newly incorporated CSX Corporation. If the ICC blessed the wedding, the resultant network integrating about 27,500 route-miles from the Great Lakes down to New Orleans and Miami would outstrip the prospective UP-MoPac-WP combine. It would be the longest in the country and almost the biggest in terms of annual revenue, marginally surpassed only by Conrail.

Naturally the threat of this massive new railroad combine sent tremors running through every railroad headquarters east of the Mississippi, for it would have ramified side-effects. Conrail's domination of the northeastern scene would no longer be so secure and it would lose its connections with the south and

southwest via the Family Lines. CSX would stand well clear as the kingpin of US railroading's freight traffic, accounting for about 30 percent of all originating tonnage – coal; the CSX annual carryings would more than double those of the next contender in the coal haulage table, Norfolk & Western, and nearly triple the aggregate tonnage of Burlington Northern. More intriguing still, by virtue of a ten percent holding in Seaboard Coast Line, Southern Pacific would be CSX's biggest single stockholder. Might not SP see the CSX conglomerate as the key to its ambitions for a new, integrated transcontinental system?

Whether or not SP joins the CSX combine, the threat in itself was enough to drive other railroads, interlocking with the CSX network, into protective merger talk. In the spring of 1979 Norfolk & Western and Southern expectedly got round a table – Southern had for some time being seeking a way to extend to Chicago – but within a few months had dropped the idea by mutual consent.

Railroad mergers of the sizes outlined above are not consummated just by presidents' signatures. In the USA railroads propose, but the ICC disposes in a whole gamut of detail, from tarification to service withdrawals and associations, under the regulatory procedures laid down to safeguard the country from monopolistic exploitation by monolithic railroads when the train had no convincing rival as a means of long-haul transportation. Although the Norfolk & Western and the Southern have abandoned their own merger, they have been seeking to have the ICC deny the CSX proposition unless they are ceded a good deal of track in CSX territory. If the ICC accepts their view, the CSX parties have agreed that their merger will not be worthwhile.

Though competition from pipelines and water-borne transport is aggressive, US railroads are still paramount in the movement of the country's bulk freight – coal, ore, minerals, grain, oil and chemicals. Since the 1950s a good deal of this traffic has been reshaped into block or unit trains running intact from shipper to consumer and bypassing marshalling yards, especially the flows of coal to public utilities, to major industries and to ports for export shipment.

To Europeans even a 100-car US freight train was a railway wonder of the world between the wars, but nowadays 200-car hauls with 10,000 tons of payload are unremarkable on the principal mineral-hauling roads. Operation of longer, heavier trains even over mountain routes has become practicable and economical in the past two decades through the evolution of efficient systems for the control of mid-train 'slave' locomotives. Stability of very long trains over curves is more assured and drawbar strain through the creation and pick-up of coupling slack at starting is almost eliminated if power is not concentrated up front or even divided between front and helper locomotives at the rear, but shared with traction inserted at a carefully chosen point within the formation. The vital requirement is that the mid-train power works in the closest concert with the head-end locomotives. This is achieved not by human remote control, but by micro-processors which continually read the state of the driver's desk controls in the master locomotive up front and immediately transmit any changes they detect by radio down train to a receiver actuating the slave's controls. Thus master and slave are guaranteed to act in perfect unison. The master-slave radio signals can be and are transmitted over the locomotive-to-brakesman radio link which, with

train-to-track radio communication, is a standard feature of US rail freight operation.

Impressive as many North American unit train operations are technically, they do not make a dramatic impact on the financial state of most railroads for two reasons. One is that most of the traffic is low-rated. The other is that many do not achieve as intensive a utilization of their equipment as the best of such exercises elsewhere in the world, partly because of slow speed enforced by poor-quality track, partly because of oppressive union work rules which enforce too frequent crew-changes en route or otherwise, seriously overman the operation. In 1977, for instance, Canadian National and Grand Trunk Western started a feed of oil from an Ontario refinery to an oil-burning power station near Bay City, Michigan, with two 60-car sets of TankTrain, which is a development by General American Transportation that interconnects tank cars of 23,150-gallon capacity apiece so that a whole train can be unloaded or loaded through a single feed within six hours (besides oil, TankTrains on other railroads convey chemicals). The length of the run was only 136 miles, yet each train needed 48 hours for an out-and-home trip.

The railroads desperately need to make bigger inroads into the higher-rated merchandise traffic. The obstacles to advance in that sector are epitomized by the experience of Coors brewery in Golden, Colorado, a rail-served plant with 1300 rail freight cars of its own and whose chairman, moreover, is himself a director of the conglomerate owning the Denver & Rio Grande Western Railroad. Half the Coors output goes to California and in 1979 the firm invested in 400hp tractor-and-trailer road rigs capable of making the 2400 out-and-home run twice a week (what is more they will come back with return loads of California produce). But the average turn-round time of his freight cars, the Coors chairman told a Denver audience in 1979, was 17 days. 'Three

The energy crisis sparked a dramatic upsurge of 18 percent in US railroads' coal carryings in 1979 and some systems expected their tonnage to double in the 1980s. Four EMD 3000hp SD40 diesels power this Denver & Rio Grande unit coal train, seen east of the Moffat Tunnel in Colorado.

A trio of Union Pacific diesels, including two of the railroad's high-horsepower giants of the 1960s, wind an all-TOFC train through the Cajon Pass. At the start of the 1980s UP was one of the railroads deeply involved in merger negotiations.

Santa Fe's lightweight, skeletal 'Ten-Pack' of articulated cars for TOFC traffic.

years ago', he went on, 'it was 15.5 days. . . . . if we just simply extrapolate out, we can assume that within five years we're going to need 2600 cars.'

The railroads' white hope in this market sector is inter-modal transport. Back in the 1950s dieseliza-

tion was only one momentous US railroad development. The other, spearheaded by the Pennsylvania, was piggyback, or trailer-on-flat-car (TOFC), in official US parlance. Pennsylvania and Norfolk & Western jointly conceived another idea that helped to popularize the concept – Trailer Train, a kind of flatcar-owning club, a railroad's payment of entry fees to which not only enabled it to lease flatcars but to run them through to destinations over other systems' tracks free of most of the bureaucratic regulations normally applied to what is called 'inter-lining'. As a result the flatcars could be loaded and circulated with much greater freedom than the majority of freight cars and were rarely to be seen on the move without cargo. Railroad after railroad joined the enterprise.

In the ensuing two decades the TOFC traffic growth curve has flattened now and then, but over the whole time-span it has moved strongly upward, in sharp contrast to that of the railroads' carrying of manufactured goods by conventional boxcars. Since the oil price explosion the TOFC upsurge has been particularly marked and it now ranks after coal as the railroads' second biggest freight business in volume. Throughout most of these two TOFC decades the railroads have attacked chiefly on the long-haul front, scoring their major successes over the 1000 miles or so between the New York and Chicago areas, and over the 2000+ miles between

Chicago and California. Roads like Chicago & North Western, Union Pacific, Santa Fe, Southern Pacific and Illinois Central Gulf have been operating unit trains dedicated entirely to intermodal traffic. Furthermore, they have been running them at 70mph where track alignment permits and ranking them as the modern equivalent of yesteryear's passenger streamliners, so that their schedules are not too pale a reflection of the bygone passenger best and their punctuality records glittering compared with many of today's Amtrak operations. These trains run from terminal to terminal, pausing en route only for crew changes.

However, although the railroads have won shares ranging from 10 to 35 percent of the potential long-haul intermodal market, they have less than two percent of the nine-times-bigger volume of traffic moving less than 1000 miles. Recently two railroads have tackled this short-haul sector: the Milwaukee (backed at the start with some government money) with an eight times-daily 'Sprint' operation of fixed-formation 20-car train-sets over the 410 miles between Chicago and Minneapolis/St Paul; and Illinois Central Gulf with up to four trains daily, brandnamed 'Slingshot', covering the 298 miles between Chicago and St Louis in seven hours. Within a year the 'Sprints' had chalked up an 80 percent load factor and were operationally in the black. Both railroads achieved a major coup in securing union agreement to cost-cutting crew reduction of these trains. Instead of the four man crew standard on most US freight trains, the 'Sprint' trains run with three and the 'Slingshots' with only two – and what is more the unions agreed that one 'Slingshot' crew should man the train throughout, whereas the work-rule tablets of stone which US railroad managements have managed only to chip at the edges since the last war demand that orthodox Chicago-St Louis freight trains change crews three times en route, with each crew's stint commanding a full day's wages!

The Milwaukee 'Sprint' project is part of a determined Federal effort to develop a more fuel-efficient and economical intermodal technology. Private enterprise is active too. One promising concept on that front is Santa Fe's 'Ten-Pack', an articulated set of ten skeletal, low-slung vehicles that consist of little more than a centre sill with side aprons to carry trailer wheels. These Santa Fe premiered in 100-car sets on a through Chicago–Los Angeles intermodal train named 'The Chief'. The 'Ten-Pack' is not only 35 percent lighter than a conventional Trailer Train flatcar, but on its low frames packs the trailers so that the loaded train has a much better aerodynamic outline; a loaded 'Ten-Pack' train saves about 5000 gallons of fuel on each 4400-mile round trip compared with normal TOFC equipment.

The new energy-conscious interest in intermodal transport has also revived a Chesapeake & Ohio invention of the late 1950s which did not make much headway in its first incarnation. This is the Road-

A Santa Fe 'Safe-Pak' covered tri-level transporter for movement of new cars from manufacturers to distributors.

railer. It is an 'amphibian', a box trailer with interchangeable road and rail running gear – so that theoretically it greatly simplifies terminal arrangements by obviating the need of costly cranage to hoist trailers or containers on and off flatcars – which in its rail mode can be close-coupled into trains of up to 75 vehicles. The substitution of one pair of wheels for another at the point of mode change is claimed to take only $2\frac{1}{2}$ minutes at most; and in the course of rigorous and prolonged rail evaluation on the Government's circular test track at Pueblo a pair of Railvans has been pushed without trouble up to a peak speed of 105mph. At least one railroad was expected to inaugurate Roadrailer service in 1980.

Four manufacturers have dominated North

This close-up of the British 1960s prototype of the Roadrailer devised in the USA by the Chesapeake & Ohio shows the application of compressed air to lower the rail running gear and raise the road wheels at the rear of the vehicle. The Roadrailer was refined and revived in the USA at the end of the 1970s and was likely to be adopted by one or more railroads for commercial operation in the 1980s, following an initial production order for 250 cars.

American diesel locomotive production since the twilight of the 1960s. Principal suppliers of US railroads are: the Electromotive Division (EMD) of General Motors (GM), the original mainspring of US dieselization; and General Electric (GE), which entered the main-line locomotive market in partnership with ALCO, but from 1960 struck out on its own, while ALCO withdrew from US traction business in 1969 in the wake of Lima-Hamilton and Fairbanks-Morse, which gave up in 1956 and 1963 respectively. ALCO's designs and worldwide licensing agreements were taken over by its former Canadian subsidiary, Montreal Locomotive Works, which is now MLW Industries, an all-Canadian company that is a division of Bombardier-MLW, and one of the two major locomotive builders in Canada. The other is General Motors of Canada.

A new name in US main-line diesel traction of late is Morrison-Knudsen, a specialist in one important branch of the industry over the past two decades or so – the re-engining and updating of obsolescent locomotives whose carcases and running gear are still serviceable as a means to escape the huge inflationary rise in the first cost of brand-new locomotives. At the end of the 1970s Morrison-Knudsen introduced Sulzer diesel engines to North America in some rebuilds of GE U25B locomotives for Southern Pacific.

Except for a short-lived sampling of German-style – and German-built – 4000hp diesel-hydraulics by Denver & Rio Grande Western and Southern Pacific in the 1960s, North American railroads have always standardized on diesel-electrics. In the 1960s and early 1970s it looked as though US diesel traction was set for unique characteristics of size and power as Union Pacific advanced from the 5000hp units which GM and ALCO had created both for this road and for Southern Pacific in the mid-1960s to the massive GM Type DDA40X 6600hp locomotives of 1969–71. These last machines, familiarly known as the 'Centennials' because their debut coincided with the 100th anniversary of the first transcontinental

In the USA's Bicentennial year, 1976, several railroads picked locomotives for special repainting in patriotic colour schemes. A Santa Fe choice was this EMD 3600hp SD45-2 Co-Co, posed alongside the preserved 2-8-0 veteran, *Cyrus K Holliday.*

route's completion, were fundamentally two standard GM locomotives encased as one. As the 1970s progressed, railroads realized that when a 'Centennial' was grounded by a fault the cost of having so much power idle outweighed any operational benefit of mammoth single-unit horsepower. By the end of the 1970s, in fact, Southern Pacific was retiring its 5000hp units. Nowadays every railroad prefers the flexibility of more compact units not exceeding about 3500hp in output which can be assembled in multiple-unit blocks of whatever size matches the load to be hauled.

The strength of the North American diesel traction industry from the start has been its enforcement of a high degree of standardization on its client railroads. Custom-building is limited to detail and livery. Thus over 2600 of EMD's first postwar general-purpose four-axle 'hood unit', the GP7, familiarly known as the 'Geep', spread the length and breadth of the USA, followed by around 3500 of the subsequent 1750hp GP9; in the 1970s at least half the country's Class I railroads were operating the 2000hp GP38. Predominant in the higher power range in the second half of the 1970s were EMD's SD40 range of 3000hp six-axle units, with a 3600hp derivative denominated SD45, and General Electric's very successful counterparts, the C30 3000hp series and the associated 3600hp C36. At the end of the decade EMD was unveiling a new range of standard designs with a new engine affording a higher power/weight ratio. Its chief models were a 3500hp four-axle type for fast merchandise freights, the GP50, and a new 3500hp

six-axle unit, the SD50, for heavy haulage. The GP50 was prefigured by 23 3500hp four-axle prototypes designated GP40X, of which ten went to Santa Fe and were conspicuously employed on the Chicago–Los Angeles 'Chief' trains of the new 'Ten-Pack' flatcar sets described earlier. In 1979 the output of the EMD plant at La Grange, Illinois, for US railroads was as high as 1299 units.

As already mentioned, disheartened by the uncertain prospects for further Amtrak orders, by aggressive European bidding for US urban rapid

Above:
Three of this Santa Fe diesel quartet are SD45-2s, but the second is one of the 3000hp SDP40Fs built by EMD to a special Santa Fe order for full-width body units in the 1970s. The TOFC train is crossing the Mississippi River at Fort Madison, Iowa.
Below:
One of Canada's luckless UAC Turbotrains in VIA Rail livery.

transit vehicle contracts and by tribulations over some of the business it had been getting, Pullman-Standard has opted out of further passenger car-building business as soon as its existing contracts have been fulfilled. Its departure was announced while it was locked in multi-million-dollar litigation with the New York Transit Authority and another manufacturer, Rockwell, over troublesome bogies (made by Rockwell) fitted to 750 cars constructed by Pullman-Standard some years earlier. The other great US car-builder, Budd, was going to retreat too, but changed its mind.

One of Budd's latest products is a new version of the RDC diesel railcar which it marketed in the 1950s as an economical solution to mounting passenger traffic losses. Offered in a number of configurations, most of them powered by a brace of 275hp underfloor engines of a type originally evolved for US military AFVs, over 350 RDCs were sold, some to foreign railways (among these were Canadian Pacific and Australia's Commonwealth Railways, of which the latter operated them on the 1051-mile desert haul between Port Augusta and Kalgoorlie). Budd's late 1970s successor, the SPV-2000 (for Self-Propelled-Vehicle with validity and life expectancy up to the year 2000 at least), is another adaptation of the versatile Metroliner bodyshell, mounted on Budd's

special design of air-sprung bogie, which can be fashioned internally for anything from high-capacity commuter operation to roomy inter-city service and for the latter could be arranged to attain up to 120mph. But up to the end of 1979 Budd had announced only one SPV-2000 purchaser, Connecticut, which is acquiring 13, all but one of them for the New Haven–Springfield service. This service, previously furnished by RDCs, is operated by Amtrak to Connecticut's order under provisions which allow states to sponsor and subsidize passenger workings within their borders that supplement Amtrak's national network. With its SPV-2000 buy, Connecticut became the first state to finance new rolling stock for an Amtrak operation of this kind.

As for new-technology rolling-stock purchases of its own Amtrak seems to have a much more eager eye on a Canadian product which is to revitalize the inter-city corridor service in the eastern half of that country. In the early 1970s Canadian long-haul passenger services were in the same state of crisis as those of the USA a decade earlier. Canadian Pacific had almost cleared house of passenger trains in the 1960s, but with the Turbotrains, purchases and refurbishing of discarded US streamliner equipment and some vigorous and astute marketing Canadian National had striven to reverse the downward curve

The mid-train helper diesels in this Canadian Pacific block grain train traversing the Rockies are under the remote control of the head-end locomotive crew. The van cut into the train ahead of the two locomotives houses the apparatus which translates the radio-wave commands from the front into appropriate activation of the 'slave' locomotive controls.

of its passenger carryings. Sadly its discounted fares did not generate enough new traffic to cover expenses and equipment depreciation, and in the early 1970s CN had to campaign vociferously for relief from mounting losses on its passenger services. As in the USA, extinction of the long-haul passenger train was politically unthinkable, so Pierre Trudeau's Liberal administration more or less followed the US example: in 1978 inter-city passenger services were regrouped and integrated under the management of an Amtrak-style Federal agency named VIA Rail, supported by Federal money. A natural corollary of the new order was a rationalized timetable, in which the most conspicuous economy was the merger of the two great Canadian transcontinentals, Canadian Pacific's (CP) 'Canadian' and Canadian National's (CN) 'Super Continental', as one over the Sudbury–Winnipeg sector.

As freight hauliers, state-owned CN and private

enterprise CP are both financially healthy – indeed CN must be the most remunerative state railway system for its size outside the Communist Bloc – and consequently VIA Rail plies its trains over track that is generally in far better shape than many of Amtrak's pathways. Nevertheless the Canadian Government was persuaded to recognize that passenger trains would not hold their own in the populous inter-city corridors without acceleration, and that that would predicate infrastructure improvements. As a start it agreed to finance upgrading between Montreal and Quebec, though the sum allocated to this pilot exercise had the look of a gesture rather than serious long-term intent when it was set against vastly larger amounts of Federal money lavished on experimentation in other modes of transport.

To operate the revamped Montreal–Quebec corridor route the government has bought Canadian-devised automatic tilt-body equipment, the LRC –

The latest version of the Budd diesel railcar, the SPV-2000 prototype, was built with an optional streamlined front end.

Canada's bid for high-speed train business – the Bombardier-MLW LRC with automatic body-tilting. This is a prototype power car and trailer; production sets are due to emerge in Canada and on some Amtrak services in the USA early in the 1980s.

All long-haul Canadian passenger trains are now run by a Government agency, VIA Rail, which by the end of 1979 had increased traffic by a third in the three years of its existence. Heading this transcontinental in the Rockies is a diesel triple-unit fronted by an EMD 3000hp full-width body F7 twin-unit of the 1950s pattern which pre-dated the road-switcher 'hood' unit in North America.

Hawker-Siddeley Canada's bi-level commuter coaches for the GO Transit system of Toronto.

for 'Light, Rapid, Comfortable' or '*Léger, Rapide, Confortable*' which has been developed by a consortium of Canadian industries with the aid of government finance and is being built by Bombardier-MLW. Like British Rail's HST, the LRC mates diesel-alternator power cars with non-powered trailers, though the LRC is not conceived as a fixed-formation unit but for flexible push-pull assemblies of one or two power cars with as many trailers as its operators may deem suitable for traffic demand or route configuration. Only the trailers have automatic body-tilting apparatus. Available in different interior layouts, each of these mounts an aluminium alloy stressed-skin body devoid of centre sill as low as is practicable on two-axle bogies and turns the scales at around 42 tonnes. Prime mover of each 83.8-tonne power car is an MLW Series 251 2900hp engine.

Like the British HST, the LRC is designed for 125mph top speed within existing signal braking

distances and on existing track, but whether this will in fact be their maximum operational speed on Canadian tracks was unconfirmed at the end of 1979. Certainly the prototype LRC has been tested at up to 129mph, thereby notching a new Canadian rail speed record in the course of Montreal–Quebec trials in February and March 1976 (its tenure of the championship was short-lived, for only a few weeks later CN whipped one of its Turbotrains up to 140.6mph between Kingston and Montreal – Canada's Transport Commission peremptorily vetoed any more high-speed pyrotechnics unless its permission had been sought and granted in advance). In Canada, as in so many other countries this book has covered, it is not only the state of the track, the efficacy of signalling and the characteristics of the rolling stock which will decide the safe limit of train speed, but the number of open level crossings.

The Montreal–Quebec route was scheduled to welcome in 1980 the first four sets of Canada's own order for 22 LRC power cars and 50 trailers, some of which are programmed for use on other inter city itineraries. In Canada the equipment is likely to be employed in either twin-power-car-ten-trailer or single-power-car-five-trailer assemblies. As already hinted, Amtrak, too, will operate LRCs. Having borrowed the prototype vehicles for tests which achieved a gratifyingly comfortable ride at 90mph over curvature limiting orthodox Amtrak vehicles to 60mph, Amtrak arranged to procure a couple of LRC sets, each of a power car and five trailers, for a two-year trial in revenue-earning service between Vancouver, Seattle and Portland. At the start of 1980 the Americans were also considering the LRC tilt-body system against that of British Rail's APT as a way of improving speed between New York and Boston after Northeast Corridor reconstruction.

If and when VIA Rail has the inclination and the resources to renew its locomotive-hauled passenger equipment, Canadian industry has a striking product to offer in that category too. This is the bi-level car designed and built by Hawker Siddeley Canada, the country's pioneers in lightweight rail vehicle construction. At present the Hawker Siddeley bi-level exists only in a high-capacity commuter version, of which 80 are operated in push-pull, diesel-powered train-sets, liveried a spectacular two-tone green and white, on the main-line short-haul services sponsored financially by the Toronto Area Transit Operating Authority under the GO Transit brandname (GO signifying Government of Ontario.

There are two crucial differences between the Hawker-Siddeley design and the bi-levels operated in commuter service south of the 49th Parallel, the locomotive-hauled cars of the Chicago & North Western and the 'Highliner' electric multiple-units of Illinois Central Gulf, both now run under the aegis of Chicago's Regional Transportation Authority. The first distinction is external shape. On the 'Highliner' power cars, the upper storey is cut off abruptly

Above:
A bi-level 'Highliner' electric multiple-unit of the fleet operated by Illinois Central in Chicago's suburbs. The cars are owned by the Chicago South Suburban Mass Transit District (CSSMTD), which bought them with the aid of a two-thirds grant from the Urban Mass Transit Administration (UMTA) of the USA, and are rented out to the railroad. Livery is a spectacular black, orange and silver-grey.
Left top and bottom:
Upper and lower decks of a Toronto GO Transit bi-level; note the remarkable roominess of the upper floor accommodation. At the end of 1979 Quebec decided to follow Ontario's example in Toronto and subsidize and redevelop CN and CP's surface commuter lines in the Montreal area to fend off their abandonment by the railroads as intolerable lossmakers

to drop the roof line and make room for a current-collection pantograph, whereas Hawker-Siddeley has adopted as the standard for every car an unusual, lozenge-shaped outline which besides creating space for pantographs on any vehicle creates a more aero-dynamically effective outline throughout a train's length. The other essential difference is that the US commuter cars are arranged internally with the upstairs seating in galleries alongside each car wall, so that downstairs there is air space from the central gangway to the car roof. At the lozenge-ends of each Hawker Siddeley bi-level, above the air-sprung bogies, the accommodation is single-storey at orthodox floor level, but in the central section of the body, where the lower floor is sunk as near rail level as feasible, the seating is properly double-deck on two separate and complete floors. This course was taken to make the design adaptable to long-haul use. As yet, however, there is no whisper of any enquiry for Hawker Siddeley bi-levels.

13.
THE METRO ROOM

A rubber-tyred train-set of RATP's Paris Metro Line 6, here seen at a

depot riding on its steel wheels. One of the horizontal rubber-tyred wheels which make contact with side rails to achieve guidance can be seen ahead of the running wheels.

A rubber-tyred MP73 train-set in action on Paris Metro Line 6. On the left-hand track the concrete strips for the tyred running wheels are conspicuous outside the running rails, as are the side guidance rails which are slightly elevated above track level.

The Paris Metro's latest MF77 design of steel-wheeled stock, at Miromesnil on Line 9.

Rapid transit, Metro, Tube, Underground, *U-Bahn* – it goes by a variety of names nowadays. But lump all these titles and types together as metropolitan railways and that spells the outstanding growth area of the railway industry since World War II. Before 1939 only 20 of the world's cities had metropolitan railways. Today, despite the vast cost of carving a new right-of-way in an urban environment, whether underground or elevated, the total is beyond 50 and still growing. Not only are most existing systems absorbed in extensions of their networks, but the total is likely to be augmented by at least 20 more cities before the century is out.

The mainspring of this expansion, naturally, has been city authorities' mounting concerns to stave off strangulation of city centres by unchecked use of private cars, or alternatively to avoid pulling down more and more buildings to make extra room for automobiles. The sterilization of large areas of down-

town Los Angeles with concrete strip awoke any number of city fathers to the ultimate price of failure to offer a smart, convenient and generally valid public transport alternative to the private car.

An incentive to make railed transport the centre-piece of the public system, despite the formidable first cost of urban railway construction, was the realization that labour-saving technology could steadily increase the margin of its comparative economy as a mass people mover. Because metropolitan railways generally operate standard train-sets repetitively over a simple route system which does not conflict with other types of rail traffic, all processes were becoming automatic. Not only were driverless trains running automatically set and signalled routes a practical possibility, but also unstaffed stations at which ticket issue and control and revenue collection and checking were entirely automated were also possible.

One of the first major innovations in metropolitan railway technique after World War II was the adoption of rubber-tyred traction by RATP, the Paris Transport Authority which presides over the Paris Metro. This Paris system – or to be specific its original inner-city core – is distinguished by the tight spacing of stations and the determination of its builders to keep the sub-surface lines as close to street level as they could, which often obliged them to curve and climb quite sharply. For smart operation these characteristics put a premium on a high adhesion factor in the design of Paris Metro train-sets and that is the cardinal virtue of rubber-tyred traction, with reduced noise and tranquillity of ride as significant bonuses.

One should add that the rubber tyre's efficiency is only realized fully underground, where rail surfaces

Paris RER electric multiple-unit, Type MS61. These deep-level underground cars are built to full surface line loading gauge dimensions.

are always dry. The technique has no real value on rapid transit lines with substantial open-air trackage; below ground its effect is dramatic. Parisian standees who have not made sure of support put their dignity in hopeless jeopardy when a rubber-tyred Paris Métro train restarts: just a touch of power in the cab and almost like a jetliner starting take-off it is up to full speed before its last car is anywhere near the tunnel-mouth, its acceleration accentuated by the dip between stations of most lines.

Rubber-tyred trains have orthodox flanged wheels and below them conventional steel rails, but these only come into play at turnouts in the track or in the event of tyre deflation, when a vehicle gently subsides on to the alternative running gear. The rubber-tyred carrying wheels are mounted outside the flanged wheels and rest on flat concrete runways laid outside and at a slightly higher level than the steel rails; at pointwork these concrete tracks are gradually dropped to lower the vehicles on to their steel wheels for negotiation of the junction. Since the concrete strip is flat-headed there has to be a guidance medium. Guidance is provided by further rubber-tyred wheels, horizontally mounted on each bogie, that ride against continuous flat rails laid sideways-on to the train, at fixed gauge, just above the level of the concrete running strips.

The penalty of the rubber-tyre system is the excessive heat generated by friction of tyres and concrete, which can be a purgatorial discomfort below ground. In Paris and in the first foreign city to buy it, Montreal, this was an intolerable nuisance until the authorities realized that an extra-powerful

ventilation plant was an indispensable concomitant of rubber-tyred trains.

The first Paris Metro route to be converted throughout to rubber tyred traction, Line 11 (Chatelet–Mairie de Lilas), was fully operative in 1957. Since then three more, Lines 1, 4 and 6, have been similarly reconstructed. However, although the French remain utterly convinced advocates of the system, the RATP has long since abandoned any thought of a rolling programme of conversion and no additional Paris routes were slated for a changeover at the end of the 1970s. The reason is that the age of so much Paris Metro rolling stock demanded its immediate replacement and this could not wait until the other lines were successfully rebuilt, for conversion of a whole line to rubber-tyred operation is a long job. Even in 1979 a quarter of the total Métro fleet of 3434 cars was of pre-World War II build, but twice as many similar antiques have now been superseded by some 1700 new, conventionally wheeled cars built since the 1950s to standard designs, of which the latest is the very elegant Type MF77, with thyristor control of traction motors. All Paris Metro lines with the exception of the lightly-trafficked No 10 are now equipped for fully automatic train operation (ATO), but each train still has a conductor in the cab. So that its trains can also be one-man operated, Line 10 has the more economical fitting of automatic train stop controls in association with each of its signals.

The earlier chapter of this book discussing the SNCF touched on the massive works which have created and are further developing new under-

The remarkably spacious deep-level Paris RER platforms at Gare de Lyon (left) and Châtelet-les-Halles (right).

McGill station on the rubber-tyred Montreal Metro.

ground, high-speed cross-city links between the suburbs on each side of the capital, the Réseau Express Régional (RER), and how these are being interconnected with the SNCF suburban network to open up not only fast through travel from the outer suburbs right to the heart of Paris along a number of vectors, but also much easier and faster journeys between suburbs. Simultaneously the RATP has been extending a number of its Metro lines deeper into the suburbs – in fact the annual amount of RATP

investment in RER and Metro improvements alone, apart from expenditure on the SNCF's Paris suburban network, was hovering around £250 million ($560 million) in the late 1970s. The earlier chapter also mentioned the superb layout and modern decor of the new interchange stations that have been created in central Paris at the intersections of the various types of sub-surface railway, especially those at Châtelet and Gare de Lyon, where the platform amenities below ground even run to a

A BART train of the San Francisco Bay Area, the first rapid transit project to attempt simultaneous automation of all functions.

snack bar with an enclosure of tables and chairs. One should add that the RATP has done some equally impressive refurbishing at many of its historic in-town Metro stations.

Montreal, Mexico City and Santiago have installed French-style rubber tyred Métros (in Japan Sapporo has a rubber-tyred system, but of a unique arrangement that was not derived from French practice) and in France itself the technique has been adopted for the new Metros of Lyons, Marseilles and Lille. The Lille system, due to open in 1981, will begin a new chapter in passenger railway history. Other systems have all the apparatus for full ATO in readiness, but the Lille management is the first to earn the red badge of courage by deliberately building train-sets without any driver's or conductor's position. The 15-station line will therefore be operated perforce with unmanned trains from the start.

Maintenance of passenger discipline during loading and unloading will be simplified in two ways. First, instead of running train-sets of six cars or more as most major city Metros do, the Lille authorities have planned to operate trains of at most four cars, though generally of one single two-car unit, at headways of no more than a minute – perhaps even less at

the peak hours. At stations passengers will not assemble on the platform, but in an adjoining concourse, from which doors opening on to the platform will open simultaneously with the doors of the train which has just arrived. Needless to say a central control room will be alert for any malfunction or passenger problem, monitoring every station continuously through closed-circuit TV cameras.

The first to attempt full ATO was BART, the Bay Area Rapid Transit Scheme of San Francisco and its neighbourhood. The idea of carrying a rapid transit line under San Francisco Bay to integrate Oakland, San Francisco, Berkeley and their outskirts, and to forestall the choking of the Bay bridges by swelling road traffic, was first aired in 1946. California eventually accepted the concept as a component of a co-ordinated transport plan for the whole Bay Area, in 1957 a BART District Authority was established to represent the five counties affected; and in 1961 BART was ready with the draft of a rapid transit

Below left:
A close-up of a unit of Montreal's rubber-tyred rolling stock.
Below right:
Marseilles is one of the two French cities to complete their first Metros in the 1970s (Lyons was the other, with Lille to follow in the 1980s). Naturally, Marseilles employed the rubber tyred system.

system with unprecedented technical sophistication.

BART got off on the wrong foot – the start of construction was stalled for two-and-one-half years through the lawsuits of some dissident taxpayers and haggling over lines of route with local authorities. The delay badly dated the original cost estimates, setting the project off on a financial slide that steepened as inflation accelerated to a pace double that anticipated by the BART planners. By 1966 the scheme was running about $150 million (£60 million) over budget and there was serious doubt of its completion, but California's legislature was finally persuaded to raise some more cash from its constituents. In the nick of time the coffers were topped up by Federal grants under the Urban Mass Transportation Act signed by President Johnson in 1964, a measure which offered two-thirds of the construction cost of infrastructure improvements in any Government-approved urban redevelopment and transportation plan.

The civil engineering of the BART project was impressive enough, with its centrepiece of the $3\frac{1}{2}$-mile Trans-Bay tube encasing twin rail tunnels and a maintenance passageway which was prefabricated in 57 sections on shore, then sunk and connected at depths up to 135ft below water level in a 60ft-wide trench on the floor of the bay. Even more impressive for the 1960s, however, was the BART team's determination to go for a railway that was capable of fully automatic operation under the control of one central, computerized apparatus. And that for a system which was breaking with convention in other ways as well: an unusual 5ft 6in gauge for, it was claimed, an assured smooth ride in trains that were intended to achieve 80mph between stops; third-rail traction current supply at the unusual value of 1000V; and train-sets created not by established rolling-stock builders, but designed by BART men and built by an aerospace firm, Rohr, (it was Rohr's first contract in its drive to penetrate the railroad car-building market).

Through coded impulses passed through the track circuiting, the central computers were to stop and start the trains, open and close their doors at stations, and govern their speed on the open track as necessary to match their progress with the timetable stored in the computer's memory bank. When the running got seriously out of gear, the computer would automatically offer the controllers the likeliest timetable improvisation to sort out the problem as quickly as possible. On its stations, moreover, BART was the first rapid transit operator to essay fully automated fare collection, or AFC.

Metros and rapid transit railways are the most inviting arena for an automated ticketing and revenue control system because their route systems are uncomplicated and in most cases their tarification is simple. The extraordinarily rapid development in micro-processors now allows a variety of instantaneous ticket-checking procedures to be built into turnstiles protecting entry to platforms, but in this equipment a reliability factor of practically 100 percent is a critical requirement – to cite one recent operational specification, British Rail is looking for apparatus that guarantees a failure rate no worse than 0.000017 percent! This is not too easy when the machines are confronted with tickets not infrequently crumpled, even chewed. But such near-infallible efficiency is vital at city-centre stations which can be processing up to a thousand passengers a minute in the peak commuting hours. As a result some operators remain wary of going for broke and entrusting everything to machines, from ticket issue and cash collection to ticket checking and automatic accounting via data links from the machines to central computers. One preferred option is to retain the human element in ticket issue – but backed by every feasible automated aid – and that way to ensure that passengers will have a fault-free ticket to present to the automated turnstile 'readers'.

BART did go for broke. It set a fashion for new US rapid transit systems with 'stored-ride' as well as single-journey ticket-issuing machines. The 'stored-ride' machine issued a ticket for $20- (£9-) worth of travel, which the entrance turnstile at the start of a journey validated and the exit turnstile at destination engrossed with details of the date and trip just finished and the money's-worth of travel left to the user. If one ended up with a cash balance too small for the next trip one had in mind, there was a facility to return the ticket to the issuing machine and have the balance credited against the full price of a new one. It was fine in concept, but much too elaborate to trust without the proof of protracted trial in the most rigorous everyday operating conditions behind it. Most of the US rapid transit authorities who followed BART's lead and adopted the 'stored-ride' facility now imply that it is one refinement they could definitely do without. Even without 'stored-ride' AFC has been one of the most difficult components of the fully automated railway to perfect to an acceptable level of reliability and passenger acceptance.

A BART train on one of the elevated sections of the San Francisco Bay Area system.

The BART designers had already put up enough hostages to fortune by packing so much untried technology in one project, but then they tempted the fates beyond endurance by building little or no provision for component failure into the closely interacting automation systems. And failures occurred right from the start. Even now, at the end of the 1970s, the railway cannot be operated to its original service specification in full, though it works serenely compared with its chaotic performance earlier in the decade, for which BART extracted substantial compensation from the designers and builders after protracted litigation.

Basic problems were (a) the unreliability of the type of track circuitry selected and of the lineside apparatus involved in the automatic train control system, (b) the fact that the train-sets proved incapable in certain conditions of achieving the deceleration rate predicated by the signal spacing, and (c) other vehicle malfunctions which sometimes cut the number available for use down to only half the total fleet. The fallibility of the automatic train control arrangements induced at least one near-catastrophe, when a train approaching a dead-end station at Fremont received a command to accelerate instead of decelerate to a stand. Not that later automated systems have proved immune to the unexpected; as this chapter was being written the US press reported an incident on the Washington Metro in which a train whose driver had dismounted got the computer command to move on, departed without him, kept its passengers imprisoned while it dutifully called at the next three stations with its doors shut tight because there was no driver to release them, and was only tamed when a desperate woman passenger picked the lock in the door from the

train to the conductor's cab and located an emergency stop button on the cab console.

The humiliating effect of BART track circuitry's shortcomings was that though the trains were driven automatically when they were on the move, for a time they could be spaced reliably from each other only by a primitive despatching through interstation telephoning. This was replaced by a computer automated block system in 1973–74, but even then trains could only be run at a six minute headway instead of the 1½ minute interval originally planned. So instead of the 105 trains once envisaged to be on the move simultaneously the limit was 30. Moreover the vast amount of work needed to rectify all the original design flaws restricted BART operation to the five working days of the week until late 1977, when at last Saturday opening was possible. Not until mid-1978 had enough been done to permit seven-days-a-week service at three-minute headway. Scarcely had the BART operators relaxed than the ill-starred system was pole-axed by a train fire in the middle of the Trans-Bay Tunnel! Although the passengers were evacuated safely, a fireman was later asphyxiated by dense, acrid smoke from the cars' burning polyurethane cushions – warning of a new hazard to safety which had a ban clapped on further operation through the underwater tunnel for 11 weeks until it had been eliminated.

The wisdom of proceeding to full automation by controlled steps, each thoroughly tested for security before making a fresh advance, has been exemplified by London Transport. Years of laboratory and field trial preceded the 1969 opening of the first Walthamstow–Victoria sector of LT's Victoria Line with automatic train operation throughout and as result it has performed with high reliability from the start.

Lake Merritt station on the BART system. Special attention was paid to both the interior and the environmental design of the BART stations and subsequent Metro schemes around the world have vied with each other for spectacular achievement in this respect.

Seven Sisters station on London Transport's Victoria Line, the first in the world to be commissioned with full provision for automatic train operation.

The style and the components of the new Washington Metro were developed and perfected in this full-scale sectional model of part of a typical station and train-set.

Though each Victoria Line train has a driver, its acceleration, shut-off of power, respect for signals and permanent speed restrictions, and its deceleration to a stand at the appointed place in each station – are automatically governed at the correct points along the line by command impulses automatically actuated through track circuitry. But for traffic regulation LT was content at first with the electro-mechanical programme machines it had successfully designed some years earlier to control and monitor actual working against the planned timetable and supersede manned signalboxes. Only in the late 1970s, in the age of the mini-computer and micro-processor or silicon chip, was it proceeding by graduated steps to automated regulation of trains throughout the whole length of one of its tube lines from a central base, leaving the control-room staff free from routine work to concentrate on unravelling any serious breakdown in the service.

LT has recognized, too, that early warning of incipient defects in trains on the move becomes more critical as automation tightens its grip on the working. It has evolved an electronic system which links key components of every vehicle in a train-set to a fault-indicator in the conductor's cab – and not only that, but a system which can ultimately be plugged into the track-to-train radio system so that a line's traffic controller will be able at any time to call up any train under his supervision and verify its technical

state. An additional value of this facility is that maintenance depots can be forewarned of any attention a specific train-set may need when it returns to base.

To be fair to BART, its conception in the 1950s was quite influential in rousing the demand for an American urban public transport revival which elicited the UMTA Act of 1964 and Federal aid for approved schemes. By far the most spectacular and ambitious project to ensue from that legislation so far – perhaps for all time, as by the late 1970s the Carter administration was grumbling that overmuch Federal money had been handed out in uncritical support of dispensable elaboration – is the Washington Metro. Construction started in 1970 and by the decade's end roughly one-third of an ultimate five-line complex of 98 route-miles, destined to serve 53 fully air-conditioned underground stations in downtown Washington and 34 more on the surface in the suburbs, was finished and operative.

Both at street level and below ground Washington Metro stations are superbly spacious and strikingly designed, with subtle combinations of colour and lighting to complement the effect of keeping sight lines clear of pillars or obstructions to the maximum extent possible. The air-conditioned trains, fully carpeted within and capable of 75mph top speed, carry a driver or conductor, but they move under the total control of a computer-based automation system, which has had its teething traumas but none anything like as crippling as BART's. The same goes for the Washington Metro's AFC, which again like that of BART features a stored-ride facility.

All the recent US rapid transit schemes, whether totally new or extensions of existing networks, have been characterized by determination to effect convenient marriages with road transport in such a way as to deter use of private cars for travel to the heart of the city. The postwar trend-setters of an effectively and attractively co-ordinated intermodal city transport system were in Europe. One example is Hamburg, with its single authority controlling water as well as road, underground rail and surface rail transport, and its simple zonal fare scheme that allows one to complete a journey by sequential use of different modes on one ticket; another trend-setter was Stockholm, which as described in Chapter 8, re-grouped its suburban and inner-city bus services into feeders into and out of the city's radial Metro lines.

In the USA authorities like Chicago and Washington have followed suit, reorienting bus services to focus on rapid transit stations, and at the same time making much more lavish provision for inter-connection between private car and train than the European norm. By the mid-1980s, for instance, the parking lots at the suburban stations of the Washington Metro will have room for a total of 30,000 cars. Besides 'park-and-ride' space, moreover, suburban station designers are careful to leave a capacious forecourt roadway for the manoeuvring of 'kiss-and-riders' – customers who are driven to the station by someone else.

In the late 1950s the Chicago Transit Authority (CTA) taught the world a new wrinkle in reduction of the first cost of a new rapid transit railway – the integration of its route plan with that of new multilane urban highways. CTA's first essay of this kind was its Eisenhower line, but the full flowering of the concept was seen with the 1969 completion of the Dan Ryan extension; this was projected down the median strip of a new expressway through 60 consecutive blocks. Subsequently CTA began in the 1970s to extend its west-northwest Milwaukee line down the centre of the Kennedy Expressway, ultimately to give direct service to the city's phenomenally busy O'Hare Airport.

By the close of the 1970s Atlanta had joined Washington in the new full-scale rapid transit league and a new system in Baltimore was well under way. Other cities were mulling over estimates – among them Los Angeles, at long last – but a good many were lowering their sights in face of Washington's more stringent criteria for Federal aid and veering to the modern version of the tram or streetcar.

A two-car train-set of the Chicago Transit Authority (CTA), a design developed by Boeing Vertol.

In the developed world Britain is the only country to have banished the tram from its big cities. Of the 108 cities with more than half-a-million population as many as 69 still have tramways, the most extensive of which are in the Eastern Bloc countries; seven substantial networks flourish in the cities of North America. World War II's devastation of so many European cities spared neither the tramways nor their rolling stock, but there was no inclination after the war to part with them. On the contrary, the need to reconstruct prompted some sagacious forward-

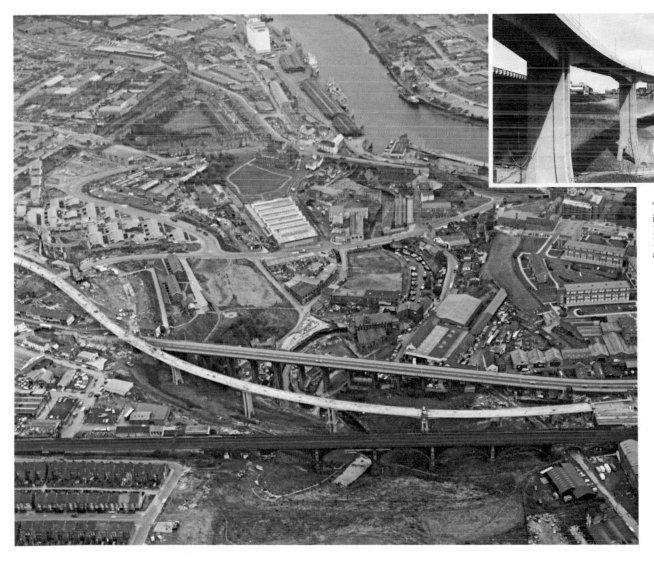

The Tyne Metro takes shape in Britain – two views of its Byker Viaduct, with British Rail's tracks alongside in the aerial scene.

Light Rail Transit in the USA – an LRV of Boeing-Vertol design at Brookline Village on Boston's Green Line of the Massachussetts Bay Transportation Authority (MBTA).

thinking both on patterns of operation and on vehicle technology, which would soon give the tramway a new dimension – that of the Light Rail Transit railway, or LRT.

The first step toward this concept was the decision of numerous urban tramway authorities to re-lay existing tracks or plan new extensions on rights-of-way segregated from main roadways wherever possible, but chiefly outside the city centres where there was room for this configuration. This kept the trams clear of the traffic aggravations which steadily accumulated as private motoring became every-man's postwar way of life. Given the protection of some very basic signalling on such segregated lengths of track, the operators could consider vehicles of substantially higher performance – and electric traction technology was ready with the models.

The tram evolved into the Light Rail Vehicle, or LRV, the articulated two- or three-section tramway unit that is now a staple of so many European cities' metropolitan transport systems. Outside Eastern Europe's builders the chief LRV constructors are the German firms of Düwag and Linke-Hofmann-Busch, Schlieren/BBC in Switzerland, Breda in Italy and La Brugeoise et Nivelles in Belgium.

The modern tram is distinguished from the LRV

proper by its low body floor, essential for ease of street-level boarding and dismounting. Light Rail Transit networks mostly operate from platformed stations, so that they need vehicles either with a height of body floor expressly suited to the system's platform dimensions or else some form of retractable steps so that they can service both platforms and street-level halts.

The Düwag design for Cologne epitomizes the capability of today's LRV. An articulated twin with seating for 72 and standing space for 108 more commuters, it has a total unladen weight of only 39 tonnes but two motored bogies with a combined output of 630hp for traction; thus its power/weight ratio is a muscular 16.2hp/tonne. That endows the unit with an acceleration rate of 1.2m/sec^2 up to its maximum speed, which is as much as 62mph.

At this point one should interpose that there is no universally accepted terminology in this fast-developing sector of modern railways. From what has just been written it is patent that the distinction between a tram and an LRV is hairline-fine. So, in mainland Europe, is the borderline between an LRT and what used to be broadly categorized as an underground railway. German cities such as Cologne, Frankfurt and Stuttgart which have lowered their tramways underground in the heart of their downtown areas to reduce street traffic and create pedestrian precincts brand these sub-surface systems as *U-Bahnen*, but to purists one or two are subterranean LRT.

Some of these city-centre tramway reconstructions, moreover, are what has become known as 'pre-Metro' schemes. In a 'pre-Metro' rebuilding, the reorientation of the tramways below ground has a long-term objective as well as the immediate one of relieving surface traffic pressures; all the sub-surface engineering is done to parameters that will allow conversion of the railway to a full-scale Metro should traffic build up to a level that warrants the more expensive medium. This second stage has already happened in Brussels, where the city's first full Metro line emerged from a pre-Metro chrysalis in 1976. Elsewhere in Belgium, Antwerp is steadily converting the tunnel sections of its tramway system to 'pre-Metro' standards.

In broad terms LRT systems can at most offer only half the carrying capacity of a full-scale Metro, but in view of their markedly lower – though still quite formidable – cost, this is enough to satisfy many cities which would otherwise have to exclude rapid rail transit from their urban transport modernization planning. Of this Newcastle-on-Tyne, in Britain, is likely to be a text-book instance for future historians.

Newcastle used to have a full-scale electric multiple-unit service from its Central station to suburbs both north and south of the Tyne River. But after World War II so much off-peak traffic ebbed away that frequent day-long service of the kind which is the economic justification for electric trac-

Pre-Metro in Brussels – tramways are relaid below ground on a scale allowing for later conversion of the system to a full Metro.

Light Rail Transit in Britain –
the prototype Tyne Metro
two-car train-set on the Tyne
& Wear PTE's test track.

tion was no longer sensible. In 1967 British Rail switched off the current and thinned out the time-table for a diesel multiple-unit operation.

The following year one of Britain's postwar sequence of Transport Acts vested the control and forward planning of local public transport in each of the country's major conurbations in new Passenger Transport Executives (PTEs). Each PTE took over the municipal bus services in each territory and, gradually, full financial liability for the losses of any short-haul rail services it contracted BR to operate within its territory. The objective, naturally, was more effective integration of public transport within each PTE area. So far as the area's local rail services were concerned, the future was now bleak unless the PTE concerned found them individually pivotal to its co-ordination plan and economically viable. If the PTE was disinterested in a service, its losses would now fall wholly on BR; and in most cases BR would inevitably move for closure.

The Tyne & Wear PTE, which covered the New-castle area, was not enamoured of the quality or the convenience of the North and South Tyneside local rail services, still less of the £1.5 million ($3.4 million) annual loss they were running up in the early 1970s. A major defect was that the historic network focus-sing on Central station did not touch the present-day heart of Newcastle itself; that could only be rectified by some dauntingly expensive engineering if the railway was to remain an orthodox BR operation. But a full-scale rapid transit railway was not the answer to the area's transport needs, even if there had been traffic potential to warrant its cost. The Tyne & Wear PTE realized that the answer was to reduce the greater part of the existing North and South Tyne local railway network to a Light Rail Transit system, with more frequent halts in the suburbs, and to knit this into a new sub-surface route through the heart of Newcastle.

The resultant Tyne Metro – in its youth popularly known as the Tyne Super-Tramway – has a fair measure of the automated refinement of the latest full-scale rapid transit systems, but in simple and more economical form. The two-car train-sets, built in Britain by Metro-Cammell, have very similar characteristics to those of a Düwag LRV unit on Frankfurt's LRT system in West Germany, but with a bigger capacity of 84 seats and standing space for 125. Capable of 50mph maximum they are intended to operate mostly in pairs at $2\frac{1}{2}$-minute headway in the downtown Newcastle sector of the system, under the control of a simple two- and three-aspect colour-light signalling system automatically operated through the track circuiting. The trains will set their own routes automatically at junctions – again by an appealingly simple device; under each two-car unit is a passive transponder set to indicate its route and this is interrogated at key points by trackside equip-ment which then sets points ahead, actuates platform train indicators and reports accordingly to the illuminated route diagram in the system's central control room. There is full two-way radio communi-cation between train drivers and control room and extensive use of closed-circuit TV to allow many stations to be unmanned but kept under the main control room's scrutiny.

Twenty years ago public opinion in some parts of the industrialized world – North America especially – was prone to regard the railway as heading for fossilization, locked in historic concepts of trains and how to run them. Light Rail Transit is one more proof to add to instances cited earlier in this book that the railway is not an inflexible medium: and that given equality of treatment with other modes of transport in the matter of covering infrastructure costs, a fair crack of the investment whip and management that is not hidebound, it has a valid solution to a great many transport dilemmas in an age of mounting world-wide concern for optimal use of energy.

PICTURE CREDITS

Swedish State Railways 6/7, 170, 171 bottom, 172 top right, 173, 174 bottom left and bottom right (MARS), 175, 176, top (MARS); British Transport Films 10/11, 24/25, 32 top, 35, 39 bottom; Fox Photos 12; Geoffrey Freeman Allen Collection 13, 14 bottom, 20 top, 22 top, 32 bottom, 33, 34 top left, right and bottom, 38 top and bottom, 40 left and right, 45, 75 top left, right and centre, 81 bottom left, 82 top and bottom, 83, 84, 85 bottom, 87, 89, 114/5, 116, 120, 122, 125, 126 top, 126/7, 130, 132 top, 155, 156 top, 157 top left, 214, 235 bottom, 237 bottom; British Railways 14 top, 16, 18/9, 20 bottom, 22 bottom, 23, 25 top and bottom, 26, 27 top, 29 inset, 36 inset, 37 top, 39 top; Derek Goss

14/5; P. Whitehouse 17, 81 top and bottom right, 154 top, 155 bottom, 157 top right, 158 top, 159 bottom, 231; Central Electricity Board 21; Brian Morrison 27 bottom, 36; L. A. Nixon 28/9, 40/1 bottom; Peter J. Robinson 31; Colourviews 37 top, 68 bottom, 162/3, 167 top, 187 bottom right, 186/7, 190 bottom, 194 bottom, 198/9, 202 top, 211, 212 bottom, 213 top, 215 bottom, 222, 228 top, 232, 238, 250 bottom; SNCF cover, 42/3, 46, 46/7, 48 top and bottom, 49, 50, 51, 52, 53, 54, 55 top and bottom, 56, 57, 58/9, 59 left and right, 60 top and bottom, 61 top and bottom, 63 top and bottom, 64, 65, 66/7, 67, 68 top left and right, 69 top and bottom; DB Mainz 73 (MARS), 74 bottom left and right (MARS), 75 bottom (MARS), 76 top left and right and bottom (MARS), 77 (MARS), 78/9 (MARS), 85 top (MARS), 86/7 (MARS), 88 (MARS), 90

top and bottom (MARS), 94 centre and bottom (MARS), 95 top and bottom (MARS), 97 (MARS); J. L. M. McIvor 74; Filmstelle 91 (MARS), 92; Krauss-Maffei 94/5 top and centre (MARS), 96 (MARS); Dutch Railways 98/9, 100, 101 top and bottom, 102, 103, 104, 105, 106/7; Belgian Railways 109, 111, 113 top; Spoorwegmateriel en Metaal-constructies 110/111 (MARS), 112/3, 113 bottom; Swiss Federal Railways 117, 118, 119, 121, 123 top and bottom, 126 bottom; BLS Bahn 127 (MARS), 128 centre and bottom, 129; SBB 128 top; MOB 129 left and right; Rhaetian R. R. 131; Werbedienst Bahnen der Jungfrau 132 bottom, 133 top and bottom (MARS); Osterreichische Bundesbahnen 134/5, 136 (MARS), 137 (MARS), 138 (MARS), 139 (MARS), 140 (MARS), 141 (MARS), 142 (MARS), 143 (MARS), 144 (MARS), 145 (MARS), 147

(MARS); Simmering-Graz-Pauker 146 (MARS); FS 148/9, 152, 153 bottom; Italian State Railways 151 (MARS), 153 top (MARS); RENFE 159 top, 160, 161; Caminhos de Ferro Portugueses 164 (MARS), 165 (MARS), 166 (MARS); Norwegian State Railways 168/9 (MARS), 174 (MARS), 176 bottom left and right (MARS), 177; AB Storstockholms Lokaltrafik 171 (MARS); Danish State Railways 178, 179, 180; Finnish State Railways 181 (MARS), 182 (MARS), 183 (MARS); Koyusha 184/5, 192; Kanesaki 187 top; S. Shimizu 187 bottom left, 197 bottom; Kazunori 2/3, 188, 189, 190 top, 191, 194, 195 top, 196, 197; Akio Noguchi 193; Fujiphotos 195 bottom; South African Railways 200, 201, 202 bottom, 204; La Vie du Rail 203; C. Garrett 205 top; Mt. Newman Mining Co. Pty. Ltd 206/7; W. Australian Railways 208 (MARS); John C. Dunn

209; Commonwealth Engineering (NSW) Pty. 210 (MARS), 212 (MARS), 213 (MARS), 215 top (MARS); Westrail 215 centre (MARS); Guild House 216/7; Union Pacific Railways 4/5 (MARS), 219 (MARS); Burl and Northern 220; J. Winkley 221, 233; Amtrak 223 (MARS), 224, 224/5 (MARS), 225, 228 (MARS); George Drury 227; Dunlop 230; Santa Fe Railway 234 (MARS), 235 top, 236, 237 top; Budd Co. 239 top (MARS); Bombardier Inc 239 bottom (MARS); Hawker Siddeley 240 (MARS), 241 centre and bottom (MARS); RATP 242/3, 244, 245, 246 top left; Montreal Metro 246 bottom; BART 247 top, 248, 249; Marseilles Metro 247 bottom; London Transport 250 top; Boeing Vertol Co. 251 top (MARS), 252 top (MARS); North East Studios 251 bottom and inset; Brussels Metro 252 bottom; All picture research by J. G. Moore